D1601097

Conjoint Measurement

Anders Gustafsson · Andreas Herrmann
Frank Huber

(Editors)

Conjoint Measurement

Methods and Applications

Fourth Edition

With 39 Figures and 68 Tables

 Springer

Professor Dr. Anders Gustafsson
Karlstad University
651 88 Karlstad
Sweden
anders.gustafsson@kau.se

Professor Dr. Andreas Herrmann
University of St. Gallen
Guisanstr. 1 a
9010 St. Gallen
Switzerland
andreas.herrmann@unisg.ch

Professor Dr. Frank Huber
University of Mainz
Jakob-Welder-Weg 9
55128 Mainz
Germany
huber@marketing-mainz.de

Library of Congress Control Number: 2007934274

ISBN 978-3-540-71403-3   Springer Berlin Heidelberg New York
ISBN 978-3-540-40479-8   3rd Edition Springer Berlin Heidelberg New York

Springer is a part of Springer Science+Business Media

springer.com

© Springer-Verlag Berlin Heidelberg 2003, 2007

Production: LE-TEX Jelonek, Schmidt & Vöckler GbR, Leipzig
Cover-design: WMX Design GmbH, Heidelberg

SPIN 12034659   42/3180YL - 5 4 3 2 1 0   Printed on acid-free paper

Table of Contents

Foreword

by
Paul E. Green

I am honored and pleased to respond to authors request to write a Foreword for this excellent collection of essays on conjoint analysis and related topics. While a number of survey articles and sporadic book chapters have appeared on the subject, to the best of my knowledge this book represents the first volume of contributed essays on conjoint analysis. The book reflects not only the geographical diversity of its contributors but also the variety and depth of their topics.

The development of conjoint analysis and its application to marketing and business research is noteworthy, both in its eclectic roots (psychometrics, statistics, operations research, economics) and the fact that its development reflects the efforts of a large variety of professionals - academics, marketing research consultants, industry practitioners, and software developers.

Reasons for the early success and diffusion of conjoint analysis are not hard to find. First, by the early sixties, precursory psychometric techniques (e.g., multidimensional scaling and correspondence analysis, cluster analysis, and general multivariate techniques) had already shown their value in practical business research and application. Second, conjoint analysis provided a new and powerful array of methods for tackling the important problem of representing and predicting buyer preference judgments and choice behavior - clearly a major problem area in marketing.

In addition, the fortuitous confluence of academic research, practictioner application, and easy-to-use software (distributed by Sawtooth Software and Bretton-Clark) provided the necessary mix for conjoint's rapid acceptance by both the private and public sectors. The rest (as they say) is history.

Recent Trends

Conjoint analysis continues to expand in terms of models, techniques, and applications. Examples include:

Prescriptive modeling: the development of normative models for finding the product/service or line of products/services that maximize the firm's return.

- Dynamic modeling: the development of normative conjoint models for representing competitive actions and reactions, based on game theoretic concepts.
- Extension of earlier models to choice-based conjoint situations, incorporating multinomial logit and probit modeling.
- Latent class, hierarchical Bayes modeling, and constrained choice modeling.
- Other new models, such as individual-level hybrid modeling, Sawtooth's ICE model, and empirical Bayes applications.
- Applications in diverse areas, including the design of lottery games, employee benefits packages, public works (such as the New Jersey E-Z Pass toll road

system), hotel and time share amenities, gasoline station layouts, and legal issues
dealing with misleading advertising, antitrust violations, etc.

- New choice simulators that include sensitivity analysis, composing and evaluating
  selected segments, computation of monetary equivalents of part worths,
  share/return optimization, including Pareto frontier analysis.
- New developments in full-profile experimental designs, including d-optimal
  designs, randomized balance designs, and Plackett-Burman design extensions.
- The coupling of conjoint analysis with virtual-reality electronic displays that
  simulate product arrays, store interiors, house, and furniture layouts, etc.
- The coupling of conjoint analysis with the perceptual and preference mapping of
  choice simulator results.

The preceding points are only illustrative of the diversity and ingenuity of
conjoint researchers/practitioners. And, clearly, more is yet to come.

The Validation Problem

Researchers and practitioners should have (and generally do have) a healthy skep-
ticism about the "latest developments" in conjoint modeling. Fortunately, this
book of essays contains a number of model comparisons and cross validation
studies. New models and application areas have proliferated over the past 30
years; it is still highly important to evaluate the host of new "whizzbangs" that
invariably accompany a rapidly growing research area.

Our Indebtedness

This new book of essays, Conjoint Measurement - Methods and Applications, is a
welcome addition to the conjoint literature. Its publication attests to the international character associated with the growth and diffusion of interest and research
in conjoint analysis. While conjoint has reached a level of popularity and maturity
that few of us in its early stages would have imagined, the methodology is still far
from becoming moribund. This book is a fitting testimonial to the sustained interest in conjoint methods and the vigor and acuity of this international gathering of
researchers.

In closing, it seems to me that we should all express our gratitude to those
early scholars -- Thurstone, Luce, Tukey, McFadden, Addelman, Kempthorne,
Lazarsfeld, to name only a few -- who planted the seeds that have led to such a
bountiful harvest for marketing researchers. And to go back even further, let's not
forget the good reverend, Thomas Bayes. Were he here today, I'm confident that
this book would merit his blessings.

Paul E. Green
Wharton School
University of Pennsylvania

1 Conjoint Analysis as an Instrument of Market Research Practice

Anders Gustafsson, Andreas Herrmann and Frank Huber

1.1 Introduction

The essay by the psychologist Luce and the statistician Tukey (1964) can be viewed as the origin of conjoint analysis (Green and Srinivasan 1978; Carroll and Green 1995). Since its introduction into marketing literature by Green and Rao (1971) as well as by Johnson (1974) in the beginning of the 1970s, conjoint analysis has developed into a method of preference studies that receives much attention from both theoreticians and those who carry out field studies. For example, Cattin and Wittink (1982) report 698 conjoint projects that were carried out by 17 companies in their survey of the period from 1971 to 1980. For the period from 1981 to 1985, Wittink and Cattin (1989) found 66 companies in the United States that were in charge of a total of 1062 conjoint projects. Wittink, Vriens, and Burhenne counted a total of 956 projects in Europe carried out by 59 companies in the period from 1986 to 1991 (Wittink, Vriens, and Burhenne 1994; Baier and Gaul 1999). Based on a 2004 Sawtooth Software customer survey, the leading company in Conjoint Software, between 5,000 and 8,000 conjoint analysis projects were conducted by Sawtooth Software users during 2003. The validation of the conjoint method can be measured not only by the companies today that utilize conjoint methods for decision-making, but also by the 989,000 hits on www.google.com. The increasing acceptance of conjoint applications in market research relates to the many possible uses of this method in various fields of application such as the following:

- new product planning for determining the preference effect of innovations (for example Bauer, Huber, and Keller 1997; DeSarbo, Huff, Rolandelli, and Choi 1994; Green and Krieger 1987; 1992; 1993; Herrmann, Huber, and Braunstein 1997; Johnson, Herrmann, and Huber 1998; Kohli and Sukumar 1990; Page and Rosenbaum 1987; Sands and Warwick 1981; Yoo and Ohta 1995; Zufryden 1988) or to
- improve existing achievements (Green and Wind 1975; Green and Srinivasan 1978; Dellaert et al., 1995), the method can also be applied in the field of
- pricing policies (Bauer, Huber, and Adam 1998; Currim, Weinberg, and Wittink 1981; DeSarbo, Ramaswamy, and Cohen 1995; Goldberg, Green, and Wind 1984; Green and Krieger 1990; Kohli and Mahajan 1991; Mahajan, Green, and Goldberg 1982; Moore, Gray-Lee, and Louviere 1994; Pinnell 1994; Simon 1992; Wuebker and Mahajan 1998; Wyner, Benedetti, and Trapp 1984),

- advertising (Bekmeier 1989; Levy, Webster, and Kerin 1983; Darmon 1979; Louviere 1984; Perreault and Russ 1977; Stanton and Reese 1983; Neale and Bath 1997; Tscheulin and Helmig 1998; Huber and Fischer 1999), and
- distribution (Green and Savitz 1994; Herrmann and Huber 1997; Oppewal and Timmermans 1991; Oppewal 1995; Verhallen and DeNooij 1982).

In addition, this method is increasingly used as an instrument of
- controlling (Green and Srinivasan 1978; Herrmann et al., 1999).

Another field of application using basic strategic decisions such as
- Market segmentation (Hagerty 1985; Akaah 1988; De Soete and Winsberg 1994; DeSarbo, Olivier, and Rangaswamy 1989; DeSarbo, Ramaswamy, and Chaterjee 1992; DeSarbo, Wedel, Vriens, and Ramaswamy 1992; Diamantopoulos, Schlegelmilch, and DePreez 1995; Gaul and Aust 1994; Gaul, Lutz, and Aust 1994; Green and Helsen 1989; Green and Krieger 1991; Kamakura 1988; Ogawa 1987; Steenkamp and Wedel 1991; Steenkamp and Wedel 1993; Wedel and Kistemaker 1989; Wedel and Steenkamp 1989; Wedel and Steenkamp 1991). A good overview for the different segmentation approaches provides Vriens (1995) and Vriens, Wedel, and Wilms (1996). Conjoint analysis can be of great use here.
- The method is further applied to simulate purchasing decisions with a focus on competitors' responses (Mohn 1991).

This brief overview may give the impression that the success of this method comes from the application to new areas, in the sense of a broadening of the concept. But this is only one side of the coin. Simultaneously, research has been initiated to deepen the knowledge in certain areas. We have particularly seen many contributions for finding the optimal price for a certain product. In this context, an important distinction in analyzing the price attribute is made by Rao and Sattler in Chapter 2. They differentiate between two functions of the price. Consumers use the price of a product both as a signal of product quality (informational role) and as a monetary constraint in choosing it (allocative role). In their paper, Rao and Sattler implement a conjoint based research approach to separately estimate these two effects of price. While in practice only the net effect of the two roles of price are usually estimated in any conjoint measurement approach or brand choice model, our methodology is able to separate the two price effects.

It is the goal of conjoint analysis to explain and predict preferences that result in an assessment of achievements. Various achievement profiles are created (both real as well as hypothetical ones) by varying specific attributes, and these profiles are to be evaluated by the test persons. The contributions (partial benefits) that the various attributes make to overall preference (overall benefit) are estimated on the basis of overall preference judgments as expressed by the test persons. Accordingly each product concept is assigned with a specific overall benefit value. Thus no attribute-specific single judgments are summarized to yield an overall judgment (compositional approach) but vice versa; the contributions of the various attributes or their manifestations are filtered out of the overall judgments (decompositional approach).

Although many people speak of 'the conjoint analysis', the number of methods understood by this term and their variants is considerable. What all these approaches have in common, however, is a flow diagram developed by Green and Srinivasan (1978) which is shown in an updated form in Figure 1; the order of typical variants has been approximately selected based on their decreasing importance for practical applications (Cattin and Wittink 1982; Wittink and Cattin 1989; Wittink, Vriens, and Burhenne 1994).

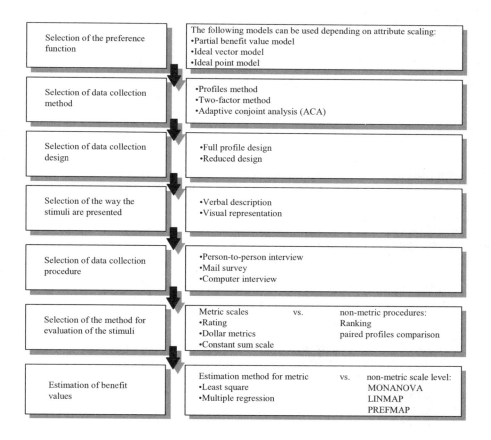

Figure 1:   Flow diagram of conjoint analysis

1.2   Research areas and future development trends of conjoint analysis

1.2.1   A flow diagram of conjoint analysis

The various options regarding the flow diagram (see figure 1) of the process of analysis should be determined before carrying out a practical conjoint analysis (Green and Srinivasan 1978; Green and Srinivasan 1990; Vriens 1995). Although each step is suitable to reveal findings and future developments of the research areas, the individual steps are not carried out one after the other and decisions are not made independently. Furthermore, good conjoint research most likely occurs if the process is hypothesis driven. Each stage of the process should be used to approve or reject potential solutions to decision problems.

1.2.2   Data collection

Selection of the preference function

The first step is the selection of the preference function based on which influence the defined attributes have on the respondents' preferences (other authors accentuate the relevance of the selection of the attributes and their levels in the first step, see Vriens 1995). This preference function therefore is the basis for determining partial benefit values for the respective attributes that reflect the preferences of the persons interviewed (Green and Srinivasan 1978; Schweikl 1985). The models that are most frequently used are the ideal vector model, the ideal point model, and the partial benefit model (See also Green and Srinivasan 1978; Vriens 1995).

When using the ideal vector model (see Figure 2) a proportional relationship is assumed between a partial benefit value and the manifestation of an attribute. This means that benefit increases ($w_{xj} > 0$) or decreases ($w_{xj} < 0$) with an increasing or decreasing manifestation of the attribute (Vriens 1995; Srinivasan, Jain and Malhotra 1983; Kamakura and Srivastava 1986; Allenby, Arora, and Ginter 1995).

If the ideal point model (see Figure 3) is used, the researcher assumes the existence of an ideal manifestation. The benefit value of a manifestation drops as soon as it falls below or exceeds the ideal point (Green and Tull 1982).

The partial benefit model (see Figure 4) is the most flexible of all three models and includes the ideal vector and the ideal point models as special cases (Green and Srinivasan 1978; Cattin and Wittink 1982; Louviere 1984; Wittink and Cattin 1989; Krishnamurthi and Wittink 1991; Green and Srinivasan 1990). This model does not assume a specific functional process and manifestations of attributes can only be interpolated if the scale level is metric.

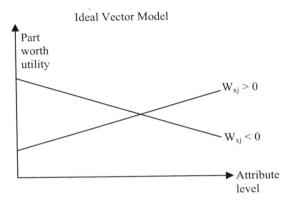

Wxj: individual weighting of attribute x by respondent j

Figure 2:   *Preference value for various manifestations of attribute x while keeping the values of the other attributes constant*

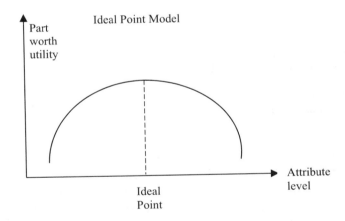

Figure 3:   *Preference value for various manifestations of attribute x while keeping the values of the other attributes constant*

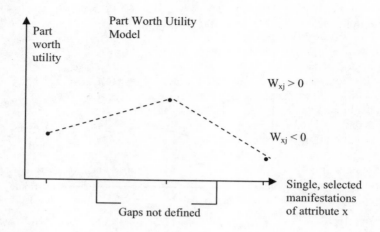

Wxj: individual weighting of attribute x by respondent j

Figure 4:   Preference value for various manifestations of attribute x while keep-
*   ing the values of the other attributes constant*

The partial benefit model is mainly used as a preference model for conjoint analysis (Green and Srinivasan 1978; Wittink and Cattin 1989; Cattin and Wittink 1982).
A linking rule is required to distinguish between the overall benefit of the product
alternative and the partial benefit values obtained using the preference function. In
principle, two types of combinations can be distinguished. Unlike noncompensatory models, compensatory models evaluate all existing attributes in
such a way that the low partial benefit of one attribute is compensated by an accordingly greater contribution to the overall benefit made by another attribute.

   If the various manifestations of attributes are interpreted as independent
(dummy) variables, the partial benefit model is formally identical to the ideal
vector model (Acito and Hustad 1981; Mahajan, Green, and Goldberg 1982;
Srinivasan 1979). The partial benefit model, however, provides greater flexibility
for designing the attribute evaluation function. But this greater flexibility has a
major setback that is not always properly taken into account in practical studies:
the number of parameters to be estimated increases for a given number of test
values. In contrast, the ideal vector model yields the smallest number of parameters to be estimated. The ideal point model ranges somewhere in between.

   The studies by Cattin and Punj (1984), Srinivasan, Jain, and Malhorta (1983),
Green and Srinivasan (1990), Krishnamurthi and Wittink (1991), and Hagerty
(1986), for example, focus on the preference function to be able to make
statements about the benefits of each model. Cattin and Punj state in their Monte
Carlo study that a limited, special model (such as the ideal vector model) yields
better predictions of preference values than a more general and flexible model

(such as the partial benefit model). Here they agree in general with the recommendations given by Srinivasan, Jain, and Malhorta (1983). Krishnamurthi and Wittink (1991) compare the partial benefit model with three other model specifications. As a result of their study in the automobile sector, they advocate the assignment of a 'continuous function' (such as the ideal vector model) to attributes for which continuous progress is expected. In this context, it appears useful to pay increased attention to the ideal vector model (viewed critically Pekelman and Sen 1979). Baier and Gaul address this in their studies presented in Chapter 3. Their essay is based on the well-known probabilistic ideal vector model (De Soete and Carroll 1983; Gaul 1989; Baier and Gaul 1996). Deterministic points for alternatives and random ideal vectors for consumer segments are used for explaining and predicting individual choice behavior in a low-dimensional attribute space where the same model formulation is employed for parameter estimation and for market simulation. Moreover, it can be used to analyze data collected via the wide-spread ACA system. To compare the new approach with traditional counterparts they conducted a Monte Carlo study. Additionally, an application for the German mobile phone market is used to illustrate further advantages.

Selection of the data collection method
After a preference model has been selected, the next step is to determine the way in which the incentives are presented to the respondents for evaluation. Among the classic data collection methods of conjoint analysis are the profile (Green and Rao 1971) and the two-factor methods (Johnson 1974; for the paired comparison approach see Srinivasan, Shocker, and Weinstein 1973), which both have repeatedly been compared to the one-factor evaluation (for some critical comments about the one-factor-method, see Vriens 1995). Although the one-factor evaluation of the self-explicated approach (Huber 1974; Srinivasan and Wyer 1989) basically conflicts with the principle of conjoint analysis to trade-off factors of combinations of factors, conjoint researchers have dedicated numerous studies to this data collection strategy. One reason for this research is that one-factor evaluation has become an integral part of the frequently used adaptive conjoint analysis. Moreover, Huber points out that one-factor evaluation is superior to data collection methods traditionally used in conjoint analysis whenever multiple attributes influence the decision, when the demanders' expectations regarding attributes and manifestations of attributes of the objects selected are stable, and when alternative choices do not exert a major influence on the decision (Huber 1997). These statements were corroborated by the study of Srinivasan and Park (1997). Another proof that the self-explication approach should be considered in conjoint analysis is provided by Sattler and Hensel-Börner in Chapter 4. In their article they give a comprehensive overview of studies comparing the self-explicated approach and conjoint measurement. On the basis of a valuable comparison of several advantages as well as disadvantages of conjoint measurement and self-explication approaches, they discuss these two approaches in great detail. After this, a broad overview of empirical studies comparing the two approaches under consideration in terms of

reliability as well as predictive validity shows the reader the state-of-the-art in that research area. Finally, they draw useful conclusions from their findings.

If the researcher decides in favor of the conjoint measurement and not the self-explicated approach he may choose between two methods of data collection. The **profile method** (synonyms are "full profile approach" or "multiple factor evaluation" (MFE), Green and Srinivasan 1978; Green and Tull 1982) describes the incentives to be evaluated by all K attributes considered. A full-profile description thus comes closer to a real buying situation (Green and Srinivasan 1978). Charts have proved their worth for representing incentives. The critical remarks by Wittink (1989) that this method was limited to approximately eight attributes requires qualification (e.g., Page and Rosenbaum 1989) as innovative forms of presenting incentives make it much easier for the individuals interviewed to carry out a preference evaluation.

The **two-factor method** (or "trade-off-analysis" or "two factor evaluation" (TFE) see Green and Tull 1982) reveals preferences for incentives only that are partially described by 2<K attributes (Mohn 1989). A typical feature of two-factor evaluations are trade-off matrices in which preferences have to be indicated in the associated matrix elements for all combinations of vertically or horizontally laid off manifestations of the two attributes considered. This approach has been criticized for being limited to ranking data (Wittink, Vriens, and Bruhenne 1994). This criticism must be qualified as well. It is true that Johnson (1974) introduced the two-factor evaluation explicitly for ranking data. However, it can easily be generalized for nearly any other evaluation scale that is common in conjoint analysis. It is a serious restriction of use, at least when using a polynomial linking function, that higher-order interaction effects cannot be taken into account (see Figure 5; Johnson 1974; Green and Tull 1982).

Two improvements of the traditional data collection methods have been used from the mid-1980s. An improvement of the profile method is called **hybrid conjoint analysis** (Green, Goldberg, and Montemayor 1981; Green 1984). It combines a direct (compositional) part of the survey in which the respondents have to give direct judgments about the importance of individual attributes, and an indirect (decompositional) part of the survey that represents the actual conjoint interview with selected combinations of attributes.

Adaptive conjoint analysis (ACA) is viewed as a modern form of the two-factor method (Johnson 1987). This method can provide a detailed analysis of the individual benefit structure of each respondent because the questions asked are adapted to previous answers in a computer-aided data collection process (Green and Srinivasan 1990).

Johnson (1974) initiated busy research activities focused on data collection methods (for a comparison of the approaches see Akaah and Korgaonkar 1983; Vriens and Wittink 1992). For example, Alpert, Betak, and Golden (1978; quoted from Green and Srinivasan 1978) and Montgomery, Witting, and Glaze (1977; quoted from Green and Srinivasan 1978) found that the two-factor evaluation had greater prediction validity. Segal (1982), however, agrees with Oppedijk van vee and Beazley (1977), Jain et al., (1979) and Rosko and McKenna (1983) that two-

The two attributes 'price' and 'warranty' are given. Please look at the manifestations of these properties and enter the number 1 into the combination you prefer most. Enter the number 2 for your second choice into one of the remaining fields. Enter the number 3 etc. for your next choices until all figures from1 to 9 have been used.

Evaluate all other pairs of attributes in this way.

Warranty

		6 months	12 months	18 months
	high			
Price	medium			
	low			

Figure 5:   Example of a two-factor matrix

and multiple-factor evaluations are equal while profile evaluation had a slight advantage

According to a study by Safizadeh, the increasing popularity of the profile approach is due to the fact that multiple-factor evaluations have less problems resulting from overvaluation of single major attributes taken out of context than the other two approaches (Safizadeh 1989; Slovic, Fleissner, and Bauman 1972). Wittink, Vriens, and Burhenne (1994), however, have shown that since Adaptive Conjoint Analysis is gaining ground, a comparison of multiple-factor and ACA approaches would be of great interest. Finkbeiner and Platz (1986) as well as Agarwal (1988) found that the results in terms of precision of prediction are alike in these two approaches. This conflicts with the findings of studies by Huber et al., (1993).

As the number of attributes that could be integrated into a conjoint design increases with the development of the ACA or hybrid procedure, it makes sense to notice studies where these attributes are the object of interest (Pullman, Dodson, and Moore 1999). The studies recently initiated by Orme, Alpert, and Chistensen (1997) and Huber, Ariely, and Fischer (1997) that focus on semantic peculiarities of the attributes used in the profile method should particularly be noted here. Their findings indicate that an affirmative or negative presentation of items may influence the evaluation of alternatives. The loss aversion effect as known from descriptive decision theory could be proved (Kahneman and Tversky 1979; Tversky and Kahneman 1991).

Selection of the data collection design

In addition to the way in which the respondents are supposed to evaluate incentives, the number of incentives is of relevance. If the objective is to have all theoretically conceivable incentives evaluated, i.e., all combinations of attribute manifestations included in the study, this will be a **complete** (factorial) **design**. In view of data collection expenses (Pearson and Boruch 1986) and the risk of wearing out the respondents, it is important to keep the number of incentives to be evaluated to a minimum, though the number of incentives, i.e., the number of observations, should at least equal the number of parameters to be estimated. From an empirical point of view, S=30 incentives seem to represent an upper limit (Green and Srinivasan 1978).

It is also desirable to have the validation of preference models supported by significance tests for the parameters and ways of cross-validation. This, however, can result in technical data collection problems. Therefore, a **reduced design** is often preferred which attempts to represent the complete design based on a smaller number of incentives (Addelman 1962a; Addelmann 1962b; Green 1974; Green and Srinivasan 1978). There are basically two ways in conjoint analysis to reduce the number of incentives, which means to fractionate the complete factorial design. The easiest way called 'random sampling' consists of taking as many incentives out of the design by random selection as is required to reach the desired scope (Green and Srinivasan 1978). This approach, however, is not used in marketing research and practice. It is common to reduce the design systematically in such a way that orthogonality, i.e., the independence of the factors (attributes) is retained (Green, Helsen, and Shandler 1988; 1989; Moore and Holbrook 1990; and Steckel, DeSarbo, and Mahjan 1990 discuss the relative advantages of the orthogonal and non-orthogonalen Design). Depending on whether the manifestations of attributes are all equal in number or whether the number of manifestations varies between attributes, we distinguish symmetrical and asymmetrical types of fractionated factorial designs (for a brief introduction see Kuhnfeld 1997). The 7 base plans provided by Addelmann (1962a) have proved to be particularly helpful for constructing asymmetrical and symmetrical main effect designs.

As there is no independence of attributes in many applications of conjoint analysis, greater attention has been recently paid to data collection design that takes into account interaction effects. Hints regarding the construction of fractionated factorial orthogonal designs with as small a number of incentives as possible were given by Cochran and Cox (1957), Winer (1973), Shah and Sinha (1989), and Assmus and Key (1992). A further contribution in this research area is made by Blomkvist, Ekdahl, and Gustafsson in Chapter 5. In their paper they use a non-geometric design to generate the concepts. Non-geometric designs represent a class of orthogonal designs that when the assumption of effect scarcity is valid, i.e., that only a few of the attributes actually influence the respondents' preferences, provide an opportunity to analyze interactions between attributes as well as the attributes themselves. In this article the use of non-geometric Plackett-Burman designs for conjoint analysis is advocated. Also, a procedure based on restricted all subsets regression for taking advantage of the special characteristics of the non-geometric designs is proposed and demonstrated using data from a conjoint study performed on cellular telephone antennas in Sweden. Blomkvist, Ekdahl, and Gustafsson also conducted a Monte Carlo simulation to further illustrate the properties of the proposed procedure and the use of non-geometric Plackett-Burman designs for conjoint analysis.

Selection of the way in which incentives are presented

There are two ways to present the incentives defined in the previous steps (Vriens 1995; Green and Srinivasan 1978). When the presentation is verbal, the incentives can be presented on product information sheets using key words, descriptive sentences, or a combination of key words and explanatory sentences.

When the presentation is visual, graphic representation using drawings or photographs has to be distinguished from physical presentation (Wedel and Steenkamp 1991; Steenkamp and Wedel 1993) where real products or prototypes are used (Aust and Gaul 1995; Vriens et al., 1998; Page and Rosenbaum 1987; 1989). Each of these three ways has its advantages and disadvantages which Green and Srinivasan (1978 and 1990) describe in some detail (Vriens 1995). The extent to which the presentation of incentives determines the responses of the test persons is the focus of a study by Holbrook and Moore (1981). The object of study of these two authors is pullovers. Pullovers most certainly are products that must be visually experienced. They are appreciated for aesthetic elements rather than objective, rational ones. The verbal description caused the respondents to attach greater importance to the interaction of attributes. When they were presented as images, the main effect was dominant. Louviere et al. 1987, however, found no differences between the two ways of presenting incentives. A survey of other studies dealing with this highly interesting, though so far virtually unexamined, area can be found in Vriens (1995).

Selection of the data collection procedure

Respondents who take part in a survey make their statements depending on the way in which the incentives are presented - either in person-to-person interviews, in writing by mail, or using a computer (Vriens 1995). According to Wittink and Cattin (1989), surveys by telephone or mail are mainly used to ensure geographic representativeness. The telephone may even be helpful in improving the usually low return rates found with written polls in market research.

Levy, Webster, and Kerin (1983) combined both ways. They first contacted the respondents by telephone. If respondents were willing to take part in the survey, they would receive the survey documents by mail. Stahl (1988) reports a commercial use of conjoint analysis via 'phone-mail-phone' and proceeds like the two authors previously mentioned. After contacting the respondents by phone, the documents would be sent to them. Eventually, the interview and data collection would again be carried out by telephone. The results of this study are encouraging and indicate that conjoint analysis by telephone is an appropriate procedure for collecting preference judgments. Still, what the respondents are asked to do should not be too straining or take too long (Stahl 1988). Based on his years of experience with conjoint analyses, Cerro (1988) lists a number of items that determine the success of a written non-personal survey used for conjoint measurement. It includes elements such as a high training level of the respondents (Tscheulin and Blaimont 1993), a call in advance to ask for their cooperation, prompt delivery of the documents, giving a telephone number where to call for advice at any time, and one to three reminder calls.

In terms of computer-aided procedures Zandan and Frost (1989), report that the respondents have a distorted perception of the duration of the interview. When asked how much time they needed to answer the questions, the participants in the survey stated clearly shorter times than would be required.

Conjoint analyses, with the help of computers, require greater attention with a view to the growing popularity of the Internet. Not only financial reasons but also new ways of designing surveys, call for a more extensive use of this survey method. Although first results of conjoint analyses carried out on the Internet are now available, this field has been sparsely examined according to Witt (1997).

Selection of the preference rating scale

The scales to be used by respondents for evaluating the existing incentives can be divided into metric (Green and Krieger 1993; for the constant-sum-rating see Mahjan, Green, and Goldberg 1982; DeSarbo et al., 1982; DeSarbo, Ramaswamy, and Chaterjee 1992) and non-metric variants. Thus a metric scale level is assumed for rating scales, a non-metric scale level for rankings, and paired profiles comparisons.

When using a **rating scale** (the so-called rating method), respondents are supposed to grade the (subjectively) perceived benefit on a numbered scale. This scale, in principle, just allows the collection of ordinal, i.e., non-metric, data. It is assumed, however, that the respondents will perceive scale spacings as being similar given appropriate graphic representation, so that preference statements are used as metric data. It is considered a benefit, compared to **ranking scales** (the so-called ranking method), that the rating scale expresses the intensity of the preference (Stegmüller 1995). This cannot be determined using the ranking method; here as well, respondents are to evaluate the incentives based on their (subjectively) perceived benefit but the outcome is just an order of preferences. Such order may express the preference-worthiness of an incentive but does not result in metric (ordinal) preference data (Green and Srinivasan 1990).

In a **paired profiles comparison**, the interviewer confronts the respondent with two incentives (product profiles) at the same time, and the respondent has to decide which of the two (s)he prefers. It is a benefit of ordinal paired comparisons that intransitiveness in the preferences collected from the respondents can be detected. For example, a respondent who knows his or her preferences and is willing and capable to express them without making mistakes would say in a graded paired comparison using a rating scale of 11 that he or she prefers incentive A to incentive B by seven units, and incentive B to incentive C by eight units. Furthermore, incentive A is superior to incentive C by 15 units but this number of units is not available to the respondent on the scale. This difficulty of a limited scale is circumvented by so-called dollar metrics. The respondent would be asked after making his or her choice in a graded paired comparison: "How much more would you be willing to pay for this product compared to the one you did not choose?"

Many researchers have dealt with selecting a scale for recording preferences since conjoint research began. What was of major interest in this context was the question of which one of the various methods was most beneficial. Cattin and Bliemel (1978) compared rating and ranking surveys in a simulation analysis. But as they processed rating data using a metric estimation method (OLS) and ranking data using a non-metric method (MONANOVA), it is impossible to tell whether the results were influenced by the way in which the data was collected or by the estimation method.

The design by Carmone, Green, and Jain (1978) is more transparent. The authors found in their studies that rating scales will provide more accurate results than ranking scales if a great error variance can be expected. Scott and Keiser (1984) state the opposite after evaluating their own data from the field of capital investment goods. When the respondents evaluated the profiles based on a ranking, the predictive validity was greater compared to rating.

In Chapter 6, Huber, Herrmann, and Gustafsson also deal with a scale for recording preferences. As a result of studies carried out so far, they found that results obtained using the rating method do not significantly deviate from those obtained using ranking. The test designs chosen by the various authors do not allow a clear statement as to whether or not the two measuring approaches yield different conjoint results. Avoiding the mistakes in the research design that some of the studies made in this area, they analyzed a potential connection between the rating and ranking methods, as well as a new hybrid approach (consisting of rating and ranking).

An interesting aspect in recording preferences comes from Teichert and Shehu in Chapter 7. They have generated the evolutionary conjoint analysis. Evolutionary conjoint develops individualized, flexible designs with an especially high degree of consumer integration. Consumer evaluations directly influence the experimental design. They continuously influence the levels of each attribute in each of the successive generations. This is in contrast to adaptive design techniques, where the design input of respondents is restricted to the first step of the self-explicated tasks. The new model-free method of Teichert and Shehu is based on interactive evolutionary algorithms. Algorithms are based on the principle of "survival of the fittest" and provide robust solutions for large dimensioned optimization problems.

In Chapter 8, Elrod and Chrzan also focused their research efforts on the question of the best way for respondents to evaluate the profiles. Their method is to avoid the lack of information in choice data by supplementing these data with information about the extent to which the chosen alternative is preferred. Following this idea, Elrod and Chrzan consider two types of choice-based conjoint designs for two alternatives: one using ordinary full profiles and the other using partial profiles. Having indicated which of two alternatives they prefer, consumers then also indicate the extent of their preference for their chosen alternative. The authors provide answers to five research questions, where they focus on the question only if the extent-of-preference information increases the efficiency of choice designs.

1.2.3   Data analysis

Estimation of partial benefit values

To analyze the preference data collected in the previous steps, the partial benefit values will have to be estimated for all manifestations of attributes. The methods that are available for analysis will depend on decisions made to date in conjoint analysis (Vriens 1995). The type of preference model and the scale level of the preference data collected, in particular, provide the framework within which the market researcher can analyze data.

Conjoint analysis was originally limited to an ordinal scale level. Estimation algorithms had to take this standard into account. In recent years, however, the metric approach has increasingly replaced the traditional ordinal data level both in marketing research and practice. Therefore, the importance of non-metric algorithms declined. Non-metric algorithms include (Mazanec, Porzer, and Wiegele 1976) PREFMAP as developed by Carroll (1972), LINMAP as programmed by Srinivasan and Shocker (1973; 1977), and POLYCON by Young (1972). In contrast to these algorithms taken from multidimensional scaling, Kruskal (1965) developed a non-metric MONANOVA approach especially for conjoint analysis. Johnson (1975) designed his program with calculating partial benefit values in mind. With a metric scale level, however, the method used most frequently is a regular dummy regression analysis (Kruskal 1964a; Kruskal 1964b). The most important estimation techniques are MONANOVA, LINMAP, and OLS. In Europe, over 80% of all conjoint-studies used these estimators (see Wittink, Vriens, and Burhenne 1994).

The most important studies on the use of the various estimation algorithms were carried out by Cattin and Wittink (1976), Cattin and Bliemel (1978), Colberg (1977), Jain et al. (1979), Carmone, Green, and Jain (1978), Wittink and Cattin (1981), and Mishra, Umesh, and Stem (1989). Cattin and Wittink (1976) compared metric and non-metric procedures. As a result they found that metric approaches can be superior to non-metric ones. These results by Cattin and Wittink are confirmed in the study by Cattin and Bliemel (1978). More precisely, the two researchers prove the superiority of MONANOVA over OLS estimation for determinist data. The opposite, however, applies to stochastic data. Carmone, Green, and Jain (1978) varied five environmental conditions for each respondent that could influence the outcome of conjoint analysis. One such factor that varies is the estimation algorithm. The Kendall's tau measure of quality is nearly identical for a MONANOVA and a modified (metric) variance analysis. The study by Wittink and Catin (1981) yields a similar result. Mishra, Umesh, and Stem (1989) analyzed precision and the dispersion of parameter estimates in a simulation study with more than 2000 respondents. They compared the algorithms LINMAP, MONANOVA, and OLS while changing the preference function, the error variance of simulated respondents, and the research design. Their conclusion is as follows: if precision and parameter dispersion are equivalent for a researcher, the LINMAP method should be preferred. If precision is decisive and the variance of estimates is of lesser interest, however, the OLS method should be used. Jain et al., (1979) compared the algorithms MONANOVA, JOHNSON, LINMAP, and OLS based on empirical data. The authors found nearly similar results for all estimation procedures.

If partial benefit values are available, the immediate question is about the quality of the results. One measurement here is reliability and the other is validity. Reliability, for example, is in focus in studies by Acito, (1977; 1979) Cattin, and Weinberger (1980) Jain, Malhtra, and Pinson (1980) McCullough, and Best (1979) Parker and Srinivasan (1976), and Segal (1982) (further studies can be found in Vriens 1995). The external validity of the conjoint results was proved, for example, by Bateson, Reibstein, and Boulding (1987), and Green and Srinivasan (1990). The studies by Robinson (1980), Benbenisty (1983), and Srinivasan et al., (1981) should be noted as well. While Robinson identified the factors that are relevant for passengers when choosing an airline, Srinivasan et al., were interested in the selection of the means of transport for getting to work. In both cases the behavior predicted by the researchers is largely congruent with real behavior. Wittink and Montgomery (1979), and Montgomery and Wittink (1980) correctly predicted the selection of a university or high school, or the career decision of a university graduate, at a predictive probability of 63%. Srinivasan (1988) even arrived at a value of 69% while Krishnamurthi (1988) correctly predicted selections at 56-61% for various preference models based on the study by Montgomery and Wittink (1980). Wright and Kriewall (1980), however, only achieved 14% and 21% of correct predictions as to which university would be chosen.

Validity is also in the center of interest for Kamakura and Ozer (Chapter 9). The way Kamakura and Ozer generate knowledge in this field of research is to compare various conjoint models across their part-worth estimates based on actual behavior. Because they are comparing those methods across their part-worth estimates, they use a Multitrait-Multimehod (MTMM) framework to assess the relationships among the methods and the part-worth estimates. To test the relationships, the authors use both the traditional MTMM analysis and a direct product methodology.

Also highly valuable in this context is the work conducted by Louviere, Hensher, and Swait presented in Chapter 10. In their article they expand the domain of conjoint analysis techniques by placing them within the more general framework of random utility theory (RUT). Based on this theoretical playground, the analyst is now able to compare and test the models and model results more rigorously. The authors illustrated these ideas in three case studies that show that even simple RUT-based stated preferences (SP) experiments can yield quite complex models; complex SP experiments can also provide new and different insights into the behavior of the random component of utility.

Different approaches to analyzing such complex models are presented by Haaijer and Wedel in Chapter 11. In a brief but detailed way they first describe the general elements in conjoint analysis and the "classic" conjoint analysis approaches. Then the conjoint choice approach is discussed more extensively and an overview is given of recent conjoint choice applications in the marketing literature. Finally they suggest approaches that can be used to estimate a conjoint choice experiment, including the MNL, the Latent Class MNL, and MNP models.

These various models will be illustrated using an application to a conjoint choice experiment on coffee makers.

To minimize remaining uncertainty in parameter estimation, new methods for conjoint designs have been proposed (Arora and Huber 2001). The most spectacular are the polyhedral and the machine-learning approaches. They are presented in Chapter 12 and 13 by Toubia, Evgeniou, and Hauser and Giesen and Schuberth. Fast polyhedral methods use a special "fast" algorithm that constructs profiles / choice sets depending on a-priori information of previous judgment tasks. Polyhedral methods can be used for both metric-paired comparison questions in ACA and CBC. Machine-learning and fast polyhedral algorithms have made it feasible to adapt both metric paired-comparison and choice-based conjoint questions to each respondent. Such questions promise to be more accurate and customized to focus precision where it is most needed. The basic concept is that each conjoint question constrains the set of feasible part-worths. A researcher's goal is to find the questions that impose the most efficient constraints where efficiency is defined as maximally decreasing the uncertainty in the estimated part-worths.

In Chapter 14 Dellaert, Borger, Louviere, and Timmermans present a new kind of estimating model. In their paper the four authors develop an experimental design heuristic to permit the estimation and testing of a proposed heteroscedastic extreme value model of modularized and traditional consumer choices. With this new way to design conjoint choice experiments the marketing researcher will be able to give an answer to the question of how consumer choices to package or bundle separate components differ (if at all) from choices among traditional fixed product options. To calculate the model parameters, separate MNL models were estimated from the choices in three experimental sub-designs. After this a heteroscedastic extreme value model was estimated by pooling data across all three sub-designs, and allowing for different random components in each. With this approach, differences in random components among the three conditions can be estimated independently.

Aggregation of utilities and market simulation

The estimation of the partial benefit values which takes place within the frame-work of the conjoint analysis serves to determine the individual attributes that contribute towards a preference. Usually, however, the attention of theoreticians and those who carry out field studies is focused on gaining an insight into the typical reactive behavior of a large group of consumers, rather than the specific behavior of individuals.

The hierarchical cluster methods (Green and Srinivasan 1978; Green and Krieger 1991) are used most frequently to classify respondents on the basis of normalized, individual, and partial benefits. The sequential use of a hierarchical and a partitioning technique is proposed by Punj and Stewart (1983) (for an application of overlapping partitioning methods see Hruschka 1986 and for an overview of different approaches see Vriens 1995). Problems are often encountered, however, when this technique is used. In our opinion, the fact that the different methods for determining the partial benefit values produce divergent results makes it more difficult to classify demanders. The objective function of the widespread OLS method, for example, minimizes the squared deviations of the estimated, metric stimulus benefits from the observed stimulus ranks. Conversely, LINMAP, another technique for measuring the partial benefits, minimizes the degree to which the observed and estimated rank orders are violated by means of linear programming. This objective criterion does not measure the benefit differences between pairs of ranks, providing the estimated benefit values coincide with the observed order. The calculated estimate, and thus also the clusters that are formed, is consequently dependent on the applied solution method.

The estimated partial benefits are moreover characterized by their relative un-reliability. This characteristic can be attributed to the reduced factorial design that is normally applied for conjoint analyses. The limited number of degrees of free-dom that are available for calculating the parameters on the level of individuals in turn affects the reliability of the estimates. Poor data reliability may lead to classi-fication errors (Vriens, Wedel, and Wilms 1996).

Another disadvantage is the possibility of "linking", i.e., if the variables that are taken into account in the study fail to differentiate clearly among the classes, the outcome is one large cluster containing the complete set of study objects (Everitt 1980). The large number of cluster methods that must be applied also proves problematic when it comes to forming classes. Hierarchical cluster tech-niques, such as single linkage, complete linkage, centroid cluster analysis, Ward's method, McQuitty's method, and the approach developed by Lance and William, tend to produce different results (Hartigan 1975). In addition, there are various ways of standardizing the data prior to the actual respondent classification proce-dure. The classification result is also influenced by the choice of method.

A further argument against the use of two-step classification methods is that two different objective criteria are optimized during the course of the calculations they entail. For example, whereas the objective of the first step is to minimize the squared deviations of the estimated metric stimulus benefits from the observed stimulus ranks by means of an OLS regression, Ward's algorithm maximizes the ratio between the inter-group variances and the intra-group variances of the indi-vidual coefficients.

In recent conjoint analysis applications designed to facilitate benefit segmenta-tion, the segment-specific partial benefit values and the segmentation are esti-mated simultaneously rather than sequentially (DeSarbo et al., 1989; De Soete and DeSarbo 1991; Ogawa 1987; Wedel and Kistemaker 1989; Wedel and Steenkamp 1989). Baier and Gaul (1995) propose a modified best-approximation method for estimating the model parameters - the segmentation and the segment-specific partial benefit values.

Ramaswamy and Cohen in their article (see Chapter 15) reviewed and pre-sented applications of the basic framework of latent class conjoint analysis, for both metric conjoint and choice-based conjoint situations. They noticed that given the problems with the tandem approach to segmentation in traditional metric con-joint and the difficulty of obtaining individual-level coefficients in the choice-based conjoint context, LSMs have proved to be a boon to market researchers. To show the strength of LSM, the authors have focused in their applications on simultaneous segmentation and prediction. Their outlook on further research areas is also remarkable.

A substantial improvement in clustering is the flexible approach to the segmentation of markets involving conjoint analysis called NORMCLUS employing various methods in combinatorial optimization, developed by DeSarbo/DeSarbo (Chapter 16). Their general approach accommodates multi-criterion objective functions, alternative types of clustering respondents, model or profile based segmentation schemes, constraints on coefficients, and constraints on segment memberships, etc. to adapt to the specific needs of the particular segmentation application being addressed. A variety of combinatorial algorithms are accommodated including genetic algorithms, simulated annealing, and various heuristics which are selected according to their efficiency in dealing with the structure and goals of the application at hand. The authors demonstrate the flexibility and practicability of their approach to develop a new industrial cleaner.

Knowledge of the benefit segments, however, is not the only important aspect in management decision-making processes. The extent to which changes in market shares can be brought about by modifying products or by altering the added values, for example, is also relevant. Depending on the object of the study various models could be used such as the first choice model, the Bradley-Terry-Luce model, the logit model, or the simulated probit model to transform the acquired partial benefits into choice decisions and thus to determine market shares (Vriens 1995). As the study conducted by Finkbeiner (1988) demonstrated, the first choice approach is the most suitable of all the previously mentioned choice models for predicting market share estimates. The findings obtained were refined on the basis of the study by Elrod and Krishnakumar (1989), and Davey and Elrod (1991). The studies revealed the advantages of first choice modeling when high-involvement products are the object of an investigation.

In Chapter 17, Huber, Orme, and Miller focus on choice simulators. They propose that effective choice simulators need three properties to effectively mirror market behavior. First, they need to display differential impact so that a marketing action at the individual or homogeneous segment level has maximal impact near a threshold but has minimal impact otherwise. Second, simulators need to reflect differential substitution, assuring that alternatives take proportionately more share from similar than dissimilar competitors. Finally, they need to exhibit differential enhancement, a property whereby a small value difference has a large impact on highly similar competitors but almost no impact on dissimilar ones. A new method that Huber, Orme, and Miller call Randomized First Choice enables simulators to closely match these properties in market behavior.

In the last Chapter (18), Whitlark and Smith focus on simulating and forecasting data on the basis of part-worth utilities. To be accurate, sales forecasts based on conjoint data should take into account possible competitive reactions, changes in product awareness and availability, and other marketplace realities such as varying usage rates and repurchase rates that unfold over time. The purpose of the article is to outline how sequential game theory and the macro-flow model can be applied to more accurately fit these assumptions when estimating market share and forecasting product sales.

1.3   Further Research

Despite many developments which have already taken place in conjoint analysis, many issues and new approaches to data collection or data analysis could be investigated. It is beyond the scope of this introduction to summarize all of them. In brief, we would only like to highlight some avenues which seem underdeveloped.

With regard to the process of data collection, one research topic is the further investigation of the use of photo-realistic pictorial representations for certain product categories. This field is becoming more relevant because new media, computer technology, and software packages in the meantime allow the use of visual stimuli. Furthermore, another fundamental message is that context still matters. The context within which judgments are made affects the utility structure that results from the analysis of those judgments, regardless of the conjoint method being used. Developing this area in more detail has the advantage that with the results, one should be able to match the context with the method used to estimate outcomes for the real world. In conjunction with the context, there is another interesting field of research. The area of conjoint analysis would benefit from research that can identify if and when bias actually occurs in model parameters, as well as if and when error variability is sufficiently large enough to offset gains from additional information per person. That is, in the absence of bias, more observations per person lead to higher statistical efficiency. In the case of choice experiments, evidence suggests that humans interact with experiments in such a way that more observations per person decreases choice consistency, which in turn decreases statistical efficiency.

In terms of the process of data analysis, more research is needed to investigate the relative capability of the various conjoint segmentation methods to recover the true segment structure (Vriens 1995). Research in this area is important, because on the one hand one-to-one marketing is too expansive and on the other hand the demand side is becoming more heterogeneous.

Little has been published in the way of formal tests to determine whether or not conjoint works in predicting significant real-world actions (Orme, Alpert, and Christensen 1997). As ancillary cases, there are interesting questions of whether or not one method works better than another, and under what circumstances each method should be preferred. Pioneering work in that area comes from Joel Huber (1997), but more meta-analysis is required.

1.4   References

Acito, F. (1977), An Investigation of some Data Collection Issues in Conjoint Measurement, *American Marketing Association Educators` Proceedings*, 82-85.

Acito, F. (1979), Industrial Product Concept Testing, *Industrial Marketing Management*, 10, 157-164.

Agarwal, M. (1988), Comparison of Conjoint Methods, *Proceedings of the Sawtooth Software Conference on Perceptual Mapping*, Sun Valley, 51-57.

22   Anders Gustafsson, Andreas Herrmann and Frank Huber

Akaah, I. P. (1988), Cluster Analysis versus Q-Type Factor Analysis as a Disaggregation Method in Hybrid Conjoint Modeling: An empirical Investigation, *Journal of the Academy of Marketing Science*, 19, 309-314.

Akaah, I. P. and P. K. Korgaonkar (1983), An Empirical Comparison of the Predictive Validity of Self-Explicated, Huber-Hybrid, Traditional Conjoint and Hybrid-conjoint Models, *Journal of Marketing Research*, 20, 187-197.

Allenby, G. M., N. Arora, and J. L. Ginter (1995), Incorporating prior Knowledge into the Analysis of Conjoint Studies, *Journal of Marketing Research*, 32, 152-162.

Alpert, M. I., J. F. Betak, and L. L. Golden (1978), *Data gathering Issues in Conjoint Measurement*, Working paper, Graduate School of Business, The University of Texas at Austin.

Arora, Neeraj and Joel Huber (2001), "Improving Parameter Estimates and Model Prediction by Aggregate Customization in Choice Experiments," *Journal of Consumer Research*, 28, (September), 273-283.

Assmus, E. F. and J. K. Key (1992), *Designs and their Codes*, Cambridge.

Baier, D., and W. Gaul (1996), Analyzing Paired Comparisons Data Using Probabilistic Ideal Point and Vector Models, in: Bock, H. H., Polasek, P., eds., *Data Analysis and Information Systems*, Berlin, 163-174.

Baier, D., and W. Gaul (1999), Optimal Product Positioning Based on Paired Comparison Data, *Journal of Econometrics*, 89, 365-392.

Baier, D. and W. Gaul (1995), Classification and Representation using Conjoint Data, in W. Gaul and D. Pfeifer eds., *From data to knowledge: Theoretical and Practical Aspects of Classification, Data Analysis, and Knowledge Organization*, Berlin, 298-307.

Bateson, J. E., D. Reibstein, and W. Boulding (1987), Conjoint Analysis Reliability and Validity: a Framework for future Research, in: American Marketing Association, ed., *Review of Marketing*, Chicago, 451-481.

Bauer, H. H., F. Huber, and R. Adam (1998), Utility oriented design of service bundles in the hotel industry based on the conjoint measurement method, in: Fuerderer, R., Herrmann, A. and Wuebker, G., eds., *Optimal Bundling - Marketing Strategies for Improving economic performance*, Wiesbaden, 269-297.

Bauer, H. H., F. Huber, and T. Keller (1997), Design of Lines as a product-policy Variant to retain Customers in the Automotive Industry, in Johnson, M., Herrmann, A., Huber, F. and Gustafsson, A., *Customer Retention in the Automotive Industry - Quality, Satisfaction and Retention*, Wiesbaden, 67-92.

Carmone, F. J., P. E. Green, and A. K. Jain (1978), Robustness of Conjoint Analysis: Some Monté Carlo Results, *Journal of Marketing Research*, 15, 300-303.

Carroll, J. D. (1972), Individual Differences and Multidimensional Scaling, in: Shepard, R. N., Romney, A. K., Nerlove, S. B., eds., *Multidimensional Scaling - Theory and applications in behavioral sciences*, Vol. 1, New York.

Cattin, P. and F, Bliemel (1978), Metric vs. Nonmetric Procedures for Multiattribute Modeling: Some Simulation Results, *Decision Sciences*, 9, 1978, 472-480.

Cattin, P. and M. Weinberger (1980), Some Validity and Reliability Issues in the Measurement of Attribute Utilities, in: Olsen, Jerry C., ed., *Advances in Consumer Research*, 7, 780-783.

Cattin, P. and D. R. Wittink (1977), Further knowledge beyond Conjoint Measurement: Toward a comparison of methods, *Advances in Consumer Research*, 4, 41-45.

Cattin, P. and D. R. Wittink (1982), Commercial Use of Conjoint Analysis: A Survey, *Journal of Marketing*, 46, 44-53.

Cerro, D. (1988), Conjoint Analysis by Mail, *Proceedings of the Sawtooth Software Conference on perceptual mapping*, Sun Valley, 139-143.

Cochran, W. G. and G. M. Cox (1957), *Experimental Designs*, New York.

Colberg, T. (1977), *Validation of Conjoint Measurement Methods: a Simulation and empirical Investigation*, Dissertation, University of Washington.

Currim, I. S., C. B. Weinberg, and D. R. Wittink (1981), Design of Subscription Programs for a Performing Arts Series, *Journal of Consumer Research*, 8, 67-75.

Darmon, R. Y. (1979), Setting Sales Quotas with Conjoint Analysis, *Journal of Marketing Research*, 16, 133-140.

Davey, K. S. and T. Elrod (1991), *Predicting Shares from Preferences for Multiattribute Alternatives*, working paper, University of Alberta.

De Soete, G., J. D. Carroll (1983), A Maximum Likelihood Method for Fitting the Wandering Vector Model, *Psychometrika,* 48, 553-566.

De Soete, G. and W. DeSarbo (1991), A latent Class Probit Model for Analyzing pick Any/N data, *Journal of Classification*, 8, 45-63.

De Soete, G. and S. Winsberg (1994) A latent Class Vector Model for Preference Ratings, *Journal of Classification*, 8, 195-218.

Dellaert, B., A. Borgers and H. Timmermans (1995), A Day in the City: Using Conjoint Experiments to urband Tourists`Choice of Activity Packages, *Tourism Management*, 16, 347-353.

DeSarbo, W. S., J. D. Carroll, D. R. Lehmann, and J. O`Shaughness (1982), Three-way Multivariate Conjoint Analysis, *Marketing Science*, 1, 323-350.

DeSarbo, W. S., R. L. Oliver, and A. Rangaswamy (1989), A simulated annealing Methodology for Clusterwise Linear Regression, *Psychometrika*, 54, 707-736.

DeSarbo, W. S., A. Ramaswamy, and K. Chaterjee (1992*), Latent Class Multivariate Conjoint Analysis with Constant Sum Ratings Data*, working paper, University of Michigan.

DeSarbo, W. S., V. Ramaswamy, and S. H. Cohen, (1995), Market Segmentation with Choice-based Conjoint Analysis, *Marketing Letters*, 6, 137-147.

DeSarbo, W. S., M. Wedel, M. Vriens, and V. Ramaswamy (1992), Latent Class Metric Conjoint Analysis, *Marketing Letters*, 3, 273-288.

DeSarbo, W., L. Huff, M. M. Rolandelli, and J. Choi (1994), On the Measurement of Perceived Service Quality, in: R. T. Rust, and R. L. Oliver (ed.), *Service Quality: New directions in theory and practice,* London, 201-222.

Diamantopoulos, A., B. Schlegelmilch, and J. P. DePreez (1995), Lessons for Pan-European Marketing? The Role of Consumer Preferences in fine-tuning the Product Market Fit, *International Marketing Review*, 12, 38-52.

Finkbeiner, C. T. (1988), Comparison of Conjoint Choice Simulators, *Proceedings of the Sawtooth Software Conference on perceptual mapping*, Sun Valley, 75-105.

Finkbeiner, C. T. and P. J. Platz (1986), Computerized versus Paper and Pencil Methods: a Comparison Study, paper presented at the *Association of Consumer Research Conference*, Toronto.

Gaul, W. (1989), Probabilistic Choice Behavior Models and their Combination With Additional Tools Needed for Applications to Marketing, in: De Soete, G., Feger, H., Klauer, K.-H., eds., *New Developments in Psychological Choice Modeling*, Amsterdam, 317-337.

Gaul, W. and E. Aust (1994), *Latent Class Inequality Constrained Least Square Regression*, working paper, University of Karlsruhe.

Gaul, W., U. Lutz, and E. Aust (1994), Goodwill towards domestic Products as Segmentation Criterion: An empirical Study within the Scope of Research on country-of-origin effects, in: Bock H. H., Lenski, W. and Richter, M., eds., Information systems and Data Analysis, *Studies in Classification and data analysis, and knowledge organization*, 4, 415-424.

Goldberg, S. M., P. Green, and Y. Wind (1984), Conjoint Analysis of Price Premiums for Hotel Amenities, *Journal of Business*, 57, 111-147.

Green, P. E. and V. R. Rao (1971), Conjoint Measurement for Quantifying Judgmental Data, *Journal of Marketing Research*, 8, 355-363.

Green, P. E. and V. Srinivasan (1978), Conjoint Analysis in Consumer Research: Issues and Outlook, *Journal of Consumer Research*, 5, 103-123.

Green, P. E. and V. Srinivasan (1990), Conjoint Analysis in Marketing: New Developments With Implications for Research and Practice, *Journal of Marketing*, 54, 3-19.

Green, P. E. and D. S. Tull (1982), *Methoden und Techniken der Marketingforschung*, Stuttgart.

Green, P. E. and Y. Wind (1975), New Way to Measure Consumers' Judgments, *Harvard Business Review*, 53, 107-117.

Green, P. E. and A. M. Krieger (1990), A hybrid Conjoint Model for price-demand Estimation, *European Journal of Operations Research*, 44, 28-38.

Green, P. E. and K. Helsen (1989), Cross-validation Assessment of Alternatives to individual-level Conjoint Analysis: a case study, *Journal of Marketing Research*, 26, 346-350.

Green, P. E., K. Helsen, and B. Shandler (1988), Conjoint Internal Validity under alternative Profile Presentations, *Journal of Consumer Research*, 15, 392-397.

Green, P. E. and A. M. Krieger (1987), A simple Heuristic for Selecting 'good' Products in Conjoint Analysis, *Application of Management Science*, 5, 131-153.

Green, P. E. and A. M. Krieger (1992), An Application to Optimal Product Positioning Model to Pharmaceutical Products, *Marketing Science*, 11, 117-132.

Green, P. E. and A. M. Krieger (1993), A simple Approach to Target Market Advertising Strategy, *Journal of the Market Research Society*, 35, 161 - 170.

Green, P. E. and A. M. Krieger (1993), Conjoint Analysis with product-positioning Applications, J. Eliashberg, G. J. Lilien eds., *Marketing, Handbooks in OR&MS*, 5, 467-515.

Green, P. E. and J. Savitz (1994), Applying Conjoint Analysis to Product Assortment and Pricing in Retailing Research, *Pricing Strategy and Practice*, 4-19.

Hagerty, M. R. (1985), Improving the predictive Power of Conjoint Analysis: The use of Factor Analysis and Cluster Analysis, *Journal of Marketing Research*, 22, 168-184.

Hagerty, M. R. (1986), The cost of simplifying Preference Models, *Marketing Science*, 5, 298-324.

Herrmann, A., B. Franken, F. Huber, M. Ohlwein, and R. Schellhase (1999), The Conjoint Analysis as an Instrument for Marketing Controlling taking a public Theatre as an Example, *International Journal of Arts Management*, forthcoming.

Herrmann, A. and F. Huber (1997), Utility orientated Product Distribution, *The International Review of Retail, Distribution and Consumer Research*, 8, 369-382.

Herrmann, A., F. Huber, and C. Braunstein (1997), Standardization and Differentiation of Services: a cross-cultural study based on Semiotics, Means End Chains and Conjoint Analysis, Academy of Marketing/American Marketing Association Proceedings of 31st Annual Conference 7th July 1997, *Manchester Metropolitan University*.

Hruschka, H. (1986), Market definition and Segmentation Using Fuzzy Clustering Methods, *International Journal of Research in Marketing*, 3, 117-134.

Huber, F. and M. Fischer (1999), Measurement of Advertising Response - Results of a conjointanalytical Study, *Proceedings of the Academy of Marketing Science World Conference, Malta*.

Huber, G. P. (1974), Multiattribute Utility Models: a Review of filed and field-like Studies, *Management Science*, 20, 1393-1402.

Huber, J. (1997), What we have learned from 20 Years of Conjoint Research: When to use self-explicated, graded pairs, full profiles or choice experiments, *Sawtooth Software Conference Proceedings*, Seattle, 243-256.

Huber, J., D. Ariely, and G. Fischer (1997), *The Ability of People to express Values with Choices, Matching and Ratings*, working paper, Fuqua School of Business, Duke University.

Jain, A. R., F. Acito, N. Malhorta, and V. Mahajan (1979), A Comparison of internal Validity of alternative Parameter Estimation Methods in decompositional Multiattribute Preference Models, *Journal of Marketing Research*, 16, 313-322.

Jain, A. R., N. Malhorta, and C. Pinson (1980), *Stability and Reliability of part-worth utility in Conjoint Analysis: a longitudinal Investigation*, working paper, European Institute of Business Administration, Brüssel.

Johnson, M., A. Herrmann, and F. Huber (1998), Growth through Product Sharing Services, *Journal of Service Research*, 1, 167-177.

Johnson, R. M. (1974), Trade-Off Analysis of Consumer Values, *Journal of Marketing Research*, 11, 121-127.

Kahneman, D. and A. Tversky (1979), Prospect Theory: An Analysis of Decision under Risk, *Econometrica*, 47, 263-291.

Kamakura, W. A. (1988), A least squares Procedure for Benefit Segmentation with Conjoint Experiments, *Journal of Marketing Research*, 25, 157-167.

Kamakura, W. A. and R. K. Srivastava (1986), An ideal-point probabilistic Choice Model for heterogeneous Preferences, *Marketing Science*, 5, 199-218.

Kohli, R. and R. Sukumar (1990), Heuristics for Product-Line-Design using Conjoint Analysis, *Management Science*, 36, 1464-1478.

Kohli, R. and V. Mahajan (1991), A reservation-price Model for optimal Pricing of Mulitattribute Products in Conjoint Analysis, *Journal of Marketing Research*, 28, 347-354.

Krishnamurthi, L. (1988), Conjoint Models of Family Decision Making, *International Journal of Research in Marketing*, 5, 185-198.

Krishnamurthi, L. and D. R. Wittink (1991), The Value of Idiosyncratic Functional Forms in Conjoint Analysis, *International Journal of Research in Marketing*, 8, 301-313.

Kuhfeld, W. D. (1997), Efficient Experimental Designs using Computerized Searches, *Sawtooth Software Conference Proceedings*, Seattle, 71-86.

Levy, M., J. Webster, and R. A. Kerin (1983), Formulating Push Marketing Strategies: a Method and Application, *Journal of Marketing*, 47, 25-34.

Louviere, J. (1984), Using discrete Choice Experiments and mulitnominal Logit Models to forecast Trial in a competitive Retail Environment: a fast food Restaurant Illustration, *Journal of Retailing*, 60, 81-107.

Luce, R. D. and J. W. Tukey (1964), Simultaneous Conjoint Measurement - A New Type of Fundamental Measurement, *Journal of Mathematical Psychology*, 1, 1-27.

Mahajan, V., P. E. Green, and S. M. Goldberg (1982), A Conjoint Model for Measuring Self and Cross-Price/Demand Relationships, *Journal of Marketing Research*, 19, 334-342.

McCullough, J. and R. Best (1979), Conjoint Measurement: Temporal Stability and Structural Reliability, *Journal of Marketing Research*, 16, 26-31.

Mishra, S., U. N. Umesh, and D. E. Stem (1989), Attribute Importance weights in Conjoint Analysis: Bias and Precision, *Advances in Consumer Research*, 16, 605-611.

Mohn, N. C. (1989), Simulated purchase 'Chip' testing versus trade-off (conjoint) analysis, *Proceedings of the Sawtooth Software Conference on perceptual mapping*, Sun Valley, 53-63.

Montgomery, D. B. and D. R. Wittink (1980), The predictive Validity of Conjoint Analysis for alternative Aggregation Schemes, Market Science Institute, ed., *Market Measurement and Analysis*, Cambridge, 298-309.

Montgomery, D. B., D. R. Wittink, and T. Glaze (1977), *A predictive Test of individual level Concept Evaluation and trade-off Analysis*, Research paper No. 415, Graduate School of Business, Stanford University.

Moore, W. L., J. Gray-Lee, and J. J. Louviere (1994), *A cross-validity Comparison of Conjoint Analysis and Choice Models at different levels of Aggregation*, working paper, University of Utah, Salt Lake City.

Moore, W. L. and M. B, Holbrook (1990), Conjoint Analysis on objects with environmentally correlated Attributes: The questionable Importance of representative Design, *Journal of Consumer Research*, 6, 490-497.

Neal, W. D. and S. Bathe (1997), Using the Value Equation to evaluate Campaign Effectiveness, *Journal of Advertising Research*, 37, 80-85.

Ogawa, K. (1987), An Approach to Simultaneous Estimation and Segmentation in Conjoint Analysis, *Marketing Science*, 6, 66-81.

Oppedijk van veen, W. M. and D. Beazley (1977), An Investigation of alternative Methods of Applying the trade-off Model, *Journal of Market Research Society*, 19, 2-9.

Oppewal, H. (1995), *Conjoint experiments and retail planning: Modeling consumer choice of shopping centre and retailer reactive behavior*, thesis, Eindhoven.

Orme, B. K., M. I. Alpert, and E. Chistensen (1997), Assessing the validity of Conjoint Analysis - continued, *Sawtooth Software Conference Proceedings*, Seattle, 209-226.

Page, A. and H. F. Rosenbaum (1987), Redesigning Product Lines with Conjoint Analysis: how Sunbeam does it, *Journal of Product Innovation Management*, 4, 120-137.

Page, A. and H. F. Rosenbaum (1989), Redesigning Product Lines with Conjoint Analysis: a reply to Wittink, *Journal of Product Innovation Management*, 6, 293-296.

Parker, B. R. and V. Srinivasan (1976), A consumer Preference Approach to the Planning of rural primary health-care facilities, *Operations Research*, 24, 991-1025.

Pearson, R. W. and R. F. Boruch (1986), *Survey Research designs: Towards a better Understanding of their Cost and Benefits*, Berlin.

Pekelman, D. and S. K. Senk (1979): Improving prediction in conjoint analysis, *Journal of Marketing Research*, 16, 211-220.

Perreault, W. D. and F. A. Russ (1977), Improving Physical Distribution Service Decisions with trade-off Analysis, *International Journal of physical Distribution and Materials Management*, 7, 3-19.

Pinnell, J. (1994), Multi-Stage Conjoint Methods to Measure Price Sensitivity, in: Weiss, S., ed., *Sawtooth News*, 10, 5-6.

Pullman, M. E., K. J. Dodson, and W. L. Moore (1999),.A comparison of conjoint methods when there are many attributes, *Marketing Letters,* 10 (2), 125-138.

Punj, G. and D. W. Stewart (1983), Cluster Analysis in Marketing Research: Review and Suggestions for Application, *Journal of Marketing Research*, 20, 134-148.

Robinson, P. J. (1980), Applications of Conjoint Analysis to Pricing Problems, in: D. B. Montgomery and D. R. Wittink eds., *Proceedings of the first ORSA/TMS Special interest conference on market measurement and analysis*, Report 80-103, Cambridge, 183-205.

Rosko, M. D. and W. F. McKenna (1983), Modelling consumer choices of health plans: A comparison of two techniques, *Social Sciences and Medicine*, 17, 421-429.

Safizadeh, M. H. (1989), The internal Validity of the trade-off Method of Conjoint Analysis, *Decision Science*, 20, 451-461.

Sands, S. and K. Warwick (1981), What product Benefits to offer to whom: an Application of Conjoint Segmentation, *California Management Review*, 24, 69-74.

Segal, M. N. (1982), Reliability of Conjoint Analysis: contrasting Data Collection Procedures, *Journal of Marketing Research*, 13, 211-224.

Shah, K. R. and B. K. Sinha (1989), *Theory of Optimal Designs*, Berlin.

Simon, H. (1992b), Pricing Opportunities - And How to Exploit Them, *Sloan Management Review*, 34, 55-65.

Slovic, P., D. Fleissner, and S. Bauman (1972), Analyzing the use of Information in Investment Decision Making: a methodological proposal, *Journal of Business*, 45, 283-301.

Srinivasan, V., A. K. Jain, and N. K. Malhotra (1983), Improving predictive Power of Conjoint Analysis by constrained Parameter Estimation, *Journal of Marketing Research*, 20, 433-438.

Srinivasan, V. and C. S. Park (1997), Surprising Robustness of the self-explicated Approach to Customer Preference Structure Measurement, *Journal of Marketing Research*, 34, 286-291.

Srinivasan, V. and A. D. Shocker (1973), Linear Programming Techniques for Multidimensional Analysis of Preferences, *Psychometrika*, 38, 337-369.

Srinivasan, V., A. D. Shocker, and A. G. Weinstein (1973), Measurement of a Composite Criterion of Managerial Success, *Organizational Behavior and Human Performance*, 9, 147-167.

Stahl, B. (1988), Conjoint Analysis by Telephone, *Proceedings of the Sawtooth Software Conference on perceptual mapping*, Sun Valley, 131-138.

Stanton, W. W. and R. M. Reese (1983), Three Conjoint Segmentation Approaches to the Evaluation of Advertising Theme Creation, *Journal of Business Research*, 11, 201-216.

Steckel, J. H., W. DeSarbo, and V. Mahjan (1990), On the Creation of acceptable Conjoint Analysis Experimental Designs, *Decision Sciences*, 22, 435-442.

Steenkamp, J. B. and M. Wedel (1991), Segmenting Retail Markets on Store Image using a consumer-based Methodology, *Journal of Retailing*, 7, 300-320.

Steenkamp, J. B. and M. Wedel (1993), Fuzzy clusterwise Regression in Benefit Segmentation Application and Investigation into its Validity, *Journal of Business Research*, 26, 237-249.

Tscheulin, D. K. and B, Helmig. (1998), The optimal Design of Hospital Advertising by Means of Conjoint Measurement, *Journal of Advertising Research*, 38, 35 - 46.

Tscheulin, D. K. and C. Blaimont (1993), Die Abhängigkeit der Prognosegüte von Conjoint-Studien von demographischen Probanden-Charakteristika, *Zeitschrift für Betriebswirtschaftslehre*, 63, 839-847.

Tversky, A. and D. Kahneman (1991), Loss Aversion and Riskless Choice: A Reference Dependent Model, *Quarterly Journal of Economics*, 6, 1039-1061.

Van der Lans, I. A., P. W. Verlegh, and H. N. Schifferstein (1999), An Empirical Comparison of various individual-level Hybrid Conjoint Analysis Models, in: Hildebrandt, L., Annacker, D. and Klapper, D., eds., *Proceedings of the 28th EMAC Conference*, Berlin.

Verhallen, T. and G. J. DeNooij (1982), Retail Attributes and shopping Patronage, *Journal of Economic Psychology*, 2, 439-455.

Vriens, M. (1995), *Conjoint analysis in Marketing*, Ph. D thesis, Capelle.

Vriens, M., H. Oppewal, and M. Wedel (1998), Ratings-based versus choice-based Latent Class Conjoint Models - an empirical comparison, *Journal of the Market Research Society*, 40, 237-248.

Vriens, M., H. R. van der Scheer, J. C. Hoekstra, and J. P. Bult (1998), Conjoint Experiments for direct mail Response Optimization, *European Journal of Marketing*, 32, 323-339.

Vriens, M., M. Wedel, and T. Wilms (1996), Metric Conjoint Segmentation Methods: a Monte Carlo comparison, *Journal of Marketing Research*, 33, 73-85.

Vriens, M. and D. Wittink (1992), *Data Collection in Conjoint Analysis*, unpublished manuscript.

Wedel, M. and C. Kistemaker (1989), Consumer Benefit Segmentation using clusterwise Linear Regression, *International Journal of Research in Marketing*, 6, 45-59.

Wedel, M. and J. B. Steenkamp (1989), Fuzzy clusterwise Regression Approach to Benefit Segmentation, *International Journal of Research in Marketing*, 6, 241-258.

Wedel, M. and J. B. Steenkamp (1991), A clusterwise Regression Method for simultaneous fuzzy market structuring and Benefit Segmentation, *Journal of Research in Marketing*, 28, 385-396.

Winer, B. J. (1973), *Statistical Principles in Experimental Design*, New York.

Witt, K. J. (1997), Best Practice in Interviewing via the Internet, *Sawtooth Software Conference Proceedings*, Seattle, 15-34.

Wittink, D. R. and P. Cattin (1981), Alternative Estimation Methods for Conjoint Analysis: A Monté Carlo Study, *Journal of Marketing Research*, 18, 101-106.

Wittink, D. R. and P. Cattin (1989), Commercial Use of Conjoint Analysis: An Update, *Journal of Marketing*, 53, 91-96.

Wittink, D. R. and D. Montgomery (1979), Predicting validity of trade-off analysis for alternative Segmentation Schemes, American Marketing Association Educator's Conference, Chicago, 69-73.

Wittink, D. R., M. Vriens, and W. Burhenne (1994), Commercial Use of Conjoint Analysis in Europe: Results and Critical Reflections, *International Journal of Research in Marketing*, 11, 41-52.

Wright, P. and M. A. Kriewall (1980), State-of-mind Effects on the Accuracy with which Utility Functions predict marketplace Choice, *Journal of Marketing Research*, 17, 277-293.

Wuebker, G. and V. Mahajan (1998), A conjoint analysis-based Procedure to measure Reservation Price and to optimally Price Product Bundles, in: Fuerderer, R., Herrmann, A. and Wuebker, G., eds., *Optimal Bundling - Marketing Strategies for Improving economic performance*, Wiesbaden, 157-176.

Wyner, G. A., L. H. Benedetti, and B. M. Trapp (1984), Measuring the quantity and mix of Product Demand, *Journal of Marketing*, 48, 101-109.

Yoo, D. I, and H. Ohta (1995), Optimal Pricing and Product Planning for new Mulitattribute Products based on Conjoint Analysis, *International Journal of Production Economics*, 38, 245-254.

Young, F. W. (1972), A model for polynomial Conjoint Analysis algorithms, in: Shepard, R., Romney, A. K. and Nerlove, S. B., eds., *Multidimensional Scaling - Theory and Applications in Behavioral Sciences*, New York, 69-104.

Zandan, P. and L. Frost (1989), Customer Satisfaction Research using disks-by-mail, *Proceedings of the Sawtooth Software Conference on perceptual mapping*, Sun Valley, 5-17.

Zufryden, F. (1988), Using Conjoint Analysis to predict trial and repeat-purchase Patterns of new frequently purchased Products, *Decision Sciences*, 19, 55-71.

2 Measurement of Price Effects with Conjoint Analysis: Separating Informational and Allocative Effects of Price

Vithala R. Rao and Henrik Sattler

2.1 Introduction

One of the most frequent purpose of conjoint analysis is the measurement of price effects (Wittink and Cattin 1989; Wittink, Vriens, and Burhenne 1994). Usually this is be done by describing a number of product alternatives on a small number of attributes, including price, and collecting some kind of preference data for these product alternatives. From the estimated part-worth function for price one can infer price effects (Srinivasan 1979).

A particular problem of this approach is that the role of price often is restricted to its function as a monetary constraint in brand choice. However, it is well known that prospective buyers use price of a brand both as a signal of quality as well as a monetary constraint in the brand choice (Erickson and Johansson 1985). These two distinct roles of price in the consumers' evaluation of alternative offerings in the marketplace can be labeled as the informational (signal) role of price and the allocative (constraint) role of price. While these roles are conceptually distinct, their measurement using conjoint analysis becomes confounded owing to the difficulties of distinctly modeling the two effects of price. In practice, only the net effect of price is estimated.

In a meta-analysis study of price elasticity covering 367 products Tellis (1988) uncovered about 50 products where the estimated price elasticity is greater than zero; given the fact that effect of price on sales (or aggregation of individual choices) is the net result of both informational and allocative effects, it is conceivable that for these 50 products, the informational effect may have dominated the allocative effect. Further, the price elasticity was between 0 and -1 for an additional 40 products possibly indicating that the magnitude of the allocative effect exceeded that of the informational effect.

The lack of a distinction between these two price effects can be seen in the different views of price in the literature. The economic theory of consumer behavior (Nagle 1984) and the research on hedonic prices (Rosen 1974) focuses on the allocative role of price, whereas the stream of marketing research investigating the relationship between price and quality (Olsen 1977; Monroe and Dodds 1988; Dodds, Monroe, and Grewal 1991) largely focus on the informational effects of price.

The fact that price may convey some information on quality had been already acknowledged by Scitovsky (1945). Since then, more than 90 studies examined the relationship between price and perceived quality (see Gardner 1977; Rao 1984 and 1993; Monroe and Dodds 1988; Gijsbrechts 1993 for reviews). In general, no uniform price-quality relationship could be observed. Several explanations have been offered for the mixed results. Besides methodological differences, contextual and situational factors and demand artifacts (Olson 1977; Monroe and Krishnan 1985; Rao and Monroe 1989), we argue that the studies could have measured the net effect of the allocative and informational role of price instead of the pure informational effect. In other words, we argue that the studies could have measured the net effect of the allocative and informational role of price instead of the pure informational effect. Depending on whether or not the informational effect is stronger than the allocative effect, a positive or negative net price effect on quality will be observed.

Gautschi and Rao (1990) proposed a methodology to estimate separate effects of price in the conjoint setting. It requires collecting data on two preference orderings on the set of choice alternatives - called unconstrained and constrained preferences - respectively obtained under no budget constraint and obtained under the budget constraint. Denoting the unconstrained and constrained preferences by $U(\mathbf{b}^*)$ and $U(\mathbf{b})$, they estimate two relationships between $U(\mathbf{b}^*)$ and the product attributes and price as well as between the difference, $U(\mathbf{b}) - U(\mathbf{b}^*)$ and attributes and price. They theoretically show that the coefficient (or part-worth function) of price in the $U(\mathbf{b}^*)$ function measures the informational effect and that in the $U(\mathbf{b})$ $- U(\mathbf{b}^*)$ as the allocative effect.

This approach was illustrated in a pretest by Gautschi and Rao (1990) using a small-scale conjoint study on laptop computers, each described on three attributes at two levels. So far there has been no systematic empirical test of the approach. The main objective of this paper is to test the model of Gautschi and Rao (1990) in an empirical setting in a large sample under various conditions; three questions are taken under consideration:

1. Do the signs of the estimated parameters for the informational and allocative effects of price behave in the expected direction for different kinds of product categories and different kinds of information about product characteristics available for the consumer?
2. How do the informational and allocative effects of price vary with respect to the budget available to consumers while choosing/evaluating brand alternatives?
3. How do the informational and allocative effects vary when brand name and/or other information are included as an additional cue in the alternative descriptions?

The rest of this paper is organized as follows. First, we develop hypotheses with respect to the three questions and describe the method used in our study. Next, we present our results and, finally, we discuss the results and provide future research directions.

2.2   Hypotheses on Roles of Price

Our discussion thus far makes it clear that price plays two distinct roles - informational and allocative - in product evaluation by consumers. The literature reviewed earlier and the general meaning of the two price effects suggest that the informational price effect is positive and the allocative price effect is negative. Further, based on a meta-analysis of over 30 years of research, Rao and Monroe (1989) found that price effects on perceived product quality will vary with product characteristics such as the price level and whether or not the products are durables. If we interpret the perceived quality judgments as equivalent to informational effects of price, it can be expected that the magnitude of this price effect will vary with product characteristics. Thus:

Hypothesis 1: The informational effect of price is positive and the allocative effect of price is negative for all types of products and different kinds of product characteristics.

The allocative price effect treats price as a monetary constraint in the brand choice; it limits how much is available for spending on other products (Erickson and Johansson 1985). The classical model derived from economic theory of consumer behavior postulates that a consumer maximizes utility by allocating a limited budget over alternative products (Lancaster 1971; Nagle 1984). Price becomes the sacrifice one makes to obtain the stream of benefits generated by the bundle of attributes that constitutes the product. The magnitude of the sacrifice is measured by the allocative price effect and should be inversely related to the amount of budget that remains after purchase of the product. However, the informational price effect is not related to the budget available for a consumer after purchase. For instance, depending on whether a product is free (e.g., because a person gets a product as a present or wins it in a lottery or gets a free sample as a part of a sales promotion) or one has to pay a certain price the allocative effect will change. But, the informational price effect will be the same independent of whether the product is free or not, because the signaling function of price information is the same - assuming one knows the market price of the free product (which is the same as for the non-free product). Several theories and conceptual models dealing with the informational effect of price emphasize that the price information depends upon the objective and perceived level of price, but is not related to the monetary budget constraint. For example, the signaling theory states that price can be used as a signal of quality when consumers are imperfectly informed which is independent on the strength of the allocative price effect (Milgrom and Roberts 1986) Similarly, several conceptual models of the effect of price on product evaluation state that higher prices lead to higher perceived quality and consequently to a greater willingness to buy; this relationship is deemed to be independent of the monetary sacrifice required for purchase of goods with higher prices (Dodds, Monroe and Grewal 1991; Monroe and Krishnan 1985; Zeithaml 1988) Thus:

Hypothesis 2: The magnitude of the allocative effect of price is inversely related to the amount of budget that remains after the purchase of the product while there will be no effect of the remaining budget on the informational price effect.

It is well known that brand name connotes information to prospective buyers (Aaker 1991; Keller 1993). Thus, one could expect the effect of price to be moderated when choices of known brands are made. Analyzing the relationship between price as a quality indicator, several authors suggest that the role of price may have been overestimated, and that other extrinsic cues such as brand name are equally or more important, especially for package goods (Zeithaml 1988; Gijsbrechts 1993). In this context, Olsen and Jacoby (1972) argued that consumers use extrinsic cues that are not related directly to product performance (e.g., price, brand name and store name) as well as intrinsic cues that are derived directly from the physical product (e.g., amount of sugar in food or RAM of a computer) to evaluate a product. If price is either the only information available („single cue") or it is in addition to a few intrinsic cues, the informational effect of price in the evaluation of a product should be higher than if brand name is used in addition (Olsen 1977). This can be expected because brand names often have a strong information or knowledge function (Keller 1993) and therefore will take at least partly the role of the price as an informational cue. However, if a brand has no or nearly no reputation (which can be typically assumed for a totally new brand) its informational effect should be (nearly) zero. Therefore, an unknown brand name should have no influence on the informational price effect. Thus:

Hypothesis 3: The informational effect of price will vary systematically with the reputation of the brand.

2.3   Method

This study was conducted among 216 „MBA" and doctoral students at the University of Kiel, Germany during the months of May to July 1991. Each subject evaluated various product descriptions in an experimental setting. Two products - marmalade and alarm clocks—were used in the study. The incentive for participation was the opportunity to receive one of several prizes in a lottery; the lottery was conducted at the end of the study and prizes were distributed to winners. The subjects took about forty minutes on the average to complete the data collection task.

The design of the study is the same for marmalade and alarm clocks and is shown in Table 1. We employed five subsamples, each subsample consisting of 38 to 46 subjects. About one-half of the subjects in each subsample evaluated products in each of the two product categories. Further, there were three information conditions. Under condition A, information about price (3 levels, i.e. 1.99 / 2.49 / 2.99 DM for marmalade and 29.- / 39.- / 49.- DM for alarm clocks) and brand name (3 levels, i.e. market leader / third in the market / fictitious for both product categories) was given; under condition B, information about price and 3 attributes (fruit content / sugar content / artificial coloring and preservatives for marmalade and format / snooze / switch off for alarm clocks, each having 2 levels); and condition C, information about price, brand name and the same 3 attributes. The chosen attributes and attribute levels were based on a pretest with salespeople and consumers. The attributes were the most important ones for the product evaluation by the consumers and were also seen as to be able to distinguish between products (Alpert 1971). The levels of the attributes were chosen according to real market conditions.

Each subsample evaluated different numbers of product profiles; for example, in the price and brand information condition, the subjects evaluated a set of nine profiles under an unconstrained and constrained budget conditions. According to Table 1, each subject in each subsample evaluated four or five stimuli sets and one additional set to evaluate the reliability of their responses.

For the evaluation task, the full profile method was used (Green and Srinivasan 1990). Initially the subjects ranked the profiles in terms of preference to buy one item in the product category and then rated each profile on a 100 point rating scale with the extreme values „I would least prefer to buy" and „I would most prefer to buy". This procedure resulted in an interval scale with values between 1 and 100 where the points indicate the relative preference to buy one item of the described products.

Table 1:   *Experimental Design*

Sub-sample	# of Subjects	Information Condition		
		A: Price & Brand 9 Profiles, 4 Parameters	B: Price & Attributes 10 Profiles, 5 Parameters	C: Price, Brand & Attributes 16 Profiles, 7 Parameters
1	45	Uncon., Con. 1	Uncon., Con. 1, R	—
2	46	Uncon., Con. 2	Uncon., Con. 2, R	—
3	46	Con. 1, Con. 2	Con. 1., Con., 2, R	—
4	41	Uncon., Con. 1	—	Uncon., Con. 1, R
5	38	—	Con. 1, Con. 2, R	Con. 1, Con. 2
Total	216			

Uncon.	=	Respondents had no budget constraint (unconstraind).
Con. 1	=	Respondents got a 50% price discount (partially constrained).
Con. 2	=	Respondents had to pay the full price (fully constrained).
R	=	Additional alternate form test of reliability.

The evaluation data were collected under three budget conditions: Unconstrained budget (free: „Assume you don't have to pay for the product at all. Somebody else (a big company where you are employed) is paying. So, you don't have to worry about who is paying."), partially constrained (50% discount: „Assume you don't have to pay the full price. You will get the product with a 50% discount.") and fully constrained (full Price: „Assume you have to pay the full price shown."). The partially constrained condition can be seen as an extreme case of price promotion which is not uncommon (but at a high level) in Germany.

When representing choice alternatives parsimoniously as bundles of character-istics Z, it is inevitable that the researcher will omit some elements of Z in a con-joint setting. Therefore, one can partition Z as (Z_o, Z_u), where Z_o is a vector of observed (or included) characteristics of product descriptions and Z_u is a vector of unobserved (or excluded) characteristics. Denoting U as the utility from consum-ing a good, V as a utility component corresponding to a representative consumer and e as a idiosyncratic deviation of the individual's utility from V in modeling utility, one can express U as:

(1) $\qquad U = V(Z_o, Z_u) + e\,(Z_o, Z_u).$

If one attempts to estimate U with no knowledge of Z_u, the estimates of the pa-rameters of V are likely to be biased. As we discussed earlier, one approach to controlling for Z_u is to use price as a proxy variable for Z_u. The problem with using price as a proxy for Z_u is that price also performs a conventional function of allocating the individual's resources. Therefore, the procedure to reduce the con-founding of the price effects requires use of two preference orderings.

Our procedure to estimate the informational and allocative effects of price may be illustrated for the situation with one product feature, Z_1, and price, P, and linear functions for the two preferences. Denoting the unconstrained and constrained preference functions as:

(2) $\qquad U(\mathbf{b^*}) = \alpha_0 + \alpha_1 Z_1 + \alpha_2 P + \in_{\mathbf{b^*}};$ and

(3) $\qquad U(\mathbf{b}) = \beta_0 + \beta_1 Z_1 + \beta_2 P + \in_{\mathbf{b}}$

where α_s and β_s are parameters to be estimated and $\in_s$ are random components. The difference equation, becomes

(4) $\qquad U(\mathbf{b}) - U(\mathbf{b^*}) = (\beta_0 - \alpha_0) + (\beta_1 - \alpha_1)Z_1 + (\beta_2 - \alpha_2)P +$

$\qquad\qquad (\in_{\mathbf{b}} - \in_{\mathbf{b^*}}).$

In our analysis, we need only to estimate the equations for $U(\mathbf{b}^*)$ and for the difference, $U(\mathbf{b}) - U(\mathbf{b}^*)$ constraining $(\beta_1 - \alpha_1)$ to zero.[1] The main allocative effect of price is then revealed by the estimate of $(\beta_2 - \alpha_2)$. The informational or signaling effect is reflected in the estimate of α_2.

The two effects of price were estimated at the individual level using data on unconstrained and one of the two constrained budget situations. Further, the estimates of price effects were also made between the two constrained budget situations. In this process, we estimated 563 regression equations of which 535 were statistically significant in terms of the goodness of fit (R-square). The models were significant for both products and for all experimental conditions. Thus, we may conclude that the proposed model works well.

2.4   Results

Reliability: The two sets of ranks for a particular product set (designed with the same attributes and attribute levels, but with no duplications) were used for separately estimating the attribute part-worth functions using the OLS method. These estimates were correlated to provide a measure of reliability of the conjoint task. This test takes four sources of error into account (Green and Srinivasan 1978): inaccuracies in the input data, variability in the set of constructed stimuli, errors in the estimation procedure, and lack of stability (variations from one time period to another). These reliability measures were statistically significant at the 10 percent level for 188 out of the 216 subjects. For more than 85% of all respondents, Pearson's product-moment correlation was higher than 0.75. Given the fact that our reliability measure takes four sources of error into account and, therefore, has a high power and the result, that for persons with a non-significant reliability score the correlation coefficient is in all but two cases higher than 0.30, we decided to exclude just two respondents from further analysis (those with a correlation coefficient lower than 0.30) and to keep the other in the sample.

Internal validity: To check the internal validity of the model we tested the goodness of fit (R-square) of each estimated equation. In total we estimated 530 regression equations of which 505 were statistically significant at the $p < 0.10$ level (i.e. 95%). The models were significant for both products and for all experimental conditions. Thus, we may conclude that the proposed model works well.

Informational and Allocative Price Effects (Test of H1): We first analyzed the informational and allocative price effects pooling the data across various experimental conditions for the subsamples 1, 2, and 4 in Table 1. As can be seen from Table 2, the informational price effect for the unconstrained–constraint 1 (partially

---

[1]   We explicitly tested the assumption of equality of effects of attributes (excluding price) in the unconstrained and constrained preferences and found that this assumption is justified for over 82 percent of the respondents at 0.10 significance level. Thus, the estimation method employed seems appropriate.

constrained) and the unconstrained–constraint 2 (fully constrained) condition is usually positive or non-significant. However, for 15 to 22% of the respondents the „informational" effect is negative indicating that these individuals are generally suspicious of the quality of higher priced products. This finding is consistent with the results of the pretest found by Gautschi and Rao (1990). The allocative effect is significant and negative or non-significant in all but very few cases; it is negative and significant in about 50% of the cases for marmalade and about 60% of the cases for alarm clocks.

We also estimated the net effect of price in the regression of constrained preference under the full budget constraint condition. As one might expect, in only a small number of cases - 4 out of 82 for marmalade and 7 out of 98 for alarm clocks - the net price effect is positive. Thus, a negative price effect estimated in a normal conjoint analysis study does not enable a researcher to infer the magnitude of the two price effects; there is no way to determine which role of price (informational or allocative) is contributing to the estimated price effect.

Table 2:   Overall information and allocative price effects (Hypothesis 1)

Product Category	Informational Effect		Allocative Effect	
	# Sub.	Mean (s.d.)	# Sub.	Mean (s.d.)
MARMALADE:				
Positive, Significant	**50**	37.09 (3.19)	0	
Nonsignificant	48	0.07 (1.46)	62	−5.49 (1.18)
Negative, Significant	28	−35.93 (4.82)	**64**	−67.31 (4.92)
Total	126	6.07 (1.71)	12 6	−36.89 (2.11)
ALARM CLOCKS:				
Positive, Significant	**78**	47.62 (2.70)	2	102.8 (17.8)
Nonsignificant	40	6.94 (2.54)	55	−6.56 (1.70)
Negative, Significant	21	−44.40 (5.80)	**82**	−77.52 (4.82)
Total	139	22.01 (2.00)	13 9	−46.8 (2.61)

Table 3:   *Informational and allocative price effects for different experimental conditions*

MARMALADE

Experi-mental Design	Comparison Used for Estimation		Informational Effect			Allocative Effect		
			Signifi-cant Posi-tive*	Non-Signifi-cant*	Signifi-cant Nega-tive*	Sig-nificant Posi-tive*	Non-Signifi-cant*	Signifi-cant Nega-tive*
Price and Brand	Unconst. Versus Const. 1	#a	23	9	11	0	20	23
		Mean	44.23	5.93	-40.63	—	-7.07	-86.80
		(SD)	(3.01)	(4.63)	(2.06)		(2.99)	(3.15)
Price and Brand	Unconst. Versus Const. 2	#	17	1	2	0	2	18
		Mean	29.41	-13.00	-19.17	—	-11.33	-70.93
		(SD)	(1.18)	(10.06)	(6.34)		(6.94)	(3.98)
Price and Attri-butes	Unconst. Versus Const. 1	#	4	12	4	0	9	11
		Mean	40.09	2.52	-52.92	—	-1.07	-45.09
		(SD)	(2.53)	(3.06)	(5.63)		(.91)	(5.04)
Price and Attri-butes	Unconst. versus Const. 2	#	2	14	4	0	12	8
		Mean	44.67	1.43	-30.83	—	-4.19	-50.08
		(SD)	(5.63)	(2.31)	(2.77)		(4.63)	(5.07)
Price, Brand and Attri-butes	Unconst. versus Const. 1	#	4	12	7	0	19	4
		Mean	21.83	2.81	-26.54	—	-6.12	-34.51
		(SD)	(4.59)	(2.08)	(3.83)		(2.91)	(5.09)

ALARM CLOCKS

Experi-mental Design	Comparison Used for Estimation		Informational Effect			Allocative Effect		
			Signifi-cant Posi-tive*	Non-Signifi-cant*	Signifi-cant Nega-tive*	Sig-nificant Posi-tive *	Non-Signifi-cant*	Signifi-cant Nega-tive*
Price and Brand	Unconst. versus Const. 1	#a	31	7	5	1	13	29
		Mean	54.62	18.4	-43.72	120.60	-8.94	-95.06
		(SD)	(1.65)	(6.42)	(6.03)	(17.8)	(3.04)	(3.14)
Price and Brand	Unconst. versus Const. 2	#	13	9	4	0	10	16
		Mean	57.18	4.68	-50.50	—	-7.22	-96.12
		(SD)	(2.09)	(7.31)	(3.51)		(5.88)	(4.55)
Price and Attri-butes	Unconst. versus Const. 1	#	13	6	4	1	13	9
		Mean	34.80	4.00	-50.20	85.00	-9.80	-54.00
		(SD)	(2.83)	(6.63)	(5.29)	(41.18)	(5.29)	(4.47)
Price and Attri-butes	Unconst. versus Const. 2	#	10	11	6	0	12	15
		Mean	50.40	4.36	-41.20	—	-3.64	-65.36
		(SD)	(2.28)	(3.58)	(5.06)		(4.10)	(3.79)
Price, Brand and Attri-butes	Unconst. versus Const. 1	#	11	7	2	0	7	13
		Mean	29.26	4.92	-31.90	—	-4.02	-45.80
		(SD)	(1.74)	(3.16)	(1.70)		(3.10)	(3.03)

[a] Number of subjects, * $p < 0.10$

Next, we investigated whether the signs of the two price effects behave in the expected direction for different kinds of product characteristics , i.e. for all experimental conditions. Table 3 shows that in general this is the case. In addition, it appears that the informational effect is stronger for the price-brand condition than for the price-attribute and the price-attribute-brand condition. Moreover, this tendency seems to be stronger for Marmalade than for Alarm Clocks. Analyzing this tendency in more detail by applying a t-test of differences between the mean t-values (t = price estimate divided by the standard error of the price estimate) of the two product categories, we found in general non-significant differences for the informational as well as the allocative price effect.

Taking all results together, Hypothesis 1 is partly supported with respect to the informational price effect and fully supported for the allocative effect of price.

Table 4:   *Price effects under different budget constraints. Mean (Standard deviations) of t-values (t = Price estimate/Standard error of price estimate*

Product Category	Experimental Design	Price Effect	n	Partially Constrained Budget[a]	n	Fully Constrained Budget[b]	Δt^c
Marmalade	Price and Brand	Informtional	43	4.42 (10.75)	20	6.21 (5.15)	0.886
		Allocative	43	-4.24 (5.99)	20	-18.01 (23.14)	2.620**
Alarm Clocks	Price and Brand	Informtional	43	4.40 (18.24)	26	6.58 (11.45)	0.601
		Allocative	43	-3.06 (2.98)	26	-10.74 (12.80)	2.954**
Marmalade	Price and Attributes	Informtional	20	0.36 (4.32)	20	0.26 (3.80)	0.078
		Allocative	20	-1.93 (1.10)	20	-5.75 (10.25)	1.657*
Alarm Clocks	Price and Attributes	Informtional	23	1.99 (5.12)	27	2.33 (5.83)	0.215
		Allocative	23	-1.95 (2.97)	27	-3.83 (4.27)	1.782*

*p < 0.10; **p < 0.01

[a]Respondents got a 50% discount; the informational price effect was estimated under the unconstrained budget condition.

[b]Respondents had to pay the full price; the informational price effect was estimated under the unconstrained budget condition.

[c]t-test of differences between partially constrained and fully constrained.

Variation Due to Budget (Test of H2): Our expectation is that the informational effect will not change with the budget, but the allocative effect of price will be inversely related to the amount of budget that remains after purchase. Table 4 shows the estimated price effects under different budget constraints. Statistical tests of these effects between the two conditions indicates that the informational price effect is independent of the budget constraint. But, the allocative price effect increases with a decrease in the budget that remains after purchase of the product; difference is statistically significant in all experimental conditions. The change in the allocative effect of price seems to be stronger for the price-brand condition than for the price-attribute condition. The individuals seem to be less price sensitive if they do have information about attributes. Thus, our results support H2.

Informational Price Effect vs. Brand Effect (Test of H3): Given our experimental design, we could investigate two particular brand effects: (i) between established brands describing the effect between the market leader and the third in the market and (ii) between unknown and established brands describing the effect between an unknown or new brand and the market leader (see Table 5). Both these effects are estimated by the coefficients of dummy variables in the estimated preference functions. If brands do have an information function in the consumer purchase decision (Keller 1993) they do directly compete with the informational price effect.

Table 5:   *Cluster centroids of significant beta values for the informational effects of price and brand under the price/brand condition*

Cluster and Interpretation		Between Established Brands				Between Market Leader and Unknown Brand			
		n	Price Effect Mean (SD)	Brand Effect Mean (SD)	Correlation between Price and Brand Effects	n	Price Effect Mean (SD)	Brand Effect Mean (SD)	Correlation between Price and Brand Effects
Product Category: **Marmalade**									
Cluster 1	B. D.	9	.285(.13)	.924(.12)	-.366	21	.230(.11)	1.041(.08)	-.452
Cluster 2	N. P. nor B. D.	18	.275(.16)	.357(.17)	-.192	6	.446(.16)	.645(.21)	.728
Cluster 3	P. D.	12	.868(.09)	.136(.08)	.671*	12	.868(.09)	.441(.12)	-.829**
Total		39	.46(.31)	.42(.32)	-.549**	39	.46(.31)	.80(.39)	-.847**
Product Category: **Alarm Clocks**									
Cluster 1	B. D.	8	.284(.25)	.629(.13)	-.051	18	.269(.13)	.983(.11)	-.435
Cluster 2	N. P. nor B. D.	18	.387(.16)	.145(.09)	-.085	22	.715(.11)	.621(.13)	-.784**
Cluster 3	P. D.	28	.826(.14)	.140(.08)	.264	14	.843(.18)	.196(.10)	-.083
Total		54	.60(.28)	.21(.20)	-.421**	54	.60(.28)	.63(.32)	-.834**

*p < 0.01   **p < 0.001
B. D. = Brand Dominated; N. P. = Neither Price

Using these two estimated effects at the individual level (specifically, the standardized regression coefficients as the measures), we clustered the subjects into three groups separately for the two experimental conditions.[2] The results are shown in Table 5.

For a three-cluster solution, a uniform structure for all conditions of the experiment can be identified: Cluster 1 represents the brand dominated cluster, for Cluster 2, neither price nor brand are dominant , and Cluster 3 represents the price dominated cluster. As predicted by H3, the brand dominated cluster becomes more important when the brand reputation increases. This is true for both products. In addition, for marmalade the „price dominated" cluster decreases when brand reputation increases which is also consistent with H3.

We expect to find a negative correlation between the measures (significant beta values) of the informational effect and the brand effect for each cluster as well as the subsamples as a whole. We also conjecture that this correlation to be lower in magnitude for the effects between established brands than for the effects between market leader and an unknown brand; this expectation is due to the fact that a known brand name versus an unknown name will be a good substitute for price as an informational signal. As shown in Table 5, the correlations are in the expected direction for the subsamples as a whole for both product categories. This is also true for the clusters in general. These additional analyses also support the hypothesis, H_3.

2.5   Discussion and Future Research Directions

This paper implemented a conjoint based methodology to separately estimate two distinct roles of price: the informational role where price serves as a signal of quality and the allocative role where price is a monetary constraint in the brand choice. While, in practice, only the net effect of the two roles of price are usually estimated in any brand choice or preference model, our methodology is able to separate the two price effects. Based on the distinction between the two roles of price and the literature on the economic theory of consumer behavior and several consumer research studies on price-perceived quality relationship, we postulated that the informational price effect is positive and the allocative effect is negative. Applying the methodology in a large scale experimental study, we found that this hypothesis is, in general, supported.

An important issue that arises from our results is whether or not the estimation of part-worth function for price in conjoint analysis should be re-examined. We recommend that researchers should collect unconstrained and constrained preference data on at least a subset of profiles in a conjoint study. This change will enable them to determine the extent of confounding of the two roles of price in the preference model. This additional data collection may require more time from the

---

[2]   The cluster algorithm used was „nearest centroid sorting" (Anderberg 1973). For a three-cluster solution, clusters all differ significantly for both price and brand effects (p < 0.05). Using the elbow-criterion of the ratio of within to total sum of squares, we found that the three cluster solutions best represent the data.

respondent and may increase costs. If so, steps should be taken to control for the confounding of the informational price effect; one approach is to instruct respondents to assume that all other aspects among the products presented (i.e., all product attributes not presented) are identical. But, practical experience with conjoint analysis indicates that instructions like these do not work well.

One way to overcome this confounding problem at least partly is to include most of the salient product attributes in the conjoint study. As can be seen from Table 3, the magnitude of the informational price effect decreases if more product attributes are available (compare the price, brand and attribute situation with the price and brand or the price and attribute situations). This approach needs to consider the issue of how to deal with correlated attributes. Experimentation with this and other approaches to separate out the price effects in conjoint setting is called for.

While we have estimated the two effects of price on preference data, there is need to determine the allocative effect of price unconfounded by the informational effect on actual brand <u>choice</u>. It is perhaps necessary to supplement the unconstrained preference data with data on choices among various choice sets and employ a combination of regression and logit analysis for estimating the two price effects. Appropriate methodologies will need to be developed to tackle this problem. The methods of designing choice experiments will be suitable in this respect (Louviere and Woodworth 1983). Further, it is unclear whether the two effects of price can be separately estimated using only longitudinal choice data as available from scanner panels.

Our research looked at buying products once. In practice, individuals buy a majority of products repeatedly over time. As an individual learns about a product, the information effect of price will change. Thus, there is a need to explore the signaling effects of price reduction particularly for frequently purchased items in a suitable dynamic model of choice.

More generally, once a defensible approach for estimating the allocative and informational effects on choices is established, models can be developed to relate them to the marketing mix decisions on price, sales promotion, distribution and advertising. It can be expected that an optimal price for a new brand will be different when the informational role of price is also included in the brand choice model. The reference price effects can be included in such a model (Putler 1992). These models can also be used for pricing new brands as well as brand extensions.

Acknowledgement

The authors thank Sönke Albers, Klaus Brockhoff, Karen Gedenk, Stephan Schrader and Douglas Stayman for their comments on an earlier draft of this paper.

2.6   References

Aaker, D. A. (1991), *Managing Brand Equity: Capitalizing on the Value of a Brand Name*, New York.

Alpert, M. I. (1971), Identification of Determinant Attributes: A Comparison of Methods, *Journal of Marketing Research*, 8, 184-191.

Anderberg, M. R. (1973), *Cluster Analysis for Applications*, New York.

Brockhoff, K. (1987), *Marketing durch Kunden-Informationnssysteme*, Stuttgart.

Brucks, M. and Zeithaml, V. A. (1991), Price and Brand Name as Indicators of Quality Dimension, *Marketing Science Institute,* Cambridge, 91-130.

Darby, M. and Karni, E. (1974), Free Competition and the Optimal Amount of Fraud, *Journal of Law and Economics*, 16, 67-88.

Dodds, W. B., Monroe, K. B. and Grewal, D. (1991), Effects of Price, Brand, and Store Information on Buyers' Product Evaluations, *Journal of Marketing Research*, 28, 307-319.

Erickson, G. M. and Johansson, J. K. (1985), The Role of Price in Multi-Attribute Product Evaluations, *Journal of Consumer Research*, 17, 195-199.

Gardner, D. M. (1977), *The Role of Price in Consumer Choice. Selected Aspects of Consumer Behavior. NSF/RA 77-0013*, Washington.

Gautschi, D. A. and Rao, V. R. (1990), A Methodology for Specification and Aggregation in Product Concept Testing, in: A. deFontenay, M. H. Shugard and D. S. Sibley, eds., *Telecommunications Demand Modeling*, Amsterdam, 37-63.

Gijsbrechts, E. (1993), Prices and Pricing Research in Consumer Marketing: Some Recent Developments, *International Journal of Research in Marketing*, 10, 115-151.

Green, P. E. and Srinivasan, V. (1978), Conjoint analysis in Consumer Research: Issues and Outlook, *Journal of Consumer Research*, 5, 103-123.

Green, P.E. and Srinivasan, V. (1990), Conjoint Analysis in Marketing: New Development with Implications for Research and Practice, *Journal of Marketing*, 54, 3-19.

Keller, K. L. (1993), Conceptualizing, Measuring, and Managing Customer-Based Brand Equity, *Journal of Marketing*, 57, 1-22.

Kihlstrom, R. E. and Riordan, M. H. (1984), Advertising as a Signal, *Journal of Political Economy*, 92, 427-450.

Lancaster, K. (1971), *Consumer Demand: A New Approach*, New York.

Louviere, J. J. and Woodworth, G. G. (1983), Design and Analysis of Simulated Consumer Choice or Allocation Experiments: An Approach Based on Aggregate Data, *Journal of Marketing Research*, 20, 350-367.

Milgrom, P. and Roberts, J. (1986), Price and Advertising Signals of Product Quality, *Journal of Political Economy*, 94, 796-821.

Monroe, K. B. and Krishnan, R. (1985), The Effect of Price on Subjective Product Evaluations, in: Jacoby, J., ed., Perceived Quality, Lexington, 209-232.

Monroe, K. B. and Dodds, W. B. (1988), A Research Program for Establishing the Validity of the Price-Quality Relationship, *Journal of the Academy of Marketing Science*, 16, 151-168.

Nagle, T. (1984), Economic Foundations for Pricing, *Journal of Business*, 57, S3-S26.

Nelson, P. (1970), Information and Consumer Behavior, *Journal of Political Economy*, 78, 311-329.

Nelson, P. (1974), Advertising as Information, *Journal of Political Economy*, 82, 729-754.

Nelson, P. (1981), Consumer Information and Advertising, in: Galatin, M. and Leiter, R. D., eds., *Economics of Information*, Boston, 42-77.

Olson, J. C. (1977), Price as an Informational Cue: Effects on Product Evaluations, in: Woodside, A. G., Sheth, J. N. and Bennett, P. D., eds., *Consumer and Industrial Buying Behavior*, New York, 267-286.

Olson, J. C. and Jacoby, J. (1972), Cue Utilization in the Quality Perception Process, *Proceedings of the Third Annual Conference Association for Consumer Research*, 167-179.

Philips, L. (1988), *The Economics of Imperfect Information*, Cambridge.

Putler, D. (1992), Incorporating Reference Price Effects into a Theory of Consumer Choice, *Marketing Science*, 11, 287-309.

Rao, A. R. and Monroe, K. B. (1989), The Effect of Price, Brand Name, and Store Name on Buyers' Perception of Product Quality: An Integrative Review, *Journal of Marketing Research*, 26, 351-357.

Rao, V. R. (1984), Pricing Research in Marketing: The State of the Art, *Journal of Business*, 57, S39-S60.

Rao, V. R. (1993), Pricing Decision Models in Marketing, in: Eliashberg, J. and Lilien, G. L., eds., *Handbooks in OR & MS , Vol. 5 (Marketing)*, Elsevier Science Publishers B.V., 517-552.

Rosen, S. (1974), Hedonic Prices and Implicit Markets: Product Differentiation in Pure Competition, *Journal of Political Economy*, 82, 34-55.

Ross, W. T. J. and Creyer, E. H. (1992), Making Inferences about Missing Information: The Effects of Existing Information, *Journal of Consumer Research*, 19, 14-25.

Scitovsky, T. (1945), Some Consequences of the Habit of Judging Quality by Price, *Review of Economic Studies*, 12, 100-105.

Shapiro, C. (1983), Premiums for High Quality Products as Rents to Reputation, *Quarterly Journal of Economics*, 98, 659-680.

Srinivasan, V. (1979), Network Models for Estimating Brand-Specific Effects in Multi-Attribute Marketing Models, *Management Science*, 25, 11-21.

Swait, J., Erdem, T., Louviere, J. and Dubelaar, C. (1993), The Equalization Price: A Measure of Consumer-Perceived Brand Equity, *International Journal of Research in Marketing*, 10, 23-45.

Tellis, G. J. (1988), The Price Elasticity of Selective Demand: A Meta-Analysis of Econometric Models of Sales, *Journal of Marketing Research*, 25, 331-341.

Wittink, D. R. and Cattin, P. (1989), Commercial Use of Conjoint Analysis: An Update, *Journal of Marketing*, 53, 91-6.

Wittink, D. R., Vriens, M. and Burhenne, W. (1994), Commercial Use of Conjoint Analysis in Europe: Results and Critical Reflections, *International Journal of Research in Marketing*, 11, 41-52.

Zeithaml, V. (1988), Consumer Perceptions of Price, Quality and Value: A Means-End Model and Synthesis of Evidence, *Journal of Marketing*, 52, 2-22.

3 Market Simulation Using a Probabilistic Ideal Vector Model for Conjoint Data

Daniel Baier and Wolfgang Gaul

3.1 Introduction

In commercial applications of conjoint analysis to product design and product pricing it has become quite popular to further evaluate the estimated individual part-worth functions by predicting shares of choices for alternatives in hypothetical market scenarios (Wittink, Vriens and Burhenne 1994 and Baier 1999 for surveys on commercial applications). Wide-spread software packages for conjoint analysis (Sawtooth Software's 1994 ACA system) already include specific modules to handle this so-called market simulation situation for which, typically, a threefold input is required: (I) The (estimated) individual part-worth functions have to be provided. (II) A definition of a hypothetical market scenario is needed that allows to calculate individual utility values for each available alternative. (III) A so-called choice rule has to be selected, which relates individual utility values to expected individual choice probabilities and, consequently, to market shares for the alternatives. In this context, the determination of an adequate choice rule seems to be the most cumbersome task. Well-known traditional choice rules are, e.g., the 1ST CHOICE rule (where the individuals are assumed to always select the choice alternative with the highest utility value), the BTL (Bradley, Terry, Luce) rule (where individual choice probabilities are related to corresponding shares of utility values), and the LOGIT rule (where exponentiated utility values are used). Furthermore, in newer choice rules implemented by various software developers, the similarity of an alternative to other alternatives is taken into account as a corrective when choice probabilities are calculated (Sawtooth Software 1994).

The application of each of the just mentioned choice rules has its specific shortcomings: The 1ST CHOICE rule is known to overstate market shares for alternatives with high individual utility values since even marginal utility differences cause highly unequal choice probabilities (Elrod and Kumar 1989). The BTL and the LOGIT rule are sensitive to scale transformations of the utility values (Green and Krieger 1988). As the part-worth functions are at best interval-scaled in most applications, this provides a severe problem (Wittink, Vriens and Burhenne 1994). Furthermore, the selection of the LOGIT rule is commonly motivated by the assumption that the utility values (and consequently the estimated part-worth functions) are superimposed by an i.i.d. extreme value distributed error. However, the unknown parameters for this distribution (and consequently the adequate monotone transformation of the utility values) are typically not estimated together with the part-worth functions. Finally, the BTL and the LOGIT rule suffer from the IIA (independence of irrelevant alternatives) property which shows the tendency to overstate market shares for similar alternatives. The newer choice rules implemented by software developers avoid the IIA problem but the chosen ad-hoc extension of the LOGIT rule fails to be properly motivated.

In order to overcome these problems, a new approach for performing market simulations is proposed. The methodology is based on the well-known probabilistic ideal vector model (De Soete and Carroll 1983; Böckenholt and Gaul 1986; 1988; Gaul 1989 and Baier and Gaul 1996). Deterministic points for alternatives and random ideal vectors for consumer segments are used for explaining and predicting individual choice behavior in a low-dimensional attribute space where the same model formulation is employed for parameter estimation and for market simulation. Moreover, it can be used to analyze data collected via the wide-spread ACA system. In section 4.2, we tackle issues concerning model formulation and parameter estimation, while market simulation together with choice prediction, advantages and methodological options of the new approach as well as related work are discussed in section 4.3. A Monte Carlo comparison of the new approach with traditional counterparts is described in section 4.4. Additionally, in section 4.5 an application to the German mobile phone market is used to illustrate further advantages. The paper concludes with an outlook in section 4.6.

3.2   A Probabilistic Ideal Vector Model for Conjoint Data

3.2.1   Model Formulation

Let be can index for C (physical) characteristics of alternatives in a conjoint analysis study (coded typically as dummy variables) to describe a so-called characteristic space and an index for A (perceptual) attributes of the alternatives under consideration $(A \leq C)$ that build up a low-dimensional attribute space. Further, let $\mathbf{z}_j = (z_{j1}, \cdots, z_{jC})'$ be the description of an alternative j in terms of (physical) characteristics that is related via a transformation matrix $\mathbf{B}$ to coordinates $\mathbf{x}_j = (x_{j1}, \cdots, x_{jA})' = \mathbf{Bz}_j$ in the attribute space. Additionally, let t be an index for T consumer segments which are described in the attribute space by ideal vectors with stochastic coordinates $\mathbf{v}_t = (v_{t1}, \cdots, v_{tA})'$ following multivariate normal distributions with mean $\boldsymbol{\mu}_t = (\mu_{t1}, \cdots, \mu_{tA})'$ and covariance matrix $\Sigma_t = ((\sigma_{taa'}))_{A \times A}$.

These probabilistic ideal vectors are used to model the fact that consumers are not always certain with respect to their preference directions in the attribute space but it can be assumed that respondents from the same segment t belong to a subsample that behaves according to the segment-specific ideal vector $\mathbf{v}_t$.

Thus the random variable $U_{jt} = (\mathbf{Bz}_j)' \mathbf{v}_t$ explains the utility assigned by consumers of segment t to alternative j.

When consumers are exposed to a set S of alternatives, their choice behavior is modeled in the following way: Firstly, they independently sample a realization $\mathbf{w}_t = (w_{t1}, \cdots, w_{tA})'$ from their corresponding segment-specific ideal vector distribution. Then, they calculate utility values $(\mathbf{Bz}_j)'\mathbf{w}_t$ for each available alternative and, finally, they select that alternative that provides the highest utility value to them.

We use

$$(1) \qquad R_{j|S} = \left\{ \mathbf{w} \in \mathfrak{R}^A \middle| \left(\mathbf{B}(\mathbf{z}_j - \mathbf{z}_s) \right)' \mathbf{w} \geq 0, \quad \forall s \in S \right\}.$$

as so-called preference region that contains all ideal vector realizations that lead to a selection of j out of the given set S of alternatives ($R_{j|S}$ is a cone with peak in the origin.) and get

$$(2) \qquad p_{jt|S} = \mathrm{Prob}\left(\mathbf{v}_t \in R_{j|S} \right)$$

as probability that consumers from segment t prefer alternative j if they are exposed to set S.

Using λ_t as the relative size of segment t ($\sum_{t=1}^{T} \lambda_t = 1$) we get

$$(3) \qquad p_{j|S} = \sum_{t=1}^{T} \lambda_t p_{jt|S}$$

as the overall probability that alternative j is selected.

It should be mentioned that this model formulation provides possibilities to explain and predict both utility values and choices among sets of presented alternatives. The first feature will be used for parameter estimation in the following, the second feature is further described in the section on market simulation.

3.2.2   Parameter Estimation from Graded Paired Comparisons

For estimating unknown model parameters in applications of conjoint analysis, the collection of graded paired comparisons has become the most popular method (Wittink, Vriens and Burhenne 1994 and Baier 1999): Consumers are subsequently exposed to pairs of alternatives and asked to evaluate the utility difference between the right and the left alternative in terms of a categorical scale. Figure 1 gives an example of such a graded paired comparison task when the interviewing module of the ACA system is used for collecting data on mobile phones. We will

also apply this data collection method to estimate the unknown model parameters
of our approach.

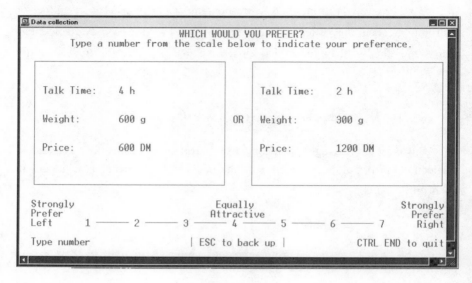

*Figure 1:   Sample graded paired comparison task when using the interviewing
              module of the ACA system for collecting data on mobile phones*

To describe the data collected, we use the following notation: Let i be an index for
I respondents and e an index for the E_i pairs of alternatives that respondent i has
evaluated. For each evaluation let $z_{ie}^{(\text{right})}$ and $z_{ie}^{(\text{left})}$ be the respective descriptions
of the right and the left alternative in terms of characteristics and
$U_{iet}^{(\text{right,left})} = \left(B\left(z_{ie}^{(\text{right})} - z_{ie}^{(\text{left})}\right)\right)' v_t$ the stochastic utility difference for the pair if
respondent i belongs to segment t. k_{ie} indicates the received response category of
the utility difference with $k_{ie} = 1$ as minimum scale value (if the left alternative is
strongly preferred) and $k_{ie} = K$ as maximum scale value (if the right one is
strongly preferred). $\alpha = (\alpha_0, ..., \alpha_K)$ with $\alpha_0 = -\infty$ and $\alpha_K = \infty$ denotes the (unknown) vector of category boundaries for the utility differences. Additionally, in
accordance with the model formulation described earlier, we assume that respondents are allocated to consumer segments via an (unknown) segmentation matrix
H with values $h_{ti} = 1$ if respondent i belongs to segment t and $h_{ti} = 0$, otherwise.

Now, we can calculate the probability that respondent i from segment t selects k_{ie} as response category in the e-th evaluation task as

(4)
$$p_{iek_{ie}t} = \text{Prob}\left(\alpha_{k_{ie}-1} \le U_{iet}^{(right,left)} \le \alpha_{k_{ie}}\right)$$
$$= \text{Prob}\left(\alpha_{k_{ie}-1} \le \left(\mathbf{B}\left(\mathbf{z}_{ie}^{(right)} - \mathbf{z}_{ie}^{(left)}\right)\right)' \mathbf{v}_t \le \alpha_{k_{ie}}\right)$$
$$= \Phi\left(f_{iek_{ie}t}\right) - \Phi\left(f_{ie(k_{ie}-1)t}\right)$$

with Φ as standard normal distribution function and fractils

(5)
$$f_{iek_{ie}t} = \frac{\alpha_{k_{ie}} - \left(\mathbf{B}\left(\mathbf{z}_{ie}^{(right)} - \mathbf{z}_{ie}^{(left)}\right)\right)' \mu_t}{\sqrt{\left(\mathbf{B}\left(\mathbf{z}_{ie}^{(right)} - \mathbf{z}_{ie}^{(left)}\right)\right)' \Sigma_t \left(\mathbf{B}\left(\mathbf{z}_{ie}^{(right)} - \mathbf{z}_{ie}^{(left)}\right)\right)}}.$$

Estimates of the model parameters $\theta = (\mu_1, \cdots, \mu_T, \Sigma_1, \cdots, \Sigma_T, \alpha, \mathbf{B})$ and the segmentation matrix $\mathbf{H}$ can be obtained by optimizing the corresponding negative log-likelihood function

(6)
$$-\ln L(\theta, \mathbf{H}) = -\sum_{t=1}^{T}\sum_{i=1}^{I} h_{ti} \sum_{e=1}^{E_i} \ln(p_{iek_{ie}t})$$

under the restriction that $h_{ti} \in \{0,1\}, \forall t,i,$ and $\sum_{t=1}^{T} h_{ti} = 1, \forall i,$ holds.

Note that in Eq. (6) an independent sampling across segments, respondents, and evaluations is assumed as in other papers that derive maximum likelihood estimates from paired comparison data (De Soete and Carroll 1983; Böckenholt and Gaul 1986; 1988; De Soete, Carroll and DeSarbo 1986; Gaul 1989; De Soete 1990 and Baier and Gaul 1996; 1999).

The negative log-likelihood function can be minimized by starting with an arbitrary adequate solution for θ and $\mathbf{H}$ followed by alternatingly improving the model parameters θ for fixed $\mathbf{H}$ and improving the segmentation matrix $\mathbf{H}$ for fixed θ. Improvements of θ for fixed $\mathbf{H}$ can be accomplished via nonlinear programming, improvements of $\mathbf{H}$ for fixed θ are carried out by checking whether a reallocation of respondent i to segment t with maximum value for $L_{it} = \sum_{e=1}^{E_i} \ln(p_{iek_{ie}t})$ is possible. Relative sizes of the segments can be calculated through $\lambda_t = \sum_{i=1}^{I} h_{ti}/I$.

Model selection, i.e. the determination of adequate values for the number of attributes A and the number of segments T in the representation, can be performed in the usual way by evaluating values of AIC (Akaike Information Criterion, see Akaike 1977) of the type

(7) $AIC = -2 \ln L(\hat{\theta}, \mathbf{H}) + 2NEP$

or of CAIC (Consistent AIC, see Bozdogan (1987)) of the type

(8) $CAIC = -2 \ln L(\hat{\theta}, \mathbf{H}) + (1 + \ln NO)NEP.$

Here, $\hat{\theta}$ denotes the maximum likelihood estimate of θ, NEP the Number of Effective Parameters and NO the Number of Observations, all with respect to some model under consideration. Even though the underlying regularity conditions for AIC and CAIC across different segmentation matrices $\mathbf{H}$ are not satisfied, these formulae have been proposed in the literature and are applied here in the same sense (see, e.g., Bozdogan 1987; 1993 and Wedel and DeSarbo 1993). NEP and NO are calculated in the following way:

(9) $NEP = TA + T\dfrac{A(A+1)}{2} + AC + (K-1) - 1 - A^2,$

(10) $NO = \sum_{i=1}^{I} E_i.$

It should be explicitly mentioned that the above described estimation procedure can also be used to analyze graded paired comparisons with partial profiles, i.e., series of independent evaluation tasks where the descriptions of the right and left alternatives only cover varying subsets of the available C characteristics. For the respondent's evaluation task it is assumed that the outcomes for omitted characteristics in partial profiles are unknown but identical for both alternatives.

Graded paired comparisons with partial profiles are quite popular within conjoint applications since this kind of data collection reduces the alternatives' complexity and simplifies the respondents' evaluation task (e.g., for applications of the ACA system's interviewing module, it is recommended to use only partial profiles with up to three characteristics instead of full profiles (Sawtooth Software 1994).

As can be seen from Eq. (4), the estimation procedure of the new approach can easily handle partial profiles if the outcomes of the omitted characteristics are (in accordance to the definition of the evaluation task) assumed unknown but identical.

3.3   Market Simulation

3.3.1   Choice Predicion in Market Scenarios

Prerequisites for an engagement with market scenarios are, e.g., the determination of the set S of underlying alternatives in terms of their characteristics and the estimation of the needed model parameters as described in the last section. Next, a calculation of the (segment-specific) expected shares of choices via Eq. (2) and (3) has to be performed. However, for $|S| > 2$ an analytical solution of Eq. (2), i.e. of

$$(11) \qquad p_{jt|S} = \int_{\mathbf{w} \in R_{j|S}} f_t(\mathbf{w}) \ d\mathbf{w}$$

with

$$(12) \qquad f_t(\mathbf{w}) = \frac{1}{\sqrt{(2\pi)^A \det(\Sigma_t)}} \exp\left(-\frac{1}{2}(\mathbf{w} - \mu_t)' \Sigma_t^{-1}(\mathbf{w} - \mu_t)\right)$$

as segment t's ideal vector density function, is not known, thus, we propose the following hypercube approximation (see Baier, Gaul (1999) for a similar suggestion with respect to probabilistic ideal point modeling):

Firstly, we transform the problem of calculating the probability mass of $\mathbf{v}_t$ over $R_{j|S}$ into an equivalent problem for

$$(13) \qquad \widetilde{\mathbf{v}}_t = \Sigma_t^{-\frac{1}{2}}(\mathbf{v}_t - \mu_t)$$

over the preference region

$$(14) \qquad \widetilde{R}_{jt|S} = \left\{ \widetilde{\mathbf{w}} \in \Re^A \ \middle| \ (\mathbf{B}(\mathbf{z}_j - \mathbf{z}_s))' \Sigma_t^{\frac{1}{2}} \widetilde{\mathbf{w}} \geq -(\mathbf{B}(\mathbf{z}_j - \mathbf{z}_s))' \mu_t, \quad \forall s \in S \right\}.$$

Then, we choose L^A grid points

$$(15) \qquad \xi_{l_1 \cdots l_A} = \left(\Phi^{-1}\left(\frac{2l_1 - 1}{2L}\right), \cdots, \Phi^{-1}\left(\frac{2l_A - 1}{2L}\right)\right)'$$

$(1 \le l_1, \cdots, l_A \le L)$ which are the mass centroids of L^A hypercubes that form an „iso-mass" representation for the random variable $\tilde{v}_t$ (L is a parameter to adjust granularity). Finally, we use the mass centroids as an (approximative) indicator whether all points of the corresponding hypercubes are assumed to belong to $\tilde{R}_{jt|S}$ or not, and approximate $p_{jt|S} = \text{Prob}(\tilde{v}_t \in \tilde{R}_{jt|S})$ as the fraction of hypercubes for which $\xi_{l_1, \cdots, l_A} \in \tilde{R}_{jt|S}$ holds.

3.3.2   Methodological Options and Advantages of the New Approach

The model formulation in section 4.2.1 provides quite a variety of methodological options. The following examples are explicitly mentioned: If the transformation matrix is restricted to the identity matrix (**B=I**) and only one segment is allowed (T=1) we get a statistical generalization of adaptive conjoint analysis at the aggregate level. For the situation (**B=I**, T>1) the new approach can be used as an alternative to other sequential or simultaneous procedures for benefit segmentation or product design based on segment level part-worth functions (DeSarbo, Wedel, Vriens and Ramaswamy 1992; Aust and Gaul 1995; Baier and Gaul 1995 and Gaul, Aust and Baier 1995). In this context, the new approach can be viewed as a simultaneous procedure for analyzing graded paired comparison data collected via the ACA system. Possibilities to fix the transformation matrix **B** in a desired way allow the derivation of results needed in QFD (Quality Function Deployment) (Hauser and Clausing 1988 and Akao 1990 for reviews and sample applications of QFD and Baier 1998 for estimation procedures).

The methodological options just mentioned are in close relationship to a series of advantages. As already mentioned, the new approach supports market simulation with the help of a choice rule that is compatible with model parameter estimation. Next, the estimation of the transformation matrix **B** supports the exploration of the relationship between the (physical) characteristics and the (perceptual) attributes of alternatives as proposed, e.g., in Brunswick's (1952) ‚lens' model. This is a feature that can be of help for the parametrization of the house of quality in QFD (Baier 1998 for an application using the ACA system). Additionally, the new approach doesn't suffer from the IIA property which assumes that the proportion of choice probabilities is independent from the available set of alternatives. This can be easily verified in terms of the well-known red bus/blue bus paradox (Ben-Akiva and Lerman 1985): Here, the starting point is a commuter mode choice situation where consumers choose between a car (alternative 1) and a red bus (alternative 2) with probabilities $p_{1|\{1,2\}} = p_{2|\{1,2\}} = 1/2$. If, additionally, a blue bus would be made available (alternative 3), one would expect that this new alternative draws especially shares of choices from its similar alternative 2.

However, models where the IIA property forces

(16) $\qquad p_{1|\{1,2\}} / p_{2|\{1,2\}} = p_{1|\{1,2,3\}} / p_{2|\{1,2,3\}}$

and $p_{2|\{1,2,3\}} = p_{3|\{1,2,3\}}$ could be expected from the description of the available alternatives (as in the red bus/blue bus example) would lead to $p_{1|\{1,2,3\}} = p_{2|\{1,2,3\}} = p_{3|\{1,2,3\}} = 1/3$.

Our new approach takes the similarity of alternatives explicitly into account. The above example can be modeled, e.g., by using T=A=C=1, $z_1 = (1)$, $z_2 = z_3 = (-1)$, $B = (1)$, $\mu_1 = (0)$, $\Sigma_1 = (1)$ that results in choice probabilities $p_{1|\{1,2,3\}} = 1/2$ and $p_{2|\{1,2,3\}} = p_{3|\{1,2,3\}} = 1/4$ which contradicts the IIA property in Eq. (16) but seems to model consumers choice behavior more realistically.

3.3.3   Related Work

The proposed approach is related to other probabilistic ideal vector models for analyzing (graded) paired comparisons (De Soete and Carroll 1983; Böckenholt and Gaul 1986; 1988; Gaul 1989 and Baier and Gaul 1996). However, to our knowledge this is the first time where the application of such an approach for analyzing graded paired comparisons to partial profiles from conjoint experiments is suggested. Moreover, it is the first time that it has explicitly been suggested and demonstrated that such an approach can be used for the prediction of shares of choices among „large" sets of alternatives.

Additionally, such a model formulation with random coefficients is related to methodologies based on the multinomial logit model (McFadden 1973; Cooper and Nakanishi 1983; Louviere and Woodworth 1983 and DeSarbo, Ramaswamy and Cohen 1995) or the multinomial probit model (Hausman and Wise 1978; Daganzo 1979 and Kamakura and Srivastava 1984). However, these approaches don't use graded paired comparisons for estimating the model parameters.

3.4   Monte Carlo Experiment

In order to examine the performance of the new approach in comparison to traditional counterparts, a Monte Carlo study was designed. Adopting much from surveys on the commercial use of conjoint analysis (Wittink, Vriens and Burhenne 1992 and Baier 1999) as well as from the design of former Monte Carlo studies in the field of conjoint analysis (Vriens, Wedel and Wilms 1996) and optimal product positioning (Baier and Gaul 1999) the following seven factors (with factor levels in brackets) were specified for synthetic data generation: number of simulated respondents (100 and 200), number of segments (2 and 4), segment heterogenity (homogeneous and heterogeneous), correlation (uncorrelated and correlated), number of alternatives in a hypothetical market scenario (4 and 8), similarity of alternatives (dissimilar and similar) and error variance (5% and 35%) where – for convenience – the abridged factor label is underlined. According to a fractionated factorial design with 32 factor-level-combinations 50 replications were performed for each combination, thus, a total of 1600 data sets was generated.

Each data set consisted of (I) simulated part-worth functions for each respondent which were drawn from segment-specific normal distributions of part-worth functions, (II) a hypothetical market scenario with individual utility values for each available alternative derived from the simulated part-worth functions, and (III) „true" market shares in this market scenario. The following steps were used for data generation: (Step 1) Segment-specific mean part-worth functions for eight characteristics each with three outcomes (dummy coded for computational convenience) were randomly drawn from a predefined range (the interval [0,1] was selected). Segment-specific variances and covariances for the (dummy coded) part-worth functions were specified according to the levels of the factors segment heterogenity and correlation. For the factor segment heterogenity variances were set to 0.05 for the level homogeneous, in the heterogeneous case a value of 0.1 was chosen. Additionally, for the factor correlation all covariances between part-worth functions were set to 0 for the level uncorrelated, in the correlated case values of 0.05 resp. 0.1 (depending on the level of the factor segment heterogenity) were chosen for the part-worth functions of four characteristics. Then, for the specified number of respondents (randomly assigned to equally sized segments) individual part-worth functions were drawn from their corresponding segment-specific normal distributions of part-worth functions. (Step 2) A hypothetical market scenario with four or eight alternatives was generated through assigning outcomes to characteristics. In the case where dissimilar was the level of the factor similarity of alternatives the assignment of the outcomes to the eight characteristics was totally random. In the other case the hypothetical market scenario was assumed to consist of two subsets of similar alternatives (with unequal subset sizes of one and three resp. of two and six according to the level of the number of alternatives). Within each subset, three characteristics were assumed to have a fixed outcome whereas the remaining five characteristics received outcomes at random. For each simulated respondent and each alternative in the hypothetical market scenario utility values were calculated. Furthermore, in order to simulate estimation errors, the drawn individual utility values were superimposed by an additive normally distributed term with mean zero. According to the already mentioned levels of the error variance, the variance of this error term was set to 5% resp. 35% of the variance of the individual utility values (Vriens, Wedel and Wilms 1996 for a similar approach). (Step 3) The „true" market shares were determined via sampling a „large" number (5000 in the underlying situation) of realizations from the simulated segment-specific distributions of the part-worth functions, via deriving error-free utility values for each realization and each alternative in the hypothetical market scenario, and via calculating for each alternative the share of realizations for which maximum utility is provided.

Each generated data set was analyzed by our new approach and selected traditional counterparts for market simulation where the following notation is used for explanation: With u_{ij} as utility value that respondent i has assigned to alternative j (through adding the respective elements of the simulated part-worth function for respondent i), d_{js} as share of different outcomes of the characteristics of the alternatives j and s ($d_{js} = c_{js}/C$ denotes the situation that c_{js} of the C characteristics have different outcomes), $w_j = 1/\sum_{s\in S}(\exp(-3d_{js}) - \exp(-3))$ as ad-hoc IIA corrective in the ACA system's choice rule (Sawtooth Software 1994), and β as additional scale parameter, the individual choice rules

$$p_{ij|S}^{(BTL)} = u_{ij}^{\beta}/\sum_{s\in S}u_{is}^{\beta} \qquad \text{with } \beta = 1, \beta = 2,$$

(17)
$$p_{ij|S}^{(LOGIT)} = \exp(\beta u_{ij})/\sum_{s\in S}\exp(\beta u_{is}) \qquad \text{with } \beta = 1, \beta = 2, \text{ and}$$

$$p_{ij|S}^{(ACA)} = w_j\exp(\beta u_{ij})/\sum_{s\in S}w_s\exp(\beta u_{is}) \quad \text{with } \beta = 2,$$

were the basis for a comparison with our new approach. The individual choice probabilitites of Eq. (17) were aggregated across respondents in traditional manner (i.e. $p_{j|S}^{(rule)} = 1/I\sum_{i=1}^{I}p_{ij|S}^{(rule)}$) to get the „simulated" market shares under different approaches for each generated data set.

Table 1: *Mean values for the performance measures MAE and RMSE under different approaches (Statistical significant differences between two means are denoted by superscript number(s) of the inferior approach(es) attached to the superior mean (p < .01))*

		MAE	RMSE
BTL	(β = 1) (1)	.0790	.0938
BTL	(β = 2) (2)	.0604[1,3]	.0723[1,3]
LOGIT	(β = 1) (3)	.0803	.0944
LOGIT	(β = 2) (4)	.0557[1,2,3]	.0656[1,2,3]
ACA	(β = 2) (5)	.0506[1,2,3,4]	.0600[1,2,3,4]
New Appr.	(6)	.0191[1,2,3,4,5]	.0232[1,2,3,4,5]

For the new approach, segment-specific means and covariance matrices were directly estimated from the simulated part-worth functions for each data set and market simulation (as described in section 4.3.1) was performed with respect to

Table 2:   Mean values for the performance measures MAE and RMSE under different approaches by levels of factors (Statistical significant differences between two means in a cell with respect to factor levels are denoted by *, superscript numbers attached to the mean of the new approach indicate significant superiority over the respective traditional approach (p < .01).

MAE		BTL (β = 1) (1)	BTL (β = 2) (2)	LOGIT (β = 1) (3)	LOGIT (β = 2) (4)	ACA (β = 2) (5)	New Approach
Respond.	100	.0829*	.0633*	.0850*	.0584*	.0536*	.0213*[1,2,3,4,5]
	200	.0750	.0575	.0755	.0529	.0477	.0169[1,2,3,4,5]
Segments	2	.0897*	.0683*	.0921*	.0629*	.0581*	.0212*[1,2,3,4,5]
	4	.0681	.0525	.0685	.0484	.0432	.0169[1,2,3,4,5]
Segment Heterog.	Homog.	.0863*	.0659*	.0910*	.0639*	.0590*	.0208*[1,2,3,4,5]
	Heter.	.0715	.0550	.0696	.0474	.0422	.0173[1,2,3,4,5]
Correl.	Uncor.	.0709*	.0540*	.0692*	.0464*	.0417*	.0154*[1,2,3,4,5]
	Correl.	.0870	.0668	.0913	.0649	.0595	.0228[1,2,3,4,5]
Alternatives	4	.0841*	.0614	.0933*	.0637*	.0592*	.0206*[1,2,3,4,5]
	8	.0737	.0594	.0673	.0476	.0420	.0176[1,2,3,4,5]
Similar. of Alternatives	Dissim.	.0732*	.0529	.0721*	.0474*	.0464*	.0168*[1,2,3,4,5]
	Sim.	.0846	.0650	.0884	.0639	.0549	.0213[1,2,3,4,5]
Error Variance	5%	.0755*	.0551*	.0779	.0504*	.0462*	.0072*[1,2,3,4,5]
	35%	.0824	.0658	.0827	.0609	.0551	.0310[1,2,3,4,5]
RMSE		BTL (β = 1) (1)	BTL (β = 2) (2)	LOGIT (β = 1) (3)	LOGIT (β = 2) (4)	ACA (β = 2) (5)	New Approach
Respond.	100	.0972*	.0747	.0986*	.0680*	.0624*	.0253*[1,2,3,4,5]
	200	.0904	.0699	.0301	.0632	.0576	.0211[1,2,3,4,5]
Segments	2	.1073*	.0826*	.1086*	.0747*	.0695*	.0262*[1,2,3,4,5]
	4	.0803	.0620	.0801	.0565	.0504	.0202[1,2,3,4,5]
Segment Heterog.	Homog.	.1025*	.0789*	.1067*	.0753*	.0700*	.0257*[1,2,3,4,5]
	Heter.	.0852	.0656	.0820	.0560	.0500	.0208[1,2,3,4,5]
Correl.	Uncor.	.0843*	.0645*	.0815*	.0547*	.0496*	.0186*[1,2,3,4,5]
	Correl.	.1033	.0801	.1072	.0766	.0704	.0278[1,2,3,4,5]
Alternatives	4	.0960	.0705	.1059*	.0725*	.0679*	.0240[1,2,3,4,5]
	8	.0916	.0740	.0828	.0587	.0521	.0224[1,2,3,4,5]
Similar. of Alternatives	Dissim.	.0867*	.0665*	.0845*	.0559*	.0564*	.0203*[1,2,3,4,5]
	Sim.	.1010	.0781	.1042	.0753	.0654	.0261[1,2,3,4,5]
Error Variance	5%	.0904*	.0665*	.0920	.0597*	.0549*	.0093*[1,2,3,4,5]
	35%	.0972	.0781	.0967	.0715	.0650	.0371[1,2,3,4,5]

the hypothetical market scenario. The resulting „simulated" market shares of the new approach as well as the „simulated" market shares of the five traditional approaches were compared to the „true" market shares using MAE (mean absolute error) and RMSE (root mean squared error) as performance measures.

As result of the Monte Carlo experiment, 9600 observations for each of the two performance measures (from 1600 generated data sets analyzed by six approaches) were available in order to show differences across approaches and factors used for the generation of the hypothetical markets. For an easy indication of superiority the approaches are, additionally, numbered from (1) to (6). Table 1 shows the mean values of the performance measures under different approaches together with indications for statistical significant differences.

In Table 2 the mean values for the performance measures under different approaches by levels of factors are depicted. Additionally, for the seven Monte Carlo factors and the approaches as main effects as well as for those first-order interaction effects in which approaches constitute one of the interacting parts, F-test results with respect to all performance measures were checked in an ANOVA context and are - as they are in agreement with the information contained in Tables 1 and 2 - not reported.

Altogether, the message from the Monte Carlo experiment is pretty clear: The new approach outperforms the traditional approaches with respect to the performance measures MAE and RMSE. Superiority also appears with respect to all factor levels. Among the traditional approaches ACA performed best, followed by the LOGIT and BTL approaches with higher β-values. We leave an interpretation of further results contained in Tables 1 and 2 to the reader.

3.5   Application

For a demonstration how the new approach competes with the traditional approaches in a real-world application, the German market for mobile phones without transmission contracts was selected. In summer 1997, major competitors in this market offered the six product alternatives P1, P2,..., P6 which are depicted in Table 3 via 11 characteristics selected on the basis of discussions with salespersons and information obtained from producers' home pages, selling brochures, and tests in technical magazines. A further alternative P2' (similar to P2) is also described in Table 3. The six respectively seven alternatives from Table 3 form market scenarios A and B which will be used in our application in order to evaluate the new approach.

Two outcomes for each characteristic were chosen for a conjoint experiment: the (assumed) advantageous outcome 600 DM and the (assumed) disadvantageous outcome 1200 DM for the characteristic price, 150 g and 300 g for weight, 180 ccm and 330 ccm for size, telescope and integrated for antenna type, 240 min. and 80 min. for talk time, 80 h and 20 h for standby time, 1 h and 2 h for recharge time as well as ++ and o for noise reduction, workmanship, branding, and automatic dialing. Graded paired comparisons were collected from 100 respondents using the ACA system. First, in a so-called importance rating part, the respondents were asked to rate the utility difference between the advantageous and the disadvantageous outcomes of each characteristic. Within this part, the outcomes of the characteristics weight and size were supported by illustrative material. Then, in the paired comparison trade-off part, each respondent had to evaluate six pairs of partial profiles covering two characteristics each and five pairs of partial profiles consisting of three characteristics each. For both parts, a similar categorical scale with seven categories was used. In Figure 1, we have already seen a sample screen from the paired-comparison trade-off part. Finally, in a further part, buying probabilitites for full profile alternatives were collected in order to predict „true" market shares with respect to the predefined market scenarios A and B. For this prediction it was assumed that each respondent would definitely buy the highest rated alternative. The predicted „true" market shares for scenarios A and B under this assumption are also shown in Table 3.

For parameter estimation using the new approach, dummy coding for the outcomes of the characteristics was introduced with a value of 1 for the advantageous and a value of 0 for the disadvantageous outcome. The data from the importance rating part in the ACA interview were viewed as paired comparisons of partial profiles covering only one characteristic which extended the observed partial profiles paired comparisons to a total number of 2200 cases. (It should be noted that part-worth estimation in the ACA system uses a similar step to combine the data from the different parts of the collection procedure.)

Table 3:   *Major competing alternatives in the German market (summer 1997)*
              for mobile phones without a transmisson contract (P1,....,P6) together
              with additional alternative (P2') forming market scenarios A and B

	P1	P2	P3	P4	P5	P6	P2
Price (DM)	950	1399	640	900	600	699	1199
Weight (g)	215	155	305	180	195	255	155
Size (ccm)	296	190	240	194	197	244	190
Antenna Type	telesc.	integr.	integr.	integr.	telesc.	integr.	integr.
Talk Time (min.)	269	97	93	146	93	128	97
Standby Time (h)	40	62	41	30	17	20	40
Recharge Time (h)	1	1	2	1	2	2	1
Noise Reduction	++	+	++	o	+	+	+
Workmanship	o	+	o	+	+	++	+
Branding	o	++	o	++	o	++	++
Automatic Dialing	o	o	o	o	o	o	o
"True" Market Shares in Scenario A:							
	16%	29%	11%	13%	4%	27%	
"True" Market Shares in Scenario B:							
	16%	27%	11%	13%	4%	27%	2%

Additionally, in order to easily compare the estimated model parameters with the results from the traditional approaches, the covariance matrices Σ_t were restricted to diagonal matrices, the transformation matrix **B** to the identity matrix, and the vector α to $(-\infty, -2.5, -1.5, -0.5, 0.5, 1.5, 2.5, \infty)$ assuming symmetrically and – except for α_0 and α_K - equidistantly distributed category boundaries around the origin.

This point should be stressed because the mentioned restrictions reduce the ability of the new approach in favor of the traditional counterparts. Table 4 shows the results of the corresponding analyses for the new approach in terms of NEP, - ln L, AIC and CAIC for the 1-, 2-,..., 8-segment solutions. We see that the CAIC values indicate that the 2-segment solution should be preferred.

Table 5 provides for this 2-segment solution (together with the corresponding results for the 1- and 3-segment solutions) the mean ideal vectors μ_t and the corresponding diagonal elements of the covariance matrices Σ_t (in brackets). It can be easily seen that the respondents provide a rather homogeneous group of potential buyers for which the characteristics price, standby time, size and noise reduction are most important. (Note, that the variances provide additional interesting insights with respect to the segment-specific assessment of characteristics).

Table 4:   *Summary of selected analyses using the new approach (Underline denotes best performance)*

	NEP	- lnL	AIC	CAIC
T = 1	22	3369.4365	6782.8730	6930.1897
T = 2	44	3234.2543	6556.5086	6851.1420
T = 3	66	3152.2879	6436.5758	6878.5258
T = 4	88	3082.5782	6341.1564	6930.4231
T = 5	110	3032.9684	6285.9368	7022.5202
T = 6	132	2992.4640	6248.9280	7132.8281
T = 7	154	2984.2547	6276.5094	7307.7261
T = 8	176	2913.3841	6178.7682	7357.3016

For market simulation via the new approach, the descriptions of the alternatives in market scenario A and market scenario B from Table 3 were converted into dummy coded characteristics using linear transformations from the [disadvantageous outcome,...,advantageous outcome]-range into the [0,1]-interval. Then, „simulated" market shares were calculated for each market scenario using the 1-, 2-,..., 8-segment solutions referred to in Table 4.

The ACA system was applied for estimating the individual part-worth functions. Again, data from the importance rating part and the paired comparison trade-off part were used together. The individual part-worth functions were standardized in the usual way (the disadvantageous outcomes get a part-worth value of 0 and the part-worth values of the advantageous outcomes sum up to 1) and used to calculate utility values for the alternatives in each market scenario. Finally, the choice rules from Eq. (17) were applied to estimate the individual choice probabilities and to predict „simulated" market shares for each scenario and each choice rule.

Table 5:   *Estimated segment-specific mean ideal vector coordinates (variances) of selected analyses using the new approach*

	T = 1	T = 2		T = 3		
	Segm. 1 (100%)	Segm. 1 (47%)	Segm. 2 (53%)	Segm. 1 (17%)	Segm. 2 (38%)	Segm. 3 (45%)
Price	2.3650 (0.9979)	2.5126 (1.3068)	2.3051 (0.7083)	1.4967 (1.1187)	2.7609 (1.0913)	2.4223 (0.6973)
Weight	1.2049 (1.1544)	1.0207 (0.5596)	1.4172 (1.5779)	0.7547 (0.6800)	1.0915 (0.5774)	1.5351 (1.4513)
Size	1.8051 (0.8670)	1.5984 (0.7719)	2.0634 (0.8853)	1.6037 (1.0590)	1.6104 (0.8917)	2.1806 (0.8371)
Antenna Type	.07608 (1.0391)	0.8992 (1.3968)	0.6700 (0.8357)	0.8794 (0.8028)	0.9253 (1.4465)	0.6409 (0.9348)
Talk Time	1.3255 (1.2685)	1.1399 (0.9948)	1.5616 (1.2772)	1.2256 (1.0932)	1.1908 (0.9666)	1.5797 (1.3096)
Standby Time	2.1050 (1.3074)	1.3586 (0.7818)	2.7776 (0.7441)	2.0508 (0.2776)	1.2707 (0.9888)	2.8511 (0.8775)
Recharge Time	0.4075 (0.6369)	0.4377 (0.7880)	0.3833 (0.5548)	1.0338 (0.5110)	0.2725 (0.6629)	0.3126 (0.4930)
Noise Reduction	1.7891 (0.6361)	2.0177 (0.6884)	1.6522 (0.4312)	1.0103 (0.8580)	2.2181 (0.3816)	1.7508 (0.3771)
Workmanship	1.4353 (0.6309)	1.7155 (0.6884)	1.2215 (0.5093)	1.5009 (0.5753)	1.7796 (0.6955)	1.2082 (0.4234)
Branding	0.3115 (0.6071)	0.6166 (0.9450)	0.1193 (0.1028)	0.5972 (0.3667)	0.5924 (1.0547)	0.1260 (0.0967)
Automatic Dialing	0.9527 (0.9403)	1.0123 (1.4188)	0.8570 (0.6708)	2.0164 (0.1506)	0.7806 (1.2310)	0.6310 (0.4926)

Again, the performance measures MAE and RMSE with respect to the „true" and „simulated" market shares were used for comparisons. Table 6 shows the results. Both, in market scenario A and market scenario B the new approach outperforms the traditional approaches. The superiority is especially striking in the case of market scenario B where products P2 and P2' are quite similar. This is not surprising since we already know about the problems of some traditional approaches to take similarity structures within alternatives into account. Even if the discussion is restricted to the 2-segment solution (suggested by the CAIC-values for model selection, see Table 4), the new approach competes well in this environment.

Table 6:   *Performance measures MAE and RMSE under different approaches for market scenarios A and B (Underline denotes best performance.)*

		Market Scenario A		Market Scenario B	
		MAE	RMSE	MAE	RMSE
BTL	($\beta = 1$)	.0826	.0705	.0762	.0897
BTL	($\beta = 2$)	.0774	.0673	.0744	.0873
LOGIT	($\beta = 1$)	.0637	.0563	.0670	.0798
LOGIT	($\beta = 2$)	.0441	.0382	.0529	.0662
ACA	($\beta = 2$)	.0468	.0389	.0525	.0658
New Appr.	($T = 1$)	.0520	.0489	.0450	.0498
New Appr.	($T = 2$)	.0492	.0443	.0406	.0464
New Appr.	($T = 3$)	.0437	.0388	.0331	.0404
New Appr.	($T = 4$)	.0442	.0388	.0364	.0427
New Appr.	($T = 5$)	.0432	.0381	.0361	.0416
New Appr.	($T = 6$)	.0478	.0391	.0389	.0478
New Appr.	($T = 7$)	.0501	.0443	.0416	.0483
New Appr.	($T = 8$)	.0483	.0465	.0432	.0462

3.6   Conclusion and Outlook

A new approach has been presented that supports product design issues, distinguishes between (physical) characteristics and (perceptual) attributes, allows an estimation of the transformation matrix between characteristics and attributes (needed, e.g., in QFD), takes the segmentation of the underlying market into account, models consumer behavior with the help of multivariate normal distributed ideal vectors, and allows an analysis of standard data obtained in conjoint applications (i.e. data collected via the ACA system). Additionally, it performs market simulation with the help of a choice rule that is compatible with the underlying model formulation and takes similarities of alternatives into account within the prediction process. Of course, further data sets need to be analyzed to demonstrate the superiority of the new approach, but already this paper provides a promising way to deal with some of the known major problems within applications of conjoint analysis.

Acknowledgements: The authors wish to thank Dipl.-Wi.Ing. Christopher Pauli and Dipl.-Wi.Ing. Andreas Schönemann for their valuable support in data collection and analysis.

3.7   References

Akaike, H. (1977), On Entropy Maximization Principle, in: Krishnaiah, P., ed., *Applications of Statistics,* Amsterdam, 27-41.

Akao, Y. (1990), QFD, *Integrating Customer Requirements into Product Design*, Cambridge.

Aust, E. and Gaul, W. (1995), A Unifying Approach to Benefit Segmentation and Product Line Design Based on Rank Order Conjoint Data, in: Gaul, W., Pfeifer, D., eds., *From Data to Knowledge,* Berlin, 289-297.

Baier, D. (1998), Conjointanalytische Lösungsansätze zur Parametrisierung des House of Quality, in: VDI-Gesellschaft Systementwicklung und Produktgestaltung, ed., *QFD: Produkte und Dienstleistungen marktgerecht gestalten,* Düsseldorf, 73-88.

Baier, D. (1999), Methoden der Conjointanalyse in der Marktforschungs- und Marketingpraxis, to appear, in: Gaul, W., Schader, M., eds., *Mathematische Methoden der Wirtschaftswissenschaften,* Heidelberg.

Baier, D. and Gaul, W. (1995), Classification and Representation Using Conjoint Data, in: Gaul, W., Pfeifer, D., eds., *From Data to Knowledge,* Berlin, 298-307.

Baier, D. and Gaul, W. (1996), Analyzing Paired Comparisons Data Using Probabilistic Ideal Point and Vector Models, in: Bock, H.H., Polasek, P., eds., *Data Analysis and Information Systems,* Berlin, 163-174.

Baier, D. and Gaul, W. (1999), Optimal Product Positioning Based on Paired Comparison Data, *Journal of Econometrics*, 89, 365-392.

Ben-Akiva, M. and Lerman, S. (1985), *Discrete Choice Analysis*, Cambridge.

Böckenholt, I. and Gaul, W. (1986), Analysis of Choice Behaviour via Probabilistic Ideal Point and Vector Models, *Applied Stochastic Models and Data Analysis,* 2, 209-226.

Böckenholt, I. and Gaul, W. (1988), Probabilistic Multidimensional Scaling of Paired Comparisons Data, in: Bock, H.H., ed., *Classification and Related Methods of Data Analysis,* Amsterdam, 405-412.

Bozdogan, H. (1987), Model Selection and Akaike's Information Criterion: The General Theory and Its Analytical Extensions, *Psychometrika,* 52, 345-370.

Bozdogan, H. (1993), Choosing the Number of Component Clusters in the Mixture-Model Using a New Informational Complexity Criterion of the Inverse-Fisher Information Matrix, in: Opitz, O., Lausen, B., Klar, R., eds., *Information and Classification,* Berlin, 40-54.

Brunswick, E. (1952), *The Conceptual Framework of Psychology,* Chicago.

Cooper, L. G. and Nakanishi, M. (1983), Two Logit Models for External Analysis of Preferences, *Psychometrika,* 48, 607-620.

Daganzo, M. (1979), *Multinomial Probit,* New York.

De Soete, G. (1990), A Latent Class Approach to Modeling Pairwise Preferential Choice Data, in: Schader, M., Gaul, W., eds., *Knowledge, Data, and Computer-Assisted Decisions,* Berlin, 240-249.

De Soete, G. and Carroll, J. D. (1983), A Maximum Likelihood Method for Fitting the Wandering Vector Model, *Psychometrika*, 48, 553-566.

De Soete, G., Carroll, J. D. and DeSarbo, W. S. (1986), The Wandering Ideal Point Model: A Probabilistic Multidimensional Unfolding Model for Paired Comparisons Data, *Journal of Mathematical Psychology*, 30, 28-41.

DeSarbo, W. S., Ramaswamy, V. and Cohen, S. H. (1995), Market Segmentation with Choice-Based Conjoint Analysis, *Marketing Letters*, 6, 137-147.

DeSarbo, W. S., Wedel, M., Vriens, M. and Ramaswamy, V. (1992), Latent Class Metric Conjoint Analysis, *Marketing Letters*, 3, 273-288.

Elrod, T. and Kumar, K. (1989), Bias in the First Choice Rule for Predicting Shares, Proceedings of the 1989 *Sawtooth Software Conference*, 259-271.

Gaul, W. (1989): Probabilistic Choice Behavior Models and Their Combination With Additional Tools Needed for Applications to Marketing, in: De Soete, G., Feger, H., Klauer, K.-H., eds., *New Developments in Psychological Choice Modeling*, Amsterdam, 317-337.

Gaul, W. Aust, E. and Baier, D. (1995), Gewinnorientierte Produktlinien-gestaltung unter Berücksichtigung des Kundennutzens, *Zeitschrift für Betriebswirtschaft*, 65, 835-854.

Green, P. E. and Krieger, A. (1988), Choice Rules and Sensitivity Analysis in Conjoint Simulators, *Journal of the Academy of Marketing Science*, 16, 114-127.

Hauser, J. R. and Clausing, D. (1988), The House of Quality, *Harvard Business Review*, 66, 63-73.

Hausman, J. and Wise, D. A. (1978), A Conditional Probit Model for Qualitative Choice: Discrete Decisions Recognizing Interdependence and Heterogeneous Preferences, *Econometrica*, 46, 403-426.

Kamakura, W. A. and Srivastava, R. K. (1984), Predicting Choice Shares Under Conditions of Brand Interdependence, *Journal of Marketing Research*, 21, 420-434.

Louviere, J. J. and Woodworth, G. G. (1983), Design and Analysis of Simulated Choice or Allocation Experiments: An Approach Based on Aggregate Data, *Journal of Marketing Research*, 20, 350-367.

McFadden, D. (1973), Conditional Logit Analysis of Qualitative Choice Behavior, Zarembka, P, ed., *Frontiers of Econometrics*, New York, 105-142.

Sawtooth Software (1994), ACA System Version 4.0, *Sawtooth Software Inc.*, Evanston, IL.

Vriens, M., Wedel, M. and Wilms, T. (1996), Metric Conjoint Segmentation Methods: A Monte Carlo Comparison, *Journal of Marketing Research*, 33, 73-85.

Wedel, M. and DeSarbo, W. S. (1993), A Latent Class Binomial Logit Methodology for the Analysis of Paired Comparison Choice Data, *Decision Sciences*, 24, 1157-1170.

Wittink, D. R., Vriens, M. and Burhenne, W. (1994), Commercial Use of Conjoint Analysis in Europe: Results and Critical Reflections, *International Journal of Research in Marketing*, 11, 41-52.

4 A Comparison of Conjoint Measurement with Self-Explicated Approaches

Henrik Sattler and Susanne Hensel-Börner

4.1 Introduction

Over the past two decades conjoint measurement has been a popular method for measuring customers' preference structures. Wittink and Cattin (1989) estimate that about 400 commercial applications were carried out per year during the early 1980s. In the 1990s this number probably exceeds 1000. The popularity of conjoint measurement appears to derive, at least in part, from its presumed superiority in validity over simpler, less expensive techniques such as self-explication approaches (Leigh, MacKay and Summers 1984). However, when considered in empirical studies, this superiority frequently has not been found (e.g. Green and Srinivasan 1990; Srinivasan and Park 1997). This issue is of major practical relevance. If, at least in certain situations, conjoint measurement is not clearly superior in validity to self-explicated approaches, it becomes highly questionable whether future applications for measuring customers' preferences should be done by conjoint measurement, as self-explicated approaches are clear advantageous in terms of time and money effort.

When comparing the validity of conjoint measurement with self-explicated approaches, one has to distinguish between different types of conjoint measurement methods which can lead to varying results in terms of validity. Most of the traditional conjoint approaches use full profile descriptions and ordinary least squares (OLS) regression to estimate partworths (Green and Srinivasan 1978; Wittink and Cattin 1989). Other types of conjoint measurement like Green's hybrid conjoint analysis (Green, Goldberg and Montemayor 1981), adaptive conjoint analysis (ACA; Johnson 1987) and customized conjoint analysis (CCA; Srinivasan and Park 1997; Hensel-Börner and Sattler 1999) combine the self-explicated task with aspects of the full profile conjoint analysis. We call all of these types "hybrid conjoint measurement". Because most of the research during the last 15 years has been focused on these hybrid conjoint methods (Green and Srinivasan 1990; Srinivasan and Park 1997), we shall include them in our analysis.

Similarly to conjoint measurement, there are different types of self-explicated approaches. However, because very simple types of self-explicated approaches like desirability ratings only have obvious limitations (Nitzsch and Weber1993), we shall include in our analysis just one type of self-explicated approach which has been applied in a number of studies (Green and Srinivasan 1990). Basically, this approach works in the following way (with some minor modifications between different applications, e.g. Srinivasan 1988). First, respondents evaluate the levels of each attribute on a (say) 0-10 desirability scale (with other attributes held constant) where the most preferred level on the attribute may be assigned the value 10 and the least preferred level assigned the value 0. Respondents then are asked to allocate (say) 100 points across the attributes so as to reflect their relative importance. Partworths are obtained by multiplying the importance weights with the attribute-level desirability ratings (Green and Srinivasan 1990).

The aim of this article is to give a comprehensive overview of studies comparing the self-explicated approach and conjoint measurement. In the following section, we shall first consider the "theoretical" perspective by comparing several advantages as well as disadvantages of conjoint measurement and self-explication approaches respectively. After this, we shall give a broad overview of empirical studies comparing the two approaches under consideration in terms of reliability as well as predictive validity. Reliability and predictive validity are taken because almost all past empirical studies used at least one of these measures. Finally, conclusions are drawn from our findings.

4.2   Theoretical Considerations

The motivation for the development of (traditional) conjoint measurement stems basically from several theoretical advantages over traditional methods of measuring customer's preference structure, especially over self-explicated approaches (Green and Srinivasan 1990). Advantages over self-explicated approaches are summarized in the upper part of Table 1 and will be discussed in more detail now. Our comparison focuses on purely decompositional methods of conjoint measurement (e.g. ranking or rating a set of stimuli), i.e. traditional conjoint measurement. Hybrid methods are not included because they combine advantages as well as disadvantages of decompositional (traditional conjoint) and compositional (self-explicated approaches) methods.

First, in contrast to self-explicated approaches (i.e. compositional approaches), conjoint measurement does not directly ask for partworths of attribute levels. Instead, conjoint methodology is based on a decompositional approach in which respondents react to a set of total profile descriptions. Profile descriptions are a (more or less) realistic representation of a real product and therefore the task for the respondents (e.g. ranking of profiles) resembles a real choice situation to a greater extent than the self-explicated approach (Green, Goldberg and Montemayor 1981). This similarity to real choice situations is a key distinction from self-explication approaches and may result in higher predictive validity, e.g. when predicting real product choices.

Second, the decompositional approach to identifying attribute partworths or importance weights is more likely to detect real importance weights than self-explicated approaches. When asking directly a question like "How important is attribute X?", it is not clear what the importance rating is supposed to mean, and different respondents are likely to interpret the question differently (Srinivasan 1988).

Table 1:   Advantages of conjoint measurement and self-explicated approaches

---

Advantages of traditional conjoint measurement over self-explicated approaches
1. Greater similarity to real choice situations
2. Greater chance of detecting real importance weights
3. Less chance of receiving only socially accepted responses
4. Greater range sensitivity
5. Better chance of detecting potential nonlinearity in the partworth function
6. Less likelihood of double-counting

Advantages of self-explicated approaches over traditional conjoint measurement
1. Less cognitive strain on the data-supplying capabilities of respondents
2. Less chance of simplifying-effects
3. Greater ease in data collection (e.g. telephone sampling)
4. Greater ease in data analysis and research design
5. Greater ability to handle a large number of attributes
6. Greater speed in data collection
7. Lower costs in data collection and data analysis

A third advantage of the decompositional conjoint measurement method over self-explicated approaches is that partworths and/or importance weights of attributes are obtained in an indirect manner. It is the job of the analyst to find a set of partworths for the attributes that, given some type of composition rule (e.g. an additive one), are most consistent with the respondent's overall preferences. For this indirect approach, only socially acceptable responses are less likely to occur than for self-explicated approaches (Hensel-Börner and Sattler 1999). For example, when respondents are asked directly for the importance of price, they might tend to underreport the importance because they possibly want to show that money does not matter much (even if it is a very important issue for them). This tendency might be weaker if respondents are asked indirectly.

Fourth, several empirical studies have shown that conjoint measurement is significantly more sensitive with respect to different ranges of attribute levels compared to self-explicated approaches, i.e. range sensitivity effects are less of a problem for conjoint measurement than for self-explicated approaches (Gedenk, Hensel-Börner, Sattler 1999). Sometimes, self-explicated approaches have been found to be *totally* insensitive to changes in attribute level ranges, which results in considerable validity problems (Nitzsch and Weber 1993).

Fifth, compared to self-explicated approaches, conjoint measurement has a better chance of detecting potential nonlinearity in the partworth function for quantitative attributes. For instance, suppose the capacity of refrigerators is varied at three levels, say 100, 125 and 150 liter. Given a 0-10 desirability scale with 0 for 100 liter and 10 for 150 liters, respondents may rate 5 for the intermediate level, making the partworth function linear. A full profile task has a better chance of detecting potential nonlinearity in the partworth function (Green and Srinivasan 1990).

Sixth, a problem with the self-explication approach is that any redundancy in the attributes can lead to double counting. For example, if energy costs and economy are two attributes of a refrigerator, there is an obvious risk of double counting because each attribute is questioned separately in the self-explicated approach. However, in a conjoint full profile approach respondents could recognize the redundancy between the attributes so that overall preference ratings would not be affected as much by double counting (Green and Srinivasan 1990).

On the other hand, there are also several advantages of self-explicated approaches over traditional conjoint measurement (lower part of Table 1). First, for self-explicated approaches there is less cognitive strain on the data-supplying capabilities of respondents, because the approach is substantially easier to handle and task complexity is much lower (Akaah and Korgaonkar 1983).

Second, there is a lower chance of simplifying-effects (Wright 1975). Especially when a larger number of attributes is used in a full profile conjoint analysis, respondents tend to focus on just a subset of attributes while neglecting the other ones. If subjects behave in this manner, severe biases in estimating partworths can occur for the conjoint analysis approach.

Third, data collection can be done much more easily for self-explicated approaches than for conjoint measurement (Srinivasan 1988). This is particularly relevant for postal and telephone surveys where complex descriptions of total profiles of conjoint measurement are hard to undertake (Srinivasan and Wyner 1989).

Fourth, there is a higher ease in analyzing the data for self-explicated approaches. Despite the fact that easy to handle software for data analysis of conjoint measurement is available, at least basic statistical knowledge is highly recommendable in conducting a conjoint analysis. In contrast, neither specialized software nor advanced statistical knowledge is necessary in analyzing the data of self-explicated approaches. The same is true for setting up an experimental design. While just basic ability is necessary for self-explicated approaches, the construction of an experimental design for conjoint measurement – e.g. in terms of stimuli construction – is rather complex.

Fifth, particularly due to advantage 1 and 2, there is a greater ability to handle a large number of attributes for self-explicated approaches compared to traditional conjoint methods (Srinivasan and Park 1997).

Sixth, also due to advantage 1, data collection can be done much faster than for conjoint measurement, especially for tasks with a large number of attributes. For this reason as well as due to advantages 3 and 4, finally, there are lower costs in data collection and data analysis for self-explicated approaches than for conjoint measurement (Green and Srinivasan 1990).

All factors taken into account, our discussion so far can be summarized as follows. Most of the reasons discussed favor conjoint measurement especially in terms of (predictive) validity, at least as long as there is a small number of attributes (six of fewer, Green and Srinivasan 1978). If, however, many attributes have to be handled, advantages 1 and 2 of self-explicated approaches (Table 1) may become crucial. Even for a small number of attributes, self-explicated approaches have considerable advantages over conjoint measurement in terms of ease of data collection, data analysis and research design as well as with respect to savings of time and costs in data collection and data analysis.

Despite the theoretical advantages of conjoint measurement in terms of (predictive) validity (for a small number of attributes), empirical research to date has produced rather mixed results. In case the advantages over self-explicated approaches can not be shown empirically, future applications of conjoint measurement seem to be at least questionable because of the advantages of self-explicated approaches in terms of ease, speed and costs. In the next section, a comprehensive overview of empirical studies which compare conjoint measurement with self-explicated approaches is given in order to determine this issue.

4.3   Empirical Comparisons

Our survey covers empirical studies comparing several types of conjoint measurement (including hybrid models) with self-explicated approaches in terms of reliability or predictive validity. In order to give a comprehensive overview, we selected all studies of this kind which have appeared in the International Journal of Research in Marketing, Journal of Marketing, Journal of Marketing Research, Marketing Letters, and Marketing Science since 1980. In addition to this, we have included available articles of the described kind which were frequently cited in these journals as well as recent available working papers.

The results of our survey are summarized in Table 2. The studies are ordered in terms of the types of methods compared, the measures investigated (i.e. reliability or predictive validity), and the results found. Unless otherwise indicated, all results are significant at the $p < 0.10$ level. Table 2 also shows the type of product investigated, the number of attributes, the sample size and the experimental design (i.e. "within" vs. "between subject design") for each study.

Out of the 23 results reported in Table 2, only 5 (22%, highlighted in Table 2) show significantly better results in terms of reliability or predictive validity for conjoint measurement compared to self-explicated approaches. The other 18 results (78%) show either non significant differences or significantly better results for self-explicated approaches. Given the theoretical advantages of conjoint measurement discussed in the previous section, these findings are surprising.

Looking exclusively at reliability, no study shows superior results for conjoint measurement. Instead, two out of four studies dealing with reliability found significantly better outcomes for self-explicated approaches. This result might be explained by the lower cognitive strain on the data-supplying capabilities of respondents for the self-explicated approach.

Table 2:   *Empirical studies comparing conjoint measurement with self-explicated approaches*

Source	Methods Compared	Measure	Results a)	Products	No of Attributes	Sample Size	Experimental Design
Srinivasan 1988	Conjoint trade-off – Self-explicated	Predictive validity (actual choices)	Non significant differences	Job offers	8	54	Within subject design
Leigh, MacKay and Summers 1984	Traditional conjoint – Self-explicated	Reliability	Non significant differences	Pocket calculators	5	122 e)	Between subject design
Heeler, Okechuku and Reid 1979	Traditional conjoint – Self-explicated	Reliability	Self-explicated better than conjoint b)	Electric blenders	10	98 e)	Between subject design
Green, Krieger and Agarwal 1993	Traditional conjoint – Self-explicated	Reliability	Self-explicated better than conjoint	Cars	8	133 e)	Within subject design
Green, Carmone and Wind 1972	Traditional conjoint – Self-explicated	Predictive validity (hypothetical choices)	No major differences b)	Discount cards	3	43	Within subject design
Leigh, MacKay and Summers 1984	Traditional conjoint – Self-explicated	Predictive validity (actual raffle choices)	Non significant differences	Pocket calculators	5	122 e)	Between subject design
Green and Helsen 1989	Traditional conjoint – Self-explicated	Predictive validity (hypothetical choices)	Non significant differences	Apartments	6	99 e)	Within subject design
Huber et al. 1993	Traditional conjoint – Self-explicated	Predictive validity (hypothetical choices)	Non significant differences	Refrigerators	5 and 9	393	Within subject design
Green, Krieger and Agarwal 1993	Traditional conjoint – Self-explicated	Predictive validity (hypothetical choices)	Mixed results for different measures	Cars	8	133 e)	Within subject design
Huber, Daneshgar and Ford 1971	Traditional conjoint – Self-explicated	Predictive validity (actual choices)	Self-explicated better than conjoint c)	Job offers	5	30 e)	Within subject design
Wright and Kriewall 1980	Traditional conjoint – Self-explicated	Predictive validity (actual choices)	Self-explicated better than conjoint	College applications	5	120	Within subject design
Green, Goldberg and Wiley 1982	Traditional conjoint – Self-explicated	Predictive validity (hypothetical choices)	Conjoint better than Self-explicated	Household appliance	7	476	Within subject design

Table 3: *Empirical studies comparing conjoint measurement with self-explicated approaches (continued)*

Source	Methods Compared	Measure	Results a)	Products	No of Attributes	Sample Size	Experimental Design
Akaah and Korgaonkar 1983	Traditional conjoint – Self-explicated	Predictive validity (hypothetical choices)	Conjoint better than Self-explicated	HMO	6	80	Within subject design
Akaah and Korgaonkar 1983	Huber hybrid – Self-explicated	Predictive validity (hypothetical choices)	Non significant differences	HMO	6	80	Within subject design
Akaah and Korgaonkar 1983	Green hybrid – Self-explicated	Predictive validity (hypothetical choices)	Non significant differences	HMO	6	80	Within subject design
Green, Goldberg and Wiley 1982	Green hybrid – Self-explicated	Predictive validity (hypothetical choices)	Green hybrid better than Self-explicated	Household appliance	7	476	Within subject design
Green, Krieger and Agarwal 1993	ACA – Self-explicated	Reliability	Non significant differences	Cars	8	133 e)	Within subject design
Green, Krieger and Agarwal 1993	ACA – Self-explicated	Predictive validity (hypothetical choices)	Mixed results for different measures	Cars	8	133 e)	Within subject design
Agarwal and Green 1991	ACA – Self-explicated	Predictive validity (hypothetical choices)	Self-explicated better than ACA d)	Apartments	6	170 e)	Within subject design
Huber et al. 1993	ACA – Self-explicated	Predictive validity (hypothetical choices)	ACA better than Self-explicated	Refrigerators	5 and 9	393	Within subject design
Hensel-Börner and Sattler 1999	ACA – Self-explicated	Predictive validity (market shares)	Non significant differences	Coffee	8	144	Within and between subject design
Srinivasan and Park 1997	Customized conjoint – Self-explicated	Predictive validity (actual choices)	Non significant differences	Job offers	8	121 e)	Within subject design
Hensel-Börner and Sattler 1999	Computerized customized conjoint – Self-explicated	Predictive validity (market shares)	Computerized customized conjoint partly better than Self-explicated	Coffee	8	144	Within and between subject design

a) Significant differences between methods b) Significance not tested c) For experienced respondents; non significant differences for non experienced respondents d) Exception: ACA better than the Self-explicated part of ACA (Green, Krieger and Agarwal 1991) e) Respondents were students

In terms of predictive validity, comparisons between *traditional* conjoint measurement and self-explicated approaches show in two cases significantly superior results for self-explicated approaches and in another two cases significantly superior results for traditional conjoint measurement, while the remaining 5 studies found no significant differences or mixed results. Comparing *hybrid* conjoint methods (Huber hybrid, Green hybrid, ACA, and customized conjoint analysis) with self-explicated approaches there are no apparent advantages of hybrid conjoint approaches.

These results can be explained only partly by the type of measure, experimental design, sample size, sampling procedure, product category and the number of attributes (see Table 2). Interestingly, findings in favor of conjoint measurement can be observed for hypothetical choices (usually holdout stimuli) only, but not for actual choices. Moreover, all studies observing superior results for conjoint measurement used a within subject design. This kind of design– as opposed to between subject designs – may cause problems because of learning effects (Campbell and Stanley 1966; Huber, Wittink, Fiedler and Miller 1993; Agarwal and Green 1991). Compared with studies which found non significant differences or results in favor of self-explicated approaches, self-explicated approaches used at least partly between subject designs or actual choices as a measure of predictive validity, thus putting more emphasis on the findings of these studies, i.e. results in favor of self-explicated approaches seem to be more trustworthy with respect to these two issues. On the other hand, studies in favor of conjoint measurement used on average a larger sample size and non-students as respondents in all cases. With respect to the product category and the number of attributes, no systematic differences between studies in favor and against conjoint measurement can be found. For instance, the same kind of product and (approximately) the same number of attributes were used by the studies of Heeler, Okechuku and Reid (1979) and Green, Goldberg and Wiley (1982), but with opposite results.

4.4   Conclusions

Comparing conjoint measurement with self-explicated approaches from a theoretical perspective, conjoint measurement possesses obvious advantages in terms of (predictive) validity. However, our comprehensive analysis of empirical studies comparing these two approaches fails to confirm the superiority of conjoint measurement. Instead, the majority of empirical comparisons (18 out of 23, i.e. 78%) found either non significant differences between methods or even higher predictive validity or reliability for self-explicated approaches. Attempts to explain these results by factors such as the type of measure, experimental design, sample size, sampling procedure, product category and the number of attributes are not promising because of mixed results.

Given the clear majority of empirical findings not in favor of conjoint measurement, future applications of conjoint measurement for measuring customers' preference structure seem to be at least questionable because of the advantages of self-explicated approaches in terms of ease, time effort and costs.

4.5   References

Agarwal, M. K. and Green, P. E. (1991), Adaptive Conjoint Analysis versus Self-Explicated Models: Some Empirical Results, International *Journal of Research in Marketing*, 8, 141-146.

Akaah, I. P. and Korgaonkar, P. K. (1983), An Empirical Comparison of the Predictive Validity of Self-Explicated, Huber-Hybrid, Traditional Conjoint, and Hybrid Conjoint Models, *Journal of Marketing Research*, 20, 187-197.

Campbell, D. T. and Stanley, J. C. (1966), *Experimental and Quasi-Experimental Designs for Research*, Chicago.

Johnson, R. (1987), Adaptive Conjoint Analysis, *Sawtooth Software Conference on Perceptual Mapping*, 253-256.

Gedenk, K., Hensel-Börner, S. and Sattler, H. (1999), Bandbreitensensitivität von Verfahren zur Präferenzmessung, working paper, University of Jena.

Green, P. E. and Helsen, K. (1989), Cross-Validation Assessment of Alternatives to Individual-Level Conjoint Analysis: A Case Study, *Journal of Marketing Research*, 26, 346-350.

Green, P. E. and Srinivasan, V. (1978), Conjoint Analysis in Consumer Research: Issues and Outlook, *Journal of Consumer Research*, 5, 103-123.

Green, P. E. and Srinivasan, V. (1990), Conjoint Analysis in Marketing: New Development with Implications for Research and Practice, *Journal of Marketing*, 54, 3-19.

Green, P. E., Carmone, F. J and Wind, Y. (1972), Subjective Evaluation Models and Conjoint Measurement, *Behavioral Science*, 17, 288-299.

Green, P. E., Goldberg, S. M. and Montemayor, M. (1981), A Hybrid Utility Estimation Model for Conjoint Analysis, *Journal of Marketing*, 45, 33-41.

Green, P. E., Goldberg, S .M. and Wiley, J. B. (1982), A Cross-Validation Test of Hybrid Conjoint Models, *Advances in Consumer Research*, 10, 147-150.

Green, P. E., Krieger, A. M. and Agarwal, M. (1993), A Cross Validation Test of Four Models Quantifying Multiattributed Preferences, *Marketing Letters*, 4, 369-380.

Heeler, R. M., Okechuku, C. and Reid, S. (1979), Attribute Importance: Contrasting Measurements, *Journal of Marketing Research*, 16, 60-63.

Hensel-Börner, S. and Sattler, H. (1999), *Validität der Customized Computerized Conjoint Analysis (CCC)*, working paper, *University of Jena*.

Huber, G. P., Daneshgar, R. and Ford, D. L. (1971), An Empirical Comparison of Five Utility Models for Predicting Job Preferences, *Organizational Behavior and Human Performance*, 6, 267-282.

Huber, J. C., Wittink, D. R., Fiedler, J. A. and Miller, R. (1993), The Effectiveness of Alternative Preference Elicitation Procedures in Predicting Choice, *Journal of Marketing Research*, 17, 53-72.

Leigh, T. W., MacKay, D. B. and Summers, J. O. (1984), Reliability and Validity of Conjoint Analysis and Self-Explicated Weights: A Comparison, *Journal of Marketing Research*, 21, 456-462.

Nitzsch, R. v. and Weber, M. (1993), The Effect of Attribute Ranges on Weights in Multiattribute Utility Measurements, *Management Science*, 39, 937-943.

Srinivasan, V. (1988), A Conjunctive-Compensatory Approach to the Self-Explication of Multiattributed Preferences, *Decision Sciences*, 19, 295-305.

Srinivasan, V. and Park, C. S. (1997), Surprising Robustness of the Self-Explicated Approach to Customer Preference Structure Measurement, *Journal of Marketing Research*, 34, 286-291.

Srinivasan, V. and Wyner, G. A. (1989), CASEMAP: Computer-Assisted Self-Explication of Multiattributed Preferences, in: Henry, W., Menasco, M. and Takada, H., eds., *New Product Development and Testing,* Lexington, 91-111.

Wittink, D. R. and Cattin, P. (1989), Commercial Use of Conjoint Analysis: An Update, *Journal of Marketing*, 53, 91-96.

Wright, P. (1975), Consumer Choice Strategies: Simplifying vs. Optimizing, *Journal of Marketing Research*, 12, 60-67.

Wright, P. and Kriewall, M. A. (1980), State of Mind Effects on the Accuracy with which Utility Functions Predict Marketplace Choice, *Journal of Marketing Research*, 17, 277-293.

5 Non-geometric Plackett-Burman Designs in Conjoint Analysis

Ola Blomkvist, Fredrik Ekdahl and Anders Gustafsson

5.1 Introduction

Design of experiments is an established technique for product and process improvement that has its origin in the 1920s and the work of Sir Ronald Fisher. Conjoint analysis shares the same theoretical basis as traditional design of experiments, but was originally used within the field of psychology and it was not until the early 1970s that the methodology was introduced into marketing research to form what is called conjoint analysis (Luce and Tukey 1964; Green and Rao 1971; Johnson 1974). Today, conjoint analysis is an established technique for investigating customer preferences.

In design of experiments, selected system parameters, sometimes referred to as experimental factors, are varied according to a carefully selected experimental design. The structure of the design then allows estimation of the influence of the experimental factors as well as interactions between them on some system output of interest. In this paper, the influence of a single experimental factor will be termed its main effect and the influence of an interaction between two or more factors will be referred to as an interaction effect.

Similar to design of experiments, the full profile approach in conjoint analysis involves presenting respondents with a set of product concepts for which a number of attributes corresponding to the experimental factors have been varied between different levels according to an experimental design. The respondents are then asked to evaluate the different product concepts, typically using some sort of rating scale. In the subsequent analysis it is possible to estimate the influence of individual product attributes and interactions between them on the preferences of the respondents. One concern when using conjoint analysis is to avoid overloading the respondents with information, i.e. too many concepts, too many attributes and too many levels. The average commercial study uses 16 concepts with eight different attributes on three levels each (Wittink and Cattin 1989). This means that there are too few degrees of freedom to estimate comprehensive models. Interactions between attributes are most often neglected in conjoint analysis. Studies show that only 10% of the commercial applications take interactions into account (Wittink et al. 1994).

In design of experiments, the identification and estimation of interactions between experimental factors is generally regarded as very important (Box 1990; Kackar and Tsui 1990; Bisgaard 1992). Within the field of conjoint analysis, on the other hand, there seems to be some confusion about whether or not conjoint analysis studies benefit from considering interactions. Certain empirical evidence indicates that including interactions often leads to lower predictive validity, i.e. that the increased model realism achieved by including interactions is small compared to the deterioration in predictive accuracy caused by including additional model parameters (Green 1984; Hagerty 1986). Nevertheless, if data is aggregated, models that include interactions tend to be superior (Hagerty 1986). Also, interactions, particularly two-factor interactions, may be of vital importance in areas where personal sensory opinions are important, e.g. for creating food products or for styling and aesthetic aspects (Green and Srinivasan 1990).

Whichever is the case, it is obvious that experimental designs allowing investigation of many attributes and at the same time enabling estimation of interaction terms without overloading the respondents would be of great value. Recent research has also indicated that by using the properties of a certain class of designs, termed non-geometric Plackett-Burman designs (PB designs) it is possible, despite the inclusion of many attributes, to identify and estimate interactions (Box and Meyer 1993; Hamada and Wu 1992).

The purpose of this paper is to illustrate how the use of non-geometric PB designs facilitates identification of models including interactions in conjoint analysis studies. Also, a procedure based on restricted all subsets regression that takes advantage of the special properties of the non-geometric PB designs is proposed and demonstrated using data from a conjoint analysis study on cellular phone antennas. The paper will provide strong indications that the estimated models that include interactions are better at explaining customer preferences than the models with only main effects. The properties of the proposed procedure are also illustrated using a Monte Carlo simulation.

5.2   Non-geometric Plackett-Burman Designs

Much work has been put into developing two-level and three-level experimental designs (see e.g., Fisher 1935; Finney 1945; Plackett and Burman 1946; Box and Behnken 1960; Box and Behnken 1961). Starting with a two-level or three-level orthogonal design, it is a straightforward process to develop more sophisticated designs, i.e. with four or more levels for each attribute. For reasons of brevity, the discussion will be limited to two-level orthogonal designs, i.e. designs in which the attributes are only tested at two levels.

Two-level orthogonal designs can be divided into geometric designs for which the number of concepts is a power of 2 (4, 8, 16, 32 etc.) and non-geometric designs. The PB designs are designs for which the number of concepts is a multiple of 4 (4, 8, 12, 16, 20 etc.). When the number of concepts in a PB design is also a power of 2, it is identical to the corresponding geometric design. It is, however, the non-geometric PB designs for which the number of concepts equals 12, 20, 24, 28 etc. that are of special interest for this paper, since they show a number of valuable properties.

The 12-run PB design is given in Table 1 following the geometric notation (Box, Hunter and Hunter 1978) in which a „-"-sign represents the low level of the attribute and a „+"-sign represents the high level. Table 1 also shows the column corresponding to the interaction between columns 2 and 3.

Table 1:   The 12-run PB design matrix

Concept	M	1	2	3	4	5	6	7	8	9	10	11	Interaction 23
1	+	+	-	+	-	-	-	+	+	+	-	+	-
2	+	+	+	-	+	-	-	-	+	+	+	-	-
3	+	-	+	+	-	+	-	-	-	+	+	+	+
4	+	+	-	+	+	-	+	-	-	-	+	+	-
5	+	+	+	-	+	+	-	+	-	-	-	+	-
6	+	+	+	+	-	+	+	-	+	-	-	-	+
7	+	-	+	+	+	-	+	+	-	+	-	-	+
8	+	-	-	+	+	+	-	+	+	-	+	-	-
9	+	-	-	-	+	+	+	-	+	+	-	+	+
10	+	+	-	-	-	+	+	+	-	+	+	-	+
11	+	-	+	-	-	-	+	+	+	-	+	+	-
12	+	-	-	-	-	-	-	-	-	-	-	-	+

The geometric designs have traditionally been preferred by experimenters, since they have relatively simple alias patterns. The alias pattern follows directly from the selected experimental design and reflects the dependencies between estimates of the effects. For the geometric designs, any two effects are either independent or completely aliased, in which case separate estimation of these effects is not possible. The alias pattern of a non-geometric PB design is considerably more complex. A specific two-factor interaction effect, for example, is partially aliased with all main effects except those comprising the interaction, which means that separate estimation of these effects is still possible, although the estimates will be correlated with each other.

The complex alias pattern has traditionally ruled out the use of the non-geometric PB designs unless the interactions could be considered of negligible importance. The alias pattern has simply been considered too complex. It turns out, however, that the complex alias pattern is also the real strength of the non-geometric PB designs.

First of all, the alias pattern allows estimation of more parameters than there are actually degrees of freedom. This is sometimes referred to as supersaturation (Wu 1993) and in principle makes it possible to estimate the impact of all two-factor interactions even though the estimates will be correlated. The 12 run PB design, for example, has $11!/(2!\cdot 9!) = 55$ two-factor interaction columns along with the eleven main effect columns that can all be distinguished from one another. To allow estimation of eleven main effects along with all two-factor interactions using a geometric design would require the use of 128 concepts, which is impossible in a normal conjoint analysis context.

Second, the alias pattern gives the non-geometric PB designs superior projectivity properties. The projectivity of a design is equal to the maximum number of arbitrary columns that can be chosen from the design matrix while maintaining a complete design between these columns; a two-level design is complete if it includes all 2^k combinations of the k attributes at two levels. See Figure 1 for an illustration. Box and Tyssedal (1996) have shown that all non-geometric PB-designs up to n = 84 are of projectivity 3 while the geometric designs are only of projectivity 2.

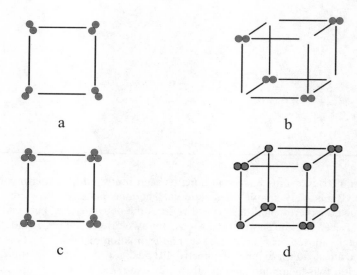

a

b

c

d

Figure 1:   *Projections of an 8-run geometric design (a and b) and the 12-run PB-design (c and d) into two and three dimensions*

Figure 1 shows how the individual runs in an 8-run geometric design and the 12-run PB design shown in Table 1 are distributed when projected into two and three dimensions. Both designs are complete when projected into two dimensions, but only the PB design remains complete in three dimensions. The projectivity property of a design is especially interesting when factor sparsity can be assumed. Under factor sparsity, it is expected that only a subset of the investigated attributes will actually be of interest and consequently it should be possible to find a satisfactory preference model from within that subset. If there is a subset of two or three attributes that are of importance for modeling the preferences of a respondent, the non-geometric PB designs will always, regardless of the subset, allow investigation of those attributes along with the corresponding interactions. For geometric designs, on the other hand, the subsets that can be investigated are already decided when choosing the actual design.

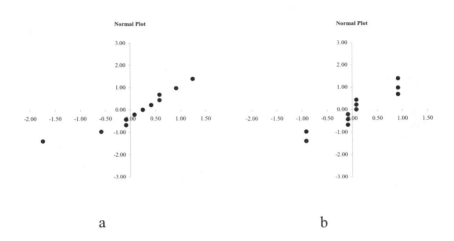

a   b

Figure 2:   *Normal plots of estimated effects for two individuals from a conjoint analysis survey using a non-geometric PB design*

When including many attributes in a geometric design, it is often impossible to demonstrate that including interactions in the preference models would improve the predictions, since the interactions will then be completely confounded with the main effects. Therefore, a third advantage of the non-geometric PB designs is that they make it possible to detect the presence of interactions without actually estimating them, as an influential interaction will cause the estimates of the main effects to group according to the structure of the alias pattern. This grouping is especially apparent when using the normal probability plotting technique, developed by Daniel (1959, 1976) and frequently applied when analyzing designed experiments. Estimates of the effects are plotted on a normal probability paper and those corresponding to influential attributes will stand out from the others. Figure 2 shows normal probability plots for two individuals in a conjoint analysis study, see section 7.4, based on the 12-run PB design.

The normal probability plot in Figure 2a displays an expected appearance, i.e. most of the effects fall along a straight line and only one or two stand out. This usually indicates that a model with main effects alone is sufficient. The normal probability plot in Figure 2b, however, shows gaps between groups of estimated effects falling along parallel lines. One possible explanation would be the presence of outliers among the observations (Box and Draper 1987), but since a rating scale was used when collecting data this is not a likely explanation. Instead, a more likely explanation would be the presence of influential interactions (Box and Meyer 1993) and further investigation in order to identify models, possibly including interactions, might be fruitful.

5.3   Proposed Procedure

Several different procedures for identifying models from experimental data have been developed over the years. Among these, the procedures due to Hamada and Wu (1992) and Box and Meyer (1986) have been advocated as especially suitable for analyzing designs with complex alias patterns. Hamada and Wu (1992) suggest a method based upon stepwise regression taking effect heredity into account when identifying the model and estimating its parameters. Effect heredity suggests that a two-factor interaction is not likely to significantly influence the response unless at least one of the two attributes that comprise the interaction also significantly influences the response. Box and Meyer (1986) propose a Bayesian approach, which identifies the important factors even if it does not include any detailed model identification. In addition, Hynén (1996) proposes a projectivity approach that investigates all possible models consisting of three main effects and the three corresponding two-factor interactions, and selects the model showing the least unexplained variation.

Hynén (1996) compares the different approaches from an „*important factors perspective*" using simulations on a 12-run PB design. He finds that for moderately large models, three main effects and one two-factor interaction, the projective approach identifies the correct influential factors and interactions, even with as many as 11 attributes in the design, whereas Hamada and Wu's method starts to fail at about 7 or 8 attributes. For larger models, three main effects and three interactions, both methods start to fail as the number of attributes increases. The projective approach seems to be reliable up to 5 attributes, while Hamada and Wu's approach frequently fails even with only 4 attributes. Hynén (1996) also concludes that if the method due to Box and Meyer (1993) is to be used to identify important attributes, it needs to be combined with normal probability plots. This more or less disqualifies the technique for analyzing data from conjoint analysis surveys, since a plot must then be made for each respondent, making it difficult to implement on a large-scale basis.

The approach proposed by Hynén (1996) considers only models with six parameters, i.e. three main effects and the three corresponding two-factor interactions. A natural extension of this approach would be to evaluate also all models consisting of possible subsets of these six parameters for all factor triplets. However, the number of candidate models grows very rapidly with the number of attributes and soon becomes unmanageable. Instead of investigating all possible models for all factor triplets, an effective way of reducing the number of candidate models would be t make a wise choice of an initial set of the attributes and then restrict the subsequent analysis to that subset.

This paper proposes a two step procedure, where the purpose of the first step is to select the most promising projection among the original attributes, relying on factor sparsity and exploiting the projective properties of the non-geometric PB designs. The purpose of the second step is then to identify the best model within the selected projection.

The first step is conducted as a restricted all subsets regression, i.e. only models including all possible two-factor interactions for all projections into one, two and three dimensions are evaluated. The projections achieving the largest R^2_{adj} for each dimension are then selected for use in the second step. The adjusted coefficient of multiple determination, R^2_{adj} is defined as:

$$(1) \qquad R^2_{adj} = 1 - \left(\frac{n-1}{n-p} \right)\left(1 - R^2\right) = 1 - \left(\frac{n-1}{n-p} \right)\left(1 - \frac{SS_R}{S_{yy}} \right),$$

where n is the number of available degrees of freedom, p is the number of parameters in the selected model including the mean, SS_R is the sum of squares due to that model and S_{yy} represents the total sum of squares. R^2_{adj} was suggested as a measure of explained variance that compensates for model complexity by for example Draper and Smith (1981). A few words of caution are in place regarding the use of R^2_{adj}. If additional parameters are included in the model, degrees of freedom are traded against explanation of variation. For R^2_{adj} to increase, it is necessary for each added parameter to explain at least as much variation as the average of those already in the model. However, this does not necessarily mean that the added parameter is significant from a statistical point of view.

The second step is also performed as a restricted all subsets regression, this time considering only models that satisfy effect heredity within the chosen projections. Note that for the proposed procedure, effect heredity has been given a more strict interpretation than that given by Hamada and Wu (1992) in that for a two-factor interaction to be considered influential both attributes comprising the interaction must also be considered influential. Finally, the model with the highest R^2_{adj} is chosen to represent the preferences of the individual respondent.

5.4 A Comparative Study

To evaluate the performance of the proposed approach and to investigate whether or not conjoint analysis studies would benefit from including interactions, models identified using the proposed procedure were compared against a number of different models with only main effects. The comparison is made in terms of R^2_{adj}, which makes it fair in the sense that R^2_{adj}, compensates to some extent for the increased model complexity.

The comparison includes three different strategies for identifying models with only main effects; (1) a full main effect model, (2) an all subsets regression with main effects only and (3) an ANOVA restricted to include only main effects. The full main effect model represents perhaps the simplest strategy for selecting models. Since some of the included attributes will most probably lack explanatory power, the R^2_{adj} may, however, decrease. Instead, a more elaborate strategy is to perform an all subsets regression on the main effects and choose the model with the highest R^2_{adj}. Finally, ANOVA was included in the comparison as a well-established technique for identifying models. ANOVA uses an estimate of the experimental error and F-tests to identify the influential attributes and is the only strategy in the comparison that includes an objective test of significance.

Data from a conjoint analysis study of the characteristics of a cellular phone antenna was used for the comparison. The survey was carried out in Sweden and the respondents were recruited from the customers in two stores. The total number of respondents was 142. Each respondent was interviewed and the responses, i.e. ratings on a scale from 1 to 10 for each concept, were given verbally. The stimuli consisted of separate lines of text and all concepts were presented on one large sheet of paper. The study included five product attributes (A, B, C, D and E) such as the price and a few technical parameters. The experimental design used in the study was the 12-run non-geometric PB design illustrated in Table 1 and the levels of the five attributes were varied according to columns 1 through 5.

5.5   Results of the Comparison

The analysis of the case study aimed at determining whether better explanatory abilities are gained by introducing interactions in the estimated models and whether the proposed procedure is well suited for identifying these interactions. Following the proposed procedure, the first step in the analysis is to find the most promising projection, i.e. that corresponding to the highest R^2_{adj} for each individual respondent. Table 2 lists the most frequently chosen projections.

It is interesting to see that they are all of size 3, which could indicate that the proposed procedure favors large models. Among the chosen projections, $\{B, C, D\}$ stands out as considerably more frequent than the others. If the choice of projection is considered to be binomially distributed, the probability that as many as 40 of the respondents would fall within the same projection is less than one in a billion.

Following the second step of the proposed procedure, the model with the highest R^2_{adj} is then identified within the restrictions of the chosen projection. Table 3 lists the models most frequently identified using the proposed procedure and the various main effect strategies in the comparison. As can be expected, the top ranking models identified using the proposed procedure fall within the $\{B, C, D\}$ projection.

Table 2:   *The projections with the highest R^2_{adj} for the individual respondents in the case data*

Attributes in the Projection			No. of Cases
B	C	D	40
A	B	D	17
B	C	E	17
C	D	E	17
A	B	C	10
A	C	E	10
A	D	E	9
A	C	D	8
B	D	E	6
A	B	E	5

Table 3:   *The models identified using the proposed procedure and the main effect strategies in the comparison (The full main effect model is omitted)*

Proposed Projective Procedure						No.of Cases	All Subsets Regression					No. of Cases	Anova		No. of Cases
B	C	D	BC	BD	CD	16	A	B	C	D		18			36
B	C	D	BD	CD		11	B	C	D	E		14	C		17
A	B	D	AB	AD	BD	9	A	B	C	D	E	14	B		12
A	D	E	AD	AE	DE	7	B	D	E			9	B	C	11
B	C	E	BC	BE	CE	7	B	C				7	E		8
A	B	C	AB	AC	BC	5	A	B	C			7	A		7
A	C	D	AC	AD	CD	5	B	C	D			7	D		7
A	C	E	AC	AE	CE	5	C	D	E			7	B	D	6
A	B	D	AB	AD		4	A	C	D	E		7	C	D	4
C	D	E	CE	DE		4	A	C	D			6	A	C	3

These attributes are also well represented in the top ranking main effect models. Perhaps more interesting is that the models identified using ANOVA, i.e. those representing significance in the statistical sense, are very small compared to the models identified using R^2_{adj} as reference. For the proposed procedure, the average number of model parameters excluding the mean is 5.18 (of which an average of 2.96 are main effects). The models identified using the all subsets regression strategy use 3.21 parameters on average, compared to 1.32 parameters for the ANOVA.

Table 4:   *The average R^2_{adj} for the proposed procedure and the main effect*
               strategies in the comparison

Technique	Proposed Projective Procedure	All Subsets Regression	Full Main Effect	ANOVA
R^2_{adj}	0.81	0.64	0.58	0.49

Table 4 shows the average R^2_{adj} for the proposed approach and the three main
effect strategies in the comparison. The results clearly indicate that the models
including interactions outperform the main effect models in terms of R^2_{adj}. In view
of the larger models identified by the proposed procedure, this result is perhaps
not surprising. Note, however, that on average the models identified by the proposed procedure use fewer main effects and that the higher R^2_{adj} achieved for these
models therefore can be attributed to the inclusion of interactions. This is a strong
indication that the inclusion of interactions contributes to superior model properties.

The proposed approach identifies interaction effects in 139 out of the 142
models, which of course indicates that the inclusion of interactions is beneficial
for the analyst. However, the frequency of interactions may also seem somewhat
suspicious, which leads to the question of whether or not they actually represent
the preferences of the respondents or if their origin should be sought elsewhere.
One possible explanation for the high frequency of interactions in the models is
the use of a rating scale as the response. When using ordinary least square regression to estimate a model it is quite possible that the estimated model will predict
outside of the rating scale for the preferred attribute settings. This way, the rating
scale might induce pseudo interactions, which could lead to serious misinterpreta-
tions. For about 30% of the respondents in the antenna case study, the identified
models predict outside the 1 to 10 rating scale. While these pseudo interactions do
not have a straightforward interpretation in themselves, they instead indicate a
scale deficiency that perhaps must be addressed before making inferences from
the study. The issues accompanying the use of rating scales are not of primary
interest here and will therefore not be discussed further in this paper.

To further illustrate the results from the comparison, Figure 3 displays scatter
plots of the R^2_{adj} for each individual model identified using the proposed approach
and the three competing main effect strategies. If one approach is superior to another, the observations will lie above the diagonal in the corresponding scatter
plot. Figure 3 also contains frequency charts showing the distribution of R^2_{adj}. Due
to the distribution of R^2_{adj} for the full main effect approach, which is occasionally
negative, the scale in Figure 3 is between -0.5 and 1, except of course for the vertical axes in the frequency charts. As can be seen from Figure 3, there are very few
cases in which the proposed approach does not produce a model with higher R^2_{adj}
than the competing strategies. It is also apparent that the variation in R^2_{adj} is considerably smaller for the proposed procedure.

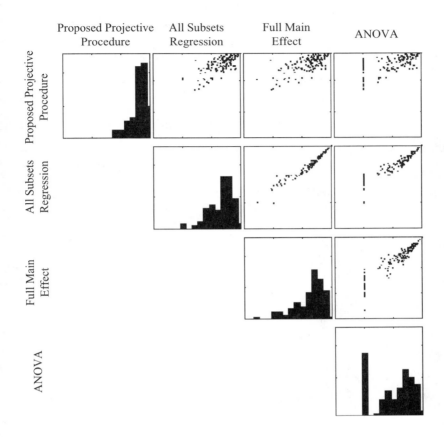

Figure 3:   A comparison of R^2_{adj} for each individual model

5.6   Some Simulation Results

To further illustrate the properties of the proposed procedure, a simulation study was conducted. Using the 12-run PB design, 2500 individual responses on a 1 to 10 rating scale were generated for each of the five different underlying models shown in Table 5. The aim when choosing the five underlying models was to illustrate a few interesting situations rather than trying to be complete. The first two cases represent two main effect extremes, i.e. an empty model and a complete main effect model. The last three represent models that include interactions in different combinations.

Table 5:   *The five underlying models used in the simulation study*

	Model Parameters
1	No active factors
2	A, B, C, D, E
3	A, B, AB
4	A, B, C, AB
5	A, B, C, AB, AC, BC

When generating the responses, each of the model parameters was given a regression coefficient of 0.5 and noise was generated from a discontinuous distribution created from $N(0,0.5)$ by concentrating the probability mass to the closest integers. In this way, the risk of predictions outside the 1 to 10 rating scale was kept very low. The results from the simulation study are shown in Table 6.

Table 6:   *Results from the simulation study. For each approach, the number of the models falling within the correct projection, the number of correctly identified models and the average R^2_{adj} is given*

	Attributes	Proposed Projective Procedure			All Subsets Regression			ANOVA		
		Proj.	Model	R^2_{adj}	Proj.	Model	R^2_{adj}	Proj.	Model	R^2_{adj}
1			8			327			2016	
2	A, B, C, D, E	n/a	n/a	0.77		1496	0.71		316	0.54
3	A, B, AB	51	51	0.76	497	n/a	0.47	240	n/a	0.24
4	A, B, C, AB	1340	382	0.75	465	n/a	0.49	99	n/a	0.25
5	A, B, C, AB, AC, BC	1992	1543	0.71	153	n/a	0.20	2	n/a	0.03

For the first underlying model, it is of course discouraging to find that when using the proposed procedure the correct model is identified in only 8 of the 2500 cases, whereas when using ANOVA the correct model is selected in about 2000 of the cases. However, a closer look at the results from the simulation reveals that the models identified with the proposed procedure are well distributed between all possible models, with a distinct preference for large models. None of the identified models represents more than 104 of the 2500 cases and there are more than twenty different models that have been identified in at least 50 cases. This result is in itself an indication of the absence of a distinct structure in the data.

For the second underlying model, i.e. the full main effect model, the correct model is identified in about 1500 of the cases when using the all subsets regression strategy, which is quite impressive considering the model complexity. Using ANOVA now only identifies the correct model in approximately 250 of the cases. In the case of the empty model, the proposed procedure identifies models that are well distributed between the possible models, although with a slightly lesser preference for large models. None of the models represents more than 192 of the cases and there are twelve different models that represent at least 70 cases.

Finally, it is interesting to note that even though the correct model cannot be identified when using the proposed procedure, since it only allows three main effects at a time, the average R^2_{adj} is still higher for the proposed procedure than for any of the main effect strategies. This result can be explained by the dependencies between estimates of the main effects and the interaction effects.

Moving on to the models that include interactions, the main effect strategies can of course no longer be used to identify the correct models and in addition the result from the simulation also indicates that they are relatively ineffective in identifying even the correct main effects. The models identified using the proposed procedure show considerably higher R^2_{adj} than the models with main effects only and it is therefore somewhat discouraging at first that for the third underlying model, i.e. two main effects and one interaction, only about 2% of the identified models are correct. Once again, the proposed procedure seems to favor large models. However, closer examination of the results shown in Table 7 reveals a more encouraging situation.

First of all, the projections that include factors A and B together represent almost 2000 of the responses. Further, attributes A, B and the AB interaction, even though complemented by other attributes and interactions, are consistently present in all top ranking models, which together represent over 1800 cases. The fact that attributes A and B along with the AB interaction consistently appear in the top ranking models is a strong indication that they together represent the correct model. In this way, a certain amount of craftsmanship, even though quite questionable from a statistical viewpoint, helps in interpreting the results.

For the second and somewhat more complex underlying model, the results are quite similar. Although the correct projection is chosen in about half of the cases only about 375 of the identified models are correct. Again, the proposed procedure seems to favor large models and the rest of the models from the correct projection are distributed between the models where one or two of the other possible interactions are also included. As before, using craftsmanship makes it possible to detect that it is actually the AB interaction that is influential. Of course, the ease of coming up with the right interpretation when actually knowing the correct answer is recognized. For the last of the underlying models, the correct projection is chosen in about 2000 of the cases and the correct model is chosen in roughly 1500 of the 2500 cases. This result, although expected in view of the fact that the underlying model closely agrees with the construct of the proposed procedure, is of course encouraging in view of the relative complexity of the underlying model.

Table 7:   Simulation results for the third underlying model, i.e. A, B and AB

Attributes in the Projection			No. of Cases	No.	Selected Model						No. of Cases
A	B	C	754	1	A	B	C	AB	AC	BC	237
A	B	D	651	2	A	B	D	AB	AD	BD	213
A	B	E	566	3	A	B	C	AB	AC		190
A	C	E	100	4	A	B	E	AB	AE	BE	188
A	D	E	79	5	A	B	C	AB	BC		186
A	C	D	78	6	A	B	D	AB	AD		167
B	C	D	67	7	A	B	D	AB	BD		159
C	D	E	66	8	A	B	E	AB	AE		152
A	B		51	9	A	B	E	AB	BE		139
B	C	E	45	10	A	B	C	AB			88
B	D	E	41	11	A	B	D	AB			73
B			1	12	A	B	E	AB			56
C	D		1	13	A	B	AB				51
				14	C	D	E	CD	CE	DE	42
				...							
				27	A	B	C	AC	BC		16
				...							
				32	A	B	D	AD	BD		12
				33	A	B	E	AE	BE		12

5.7   Conclusions

This paper illustrates the use of non-geometric PB designs for conjoint analysis and it is suggested that these designs are in many senses superior to those more commonly used in conjoint analysis studies. It is foremost the projectivity characteristics of the non-geometric PB designs and the fact that they allow supersaturation that have been argued to be in their favor. The reason is that these properties make the non-geometric PB designs well suited for estimating models that include interactions, even when including many attributes.

Whether or not including interactions actually improves inference has been the subject of much discussion. Using R^2_{adj} as reference, the results in this paper clearly indicate that by including interactions a large increase in explained variance can be achieved. This result should be compared to other studies that have come to the opposite conclusion or at least produced mixed results when including interactions (Green 1984; Hagerty 1986).

The paper also introduces a procedure that makes use of the advantages of the non-geometric PB designs and identifies models that include interactions. It is found that the proposed procedure has a tendency to favor large models, which may be a result of the structure in the data resulting from the use of rating scales, and some craftsmanship is necessary in order to interpret the results correctly. The proposed procedure should therefore primarily be seen as a complement to traditional analysis rather than a substitute. By comparing findings from different analysis procedures, it should be possible to achieve better and more reliable results.

The non-geometric PB design used in this study is fairly simple. Generally, it is not common to use only two levels for the attributes in a conjoint survey. Furthermore, only five attributes were tested compared to the average conjoint analysis application that includes six or seven attributes. The data analyzed in the simulation study was also completely homogeneous, i.e. it only contained one market segment with similar preferences. Future research regarding the use of non-geometric PB in conjoint analysis should be focused on the issues of including more attributes and to explore how interactions should be dealt with effectively when the attributes have more than two levels. The special problems that arise when the respondents represent different market segments are of course also of interest.

There is also more work to be done on the proposed procedure regarding the tendency to favor large models. Both the selection of the initial projection and the subsequent model selection need more work. Convenient means for verification of the selected model are also of interest. Finally, the issues accompanying the use of rating scales need to be analyzed further, especially in view of the extensive use of rating scales in commercial applications of conjoint analysis.

5.8   References

Bisgaard, S. (1992), Industrial Use of Statistically Designed Experiments: Case Study References and Some Historical Anecdotes, *Quality Engineering*, 4, 547-562.

Box, G. E. P. and Behnken, D. W. (1960), Some New Three Level Designs for the Study of Quantitative Variables, *Technometrics*, 2, 455-475.

Box, G. E. P. and Behnken, D. W. (1961), Corrections, *Technometrics*, 3, 576-577.

Box, G. E. P., Hunter, W. G. and Hunter, J. S. (1978), *Statistics for Experimenters - An Introduction to Design, Data Analysis, and Model Building*, New York.

Box, G. E. P. and Draper, N. R. (1987), *Empirical Model-Building and Response Surfaces*, New York.

Box, G. E. P. (1990), George's Column - Do Interactions Matter? *Quality Engineering*, 2, 365-369.

Box, G. E. P. and Meyer, R. D. (1993), Finding the Active Factors in Fractionated Screening Experiments, *Journal of Quality Technology*, 25, 94-105.

Box, G. E. P. and Tyssedal, J. (1996), Projective Properties of Certain Orthogonal Arrays, *Biometrika*, 83, 950-955.

Daniel, C. (1959), Use of Half-Normal Plots in Interpreting Factorial Two-Level Experiments, *Technometrics*, 1, 311-341.

Daniel, C. (1976), *Application of Statistics to Industrial Experimentation*, New York.

Draper, N. R. and Smith, H. (1981), *Applied Regression Analysis*, New York.

Finney, D. J. (1945), The Fractional Replication of Factorial Arrangements, *Annals of Eugenics*, 12, 291-301.

Fisher, R. A. (1935), *The Design of Experiments*, Edinburgh.

Green, P. and Rao, V. (1971), Conjoint Measurement for Quantifying Judgemental Data, *Journal of Marketing Research*, 1, 61-68.

Green, P. (1984), Hybrid Models for Conjoint Analysis: An Expository Review, *Journal of Marketing Research*, 21, 155-169.

Green, P. and Srinivasan, V. (1978), Conjoint Analysis in Consumer Research: Issues and Outlook, *Journal of Consumer Research*, 5, 103-123.

Green, E. P. and Srinivasan, V. (1990), Conjoint Analysis in Marketing: New Developments with Implications for Research and Practice, *Journal of Marketing,* 17, 3-19.

Hagerty, M. R. (1986), The Cost of Simplifying Preference Models, *Marketing Science*, 5, 298-319.

Hamada, M. and Wu, C. F. J. (1992), Analysis of Designed Experiments with Complex Aliasing, *Journal of Quality Technology*, 24, 130-137.

Hynén, A. (1996), Screening for Main and Interaction Effects with Plackett and Burman's 12 Run Design, (Submitted) (A preprint is available as RQT&M Research Report No. 1, Division of Quality Technology and Management, Linköping University, Sweden.).

Johnson, R. (1974), Trade-off Analysis of Consumer Values, *Journal of Marketing Research*, 11, 121-127.

Kackar, R. N. and Tsui, K. L. (1990), Interaction Graphs: Graphical Aids for Planning Experiments, *Journal of Quality Technology*, 22, 1-14.

Luce, D. and Tukey, J. (1964), Simultaneous Conjoint Measurement: A New Type of Fundamental Measurement, *Journal of Mathematical Psychology*, 1, 1-27.

Myers, R. H. and Montgomery, C. M. (1995), *Response Surface Methodology,* New York.

Plackett, R. L. and Burman, J. P. (1946), The Design of Optimum Multifactorial Experiments, *Biometrika*, 33, 305-325.

Sun, D. X. and Wu, C. F. J. (1994), Interaction Graphs for Three-Level Fractional Factorial Designs, *Journal of Quality Technology,* 26, 297-307.

Wittink, R. D. and Cattin, P. (1989), Commercial Use of Conjoint Analysis: An Update, *Journal of Marketing*, 53, 91-96.

Wittink, D. R., Vriens, M. and Burhenne, W. (1994), Commercial Use of Conjoint Analysis in Europe: Results and Critical Reflections, *International Journal of Research in Marketing*, 11, 41-52.

6 On the Influence of the Evaluation Methods in Conjoint Design - Some Empirical Results

Frank Huber, Andreas Herrmann and Anders Gustafsson

6.1 The Problem

It is the goal of conjoint analysis to explain and predict preferences of customers (Schweikl 1985). Variants of predefined manifestations of attributes of various product concepts (both rea! and hypothetical) are created, and these are presented to test persons for evaluation. The contributions (partial benefits) the various attributes make to overall preference (overall benefit) are estimated on the basis of overall preference judgments (Green and Srinivasan 1978).

Market researchers have several options when designing a conjoint analysis for determining overall or partial benefit values. Although this freedom enhances an adequate research design for achieving the goal of the study in question, it should be noted that the sequence of steps taken in a conjoint analysis may influence the estimated results (Green and Srinivasan 1990; Schweikl 1985; Schubert 1991; Vriens 1995).

It is the subject of this paper to give a survey of those factors of a research design that may determine the behavior of respondents when carrying out a conjoint analysis. The estimation algorithm was not taken into consideration although Cattin and Wittink (1977), Cattin and Bliemel (1978), Colberg (1977), Carmone, Green and Jain (1978), Jain et al. (1979), Wittink and Cattin (1981) and Mishra, Umesh and Stem (1989) have proved the dependence of conjoint results on the calculation procedure used. The influence of incentive evaluation (rating vs. ranking vs. hybrid form, i. e. a combination of rating and ranking) on the results of a conjoint analyses will be analyzed in some detail in an empirical study of our own.

6.2 The Influence of Survey Design on the Results of Conjoint Analysis as Reflected in the Relevant Literature

6.2.1 The Schedule of Conjoint Analysis

If a conjoint analysis is used for collecting preferential judgments, several alternatives have to be determined regarding the sequence of the survey method (Hausruckinger and Herker 1992). The steps are shown in Table 1.

Table 1: *The schedule of conjoint analysis and a survey of selected studies to determine the connection between the influence of survey design and the result of conjoint measurement*

Process step	Options	
1. Determining attributes and manifestations of attributes	can be influenced no k.o. criteria compensatory relation independence limitedness feasibility relevance	
Studies		
Number of attributes: Acito (1979) Cattin/Weinberger (1980) Mishra/Umesh/Stern (1989) Weisenfeld (1989)	*Number of manifestation stages*: Currim/Weinberg/Wittink (1981) Wittink/Krishnamurthi/Nutter (1982) Creyer/Ross (1988) Wittink/Krishnamurthi/Reibstein (1989) Wittink/Huber/Zandan/Johnson (1992) Steenkamp/Wittink (1994) Perrey (1996)	*Range of manifestation stages*: Helson (1964) Parducci (1965) Hutchinson (1983) Mellers (1982) Chakravarti/Lynch (1983) Creyer/Ross (1988)
2. Selection of the preference function	Ideal point model Ideal vector model Partial benefit model	
Studies		
Krishnamurthi/Wittink (1991) Green/Srinivasan (1990)		
3. Selection of the data collection method	Profile method Two-factor method Hybrid/adaptive method	
Studies		
Survey method: Oppedijk van Veen/Beazley (1977) Jain/Acito/Malhotra/Mahajan (1979) Segal (1982; 1984) Reibstein/Bateson/Boulding (1988) Müller-Hagedorn/Sewing/Toporowski (1993) Agarwal (1988) Huber/Wittink/Fiedler/Miller (1993; 1991)	*Positional effect*: Acito (1977) Hong/Wyer (1989) Johnson (1982; 1989) Chapman/Bolton (1985) Kumar/Gaeth (1991) Tharp/Marks (1990) Chrzan (1994) Perry (1996)	
4. Selection of the data collection design	Complete design Reduced design	
Studies		
Number of incentives: Carmone/Green/Jain (1978) Cattin/Weinberger (1980) Acito (1979)	Leigh/MacKay/Summers (1981) Weisenfeld (1989) Mishra/Umesh/Stern (1989)	

Process step	Options		
5. Selection of incentive presentation	Verbal description Visual representation		
Studies			
MacKay /Ellis/ Zinnes (1986) Holbrook /Moore (1981) Domzal /Unger (1985)	Smead /Wilcox /Wilkes (1981) Anderson (1987) Louviere /Schroeder /Louviere /Woodworth (1987)	Vriens (1995) Sattler (1994) Weisenfeld (1989)	
6. Selection of the data collection procedure	Person-to-person interview Mail survey Computer interview		
7. Selection of the method for evaluating incentives	Metric rating scales Dollar metrics Constant sum scale	vs. non-metric methods Ranking Paired profiles comparison	

The table also gives a survey of authors who have dealt in their studies in some with the influence of individual elements of the research design on the results of conjoint analysis. There are some obvious focuses. Research efforts were concentrated on determining the connection between the number of attributes or manifestations of attributes, the data collection method, dependence of the findings on survey design as well as the presentation of incentives and estimation of benefit values.

As the analyses of some studies show, the number of attributes and the number of manifestation stages can influence the results of a conjoint analysis. In particular, the effect of „information overload" and decreasing reliability with an increasing number of properties were found (Acito 1979).

To minimize a potential information overload for the respondents, Thomas suggests that no more than 5 attributes should be included in a survey in the field of consumer goods marketing. In addition, he thinks it is not very realistic to use more than 20 incentives (Thomas 1979). Malhotra, however, thinks after analyzing his study that respondents are capable of processing 10 attributes without excessive strain (Malhotra 1982). Green and Srinivasan recommend on the basis of the experience they gained using their profile method that no more than 6 attributes be used simultaneously in a study (Green and Srinivasan 1978).

The authors who examined the influence of the data collection method on the results of conjoint analysis in their empirical studies cannot make any definite statements based on their findings (Segal 1982; Oppedijk van vee and Beazley 1977 and Jain et al.1979). If a connection was found, it is rather weak and/or not significant (Vriens 1995). In view of these findings, experts recommend to apply an adaptive interviewing method or profile method rather than the two-factor method (Gutsche 1995). Investigators say that the increased interest of the respondents due to the interactive conduct of the interview was a positive effect. Furthermore, focusing on attributes that are important to the respective person enables processing of a greater number of attributes and their manifestations (Green and Srinivasan 1990).

Selection of a particular data collection design, however, can influence the results of a conjoint analysis (Kuhlfeld et al. 1994). If a complete design is used, this can be done in smaller studies only involving not too many attributes and manifestations of attributes (Vriens 1995). If a reduced design is used, the number of incentives has to be determined independently based on desired main factorial and interactive effects.

Moreover, an interdependence could be shown between verbal or visual representation and the results of conjoint analysis. Especially with design attributes, i. e. attributes that are not easily described in words, the order of purchasing-relevant attributes was frequently changed depending on the form of presentation (Vriens 1995). Maybe this effect can be explained by the fact that respondents were biased in favor of visual incentives as these are more easily processed than verbal descriptions. What is important, however, is that the respondents are primarily evaluating the styling and design of incentives presented visually while neglecting other objective attributes. Therefore, Aust recommends the use of highly abstract forms of visual representation rather than photo-realistic images (Aust 1996). More studies are to follow to investigate the influence of various forms of presentation in some greater detail.

6.2.2   Effects Depending on the Selection of the Method of Preference Measurement

Selection of the scale used for recording preference is the last planning step of a survey design. As Wittink, Vriens and Burhenne reported, a rating scale comprising a metric scale level and a ranking that produces non-metric data are used in more than 90% of all cases[1]. Although the respondents thus express their preferences in rather different ways, the potential influence of these various approaches on the results of conjoint analysis to date has rarely been in the center of interest. Only five studies deal with this topic. The rather low research activity in this field is surprising because Green and Srinivasan emphasized the influence of the method of measurement on the quality of the result as early as in 1978. They hold the view that data collected by ranking are more reliable than those preference judgments obtained using a metric scale (Green and Srinivasan 1978). This assumption was not tested in a study, however, but just based on the fact that respondents are usually much more capable of stating what they prefer rather than additionally judging the strength of their preferences. The authors did not answer the question whether a conjoint analysis really yields different results depending on using a rating or ranking method.

---

[1]   The rating scale (including its use in adaptive conjoint analysis) was used in Europe in the period from 1986 to 1991 in 70%, and ranking in 22% of all analyses carried out. Cf. Wittink,Vriens and Burhenne 1994; see also Wittink and Cattin 1989.

Leigh, MacKay and Summers, however, have proved empirically that reliability is increased when ranking is used instead of rating. In their study, 52 students had to evaluate 13 incentives by either ranking them or evaluating them on a rating scale of 11. One month later, these 52 students were asked again to express their preferences. The authors found that ranking was more reliable (Leigh, MacKay and Summers 1981). So their study focused on determining test-retest reliability and validity. The two authors, however, do not make a statement regarding the influence of the survey method on the result of conjoint analysis as the same respondents were asked twice using the same method each time. To detect potential influences, it would have been required to have the respondents make their statements using the two methods alternately.

Carmone, Green and Jain also dealt with the effect of the survey method on the results of conjoint measurement. The authors carried out a simulation study in which they compared a rating scale of 6 with ranking (using 18, 27, 54, and 243 incentives to be ranked), and they found little or no differences between the partial benefit values obtained (Carmone, Green and Jain 1978). They could make this statement after comparing the partial benefit values with a simulated design (using the rating as well as the ranking methods). The Kendall's tau correlation coefficient was used to determine the degree of agreement. This value is 0.795 for ranking and 0.782 for the rating method. While this study provides a clear result, it has the disadvantage that it is just a simulation. Compared to a real empirical study, situational influences (such as advertising) or respondents' influences (such as lack of interest and low motivation on the part of respondents) can be excluded. An „optimized" situation is created that leaves it open to what extent such a result has general validity as regards the influence of the respective survey methods on the result of the analysis.

Kalish and Nelson (1991) confronted 255 students with 12 hypothetical products whose preferential evaluation was carried out based on the „reservation price", ranking and the rating method (they used a scale ranging from 0 to 100 points divided into 5-point intervals). The study focused on comparing the rating and ranking methods based on prediction validity. As the results show, a significant difference between rating and ranking cannot be proved but was detected between rating and ranking on the one hand and the „reservation price" method on the other. As the survey design shows, a simulation is used again to predict the respective product ranks or preferences. The authors said they did not want to ask the students twice using different methods because various studies have significantly proved that learning effects occur.

As a result of studies carried out so far we can state that results obtained using the rating method do not significantly deviate from those obtained using ranking. The test designs chosen by the various authors do not allow a clear statement as to whether the two measuring approaches yield different conjoint results or not. The deficits shown here require an empirical study that analyzes a potential connection between the rating, ranking, and hybrid methods (consisting of rating and ranking) and the results of a conjoint analysis.

6.3   An Empirical Study of the Influence of Various Interviewing Designs

6.3.1   Propose of the Study

To determine a potential influence of the survey method on the results of a conjoint analysis, the following three methods shall be compared:

- the rating method,
- ranking, and
- a hybrid form (consisting of rating and ranking)

When using the rating method, respondents are asked to express preference, that is, liking or desire to purchase on a scale that allows to judge the intensity of the preference (Gutsche 1995). We used a rating scale of 10 in our study. Ranking, i. e. determining the preferential order of all incentives, just indicates the preference-worthiness of the incentives and does not allow a statement of their intensity (Green and Srinivasan 1990; Schweikl 1985). The hybrid method has the respondent compare because (s)he has to evaluate the product profiles generated in relation to a reference object. The respondents can express their opinion on a scale ranging from -10 „I like the TV set shown on this card ... much less than the reference TV set" to +10 „I like the TV set shown on the card ... much better than the reference TV set."

6.3.2   Experimental Design

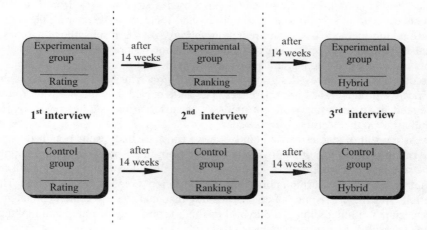

Figure 1:   The experimental design of the empirical study

The design used in this study can be characterized as follows (Figure 1).

1. Two groups shall be formed, i. e. an experimental group and a control group, to determine any potential influence of the survey method.
2. All participants should state their preferences three times (at an interval of at least 14 weeks) on the same object of study, each time using a different method of measurement.
3. The respondents shall be grouped in the two groups by random selection.
4. Each group should consist of at least 50 respondents to ensure an adequate informative value of the results.

Unlike the studies carried out so far that dealt with using different survey methods, this approach allows to draw conclusions about potential influences of the survey design on the results of conjoint analysis, as the same respondents express their changing preferences several times using different measuring techniques. In addition, the interviews were carried out 14 weeks apart. This should rule out any learning effects among the respondents.

6.3.3   The Course of the Study

Pilot Study
The object of study was a TV set. This consumer good was selected based on the assumption that all respondents have had experience with this product, and that it is a specialty good where low cost is not necessarily a major factor. It is assumed with such specialty goods that those consumers have a very precise idea of the product who strive for maximum product benefit. Brochures and interviews of experts proved valuable for determining the attributes that contribute to the purchasing decision. We identified a total of 31 attributes.

- **Price**

The price is DM 1200

The price is DM 1500

The price is DM 1800

- **Warranty**

Warranty is granted for a period of **6 months**

Warranty is granted for a period of **12 months**

Warranty is granted for a period of **18 months**

• User friendliness

User-friendliness of the TV set is **high**, i. e.

> channels are tuned and sorted automatically, even at first startup; it has a remote control unit and a convenient screen menu system that guides and instructs the user

User-friendliness of the TV set is **average**, i. e.

> it has a remote control unit and a convenient screen menu system that guides and instructs the user

User-friendliness of the TV set is **low**, i. e.

> it just has a remote control unit

• CRT design

CRT design is **advanced**, i. e.

> the TV set has 16:9 format, 100 Hz technology to prevent flickering and line jitter, a PAL comb filter for improved definition and an advanced type of CRT as compared to conventional tube technology

CRT design is **conventional**, i. e.

> the TV set has the conventional 4:3 format and a black matrix CRT as used in most conventional TV sets

• Videotex

Videotex is available

Videotex is not available

To determine the purchase-relevant attributes from the point of view of the consumers, we asked 49 respondents that were selected at random to indicate the importance of all 31 attributes for a purchasing decision on a scale ranging from 1 to 9. Then we generated 12 independent factors using factor analysis. These had to be evaluated again by the respondents. As the results of the evaluation process show, the following product attributes influence the purchasing decision most: price, warranty, videotex, user friendliness and CRT design.

The research design of the main investigation was based on the five most important attributes for each of which 2 or 3 manifestations were defined to prevent respondents from having to deal with too much information (Green and Srinivasan 1978).

Main Study

The reduced profile method was used to keep interview time endurable for the respondents (Vriens 1995; Green and Srinivasan 1990). Two holdout cards were used to determine internal validity. The respondents had to evaluate a total of 18 incentives (including the 2 holdout cards). The data was collected in the period from January to November, 1998. 154 took part in the study and were assigned at random to either the experimental or the control group. Answers provided by 10 respondents were not included in the analysis because they could not take part in all three interviews. While only three respondents had to be excluded from the control group, the remaining 7 respondents to be excluded were members of the experimental group which thus included 70 respondents.

The two groups were to grade all 18 product cards on a monopolar scale inter-preted as metric and ranging from 1 („I like it very much") to 10 („I don't like it at all"). After 14 weeks, preferences were given by means of ranking. This time the respondents were to pile all product cards in such a way that the topmost card indicates the TV set that is most preferred while the card at the bottom of the pile shows the least preferred TV set. Preference was to decrease continually from the top to the bottom. After another 14 weeks, the respondents were asked once again to give their product preferences on a scale. This time we used a hybrid form consisting of a rating and a ranking task. Scaling was to be done in relation to a reference product. We therefore used a bipolar scale ranging from -10 („I like the TV set on the card ... much less than the reference TV set") to +10 („I like the TV set on the card ... much better than the reference TV set"), and the reference TV set represented the zero point of the scale. We selected a model of which experts thought it represented attributes in average manifestation. Moreover, this TV set differed in at least two manifestations from the 18 alternative products to be evaluated.

When checking correlation coefficients we found that the preference data from 15 respondents showed a correlation <0.5. The data from these people were there-fore not included in the study (Table 3). The correlation values of the holdout cards showed high correlations (Kendall's tau 0.9) for all survey methods in both groups.

Table 2:   *Composition of the respondents in the experimental and control groups after data analysis*

		Experimental group (group 1)	Control group (group 2)
Sex	male	31	37
	female	30	31
	(total)	(61)	(68)
Age	16-25	5	7
	26-40	23	26
	41-55	27	22
	> 55	6	13

While the number of respondents decreased by 9 to 61 people in the experimental group, the control group was reduced to 68 respondents.

6.3.4   Analysis of the Conjoint Results

Effects of Survey Design on Attribute Importance and Partial Benefit Values

As reflected in Table 3, there are some great differences in attribute importance depending on the survey method. Most striking here are the importances in the hybrid form which differ markedly from the two other methods. The rating and the ranking methods provide very similar results that deviate in the comparatively small range of 2.06% (see Table 4). The hybrid survey shows a significant difference for the videotex attribute: its difference from ranking is 5.96%, from rating even 7.21%.

Table 3:   *Attribute importances for the experimental group and their order as a function of the data collection method*

	Price im-port.	rank	Warranty im-port.	rank	User-friendly im-port.	rank	CRT design im-port.	rank	Videotex im-port.	rank
Rating	19.66	2	19.3	3	27.58	1	15.73	5	17.73	4
Ranking	19.64	2	17.24	4	27.41	1	16.7	5	18.98	3
Hybrid	17.04	4	18.33	3	25.01	1	14.68	5	24.94	2

While user-friendliness is the decisive attribute for purchasing a TV set using the rating, ranking, and hybrid methods (27.58%, 27.41%, and 25.01%, respectively; rank 1) and CRT design (15.73%, 16.7%, and 14.68%, respectively; rank 5) is the least important attribute, there is a difference in the order of the remaining attributes. According to both the rating and the ranking methods, the price comes second in importance after user-friendliness (19.66% and 19.64%). Both methods show it at rank 2. Furthermore, the warranty attribute holds rank 3 (19.3%), and videotex holds rank 4 (17.73%) using the rating method. This order is reversed according to the ranking method: videotex (18.98%) takes rank 3, and warranty (17.24%) takes rank 4. The results of the hybrid form are different, however. After rank 1 for user friendliness (25,01%), videotex had an importance 24.94% and rank 2, followed by warranty and price 18.33% and 17.04%, respectively) on ranks 3 and 4.

An influence of the survey method on the results of a conjoint analysis can also be stated for the control group. However, Table 4 indicates that the control group shows greater differences in importance percentages of the attributes. The greatest differences as compared to the experimental group can be found with the attributes price and user friendliness. Thus the price attribute deviates 7.34% between rating and ranking, and 5.66% between rating and hybrid. The differences in user friendliness percentage when comparing rating and hybrid are even 7.69%.

These great deviations result in greater differences in the order of attribute importances as compared to the experimental group across all surveying methods. For example, user friendliness is the most important attribute (28.88%) according to the rating method while CRT design is least important for forming preferences (16.65%). The medium ranks are taken by videotex, price, and warranty and show only minor variation (18.75%, 17.87%, and 17.85%).

Table 4:   *Attribute importances for the control group and their order as a function of the data collection method*

	Price import.	rank	Warranty import.	rank	User-friendly import.	rank	CRT design import.	rank	Videotex import.	rank
Rating	17.87	3	17.85	4	28.88	1	16.65	5	18.75	2
Ranking	25.21	2	13.26	5	26.86	1	14.21	4	20.46	3
Hybrid	23.53	1	16.65	5	21.19	2	17.09	4	21.14	2

According to the ranking method, user friendliness also has special importance for taking the purchasing decision (26.86%). The two approaches differ, however, in the remaining attributes. For example, the price was identified here as second in importance for forming preferences (25.21%). Videotex receives much more attention (20.46%) here than CRT design (14.21%) and the warranty period (13.26%) of a TV set.

According to the hybrid method, the price was most important (23.53%). Videotex (21.14%) and user friendliness - the most important attribute with rating and ranking - were of medium importance only. The warranty period of a TV set (16.65%) has the least influence on forming preferences according to the hybrid method.

Marked differences were found in viewing the percentages of attribute importance and the resulting order of attributes for all three surveying methods within both groups. The control group shows greater deviation between data collection methods than the experimental group, which can only be explained by the composition of the groups.

To be able to make further statements about the influence of the method of measurement on the estimates obtained using a conjoint analysis, various sample tests were applied to check the null hypothesis according to which the partial benefit values of the interview rounds should not differ. As the interview dates for rating and ranking as well as for ranking and the hybrid method were 14 weeks apart, it is assumed that the evaluating tasks using the various methods were carried out with little or no interference. This implies that the results derived from them are also practically free of interferences and therefore independent.

Check Using a T-test

The T-test checks whether there are significant differences in the mean values of two groups or not. As it is assumed that the various surveying methods are independent of each other, the T-test can be applied to test mean value comparisons with regard to these three methods. While the respective surveying methods were defined as group variables for the mean value comparison, the manifestations of attributes are the test variables. It thus becomes possible to examine each attribute manifestation for each surveying method for statistically significant differences in mean values. The so-called null hypothesis is tested here according to which there is no difference between the mean values of a pair of surveying methods. Table 5 shows the results for the experimental group of applying the T-test for comparing the rating and ranking, rating and hybrid, and ranking and hybrid methods.

Table 5:   *T-test results of the experimental group*

		Comparison of rating and ranking		Comparison of rating and hybrid		Comparison of ranking and hybrid	
		t-value	signifi-cance	t-value	signifi-cance	t-value	signifi-cance
Price	DM 1200	- 1.714	0.089	- 1.567	0.120	0.225	0.822
	DM 1500	0.048	0.962	- 1.370	0.173	- 1.451	0.149
	DM 1800	1.360	0.176	4.562	*0.000*	3.474	*0.001*
Warranty	6 months	3.340	*0.001*	2.408	*0.018*	- 1.277	0.205
	12 months	0.350	0.727	1.031	0.305	0.699	0.486
	18 months	- 0.169	0.866	- 0.461	0.646	- 0.222	0.824
User friendli-ness	high	- 0.409	0.684	0.127	0.899	0.520	0.604
	average	2.030	*0.045*	1.245	0.215	- 1.028	0.306
	low	- 1.681	0.096	- 0.801	0.425	1.026	0.307
CRT design	advanced	1.156	0.250	0.420	0.675	- 0.702	0.484
	conventnl	- 3.195	*0.002*	- 0.368	0.713	2.980	*0.004*
Videotext	equipped	- 0.703	0.483	- 2.298	*0.024*	- 1.608	0.109
	unequipped	0.560	0.576	- 0.166	0.868	- 0.771	0.442

With the selected level of significance of 5% (10%), there was a total of 8 (11) significance values (of 39, i. e. approx. 20% or 28%) for all three method comparisons that were below this level, and for which the null hypothesis had to be rejected. A detailed analysis of these values for the respective method comparisons does not provide a uniform picture, however. For example, significant differences in the rating-ranking comparison could only be detected for the manifestations „6 months warranty period", „average user-friendliness", and „conventional CRT design." The rating-hybrid comparison however shows significant differences for the manifestations months warranty period", „price DM 1800," and „videotex equipped." In the ranking-hybrid comparison, significant differences are detected for two mean value comparisons („price DM 1800" and „conventional CRT design").

If we look at the 39 partial benefit values of the control group in Table 6, it becomes apparent that a total of 8 (14) significance values was detected for all three method comparisons at the selected level of significance of 5% (10%) (of 39, i. e. approx. 20% or 36%) that fell below this level. It can further be stated that the mean value comparison of the ranking and hybrid methods shows a significant difference for the attribute „18 months warranty period" only. The rating-ranking comparison, however, results in two significant differences for the attributes „price DM 1200" and „18 months warranty period." Other significant differences in the mean values of the manifestations of attributes could not be detected.

Table 6:   *T-test results of the control group*

		Comparison of rating and ranking		Comparison of rating and hybrid		Comparison of ranking and hybrid	
		t-value	signifi- cance	t-value	signifi- cance	t-value	signifi- cance
	DM 1200	- 2.669	*0.009*	- 3.272	*0.001*	- 0.257	0.797
Price	DM 1500	- 1.669	0.098	- 1.910	0.058	- 0.177	0.86
	DM 1800	- 0.35	0.727	1.831	0.069	1.68	0.096
	6 months	- 0.425	0.672	- 1.464	0.146	- 1.11	0.269
Warranty	12 months	1.411	0.161	2.202	*0.029*	0.796	0.428
	18 months	2.283	*0.024*	0.268	0.789	- 2.154	*0.033*
User	high	0.871	0.385	3.431	*0.001*	1.958	0.053
friendli-	average	1.136	0.258	1.926	0.056	0.667	0.506
ness	low	- 1.08	0.282	- 2.168	*0.032*	- 1.24	0.217
CRT	advanced	1.317	0.19	0.115	0.908	- 1.096	0.275
design	conventnl	- 0.459	0.647	- 1.003	0.318	- 0.626	0.532
Videotext	equipped	- 0.410	0.682	- 0.45	0.654	- 0.24	0.981
	unequipped	- 1.185	0.239	- 2.087	*0.04*	- 1.027	0.306

The T-test result of the rating-hybrid comparison is particularly interesting. This comparison yielded a total of 5 (8) manifestations of attributes that showed significant differences. This outcome gives rise to the assumption that there may be a dependence of conjoint results from the surveying methods used (rating or hybrid).

Even if we look at the results from the experimental group we cannot derive a definite proof that the application of the rating or the hybrid method to conjoint analyses will invariably yield different results. It seems reasonable to assume that this result of the rating-hybrid comparison occurs due to the group only. It was found when looking at the average relative importance values that the control group showed greater differences in all importance percentages than the experimental group.

The question comes up in this context why this group-related influence is restricted to the rating-hybrid comparison and has a clearly weaker effect on the other two method comparisons. The answer could be found in the experimental sequence of the study. The rating method was the first, the hybrid the last survey carried out. As has been assumed, it cannot be excluded that the participants in the study have learned in the meantime and have memorized various manifestations of attributes and their composition. Still, the rating-hybrid comparison will be watched especially closely below.

The results of the rating-ranking and ranking-hybrid comparisons do not allow any conclusions to be drawn for the results of the experimental and control groups to the extent that these results of a conjoint analysis could be influenced by the selection of a specific surveying method (ranking rather than rating or hybrid method). Only a small number of attribute manifestations show significant differences in their mean values when using the T-test on both groups. These do not let it seem reasonable to assume an influence of the surveying methods on the result. Thus, a general influence of surveying methods on the results of conjoint analyses could not be detected.

Check Using the Mann-Whitney Test

The Mann-Whitney test is from the group of non-parametric tests. Most non-parametric tests are characterized in that it is sufficient if the variables to be tested comprise ordinal scale levels; an interval scale level is not required. Like the T-test, the Mann-Whitney-Test checks whether there are differences between attributes between a pair of surveying methods. While the T-test checks the mean values of attribute manifestations, the Mann-Whitney-Test compares the average ranks of attribute manifestations while comparing the methods. A rank is assigned to average normalized partial benefit values which orients towards the position of values in joint ascending order for the respective comparative methods. If we assume that using different surveying methods will not produce different results, these values should be about equal in their order, which would result in approximately equal ranks of attribute manifestations. So the Mann-Whitney test checks the null hypothesis, that the distribution of partial benefit values is similar when comparing surveying methods, and that the average ranks are nearly of equal size. Table 8 shows the results determined in the experimental group for all method comparisons.

The result is analyzed using the Z-value and the significance. Like with the t-value, the null hypothesis H_0 is tested using the Z-value. This value will only be 0 when the rank distributions of the average normalized partial benefit values are exactly equal. When the Z-value becomes greater than $|1,95|$, significance assumes a level ($\geq 0,05$) at which the assumption of equal rank distributions for the two methods compared is rejected. In our study, 5 (14) out of 39 Z-values exceeded the selected level of 5% (10%).

Only two significance values that are this low were found for the rating-ranking comparison. The attributes „average user friendliness" and „conventional CRT design" show significant rank distribution differences (0.013 and 0.004, respectively). No significant differences were detected for the other attributes. The rating-hybrid comparison has even only one attribute manifestation („Price DM 1,800") that is significantly different. Two significant differences in attributes were detected for the ranking-hybrid comparison. The manifestations „Price DM 1,800" and „conventional CRT design" have significance values of 0.006 and 0.028.

When we look at all three comparisons of methods, we have to conclude after applying the Mann-Whitney test that the respective surveying method does not have an influence on the result of the analysis. Only few manifestations of attributes showed significant differences. There are no hints at a more general influence that surveying methods could exert on the results of conjoint analyses as the number of significantly differing manifestations of attributes was low.

Table 7:   *Mann-Whitney test results for the experimental group*

		Comparison of rating and ranking		Comparison of rating and hybrid		Comparison of ranking and hybrid	
		Z-value	signifi-cance	Z-value	signifi-cance	Z-value	signifi-cance
Price	DM 1200	- 1.627	0.104	- 1.702	0.089	- 0.097	0.923
	DM 1500	- 0.182	0.855	- 1.740	0.082	- 1.801	0.072
	DM 1800	- 1.01	0.313	- 3.829	*0.000*	- 2.743	*0.006*
Warranty	6 months	- 1.913	0.056	- 1.467	0.142	- 0.610	0.542
	12 months	- 0.072	0.943	- 0.956	0.339	- 0.844	0.399
	18 months	- 0.117	0.907	- 0.561	0.575	- 0.921	0.357
User friendli-ness	high	- 0.029	0.977	- 0.021	0.983	- 0.094	0.925
	average	- 2.489	*0.013*	- 0.803	0.422	- 1.782	0.075
	low	- 1.927	0.054	- 0.829	0.407	- 1.122	0.262
CRT design	advanced	- 1.907	0.057	- 0.859	0.39	- 1.11	0.267
	conventnl	- 2.862	*0.004*	- 0.792	0.428	- 2.193	*0.028*
Videotext	equipped	- 0.622	0.534	- 1.775	0.076	- 0.971	0.332
	unequipped	- 1.442	0.149	- 0.447	0.655	- 0.932	0.351

Approximately in agreement with the results of the rating-hybrid comparison using the T-test, the Mann-Whitney test proves a significant influence of the surveying method for the user friendliness attribute. But the Mann-Whitney test cannot provide more indications for assuming that the significant influences of the control group are group-specific. So the significantly different manifestation of attributes of the rating-ranking and the ranking-hybrid comparisons do hardly correspond to the five significant values of the rating-hybrid comparison.

Taking into account the results of the experimental group, however, we can state that the use of the rating rather than the hybrid method will yield different results. As could be proved unambiguously, the other comparisons of methods, i. e. rating-ranking and ranking-hybrid, in both the experimental and the control group do not suggest that there are influences on the results of conjoint analyses due to the selection of the surveying method. To summarize, it may therefore be assumed that the selection of the surveying method has little or no influence on the results of conjoint analyses.

Like in the T-test, the results of the control group presented in Table 8 are rather disparate. While the rating-ranking and ranking-hybrid comparisons together comprise just four significantly differing manifestations of attributes („price DM 1,200," „18 months warranty period," and „advanced CRT design" for the rating-ranking comparison as well as „18 months warranty period" for the ranking-hybrid comparison), the comparison of rating and hybrid methods comprises five significance values that are smaller or equal 0.05.

Table 8:   *Mann-Whitney test results for the control group*

		Comparison of rating and ranking		Comparison of rating and hybrid		Comparison of ranking and hybrid	
		Z-value	signifi-cance	Z-value	signifi-cance	Z-value	signifi-cance
Price	DM 1200	- 2.279	*0.023*	- 3.207	*0.001*	- 0.591	0.555
	DM 1500	- 1.447	0.148	- 1.73	0.084	- 0.174	0.862
	DM 1800	- 0.293	0.77	- 1.9	0.057	- 1.499	0.134
Warranty	6 months	- 1.334	0.182	- 1.558	0.119	- 0.419	0.675
	12 months	- 1.396	0.163	- 2.074	*0.038*	- 0.891	0.373
	18 months	- 2.505	*0.012*	- 0.015	0.988	- 2.648	*0.008*
User friendli-ness	high	- 1.307	0.191	- 3.437	*0.001*	- 1.445	0.149
	average	- 1.401	0.161	- 1.957	*0.05*	- 0.488	0.626
	low	- 1.893	0.058	- 2.568	*0.01*	- 0.788	0.430
CRT design	advanced	- 2.146	*0.032*	- 0.775	0.438	- 1.458	0.145
	conventnl	- 0.071	0.943	- 0.404	0.686	- 0.325	0.745
Videotext	equipped	- 0.198	0.843	- 0.013	0.989	- 0.029	0.977
	unequipped	-0.12	0.904	- 1.466	0.143	- 1.281	0.2

6.4   Summary and Outlook

The first part of this paper discussed factors that may influence the results of conjoint analyses. These variables were discussed based on findings reported in several references. These did not only present the influencing factors and their effect on results, but suggested potential solutions for preventing or reducing such influences. The empirical study we carried out subsequently focused on a potential connection between the selection of a surveying method and the result of a conjoint analysis. Results from using three surveying methods were compared. Concludingly, we could state that there hardly are any significant influences on results depending on the selection of a specific surveying method. Based on these findings, we can even say it is unimportant which of these three methods is used for a conjoint analysis.

Still, some aspects were discovered in the course of our study which could not be presented in greater detail here but could be interesting for future research activities:

1.   154 people were included in the study that were consciously selected for reasons of time, money, and organization. Although these people were assigned to the two groups at random we found that there were some marked differences in group results. This gives rise to the question whether the composition of the groups, i. e. their age structure, may have influenced our results.

2.   The research design was based on three rounds of evaluating 18 product cards at intervals of at least 14 weeks. The results suggest that, despite the long time in between, respondents apparently changed their evaluation of product attributes, which may be due to a change in their knowledge about the object of

study (in particular its technological parameters) caused by the respective interviews.
3. It would also be interesting to study the influence that may result from applying the problem of this study to other objects of study.

6.5   References

Acito, F. (1977), An Investigation of some Data Collection Issues in Conjoint Measurement, in: Greenberg, Barnett. A. and Bellenger, D. N., eds., *Contemporary marketing thought* (Educators Conference Proceedings), Chicago, 82-85.

Acito, F. (1979), An Investigation of the Reliability of Conjoint Measurement for Various Orthogonal Designs, in: Franz, R. S., Hopkins, R. M. and Toma, A., eds., Southern Marketing Association Conference Proceedings, University of Southwestern Louisiana, 175-178.

Agarwal, M. (1988), Comparison of conjoint methods, Proceedings of the *Sawtooth Software Conference on perceptual Mapping, Conjoint Analysis and Computer Interviewing*, Sun Valley, 51-57.

Anderson, J. C. (1987), The Effect of Type of Presentation on Judgments of New Product Acceptance, *Industrial Marketing and Purchasing*, 2, 29-46.

Aust, E. (1996), *Simultane Conjointanalyse, Benefitsegmentierung, Produktlinien- und Preisgestaltung*, Frankfurt am Main.

Anderson, J. C. (1987), The Effect of Type of Presentation on Judgments of New Product Acceptance, in: *Industrial Marketing and Purchasing*, 2, 29-46.

Carmone, F. J., Green, P. E. and Jain, A. K. (1978), Robustness of Conjoint Analysis: Some Monté Carlo Results, *Journal of Marketing Research*, 15, 300-303.

Cattin, P. and Bliemel, F. (1978), Metric vs. Nonmetric Procedures for Multiattribute Modeling: Some Simulation Results, *Decision Sciences*, 9, 472-480.

Cattin, P. and Weinberger, M. (1980), Some Validity and Reliability Issues in the Measurement of Attribute Utilities, in: Olsen, J. C., ed., *Advances in Consumer Research*, Ann Arbor, 7, 780-783.

Cattin, P. and Wittink, D. R. (1982), Commercial Use of Conjoint Analysis: A Survey, *Journal of Marketing*, 46, 44-53.

Chapman, R. G. and Bolton R. N. (1985), Attribute Presentation Order Bias and Nonstationarity in Full Profile Conjoint Analysis Tasks, in: Lusch, R. F. et al., ed., AMA Educators Conference Proceedings, Chicago, 373-379.

Chrzan, K. (1994), Three Kinds of Order Effects in Choice-Based Conjoint Analysis, *Marketing Letters*, 5, 165-172.

Colberg, T. (1977), *Validation of Conjoint Measurement Methods: a simulation and empirical Investigation,* dissertation, University of Washington.

Creyer, E. H. and Ross, W. T. (1988), The Effects of Range-Frequency Manipulations on Conjoint Importance Weight Stability, in: Houston, M. J., ed., Advances in Consumer Research, Provo, 15, 505-509.

Currim, I. S., Weinberg, C. B. and Wittink, D. R. (1981), Design of Subscription Programs for a Performing Arts Series, *Journal of Consumer Research*, 8, 67-75.

Domzal, T. J. and Unger, L. S. (1985), Judgments of Verbal versus Pictorial Presentations of a Product with Functional and Aesthetic Features, Hirschman, E. C. and Holbrook, M. B., eds., Advances in Consumer Research, Provo, 12, 268-272.

Green, P. E. and Srinivasan, V. (1990), Conjoint Analysis in Marketing: New Developments With Implications for Research and Practice, *Journal of Marketing*, 54, 3-19.

Green, P. E. and Srinivasan, V. (1978), Conjoint Analysis in Consumer Research: Issues and Outlook, *Journal of Consumer Research*, 5, 103-123.

Gutsche, J. (1995), *Produktpräferenzanalyse: Ein modelltheoretisches und methodisches Konzept zur Marktsimulation mittels Präferenzerfassungsmodellen*, Berlin.

Hausruckinger, G. and Herker, A. (1992), Die Konstruktion von Schätzdesigns für Conjoint-Analysen auf der Basis von Paarvergleichen, *Marketing ZFP*, 14, 99-110.

Helson, H. (1964), *Adaptation-level Theory: An experimental and systematic approach to behavior*, New York.

Holbrook, M. B. and Moore, W. L. (1981), Feature Interactions in Consumer Judgments of Verbal Versus Pictorial Presentations, *Journal of Consumer Research,* 8, 103-113.

Hong, S. and Wyer, R. S., Jr. (1989), Effects of Country-of-Origin and Product-Attribute Information on Product Evaluation: An Information Processing Perspective, *Journal of Consumer Research*, 16, 175-185.

Huber, J. C., Wittink, D. R., Fiedler, J. A. and Miller, R. L. (1991), An Empirical Comparison of ACA and Full Profile Judgements, *Sawtooth Software Conference Proceedings*, Ketchum, 1991, 189-202.

Huber, J. C., Wittink, D. R., Fiedler, J. A. and Miller, R. L. (1993), The Effectiveness of Alternative Preference Elicitation Procedures in Predicting Choice, *Journal of Marketing Research*, 30, 105-114.

Hutchinson, J. W. (1983), On the Locus of Range Effects in Judgment and Choice, Bagozzi, Richard and Tybout, A., eds., *Advances in Consumer Research*, Ann Arbor, 10, 305-308.

Jain, A. R., Acito, F., Malhorta, N. and Mahajan, V. (1979), A comparison of internal validity of alternative parameter estimation methods in decompositional multiattribute preference models, *Journal of Marketing Research*, 16, 313-322.

Johnson, R. M. (1982), Problems in Applying Conjoint Analysis, in: Srivastava, R. K. and Shocker, A. D., eds., Analytical Approaches to Product and Marketing Planning: The Second Conference, Cambridge, 154-164.

Johnson, R. M. (1989), Assessing the Validity of Conjoint Analysis, *Sawtooth Software Conference Proceedings*, Ketchum, 273-280.

Kalish, S. and Nelson, P. (1991) A Comparison of Ranking, Rating and Reservation Price Measurement in Conjoint Analysis, *Marketing Letters*, 2, 327-335.

Krishnamurthi, L. and Wittink, D. R. (1991), The Value of Idiosyncratic Functional Forms in Conjoint Analysis, *International Journal of Research in Marketing*, 8, 301-313.

Kumar, V. and Gaeth, G. J. (1991), Attribute order and product familiarity effects in decision tasks using conjoint analysis, *International Journal of Research in Marketing*, 8, 113-124.

Louviere, J- J., Schroeder, H., Louviere, C. H. and Woodworth, G. G. (1987), Do the Parameters of Choice Models Depend on Differences in Stimulus Presentation: Visual versus Verbal Presentation?, Wallendorf, M.and Anderson, P. F., eds., *Advances in Consumer Research,* Provo, 14, 79-82.

Leigh, T. W., MacKay, D. B. and Summers, J. O. (1981), An Alternative Experimental Methods for Conjoint Analysis, in: Monroe, K. B., ed., *Advances in Consumer Research*, Ann Arbor, 8, 317-322.

MacKay, D. B., Ellis, M. and Zinnes, J. L. (1986), Graphic and Verbal Presentation of Stimuli: A Probabilistic MDS Analysis, in: Lutz, R. J., ed., *Advances in Consumer Research,* Provo, 13, 529-533.

Malhotra, N. K. (1982), Structural Reliability and Stability of Nonmetric Conjoint Analysis, *Journal of Marketing Research*, 19, 199-207.

Mellers, B. A. (1982), Equity Judgment: A Revision of Aristotelian Views, *Journal of Experimental Psychology*, 111, 242-270.

Mishra, S., Umesh, U. N. and Stem, D. E. (1989), Attribute importance weights in conjoint analysis: Bias and Precision, *Advances in Consumer Research*, 16, 605-611.

Müller-Hagedorn, L., Sewing, E. and Toporowski, W. (1993), Zur Vali-dität von Conjoint-Analysen, *Zeitschrift für betriebswirtschaftliche Forschung*, 45, 123-148.

Oppedijk van veen, W. M. and Beazley, D. (1977), An Investigation of alternative Methods of applying the trade-off Model, *Journal of Market Research Society*, 19, 2-9.

Parducci, A. (1965), Category Judgment: A Range-Frequency Model, *Psychological Review*, 72, 407-418.

Perrey, J. (1996), Erhebungsdesign-Effekte bei der conjoint analysis, *Marketing ZFP*, 18, 105-116.

Reibstein, D., Bateson, J. E. G. and Boulding, W. (1988), Conjoint Analysis Reliability: Empirical Findings, *Marketing Science*, 7, 271-286.

Sattler, H. (1994), Die Validität von Produkttests - Ein empirischer Vergleich zwischen hypothetischer und realer Produktpräsentation, *Marketing ZFP*, 16, 31-41.

Schubert, B. (1991), *Entwicklung von Konzepten für Produktinnovationen mittels Conjoint Analysis*, Stuttgart.

Schweikl, H. (1985), *Computergestützte Präferenzanalyse mit individuell wichtigen Produktmerkmalen,* Berlin.

Segal, M. N. (1982), Reliability of Conjoint Analysis: contrasting Data Collection Procedures, *Journal of Marketing Research*, 13, 211-224.

Segal, M. N. (1984), Alternate Form Conjoint Reliability: An Empirical Assessment, *Journal of Advertising*, 13, 31-38.

Smead, R. J., Wilcox, J. B. and Wilkes, R. E. (1981), How Valid are Product Descriptions and Protocols in Choice Experiments, *Journal of Consumer Research*, 8, 37-42.

Steenkamp J. B. E. M. and Wittink D. R. (1994), The Metric Quality of Full-Profile Judgments and the Number-of-Attribute-Levels Effect in Conjoint Analysis, *International Journal of Research in Marketing*, 11, 275-286.

Tharp, M. and Marks, L. (1990), An Examination of the Effects of Attribute Order and Product Order Biases in Conjoint Analysis, in: Goldberg, M. E., Gorn, E., Pollay, R. W., eds., *Advances in Consumer Research*, Provo, 17, 563-570.

Thomas, L. (1979), Conjoint Measurement als Instrument der Absatzforschung, *Marketing ZFP*, 1. 199-211.

Vriens, M. (1995), *Conjoint analysis in Marketing*, ph.D thesis, Capelle.

Vriens, M., Oppewal, H. & Wedel, M. (1998), Ratings-based versus choice-based latent class conjoint models - an empirical comparison. *Journal of the Market Research Society*, 40, 237-248.

Weisenfeld, U. (1989), Die Einflüsse von Verfahrensvariationen und der Art des Kaufentscheidungsprozesses auf die Reliabilität der Ergebnisse bei der Conjoint Analysis, Berlin.

Wittink, D. R., Huber, J., Zandan, P. and Johnson, R. M. (1992), The Number of Levels Effect in Conjoint: Where does it come from, and can it be eliminated?, *Sawtooth Software Conference Proceedings*, Ketchum, 355-364.

Wittink, D. R., Krishnamurthi, L. and Nutter, J. B. (1982), Comparing Derived Importance Weights Across Attributes, *Journal of Consumer Research*, 8, 471-474.

Wittink, D. R., Krishnamurthi, L. and Reibstein, D. J. (1989), The Effect of Differences in the Number of Attribute Levels on Conjoint Results, *Marketing Letters*, 1, 113-123.

Wittink, D. R. and Cattin, P. (1981), Alternative Estimation Methods for Conjoint Analysis: A Monté Carlo Study, *Journal of Marketing Research*, 18, 101-106.

Wittink, D. R. and Cattin, P. (1989), Commercial Use of Conjoint Analysis: An Update, *Journal of Marketing*, 53, 91-96.

Wittink, D. R., Vriens, M. and Burhenne, W. (1994), Commercial Use of Conjoint Analysis in Europe: Results and Critical Reflections, *International Journal of Research in Marketing*, 11, 41-52.

7 Evolutionary Conjoint

Thorsten Teichert and Edlira Shehu

7.1 Introduction

Preference analysis and utility measurement remain central topics in consumer research. Although the concept of utility and its measurement was investigated in a large number of studies, it still remains ambiguous due to its unobservability and lack of an absolute scale unit (Teichert 2001a: 26): Whereas utility is praised as a quantitative indicator of consumer behavior, only preference judgments can be observed. These judgments contain error terms stemming from different sources which cannot be separated. This inherent methodological problem of utility measurement has not been handled consistently over years of empirical application.

A large number of compositional and decompositional methodological approaches have been developed and applied over years. Conjoint analysis (CA) is the most prominent method for utility measurement (Green & Srinivasan 1978). It enjoys large popularity among marketing researchers, as it combines easy-to-handle data collection with sophisticated evaluation methods (Hartmann and Sattler 2006). Dating back to the 70th, conjoint analysis is based on the theoretical frame of axiomatic conjoint measurement (Green and Rao 1971). Despite major advances in modeling and designing, an increasing number of studies show that there are some inherent limitations concerning the accuracy of part-worth estimates. While part of the shortcomings is attributable to respondent behavior, the major reason for these shortcomings lies in unfulfilled model axioms of the conjoint analysis (Louviere 2006, Louviere et al. 2002).

We propose evolutionary conjoint as a new model-free method based on interactive evolutionary algorithms. Evolutionary algorithms transfer principles of Darwin's evolution theory (1859) to optimization problems of other disciplines. Algorithms are based on the principle of "survival of the fittest" and provide robust solutions for large dimensioned optimization problems. By combining evolutionary algorithms with conjoint analysis we overcome some limitations of traditional conjoint analysis.

This contribution is structured as follows: We first discuss the state of the art of conjoint analytical developments. Interactive evolutionary algorithms are presented and their potential to improve conjoint analysis is discussed. We conduct an exemplary empirical application of evolutionary conjoint and compare findings with choice-based-conjoint analysis. Robust statistical tests are used to validate the feasibility of this new approach. A comparison of the quality of estimation outcomes indicates superiority of the evolutionary conjoint approach. Implications and outlook for further research are discussed and presented.

7.2   State of the art and limitations of conjoint analysis

While it is not the purpose of our study to deliver a complete review on all aspects of the method of conjoint analysis (see e.g. Hauser and Rao 2004), we will focus our discussion on three dimensions: data modeling, experimental design and application fields of conjoint analysis. The first two aspects are highly relevant themes of the actual discourse. In addition we use the application field as an indicator for the practical relevance of the method for real world problems. In the following we will discuss unresolved issues of this method and deduce requests for future research which are based on these limitations.

7.2.1   Data modeling

The methodological roots of conjoint analysis refer back to the axiomatic conjoint measurement, which has psychometric origins (Green and Rao 1971). It was initially developed to decompose an ordinal scale of holistic judgment into interval scales for each component attribute. A major limitation of the axiomatic conjoint measurement is that it lacks an error term model. This implies the very restrictive and unrealistic assumption that conjoint analysis estimators are only efficient in case of error-free rank order data (Barron 1977). Fischer (1976) shows that even minor error terms may lead to substantial violation of the additivity axiom, even in case of true additive utility functions. Emery et al. (1982) prove these confounding effects mathematically and show that a separation of the two effects in conjoint measurement is impossible. Confounding effects between error term distribution and model misspecifications lead to inherently ambiguous estimators (Louviere 2006).

Green and Rao (1971) adapt the conjoint measurement theory to the solution of marketing and product-development problems. Green and Srinivasan (1978) were the first to propose the term CA for marketing problems to distinguish it from the use of "conjoint measurement" in mathematical psychology. The primary objective of CA is to improve the predictive fit of models which are presupposed to be valid. To this end, complex statistical models (e.g., random coefficient models, latent class or Hierarchical Bayes methods) improve the forecasting power by taking preference heterogeneity at a segment or individual level into account (Allenby et al. 2005, Teichert 2001b). Heterogeneity is modeled as discrete or continuous distribution of estimated partworth values. However, most of these models ignore heterogeneity of error variances of parameters across individuals and evaluation tasks. This may lead to confounding of effects and thus to biased estimators (Louviere and Eagle 2006, Louviere et al. 2002).

To overcome problems of traditional conjoint analysis, the method of choice based conjoint (CBC) is based on discrete choice models. It leads to improved predicted accuracy, especially in market simulations (Chakraborti et al. 2002). Despite the suggested higher internal and external validity of CBC it is not always given that the results are consistent to random utility models (Louviere and Eagle

2006). Generalizability remains unexplored, since many models are only evaluated on fit and predictive ability. Furthermore, cross-validations or out-of-sample validations provide little information about the scientific validity of models. An additional problem of CBC is the potential confounding stemming from estimating aggregate parameters, since individuals may have different random components causing different scale effects. Aggregated estimates are inherently erroneous, unless all individuals are rescaled individually to take scale differences into account. According to Louviere (2006) there are two possible solutions to this problem: individual level analysis and development and application of model-free approaches.

To sum up, fitting statistical models on data sets does not automatically lead to efficient results. Models require valid assumptions from a behavior-theoretical perspective. The issues of insufficiently validated model propositions, problems of ambiguous and biased parameters due to specification of error terms in complex statistical models remain unresolved (Teichert 2001a:38).

> ***Request****: Model-free approaches should be developed to avoid possible mis-specifications of utility functions and resulting estimation biases.*

7.2.2   Experimental design

Generating efficient designs is fundamental to the performance of CA. The majority of empirical applications assume model axioms, such as a polynomial additive function form and preferential independence of investigated features to be true (Keeney and Raiffa 1976). Whenever preferential independence is not satisfied, the conjoint function is more difficult to estimate and interaction among features must be specifically estimated (Hauser and Rao 2004). Modeling interaction effects requires especially in CBC-experiments larger designs, since the design dimensions rise exponentially (Hauser and Rao 2004, Street et al. 2005). Thus, many empirical applications use fractional-design based approaches without testing for preferential independence. While traditional approaches mainly rely on fractional factorial designs (Addelman 1962), the recent discourse proposes new methods to improve design efficiency. Two research streams can be identified: adaptive designs for traditional CA and special designs for CBC.

Traditional CA is improved by combining different survey elements, such as self-explicated tasks and orthogonal designs. There are various approaches for this, such as the adaptive or so-called polyhedral methods. Adaptive conjoint analysis (ACA) aims to generate flexible designs by adapting questionnaire design within one respondent, using the respondent's own answers to previous questions. It is a two-step approach in which respondents first eliminate unacceptable products, unacceptable attributes, or use prior sorting tasks to simplify the holistic evaluation task (e.g. Hauser and Toubia 2005, Green et al. 1991). ACA uses metric paired-comparisons and relies on balancing utility between the pairs subject to orthogonality and feature balance. Recently, new methods for adaptive designs have been proposed, which iteratively adapt evaluation tasks to minimize remaining uncertainty in parameter estimation. Fast polyhedral methods use a special "fast" algorithm that constructs profiles / choice sets depending on a-priori information of previous judgment tasks. Polyhedral methods can be used for both metric-paired comparison questions in ACA and CBC (Toubia et al. 2004). All adaptive designs bear the potential of endogeneity bias, that is, the profiles of the nth question and hence of the respective set of independent variables depend upon the answers and hence the errors of the first n-1 questions (Hauser and Rao 2004). This major shortcoming leads to limited validity and generalizability of ACA results (Sattler 2006).

The second stream of research investigates how to improve the efficiency of CBC designs (e.g. Sándor and Wedel 2005; Street et al. 2005). CBC has become the most frequently applied conjoint approach (Hauser and Rao 2004). Generation of efficient CBC designs has shown to be more complex than traditional conjoint designs, as two steps of design creation are needed. Many studies have focused on efficient CBC design strategies (for a review see Louviere et al. 2004). Most designs considered in these studies are fixed, insofar as each respondent is confronted with the same set of choice tasks. An exception is the study of Sándor and Wedel (2005), in which individualized designs based on Bayesian priors are generated.

Overall, design generation is part of the sequential process of CA: In any type of conjoint analysis scientists typically formulate hypotheses, generate the experimental design, collect data and then test the deducted hypotheses by estimating the data set. This course of action implies that inefficiencies in design generation can mainly be noticed after estimation. At this point of time the empirical study can not be revised, but an improved survey-process must be replicated. This would cause time and cost intense successive data collections.

Relatively new forms of web CA make use of the internet as a data source and exploit the advantages of technological progress. Web-based surveys allow for time-efficient data collection and preparation processes. They allow conducting large scaled surveys within short periods of time. The interactivity and the multimodal presentation of stimuli open new possibilities for developing new experimental designs. Several studies, mainly from the context of new product development, apply web based conjoint surveys (Dahan and Hauser 2002). These methods make use of the internet as data collection modus, but use traditional conjoint approaches without basic improvements in experimental design.

To conclude, design remains one of the most relevant research topics in CA. Despite advances in experimental design research in recent years, there are still limitations, such as the lack of consumer interaction, lack of flexibility as well as limitations in integrating interaction effects.

> *Request:* Adaptive-recursive flexible designs should be developed which further exploit the possibilities of the internet as a new data source.

7.2.3   Areas of application

Conjoint approaches have been applied in different fields, comprising environmental economics, transportation research, scanner data analysis, health-care, telecommunication etc. CA is undoubtedly a well-established method in social and economical sciences and especially in consumer research. Reviews of application fields can be found e.g. in Hauser and Rao (2004). Despite its flexibility, CA can only investigate a finite (small) number of discrete attributes.

A careful selection of attributes and attribute levels is crucial for the success of any conjoint experiment. Attributes are commonly assumed to be independent, because if they were not, the problem of modeling interaction effects would arise. The modeling of interaction effects requires larger experimental designs, since there are many decompositional forms and related independence conditions (Hauser and Rao 2004; Street et al. 2005). As a consequence, traditional CA as well as CBC are ill suited for high dimensioned problems. ACA and other hybrid methods overcome this shortcoming by integrating self-explicated tasks.

Continuous attributes are approximated by specifying a small subset of discrete attribute levels. Typically, a worst and a best case as well as an intermediary level is chosen. An optimization of the underlying continuous variable is achieved by interpolating gained estimates. This assumes a linear function in between the chosen attribute levels which need not be the case (e.g. sugar content in a coffee mug). Presenting extreme points of the solution range endangers the face validity of provided answers: Respondents are confronted with abstract as well as irrelevant evaluation tasks, if the given levels depart significantly from their optimum level. This may be well the case for attributes with "feel and see" features. As an example, the optimal taste of coffee is hardly to be anticipated based on positive and negative extreme points of sugar content.

To sum up, although CA is a well established method of consumer research, it still shows some limitations in applications. Major shortcomings are to be diagnosed for continuous as well as "feel and see" features. Experimental designs which approximate these variables with discrete attribute levels are likely to fail short in estimation accuracy.

> **Request:** New conjoint analytical approaches should be developed for continuous as well as "feel and see" features.

7.2.4   Summary of state of the art

In spite of the high relevance of CA for survey research and its large number of applications there still are unresolved issues in data analysis and modeling, design and application areas. New approaches should be developed which fulfill requests that need to be clarified (Table 1). In the following we test the new method of evolutionary conjoint, which connects aspects of evolutionary algorithms and conjoint analysis.

Table 1: Unresolved issues of conjoint analytical approaches

Feature	ACA	CBC	Requests
I Modeling			
i. Model premises	Based on axioms (compositiona l& decompositional)	Based on axioms (decompositional)	*Model-free approaches should be developed to avoid possible misspecifications of utility functions and resulting estimation biases.*
ii. Estimation	Low external validity/Endogeneity bias	Confounding effects/ Individual scale effects	
iii. Error term modeling	Risk of confounding effects	Risk of confounding effects	
II Design			
i. Flexibility	Endogeneity bias	No learning effects	*Adaptive-recursive flexible designs should be developed which further exploit the possibilities of the internet as a new data source.*
ii. Consumer interaction	Adaptive designs	None	
iii. Interaction effects	Generally not considered	Need explicit modeling/ Exponential design growth	
iv. Time & cost intensity	Sequential surveys (t=>>)	Sequential surveys (t=>>)	
III. Application areas			
i. Suitability for high dimensioned problems	Yes	<<(exponential design growth)	*New conjoint analytical approaches should be developed for continuous as well as "feel and see" features.*
ii. Continuous attributes	Coarse-grained	Coarse-grained	
iii. "Feel and see" features	Unrealistic self-explicated part	Potentially unrealistic evaluation tasks due to fixed end-point design	

7.3   Evolutionary algorithms

Charles Darwin (1809-1882) can be considered father of the biological model of evolution. The core message of his theory is embodied in the principle of "survival of the fittest". This describes the adaptation of organisms to their environment. Evolutionary pressure typically forces systems to become highly optimized and efficient. Accordingly, methods and systems found in nature are applied to the optimization of problems in other disciplines. First applications of EA go back to the 60s (Holland 1962, Rechenberg 1973). In the 70s and 80s different schools of thought were formed with a strong focus on optimization. The four main streams, genetic algorithms, evolutionary strategies, evolutionary programming and genetic programming are comprehensively known as evolutionary computation. Recently hybrid forms connecting aspects of different streams are becoming more and more relevant and the boarders between the separate classes are becoming smoother (Figure 1).

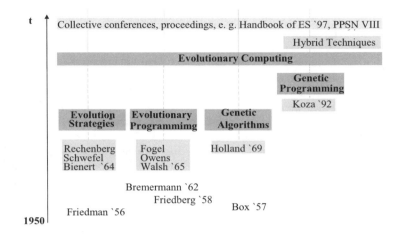

Figure 1:   Historical development of evolutionary algorithms

In contrast to traditional marketing research methods, evolutionary algorithms (EA) are model-free in content but model-driven in the algorithm of solution search. While randomized, EA are no simple random walk. They efficiently exploit past information to speculate on new search points with expected improved fitness. At the end, EA identifies promising product concepts directly, whereas CA deducts those solutions by first estimating partworth values.

Rechenberg (1973) sets up the basic assumption of the EA "...that the quality of an engineering system can be compared with the fitness of a living organism...". Still the argument "nature does it better" is not the only argument for the efficiency of EA. Both theory and practice show that EA provide robust search results in complex spaces (Goldberg, 1989: 2). A large number of methodological developments and empirical applications in different fields indicate the validity of the technique in optimization problems (Herdy 2000, Nissen 1997). Algorithms are not inherently limited by restrictive assumptions about search space, such as continuity, existence of derivatives, unimodality of optimization problems etc. All algorithms make use of biological operators of selection, recombination and mutation in order to solve complex optimization problems (Weicker 2002):

- Selection is the process of choosing those alternatives which operate as parents of the next generation. According to the biological principle of survival of the fittest, better individuals have higher selection probabilities. The selection process drives the total population and the experimental design towards better alternatives in solution space.
- Recombination is an operator which generates offspring by combining the genetic material of the parents.

- Mutations are randomized changes which make sure that new genetic material is used in the following generation thus avoiding the risk of local minima.

Despite the large number of empirical applications, EA have been used in marketing only recently. According to a meta-analysis (Wong & Bondovich 1999) on management applications of genetic algorithms, the first marketing study was published in 1988. Since then, EA were used in new product development for optimization of separate products as well as product lines. Earlier heuristics-based studies (Kohli and Krishnamurthi 1987) used elements of EA for optimizing product design under the restriction of maximizing market shares (the so-called share of choice problem). The major limitation of these first applications is their sensitivity to sequencing effects (Balakrishnan and Jacob 1996). Balakrishnan and Jacob (1996) propose the application of genetic algorithms for product design optimization, which simultaneously optimize all attributes. This work was later extended for optimizing product line decisions (e.g. Camm et al. 2006, Balakrishnan et al. 2006).

All studies use EA in a second evaluation phase without any customer interactivity. Customer partworths are generated a-priori by means of traditional CA. These partworths are used as input to the multimodal optimization problem of the share of choices. Thus, customer evaluation judgments are not an active part of the optimization problem. The CA is not improved in this two-step approach, so that traditional fractional experimental designs are not improved and potential biases of CA-estimators remain. Thus we conclude that EA are not fully established in survey research despite their potential: The model-free approach of EA could be an alternative for avoiding biases due to misspecifications of utility models. The possibility of adaptive-recursive designs could lead to improved designs.

7.4   Evolutionary Conjoint

7.4.1   Basic scheme of interactive evolutionary algorithms

Evolutionary conjoint is strongly aligned with the technique of interactive evolutionary algorithms (IEA). IEA use customer evaluations as selection criterion in the course of the optimization process (Figure 2) on the Darwinian principle of natural selection, IEA consist of the following basic pattern (Bäck 1996: 8):

1. *Solution representation:* IEA consider a product as a bundle of features. Accordingly, the first step is the selection of a structure for representing product alternatives. This leads to a set of parameters known as genes or chromosomes.
2. *Initialization:* The initial population is generated by combining different levels of features in order to create product alternatives. The initial population can be generated randomly or by using *a priori* information.

3. *Evaluation of the current population:* All alternatives are evaluated by the respondents according to their preferences. This serves as a fitness function by which a measure of quality is assigned to each product alternative in the current population.

4. *Selection of parents:* Alternatives with highest fitness values are chosen as parents for following offspring generations.

5. *Recombination:* New product alternatives are generated by applying the operators of recombination and mutation. The mutation radius can be varied in each generation. Generally it is advisable to use high radiuses in the early generations in order to avoid local minima. Smaller radiuses can be used in latter generations in order to finely specify the optimal solution point in the area of "survivors".

6. Steps 3 and 4 are repeated until convergence is achieved. Convergence criteria (e.g. similarity of best alternatives of following populations etc.) can be determined *a priori*.

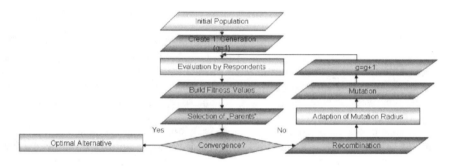

Figure 2:   The IEA Approach

The parameterization of IEA is complex and contains numerous elements such as the number of parents and children, the fitness function, mutation rate and radius, type of recombination, convergence criterion. It is to be adapted to the specific problem type (Rechenberg 1994: 91-105). Pretests are required for optimizing the parameterization before each empirical application.

7.4.2   Data modeling

Evolutionary conjoint uses the basic principles of IEA. By this means, it is a technique that embeds consumer preferences directly into the target optimization process. As in CA, each product is represented by its features, which are reinterpreted as "genes." A respondent is shown a representative set of concepts, each of which is a set of genes. Respondents evaluate the products by rating, ranking or choosing the most preferred alternative. This evaluation determines the likelihood that the product concept will "reproduce" into the next generation. Then, following an evolutionary algorithm, offspring is generated based on the genes of their parents. This process continues until the population stabilizes on a small set of product concepts.

The application of evolutionary conjoint has the great advantages of not needing restrictive assumptions concerning functional form and continuity. It also should benefit from a good fit for optimization problems in high dimensioned solution spaces. This however must be investigated because the factor of human fatigue should diminish this possibility. Due to the model-free optimization approach and the model-driven search process no statistical analysis is necessary for determining optimal solutions. The suitability of the alternative optimization approach of IEA for utility measurement has to be investigated. Analogous to the EA approach there is no explicit error term modeling up to now. Error term modeling and modeling preference heterogeneity are important issue which have to be explored in future research.

7.4.3   Experimental design

Evolutionary conjoint develop individualized flexible designs with an especially high degree of consumer integration. Consumer evaluations directly influence the experimental design. They continuously influence the levels of each attribute in each of the successive generations. This stays in contrast to adaptive design techniques, where the design input of respondents is restricted to the first step of the self-explicated tasks.

Because of the interactive nature the search space is narrowed sequentially, so that individual optima are identified. The risk of local optima is reduced by a mutation operator, which injects variance in the solution space. At the same time, it acts recursively on design evolution as a bumper for unconscious response effects, such as inconsistencies due to emotional trade-offs, context and framing effects etc. This may well be an advantage of evolutionary conjoint compared to traditional CA surveys.

Evolutionary conjoint has the advantage of high design flexibility by being able to integrate continuous attributes in the optimization processes. Consequently, there is no need for pre-selecting attribute levels, which helps to avoid problems such as threshold values or other non-linearities of utility functions. There is no need for explicitly modeling interaction effects between independent variables: Interaction effects are rather implicitly taken into account in course of the model-driven search in solution space.

Owing to the model-driven search design, data collection and model specification in evolutionary conjoint are inseparably intertwined.

The recursive pattern of evolutionary conjoint designs leads to improvements within the course of the investigation. Thus, design inefficiencies which in CA surveys are irreversible after the data is collected, have milder consequences in case of evolutionary conjoint. This indicates potential cost and time saving effects.

In short, evolutionary conjoint is based on different principles than traditional CA designs. Its dynamic design may be different for each individual. Interaction effects need not be modeled. Furthermore the adaptive-recursive nature should lead to time and cost saving advantages. These expected advantages are to be explored empirically.

7.4.4   Areas of application

Despite its potential evolutionary conjoint has not yet been established in marketing. There are numerous methodical publications on the improvement of convergence capability of IEA (e.g. Saez et al. 2005). However, there is no scientific application of these algorithms in preference modeling and no direct comparison to other conjoint methods. Sporadic applications are to be observed in special areas of prototype testing, such as hearing devices (Ohsaki and Tagaki 2000), shape of eyeglasses (Yanagisawa & Fukuda 2004), 3-D lighting systems (Aoki and Tagaki 1997), and coffee mixtures (Herdy 1998). These initial applications rely on very small samples and lack a theoretical frame.

Table 2:   Potential of evolutionary conjoint

Requests	Feature	Evolutionary CA	Potential
	I Modeling		
Model-free approaches should be developed to avoid possible misspecifications of utility functions and resulting estimation biases.	i. Model premises	Quasi model free	++
	ii. Estimation	Not applicable	?
	iii. Error term modeling	To be explored	?
	II Design		
Adaptive-recursive flexible designs should be developed which further exploit the possibilities of the internet as a new data source.	i. Flexibility	Adaptive design & mutation radius	++
	ii. Consumer interaction	Iterative-recursive	++
	iii. Interaction effects	Automatically integrated	++
	iv. Time & cost intensity	Online surveys (t=<<)	++
	III. Application areas		
New conjoint analytical approaches should be developed for continuous as well as "feel and see" features.	i. Suitability for high dimensioned problems	To be explored	?
	ii. Continuous attributes	>>(continuous features)	++
	iii. "Feel and see" features	Yes	++

7.4.5   Outlook

Rechenberg (1994: 18), one of the fathers of evolutionary computing, praises the human element in interactive EA:

"Conscious interference with an evolution strategic optimization process should not be a taboo. I am all in favor of Interactive Evolutionary Computation (IEC) Just slightly change the mutation radius, raise the number of offspring, make the parents immortal ... The layman gets a feeling for the effects of evolutionary parameters, and the EA expert whounderstands the art of IEC may be able to work wonders." (Author's translation).

We argue that the model-free optimization and the dynamic design promise important contributions and help to avoid potential limitations of traditional CA (Table 2)

7.5   Empirical application

The potential evolutionary conjoint is empirically tested in a simple experiment. We apply the new method in a new product development setting and test its adequacy for identifying utility maximizing products. Results are compared with those of CBC. Findings should indicate the adequacy of evolutionary conjoint for preference analysis and for the generation of utility optimizing product alternatives.

7.5.1   Objectives

The primary goal of our empirical research is to explore the adequacy of the new method of evolutionary conjoint. Since there is no comparable study in this field, we streamline our explorative approach along the basic scheme of the research paradigm in three steps: existence, contingency and success analysis.

1.   First of all we investigate the adequacy of evolutionary conjoint for identifying optimal product alternatives according to customer preferences. For this, we analyze the feasibility of "survival of the fittest" as the basic principle of EA. This principle implies that product alternatives which belong to more recent populations should be preferred over alternatives stemming from former populations. In order to test for this hypothesis we use paired comparisons of alternatives from different generations of individual optimization tracks.
2.   In a second step, we search for potential differences between solutions derived with evolutionary conjoint and CBC. Due to their fundamental methodical differences, we expect differences in estimated optimal product alternatives. To test this hypothesis, we present respondents with solutions derived with evolutionary conjoint and CBC and ask them about the perceived similarity of both alternatives.

3. Finally, we expect evolutionary conjoint solutions to better fit customers' preferences than those generated with CA because it directly integrates customers' preferences in the optimization process. This leads us to our third hypothesis that evolutionary conjoint solutions are closer to customers' preference optima. In order to test for this hypothesis we use ex-post choice decisions between the optima derived from both methods.

Table 3:   Hypotheses for the empirical study

Steps of Research	Hypothesis
Existence Analysis	*H1: The basic principles of evolutionary conjoint are suited for preference elicitation.*
Contingency Analysis	*H2: Evolutionary conjoint generates different optimal products than traditional CA.*
Success Analysis	*H3: Evolutionary conjoint solutions are closer to customers optimum than CA.*

7.5.2   Experimental design

Our empirical application comprises three consecutives interviews (Figure 3): two computer-based surveys with CBC and evolutionary conjoint and one in-depth personal interview. The sample consists of 50 respondents, most of them students with homogeneous sociodemographic features. The design of a bottle is chosen as application object. This enables to explore the potential of evolutionary conjoint for continuous as well as "feel-and-see-me" attributes. Three attributes were varied: the color intensity of the bottle, the color intensity of the bottle label and the position of the label. The color intensity of both bottle and label was varied between transparent and brown. The vertical position of the label was varied from bottom to top.

Discrete attribute levels were generated for the CBC design as follows: A prestudy was conducted to determine values with high discriminant power. The interviews indicated that color brightness can be represented by each four levels: transparent, beige, light brown and dark brown. Label position was represented by three levels: above, central and down. A 96% efficient orthogonal design was generated which consists of 16 choice sets with 4 alternatives each (Street et al. 2005). Two hold-out choice sets were added for validation purposes.

A Java based software prototype was programmed for the evolutionary conjoint tasks. The parameterization was specified as closely as possible to the CBC design. Generations consisted of four different product alternatives each. The two most preferred alternatives served as parents for the next generation. The evolutionary process was repeated until the respondent was fully satisfied with the product layout and stopped the interview.

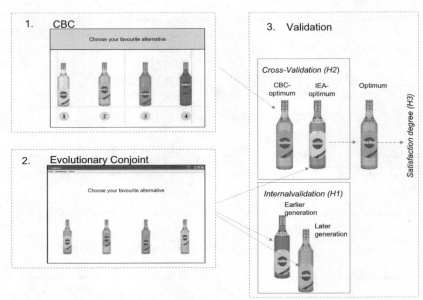

Figure 3:   Experimental setup

A week later, an in-depth interview was conducted for cross-validating both methods. The in-depth interview consists of two main question blocks (Figure). The first block concerns the internal validation of IEA (H1). Respondents had to choose between alternatives from different generations of evolutionary conjoint. The second question block investigated the differences between evolutionary conjoint and CBC: The derived optimal solutions from both methods were presented to the respondents. Respondents evaluated their similarity to test for the discriminative power of both methods (H2). To finally test the superiority of estimation outcomes, respondents had to choose the most preferred alternative and state their overall satisfaction with the outcome (H3).

7.5.3   Data collection and estimation

The CBC data was analyzed with a hierarchical Bayes model using the statistical software GAUSS. The model consists of three hierarchical levels with partworths assumed to be normally distributed with normally distributed means and Wishart distributed standard deviations (Train 2003, 285:302). The model was estimated under the assumption of correlated model parameters.

In-sample and out-of-sample validity are used to assess model performance. Fits are calculated by the prediction success index (McFadden 1979). The in-sample validity of 80% indicates a good fit of the model. The external validity of

68% is calculated by using the hold-out choice tasks. This indicates a significantly better forecasting power of the model compared to a random model ($\alpha=0.01$).

Figure 4:   Optimization with evolutionary conjoint

The evolutionary conjoint interviews were conducted by using a software programmed for this purpose (Figure 4). The software saved the entire searching track and the optimal alternatives for each individual. In average 13 generations were needed to reach convergence. This indicates that the search process was neither trivial nor suffering under consumer fatigue.

7.5.4   Results

In-depth interviews were conducted for cross-validating both methods, as described above. The results support our hypotheses (Table 4).
1. Respondents prefer in 90% of all cases alternatives from more recent generations against those from earlier ones. This indicates a good face validity of the optimization process and shows, that the basic principle of evolutionary conjoint ("survival of the fittest") can be applied to preference based optimization. These results are supported by a non-parametric sign test ($\alpha=0.01$).
2. Respondents consider the optimal solutions derived by either evolutionary conjoint or CBC to be significantly different ($\alpha=0.01$). The perceived

differences are significantly larger for respondents who prefer the evolutionary conjoint solutions. This result is supported by a non-parametric Man-Whitney U-test. To further assess the extent of the revealed differences, a difference score is calculated at the attribute level and normalized between 0 and 100. The average differences amount $\Delta=27$ for bottle color, $\Delta=25$ for etiquette color and $\Delta=30$ for etiquette position. All three values are significantly different from 0 ($\alpha=0.01$), so that our second hypothesis is supported.

3. Comparing the derived optimal products, 34 respondents out of 50 prefer the solution of evolutionary conjoint against the CBC solution. The quotient of respondents who prefer IEA over CA (68%) is significantly different from a randomized model ($\alpha=0.01$). The results confirm our hypothesis that evolutionary conjoint solutions reflect better consumers' preferences and wishes. Customers who chose evolutionary conjoint alternatives are in average significantly more satisfied with their choice as those who prefer CBC solutions ($\alpha=0.01$). An in-depth investigation revealed that respondents appraise the ability of IEA to derive finely specified colors. This shows the potential of evolutionary conjoint for continuous attributes. All these results support our third hypothesis that evolutionary conjoint may generate product optima that are more superior to CBC solutions.

Table 4:   Results

Steps of Research	Results	Hypothesis
Existence Analysis	90% of all tasks consumer prefer alternatives from more recent generations (non-parametric sign test $\alpha=0.01$)	*H1: The basic principles of evolutionary conjoint are suited for preference elicitation.* √
Contingency Analysis	32 respondents out of 50 consider the CBC and IEA solutions to be dissimilar (t-test $\alpha=0.01$)	*H2: Evolutionary conjoint generates different optimal products than traditional CA.* √
Success Analysis	34 respondents out of 50 prefer the IEA-solutions (t-test $\alpha=0.01$; Man-Whitney U-test $\alpha=0.05$)	*H3: Evolutionary conjoint solutions are closer to customers' optimum than CA.* √

7.6 Discussion and outlook

We propose evolutionary conjoint as a new model-free method, which combines aspects of evolutionary algorithms with those of conjoint analysis. By transferring the principles of Darwin's evolution theory of "survival of the fittest" to utility optimization problems, these algorithms can help avoiding some limitations of conjoint analysis. Requests concerning the modeling, design and application can be fulfilled by evolutionary conjoint.

We conduct an initial empirical comparison of evolutionary conjoint with CBC. This basic empirical application indicates the potential of evolutionary conjoint as a new method for consumer integration in new product development. Since this study is the first of its kind, we firstly explore the adequacy of evolutionary conjoint for deriving new products according to customers' preferences. Our results clearly support this thesis. Furthermore, we find that evolutionary conjoint and CBC lead to significantly different optima. Evolutionary conjoint generates solutions which are more fine tuned and thus significantly superior to CBC solutions.

This study investigates evolutionary conjoint as a new method for consumer research. It is a first contribution in an interesting and highly promising research field. Both conceptual foundations as well as empirical effects need to be further investigated. Conceptual work is needed for modeling error terms and taking consumer heterogeneity into account. Cross-validations with state-of-the-art methods should be conducted and the potential of evolutionary conjoint for improving forecasts should be further quantified.

7.7 References

Addelman, S. (1962), Symmetrical and Asymmetrical Fractional Factorial Plans, *Technometrics*, 4, 47-58.

Allenby, G., Fennell, G., Huber, J., Eagle, T., Gilbride, T., Horsky, D., Kim, J., Lenk, P., Johnson, R., Ofek, E., Orme, B., Otter, T. and Walker, J. (2005), Adjusting Choice Models to Better Predict Market Behaviour, *Marketing Letters*, 16(3-4), 197-208.

Aoki, K. and Tagaki, H. (1997), 3–D CG Lighting with an Interactive GA, *KES'97*.

Bäck, T. (1996), *Evolutionary Algorithms in Theory and Practice*, New York.

Balakrishnan, P. and Jacob, V. S. (1996), Genetic Algorithms for Product Design, *Management Science*, 42(8), 1105-1117.

Balakrishnan, P., Gupta, R. and V. Jacob (2006), An Investigation of Mating and Population Maintenance Strategies in Hybrid Genetic Heuristics for Product Line Designs, *Computers & Operation Research*, 33, 639-659.

Barron, F. (1977), Axiomatic Conjoint Measurement, *Decision Sciences*, 8, 548-559.

Camm J., Cochran J., Curry D., and Kanan, S. (2006), Conjoint Optimization, an Exact Branch-and-Bound Algorithm for the Share-of-Choice Problem, *Management Science*, 52, 435-447.

Chakraborty, G., Ball, D., Gaeth, G., and Jun, S. (2002), The Ability of Ratings and Choice Conjoint to Predict Market Shares-A Monte Carlo Simulation, *Journal of Business Research*, 55, 237-249.

Dahan, E. and Hauser, J. (2002), The Virtual Customer, *Journal of Product Innovation Management,* 19 (5), 332-353.

Darwin, C. (1859), *On the Origin of Species by Means of Natural Selection, or the Preservation of Favoured Races in the Struggle for Life.* London.

Emery, D., Barron, F. and Messier, W. Jr. (1982), Conjoint Measurement and the Analysis of Noisy Data, A Comment, *Journal of Accounting Research*, 20(2), Part I, 450-458.

Fischer, G. (1976), Multidimensional Utility Models for Risky and Riskless Choice, *Organizational Behavior and Human Performance*, 17, 127-146.

Goldberg, D. (1989), *Genetic Algorithms in Search Optimization and Machine Learning*, Addison Wesley Longman.

Green, P. and Srinivasan, V. (1978), Conjoint Analysis in Consumer Research, Issues and Outlook, *Journal of Consumer Research*, 5, 103-123.

Green, P. and Rao, V. (1971), Conjoint Measurement for Quantifying Judgmental Data, *Journal of Marketing Research*, 8, 355-363.

Green, P., Krieger, A. and Agarwal, M., (1991), Adaptive Conjoint Analysis, Some Caveats and Suggestions, *Journal of Marketing Research*, 23, 215-222.

Hartmann, A. und Sattler, H. (2006), *Commercial Use of Conjoint Analysis in Germany, Austria and Switzerland*, in: A. Gustafsson, A. Herrmann und F. Huber (Hrsg.), *Conjoint Measurement, Methods and Applications*, Berlin et al.

Hauser, J. and Rao, V. (2004), *Conjoint Analysis, Related Modeling, and Applications*, in: Y. Wind and Green, P. (Eds.), *Marketing Research and Modeling, Progress and Prospects, A Tribute to Paul Green*, Dordrecht.

Hauser J. and Toubia O. (2005), The Impact of Utility Balance and Endogeneity in Conjoint Analysis, *Marketing Science*, 24 (3), 498-507.

Herdy, M. (1998), *Evolutionsstrategie mit Subjektiver Selektion zur Optimierung von Kaffeemischungen*, in: Hafner, S., *Industrielle Anwendungen evolutionärer Algorithmen*, München.

Herdy, M. (2000), *Beiträge zur Theorie und Anwendung der Evolutionsstrategie*. Berlin.

Holland, J. (1962), Outline for a Logical Theory of Adaptive Systems, *Journal of the Association for Computing Machinery*, 3, 297-314.

Keeney, R. and Raiffa, H. (1976), *Decisions with Multiple Objectives*, New York.

Kohli, R. and Krishnamurti, R. (1987), A Heuristic Approach to Product Design, *Management Science*, 33 (12), 1523-1533.

Louviere, J. (2006), What You Don't Know Might Hurt You, Some Unresolved Issues in the Design and Analysis of Discrete Choice Experiments, *Environmental & Resource Economics*, 34, 173-188.

Louviere, J. and Eagle, T. (2006), Confound it! That Pesky Little Scale Constant Messes up, *Working Paper*, Centre for the Study of Choice, Faculty of Business, University of Technology, Sydney.

Louviere, J., Street, D. and Burgess, L. (2004), Y. Wind and Green, P. (Eds.), *Marketing Research and Modeling, Progress and Prospects, A Tribute to Paul Green*, Dordrecht.

Louviere, J., Street, D., Carson, R., Ainslie, A., DeShazo, J., Cameron, T., Hensher, D., Kohn, R. and T. Marley (2002), Dissecting the Random component of Utility, *Marketing Letters*, 13, 3, 177-193.

McFadden, D. (1979). Modelling the Choice of Residential Location., *Transportation Research*, 673, 72-78.

Nissen, V. (1997), *Einführung in evolutionäre Algorithmen. Optimierung nach dem Vorbild der Evolution*. Braunschweig/Wiesbaden.

Rechenberg, I. (1994), *Evolutionsstrategie '94*, Stuttgart.

Rechenberg, I. (1973), *Evolutionsstrategie. Optimierung Technischer Systeme nach Prinzipien der biologischen Evolution*, Stuttgart.

Saez, Y., Isasi, P., and Hernandez, J.C. (2005), Reference Chromosome to Overcome User Fatigue, *IEC New Generation Computing*, 23, 129–142.

Sattler, H., (2006), Methoden zur Messung von Präferenzen für Innovationen, *Zeitschrift für betriebswirtschaftliche Forschung (zfbf)*, 54/06, 2006, 154-176.

Street, D., Burgess, L. and Louviere, J. (2005), Quick and Easy Choice Sets, Constructing Optimal and Nearly Optimal Stated Choice Experiments, *International Journal of Research in Marketing*, 22, 4, 459-470.

Teichert, T. (2001a), *Nutzenschätzung in Conjoint-Analysen*, Wiesbaden.

Teichert, T. (2001b), Nutzenermittlung in wahlbasierter Conjoint-Analyse, ein Vergleich zwischen Latent-Class- und hierarchischem Bayes-Verfahren, *Zeitschrift für betriebswirtschaftliche Forschung*, 53, 798-822.

Toubia, O., Hauser, J., Simester, D. and Duncan, I. (2004), Polyhedral Methods for Adaptive Choice-Based Conjoint Analysis, *Journal of Marketing Research*, 41, 1, 116-131.

Train, K. (2003), *Discrete Choice Methods with Simulation*, Cambridge.

Weicker, K. (2002), *Evolutionäre Algorithmen*, Stuttgart.

Wong, B. and Bodnovich, T. (1999), A Bibliography of Genetic Algorithm Business Application Research, 1988 June 1996, *Expert Systems*, 15, 2, 75-83.

Yanagisawa, H. and Funkuda, S. (2004), Development of Interactive Industrial Design Support Systems Considering Customers' Evaluations, *JSME International Journal, Series C*, 47, 2, 762-770.

8 The Value of Extent-of-Preference Information in Choice-Based Conjoint Analysis

Terry Elrod and Keith Chrzan

8.1 Introduction

It is clear that conjoint analysis has had a substantial impact upon research practice (Wittink and Cattin 1989; Wittink, Vriens and Burhenne 1994). Conjoint analysis has evolved, and along with that evolution has been a gradual shift in the types of responses collected, from rankings to ratings to choices.

A brief contrast of ratings and choice data for conjoint purposes is as follows (cf. Elrod, Louviere and Davey 1992; Vriens, Oppewal and Wedel 1998). The first advantage of choice data is greater face validity. Making choices is what consumers do and it is the type of behavior that marketers usually seek to predict. An important benefit of collecting choice data has been that the models commonly used to analyze such data—multinomial choice models—readily generate predicted shares for any combination of brands provided only that all brands may be fully described in terms of the attributes and attribute levels included in the study.

As traditionally applied, choice-based conjoint studies, often also referred to as discrete choice experiments, have some drawbacks. First, although multinomial choice models may allow part worths to vary systematically with observed consumer characteristics, consumers typically differ in terms of their part worths more than can be accounted for by consumer demographics. Explicitly allowing for unexplained consumer hetero-geneity in multinomial logit models is computationally intensive and fussier to estimate, although recent advances have helped to reduce this difficulty (Vriens, Oppewal and Wedel 1998).

A second problem is that choice data contain minimal information about consumer preferences. A choice simply indicates which alternative is most preferred; it does not provide an estimate of the utility of any of the alternatives, not even of the one chosen.

A final difficulty is that choices implicitly entail consideration of more than one alternative. Including just two alternatives in each choice question entails a doubling of the amount of information about brands that is presented to respondents relative to a ratings-based conjoint study. It is not uncommon for choice-based conjoint studies to include three or more alternatives, each described on all attributes, for each choice question.

We employ here two choice designs for paired alternatives: one design uses ordinary full profiles and the other uses partial profiles (Chrzan and Elrod 1994; 1995). The partial profile design requires that the two alternatives in each question differ on only a researcher-specified number of attributes which may be as few as three. Respondents are told that the alternatives are identical on the remaining attributes and, under fairly general conditions, the values imputed to these attributes are irrelevant to choice. Since far less attribute information needs to be presented to respondents per choice question, greater precision of model estimates can be obtained for a given number of respondents by being able to ask more choice questions using a questionnaire of given length.

This article investigates another possible advantage that can accrue to studies that collect choice on paired alternatives. Having indicated which of two alternatives is preferred, consumers then also indicate the extent of their preference for their chosen alternative. We use a single data set to answer five questions pertaining to use of this extent-of-preference information:

1. Is there any evidence that including extent-of-preference information in an ordinal logistic model leads to coefficient estimates that are any different from those obtained by simply analyzing the binary choice information? That is, does including the extent-of-preference information bias the estimates of the part worths that drive choice?
2. To what extent does analyzing the extent-of-preference information along with the choice information improve the efficiency of the estimates of the part worths?
3. Is there evidence of biased use of the scale? That is, do consumers favor either the first or the second alternative after controlling for the attributes of these alternatives?
4. Is there evidence of asymmetric use of the scale? That is, are the intervals between adjacent cutoff values symmetric about the central cutoff that separates choice between the two alternatives?
5. Do the answers to the four questions above differ for full profile and partial profile designs?

8.2   The Data

A total of 52 consumers each filled out two of four versions of a conjoint study of over-the-counter analgesics that were defined in terms of seven binary attributes. A total of 22 conjoint questions were asked. For fourteen of the questions the two alternatives in each choice set differed on only three attributes; for the other eight choice questions the two alternatives differed on all seven attributes. The 15 missing responses (out of 1144 possible) were excluded from the analysis.

8.3   The Model

We adopt what is known as the proportional odds ordinal logistic model (McCullagh 1980), of which the logit model is a special case. Underlying all model variants considered herein is the random utility model of consumer evaluation of brands. Let U_i be the utility of the i-th alternative in a choice set. It may be represented as:

$$U_i \equiv v_i + \varepsilon_i,$$

where v_i is a constant specific to the alternative, and ε_i is a random error term that is independently and identically distributed over all alternatives, questions and subjects according to a double exponential distribution. Often, as here, the deterministic component of utility, v_i, is a linear-in-parameters function of stimulus characteristics contained in a row vector $\mathbf{x}$:

$$v_i \equiv \mathbf{x}\beta.$$

We consider only the case of paired alternatives; i.e., $i \in \{1, 2\}$.

8.3.1   Explaining Choice

The probability that the first alternative is chosen in favor of the second is equal to the probability that the utility of the first is greater than the utility of the second, or $\text{Prob}[U_1 > U_2 + \alpha]$, where α is a bias term reflecting a possible tendency to choose the first or second alternative in each pair. This can be simplified to:

$$\text{Prob}[Y \geq +1] \equiv \text{Prob}[\varepsilon > \alpha - v],$$

where $Y \in \{+1, -1\}$ indicates whether the first $(+1)$ or the second (-1) alternative is chosen, $v \equiv v_1 - v_2 \ (\equiv [\mathbf{x}_1 - \mathbf{x}_2] \ \beta) \equiv \mathbf{x}\beta)$, and $\varepsilon \equiv \varepsilon_1 - \varepsilon_2$, which then has the logistic distribution, yielding the simple formula:

(1) $$\text{Prob}[Y \geq +1] = 1 / [1 + \exp(\alpha - \mathbf{x}\beta)].$$

Consumers have a tendency to choose the first/second alternative, even after controlling for the attributes of the alternatives, according to whether α is negative/positive. One might hope that no such tendency exists (i.e., $\alpha = 0$), which is testable. The parameter α may be interpreted as a cutoff value that U must exceed if the first alternative is to be chosen instead of the second.

8.3.2   Incorporating Extent-of-Preference Information

For the ordinal logistic regression model, Y may take on more than two values. For our study, respondents indicated not only the brand chosen but also the extent of their preference using a three-point scale. These two types of information can be represented as a single ordinal response Y from the set $\{-5, -3, -1, +1, +3, +5\}$. This particular representation for Y communicates an expectation of symmetry and unbiasedness in scale usage, but this expectation is not imposed untested upon the data. The scale must possess only one property in addition to ordinality: the lower/upper half of the scale must correspond to choice of the second/first alternative, as indicated by the sign of Y. This property is assured by collecting information about choice and extent-of-preference using two separate questions, as in:

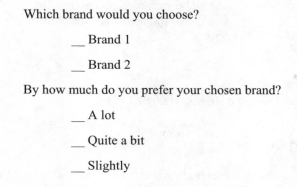

No information is lost vis-à-vis the paired choice model. The essential question is whether the extent-of-preference information contains appreciable and unbiased information about the part worths that explain choice.

For K categories of the response (K even), we define K + 1 threshold values designated $-\infty \equiv \alpha_0 < \alpha_1 < \ldots < \alpha_{K-1} < \alpha_K \equiv +\infty$. Furthermore the possible values of Y may be indicated as $y_1 < \ldots < y_K$. Then:

$$(2) \qquad \text{Prob}[Y \geq y_k] = \{1 / [1 + \exp(\alpha_{k-1} - v)]\} - \{1 / [1 + \exp(\alpha_k - v)]\}.$$

When there are only two categories, this equation simplifies to the case of binary choice.

With K possible values for Y, let m = K/2. Then the cutoff value α_m represents the bias towards choice of the second alternative. As with binary choice, the hypothesis $\alpha_m = 0$ is testable. We may also test whether the intervals between adjacent cutoffs are symmetric about α_m, as explained in the next section.

8.4   Results

For a given number of ordinal levels K, the logit choice model is not a special case of the ordinal extent-of-preference model. That is, for K > 2 there are no estimates of the cutoffs $\alpha_1, \ldots, \alpha_K$ that reduce equation 2 to equation 1. The binary model of choice assumes that an ordinal response contains no information beyond its sign, which reveals the brand chosen. Thus a response scale of $\{-5, -3, -1, +1, +3, +5\}$ may be recoded as $\{-1, 1\}$. This recoding of the response is not a strictly monotonically increasing function, so the Jacobian of the transformation, necessary to allow comparisons of likelihood-based measures of model fit, does not exist. Rigorous statistical tests of the first two research questions (Q1 and Q2) would require a general model that subsumes both the binary and ordinal logistic models. Fortunately, simpler analyses yield clear answers to these two questions. Statistical tests for questions Q3 and Q4 are available.

Binary and ordinal logistic models were fit to both the partial and full profile data. The fits of these four models are shown in Table 1. The estimates were obtained using the S function lrm written by Frank E. Harrell and included in his design library available from Statlib.[1] The top half of the table shows the estimates for the partial profile choice sets, the bottom half for the full profile choice sets, the left half for the ordinal model, and the right half for the binary model.

Table 1:   *Estimates for the Four Models*

	Partial profiles							
	Extent of Preference				Choice			
	Coef	S.E.	Z	P	Coef	S.E.	Z	P
y>=-3	−1.80	0.11	−16.62	0				
y>=-1	−0.85	0.09	−9.73	0				
y>=1	0.03	0.08	0.40	0.69	0	0.09	0.04	0.97
y>=3	0.80	0.09	9.26	0				
y>=5	1.56	0.10	15.81	0				
Fast	0.48	0.11	4.25	0	0.64	0.14	4.67	0
Caplets	−0.16	0.12	−1.41	0.16	0.11	0.14	0.75	0.45
Coated	0.02	0.11	0.22	0.82	0.16	0.14	1.14	0.26
Strong	0.47	0.11	4.17	0	0.59	0.13	4.43	0
SA	0.52	0.12	4.50	0	0.60	0.15	4.10	0
Gentle	1.58	0.12	12.82	0	1.87	0.17	10.94	0
notPM	0.42	0.11	3.73	0	0.46	0.14	3.22	0

---

[1]   S programs for Windows operating systems are available from Statlib at http://lib.stat.cmu.edu/DOS/S/ (http://stat.cmu.edu/S/ for Unix). The design library is available under the listing Harrell/design. The design library requires the hmisc library, available under the listing Harrell/hmisc. (Accessed 7 April 1999.) The function lrm defines the α values differently—they are preceded by minus signs in equations 1 and 2, which is equivalent to specifying them as category-specific intercepts rather than as cutoff values. The estimates shown in Table 1 were made consistent with the cutoff interpretation used here by reversing the signs of the α estimates returned by lrm.

Full profiles

	Extent of Preference				Choice			
	Coef	S.E.	Z	P	Coef	S.E.	Z	P
y>=-3	–2.10	0.15	–13.77	0				
y>=-1	–1.22	0.13	–9.64	0				
y>=1	–0.27	0.11	–2.37	0.02	–0.22	0.12	–1.86	0.06
y>=3	0.60	0.12	5.50	0				
y>=5	1.80	0.14	12.59	0				
Fast	0.37	0.09	4.08	0	0.46	0.13	3.61	0
Caplets	0.04	0.09	0.46	0.64	0.02	0.13	0.19	0.85
Coated	0.21	0.09	2.32	0.02	0.23	0.12	1.85	0.06
Strong	0.22	0.09	2.45	0.01	0.04	0.13	0.30	0.76
SA	0.44	0.09	4.84	0	0.42	0.13	3.33	0
Gentle	1.10	0.10	10.93	0	1.20	0.13	9.38	0
notPM	0.19	0.09	2.16	0.03	0.33	0.12	2.68	0.01

Note: The signs of Coef and Z for the cutoff values returned by the lrm function are the reverse of those shown in the table.

8.4.1   Test for Unbiasedness and Symmetry

The extent-of-preference model estimates five cutoff values that separate the 6 categories of the response. The cutoff labeled y>=1 in Table 1 separates choice of the first alternative from choice of the second. This cutoff corresponds to the cutoff for the binary choice model. We now consider tests of symmetry and unbiasedness.

If respondents use the six-point extent-of-preference scale in a symmetric and unbiased manner, then the following three equalities would hold: $\alpha_1 + \alpha_5 = \alpha_2 + \alpha_4 = \alpha_3 = 0$. A chi-square test of this null hypothesis for the partial profile and full profile data sets is shown in Table 2. This null hypothesis is accepted for the partial profile data but not for the full profile data.

It is possible to test for symmetry and unbiasedness separately. Symmetry may be claimed if the following two equalities hold: $(\alpha_1 - \alpha_2) + (\alpha_5 - \alpha_4) = (\alpha_2 - \alpha_3) + (\alpha_4 - \alpha_3) = 0$. Table 2 shows that this hypothesis is rejected for neither data set. The joint test for unbiasedness and symmetry is obtained by adding to the test for symmetry the test that $\alpha_3 = 0$. This test, which is equivalent to the test for this cutoff differing from zero in Table 1, is also shown for completeness in Table 2. We see that symmetry can be accepted for both data sets but there is evidence of a tendency to choose the first alternative in each pair for the full profile choice sets but not for the partial profile. The bias estimate for the ordinal partial profile data of 0.27 is close to the bias estimate for the choice partial profile (0.22), the latter being marginally significant (p = .06). Thus it appears that bias in favor of choice of the first alternative is a property of the full profile design and is not due to utilization of extent-of-preference information.[2] It may be that the full profile choices, which present respondents with more attribute information per choice question, tend to induce a choice heuristic that includes a tendency to choose the first alternative irrespective of the attribute values of the two alternatives. Such a tendency is of course a departure from the multiattribute utility model.

Table 2:   *Tests of Unbiasedness and Symmetry for the Ordinal Models*

	Unbiased and Symmetric	Symmetric	Unbiased
Partial Profile	4.43[a]	3.87	0.16
	3[b]	2	1
	.22[c]	.14	.69
Full Profile	10.39	3.63	5.61
	3	2	1
	.02	.16	.02

[a]chi-square value. [b]degrees of freedom. [c]p value.

It would appear that the assumption of symmetric use of the extent-of-preference scale may be imposed for both data sets. Imposition of this assumption would allow fitting of the ordinal logistic model by estimating 10 parameters rather than 12. Imposing unbiasedness on the partial profile data is also justifiable, saving estimation of an additional parameter. Imposing statistically justified constraints on a model increases the precision with which the parameters are estimated. We do not exploit this possibility here because it is not an option in the ordinal logistic program used for estimation and would require programming to be implemented, something many practitioners (and academics) would rather avoid. However this does mean that our calculation of the increase in efficiency that results from using extent-of-preference information will be conservative relative to what is obtainable when assumptions of unbiasedness and/or symmetry are warranted and utilized.

8.4.2   Estimates of Part Worths

The information of greatest interest has to do with the part worth estimates for the seven attributes. If the extent-of-preference information is to be of value, the coef-

---

[2]   It is not clear that biasedness could arise due to utilization of extent-of-preference information since the cutoff value that is used to test for bias (α_3) divides the responses identically in the two analyses.

ficient estimates should be proportional to those for the binary choice estimates, and the z-values should be greater (Swait and Louviere 1993). Since the standard errors are all very similar for the part worths within model, the z values are almost exactly proportional to the coefficients and can therefore be used to answer both questions.

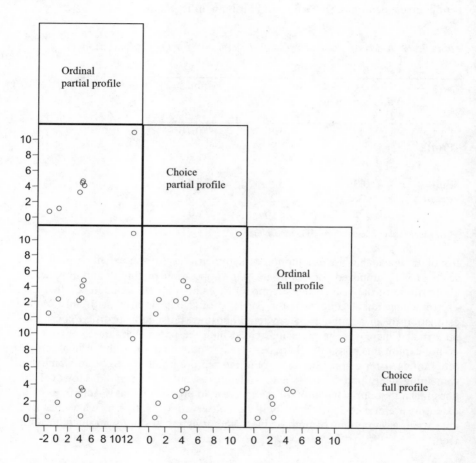

Figure 1:   *Scatterplot Matrix for Z Values for the Four Sets of Part Worth Estimates*

Figure 1 shows a scatter plot matrix of the z values for the four models. Careful examination of the figure reveals that a linear relationship through the origin appears to be appropriate, although somewhat less so for the left two figures of the bottom row, which show the relationship between the estimates based on choices for the full profiles with the estimates for the partial profiles. Table 3 bears this out. It shows the correlations, about zero rather than about the coefficient means, for all pairs of estimates.[3] The correlations are all at least 0.95, the lowest being between choice full profile and the two partial profile estimates. Examination of Figure 1 shows an outlying observation (for the attribute Strong) in the two left-most figures for the bottom row. The choice full profile model provides a z value for Strong that is only 0.30, whereas the z values for Strong for the two partial profile models are 4.43 and 4.17 for ordinal and choice, respectively (Table 1).

Table 3:   *Correlations (About the Origin) for the Z Values*

	Ordinal Partial Profile	Choice Partial Profile	Ordinal Full Profile	Choice Full Profile
Ordinal Partial Profile	1.00			
Choice Partial Profile	0.98	1.00		
Ordinal Full Profile	0.97	0.98	1.00	
Choice Full Profile	0.95	0.95	0.98	1.00

Given the apparent appropriateness of the perspective that the estimates from the four models are proportional to each other, a good assessment of the coefficients of proportionality can be obtained by a principal components analysis, again through the origin.[4] The first principal component explains 98% of the total variance about the origin in the z values. Assuming that the remaining 2% of the variance is estimation error, this analysis confirms our belief that no model provides a biased estimate of the part worths, although some may provide more efficient estimates than others.

The loadings of the four model estimates onto the first component are, from highest to lowest: Ordinal partial profile: .571, Choice partial profile: .514, Ordinal full profile: .494, Choice full profile: .407. The lowest loading for the choice full profile model reflects the somewhat poorer correlation of its estimates

---

[3]   The correlations are based upon a matrix Σ of variances and covariances calculated about the origin. That is, if the z values for the four different models are placed in the four columns of a matrix Z with n rows, then $\Sigma = Z'Z/n$.

[4]   The analysis is performed on the variance-covariance matrix calculated as described in the preceding footnote.

with those of the other models. These loadings provide our best estimate of the relative efficiency of estimates from the four models because the first principal component is proportional to a best estimate of the part worths and the loadings for this component provide for each model that multiplier which most closely reproduces its estimates.[5]

Thus the z values for the ordinal partial profile data are .571 / .514 = 1.112 times as large as for the choice partial profile data. This means that a study utilizing only choice information would have to sample $1.112^2 - 1 = 24\%$ more respondents to obtain equal precision in the part worth estimates.[6] For the more common full profile design the difference is greater: utilizing only choice information would require that data be collected for $(.494 / .407)^2 - 1 = 48\%$ more respondents than if extent-of-preference information is also collected. Given that the respondents must process full profile information before determining each choice, the extra work of having them rate their degree of preference for the chosen alternative would seem to be warranted.

8.5   Conclusion

The analysis in this paper provides answers, albeit based on a single data set, to several questions of interest to those who wonder whether paired choice data ought to be supplemented with extent-of-preference information.

- Consumers use extent-of-preference scales in a symmetric manner with respect to the two alternatives. It appears that an assumption of symmetry may be imposed in order to improve precision of part worth estimates, although perhaps not by enough to warrant the extra effort involved in estimation.
- There is some evidence that respondents favor choice of the first alternative in each pair when using full profile, but not partial profile, choice questions. This is consistent with a belief that full profile choice tasks are more likely to overburden respondents with information, inducing them to utilize a choice heuristic that departs from the assumption of multiattribute utility maximization that underlies choice based conjoint studies.
- It does not appear that utilizing extent-of-preference information introduces a bias into the part worth estimates relative to those estimates obtained from choice information alone. No formal statistical test of the hypothesis of bias is presented,

---

[5] Let V be the matrix of eigenvectors („loadings") that yields the principal components Y through the equation $Y = ZV$. Then $Z = YV'$ (because $VV' = I$). Hence the first principal component (column) of Y, denoted y, provides a best (least squares) approximation to the matrix Z by yv', where v is the first eigenvector (column) of V.

[6] The elements of the vector v (footnote one) are proportional to the error standard deviations, or scale parameters (Ben-Akiva and Lerman 1985; Swat and Louviere 1993), and the relative efficiencies of estimates are given by their squares. Taking sample sizes proportional to the inverses of relative efficiencies yields estimates of equal precision.

but the evidence of the adequacy of the notion that part worth estimates obtained from the four models analyzed are all proportional is nonetheless quite strong.

- Part worth estimates obtained by utilizing extent-of-preference information are more efficient. The gain in efficiency is greatest for full profile designs. There it is estimated that analyses utilizing choice information only must be based upon 48% more respondents than those that also collect and utilize extent-of-preference information. The difference is less striking for partial profile designs. There, choice-only analyses would require 24% more respondents to provide the same precision.

We can only conclude that supplementing paired choice conjoint data with extent-of-preference information warrants consideration. It is most attractive when many attributes are being studied simultaneously because in such settings choice sets of size two greatly reduce the burden placed upon respondents. Other work has shown, using three different data sets, that paired choice designs can lead to efficient part worth estimates (Chrzan and Elrod 1994). We find here that extent-of-preference information further increases the efficiency of these designs. The ability to analyze extent-of-preference information using available ordinal logistic regression software is also a plus. We show how simple analyses can determine whether the extent-of-preference information is providing valid information about the determinants of choice. Although the indication here is that it does, utilizing only the choice information from a study that also collects extent-of-preference information always remains an option. Finally, it must be remembered that all the advantages of choice-based conjoint studies cited at the beginning of this article are retained. In particular, the same formula is used to obtain choice share predictions for choice sets containing any number of alternatives.

8.6   References

Ben-Akiva, M. and Lerman, S. (1985), *Discrete Choice Analysis: Theory and Application to Travel Demand*, Cambridge.

Elrod, T. and Chrzan, K. (1994), *Partial Profile Conjoint Analysis: a Choice-Based Approach for handling large Numbers of Attributes,* Faculty of Business, University of Alberta, Canada.

Elrod, T. and Chrzan, K. (1995), Choice-based Approach for large Numbers of attributes, *Marketing News*, 29, 20-30.

Elrod, T., Louviere, J. and Davey, K.S. (1992), An empirical Comparison of ratings-based and choice-based Conjoint Models, *Journal of Marketing Research*, 24, 368-377.

McCullagh, P. (1980), Regression Models for Ordinal Data, with Discussion, *Journal of the Royal Statistical Society*, 42, 109-142.

Swait, J. and Louviere, J. (1993), The role of the Scale Parameter in the Estimation and Comparison of Multinomial Logit Models, *Journal of Marketing Research*, 30, 305-314.

Vriens, M., Oppewal, H. and Wedel, M. (1998), Ratings-based versus Choice-Based Latent Class Conjoint Models - an empirical Comparison, *Journal of the Market Research Society*, 40, 237-248.

Wittink, D.R., and Cattin, P. (1989), Commercial Use of Conjoint Analysis: An Update, *Journal of Marketing*, 53, 91-96.

Wittink, D.R.,Viens, M. and Burhenne, W. (1994), Commercial Use of Conjoint Analysis in Europe: Results and critical Reflections, *International Journal of Research in Marketing*, 11, 41-52.

9   A Multi-trait Multi-method Validity Test of Partworth Estimates

Wagner Kamakura and Muammer Ozer

9.1   Introduction

Conjoint analysis has already been widely accepted by marketing researchers as a popular instrument for the measurement of consumer preferences. Typical applications of conjoint analysis include new product design based on the relationship between product features and predicted choice behavior, benefit segmentation based on attribute preferences, etc. The popularity of conjoint analysis among marketing researchers hinges on the belief that it produces valid measurements of consumer preferences for the features of a product or service, and that it provides accurate predictions of choice behavior.

Given this importance, a vast literature has already emerged on the validity of conjoint analysis for the measurement of preferences. However, as we will discuss it in more details in our literature review section, these tests usually involve collecting data from two separate conjoint tasks (usually in the same interview), estimating partworths based on the first task, using the estimates to make predictions about the second task, and measuring predictive fit. We argue that these tests are more akin to test-retest reliability assessments than validation tests. Our literature review also indicates that comparative conjoint studies have yielded inconclusive results partly due to the different validity measures used as a basis for validation.

The purpose of this chapter is to compare various conjoint models across their partworth estimates based on actual behavior. Because we are comparing those methods across their partworth estimates, we use a Multitrait-Multimehod (MTMM) framework to assess the relationships among the methods and the partworth estimates. We test the relationships by using both the traditional MTMM analysis and a direct product methodology. The following section presents our literature review. After that, we provide a summary of the MTMM and direct product methodologies. Then, we present details about our research design and the conjoint models that we used to generate partworth estimates. Finally, we discuss our results and conclude the chapter with managerial and research implications.

9.2   Literature Review

Previous studies have proposed a number of methods to improve the validity and reliability of conjoint analysis. For example, Hagerty (1985) used a Q-type factor analysis to determine optimum weights that optimize the expected mean squared error of prediction in a validation sample. He tested his methodology by using both synthetic and real data. He manipulated the amount of overlaps in the clusters of partworth estimates in two Monte Carlo simulations. He also asked student subjects to rank-order eighteen job descriptions based on five attributes. Two of the eighteen job descriptions were used as a holdout sample. He compared his results with those of non-overlapping clustering and individual-level clustering. Based on Mean Squared Error (MSE) and the first choice prediction criteria, he showed that his methodology yielded higher predictive accuracy.

In another study, Kamakura (1988) used an agglomerative hierarchical method for simultaneous segmentation and estimation of conjoint models. He used a least squares procedure to identify segments that maximize the predictive validity of the segment-level partworth estimates. He compared his results with those of the two-stage segmentation procedure (individual-level estimation and clustering of sub-jects based on partworth estimates) by using both synthetic and empirical data based on holdout samples. His synthetic data included simulated preference rank-ings whereas his real data consisted of preference ratings of twenty-seven full-profile descriptions of checking account services. The holdout sample included eight profiles with the same attributes. He concluded that his methodology and the two-stage segmentation procedure yielded similar partworth estimates, but his proposed methodology gave consistently more accurate results. Ogawa (1987) also suggested a similar procedure, but used a logit-based estimation methodol-ogy. By using both simulated data and a set of preference data for Japanese auto-mobiles, he was able to show that his partworth estimates were internally valid. Similar to earlier studies, his validity assessment was also based on a holdout sample.

Wedel and Steenkamp (1989) proposed a fuzzy clusterwise regression algo-rithm to allow consumers to possess partial membership in multiple segments. Wedel and Steenkamp (1989) compared their procedure with a clusterwise regres-sion and Hagerthy's optimal weighting method. They first used a simulated data to validate the computational efficiency of their method. They later used a data set about customer satisfaction with respect to eight stock market scenarios and an-other data set for meat products. The results of the simulation showed that the methodology was computationally sound. In addition, judging by the percentage of first choices accurately predicted in a holdout sample with similar tasks, they concluded that their method and the clusterwise regression gave consistent results. They also concluded that their results were slightly better than those of Hagerty's method for well-defined clusters, but were worse for diffuse clusters. Similarly, DeSarbo et al. (1992) introduced a latent class methodology that allowed overlap-ping clusters for simultaneous segmentation and parameter estimation by using a mixture of multivariate conditional normal distributions. They successfully ap-plied the methodology to a conjoint experiment on remote controls for cars, simul-taneously identifying segments and generating partworth estimates within each segment. When they compared their methodology with various OLS procedures, they found that their latent class procedure outperformed them based on a likeli-hood-ratio test and a goodness of fit index (R-square).

As an example of incorporating exogenous variables into the segmentation process, Kamakura, Wedel and Agrawal (1994) presented a multinomial mixture model for the external analysis of rank-order, pick-any and conjoint choice data. They used their model to simultaneously determine market segments based on consumer characteristics and to generate partworth estimates for each segment. They used synthetic data to assess the performance of their methodology in recovering „true" parameters in a sample. They also used a conjoint experiment about banking services to assess the predictive validity based on a holdout sample. Both the estimation and the holdout samples included nine profiles that were equivalent, but distinct. They compared their model with a naïve model, an aggregate rank order logit model with dummy variables, and a latent class rank order logit model without concomitant variables. The results provided support for the internal and predictive validity of the proposed methodology.

Despite the proven performance of the models, the results of the comparative studies have been inconclusive. For instance, Hagerty (1985) and Kamakura (1988) found that their proposed methodologies outperformed the alternative OLS methodology. However, Green and Helsen (1989) conducted a conjoint experiment about student apartments and concluded that neither Hagerty's optimal weighting methodology nor Kamakura's method led to higher predictive validities than were obtained by conventional OLS. Their validation was based on a holdout data that was collected during the same experiment. The estimation set included eighteen full profile descriptions whereas the holdout sample had sixteen profiles with the same attributes. Similarly, Green, Krieger and Schaffer (1993) used three different studies to compare the predictive accuracy of Hagerty's optimal weighting methodology with those from individual OLS estimation. Based on a holdout validation sample, they showed that the optimal weighting methodology did not outperform the OLS method.

In an extensive Monte Carlo study, Vriens, Wedel and Wilms (1996) manipulated the number of subjects, number of profiles, number of segments, error variance, segment homogeneity, and segment similarity to compare nine methods of metric conjoint segmentation based on parameter recovery, goodness of fit and predictive power. The methods included the traditional two-stage approaches with (TTSWA) and without (TTSKM) hierarchical clustering, the alternative two-stage methods using Ward's clustering (ATSWA) and a K-means clustering procedure (ATSKM), the optimal weighting methods (OW), the optimal weighting method followed by a K-means clustering procedure (OWKM), the clusterwise regression procedure (CR), the fuzzy clusterwise regression procedure (FCR), and the latent class normal distribution model (LCN). In terms of goodness of fit, the results indicated that the two-stage clustering procedures (TTSWA, TTSKM, ATSWA, and ATSKM) outperformed OWKM, FR, and LCN. However, with respect to parameter recovery, methods that integrate segmentation and estimation aspects of conjoint analysis (integrated conjoint segmentation methods) outperformed the two-stage clustering procedures; most notably, the latent class methodology of DeSarbo et al. (1992) performed best among the integrated methods. Finally, the tested methods had similar predictive power based on an assessment with a holdout sample.

9.2.1   Validation of Partworth Estimates

Among the important managerial applications of conjoint analysis are the design
of new products, development of advertising and marketing strategies, and the
identification of relevant market segments for product targeting and positioning.
Managers achieve these objectives by considering the partworth estimates obtained from a conjoint study. Despite the importance of partworth estimates in
marketing, most research studies have investigated the ability of conjoint models
in predicting overall preferences for bundles of attributes, as opposed to investigating the validity of partworth estimates. Previous researchers such as Vriens,
Wedel, and Wilms (1996) looked at parameter recovery measured by the root-
mean-squared-error between the „true" (simulated) and estimated values of the
partworths. Our study aims to compare the partworth estimates obtained from
different conjoint models with actual consumer behavior that is directly related to
these estimates.

There are a few studies that have already looked into the validation of part-
worth estimates. However, they have primarily focused on the consistency of the
partworth estimates across estimation procedures. For example, in an earlier study
about consumer preferences for banks in which to open a checking account, Jain et
al. (1979) compared the partworth estimates obtained from different conjoint
estimation techniques such as MONANOVA, JOHNSON, LINMAP, LOGIT, and
OLS. Based on a holdout sample of conjoint profiles, they showed that the methods yielded significantly different partworth estimates across different data collection methods. In addition, they showed that the LINMAP procedure was effective
in predicting the first choice in the holdout sample whereas the OLS procedure
was more effective in predicting the least preferred choice in the sample. Leigh et
al. (1984) also compared the partworth coefficients estimated by using different
procedures such as rank-order, paired comparison, graded paired comparison, and
ranking scale with the weights elicited through a self-explicated procedure for
hand-held calculators. The results failed to provide support for the presumed
greater reliability and validity of the tested procedures over the self-explicated
procedure. The reliability was assessed by test-retest comparison whereas the
predictive validity was measured based on a simulated choice (raffle) in a separate
interview.

In a conjoint experiment involving student apartments, Akaah (1991) compared the predictive performance of self-explicated, traditional conjoint and hybrid
conjoint models under alternative data collection modes including in-person interviews, mail questionnaires and telephone interviews. By using eighteen estimation
profiles and six holdout profiles, they showed that the self-explicated and traditional conjoint models gave fairly similar attribute importance weights across the
different data collection modes. In addition, Darmon and Rouzies (1991) conducted a conjoint simulation to investigate the internal validity of part worth estimates across different design (full vs. fractional) and different estimation procedures (LINMAP, MONANOVA and OLS). By comparing the partworth estimates
generated by known functional forms („true" values) with those generated by a
conjoint analysis procedure, they showed that the partworth estimates were more

valid with full design rather than with a fractional factorial design, and with OLS rather than other estimation procedure when a fractional design was mandatory. In a subsequent simulation study, Darmon and Rouzies (1994) also investigated the role of error in the reliability and internal validity of part worth estimates. The results indicated that when there is a low level of error in the input data less important attributes are underestimated whereas when there is a high level of error in the input data less important attributes are overestimated.

9.2.2 Validation Measures

Researchers argued that the inconclusive results of previous comparative studies could be due to several factors. Among the most important factors affecting the results is the use of one or two data sets and/or the use of a small holdout sample (Hagerty 1993; Vriens, Wedel and Wilms 1996). For example, Hagerty (1993) stated that the type of brands included in a holdout sample could affect the validity results and urged researchers to consider multiple holdout samples for cross validation. It can also be due to various validation measures used in the literature.

Previous studies have used different validity measures. Given the difficulties in externally validating conjoint experiments, many studies have emphasized internal validity which can be measured by a test/re-test reliability analysis and/or cross-validation, i.e., the ability of a model to predict the rankings or the first choice in a hold-out sample (Green, Krieger and Agarwal 1993). Alternatively, some studies also used Monte Carlo simulations to validate or compare alternative conjoint methodologies (Vriens, Wedel and Wilms 1996) on synthetic data.

In this chapter, we attempt to assess the external and convergent validity of the preference measurements obtained from various conjoint methods. We used actual behavior of individuals for comparison. More specifically, we compared the preferences of customers of a major bank for a factorial design of account characteristics with their actual banking behavior on those dimensions that were measured immediately prior to the conjoint study and were totally independent from the conjoint task. We believe that using actual behavior for validating and/or comparing alternative conjoint methods can reduce some of the concerns associated with holdout samples and other alternative validation measures.

There are a few studies that have already used actual behavior for validation. For example, Krishnamurthi (1988) asked MBA students and their spouses to rank-order 28 hypothetical job descriptions. Three months later, he asked the couples to rank-order the job offers that they received. The predictive validity was calculated based on the actual job choices that the models predicted. Similarly, Srinivasan and Park (1997) conducted a conjoint study to identify how important different factors were for MBA students in choosing among job offers. Three months later they asked the participants about the number of job offers they had and the one they selected. The predictive validity was assessed based on a comparison between the actual job choices and the predictions of the conjoint model. Although this can also be a useful measure, the three-month time lag can involve changes in the environment and in individuals' preferences.

Some researchers have also used raffles to simulate an actual choice environment. For example, Leigh et al. (1984) first conducted a conjoint experiment for hand-held calculators. Two weeks later, their subjects participated in a raffle for a calculator of their choice from a predetermined set of ten calculators. The subjects' choice in the raffle represented actual behavior and was a base for predictive validity. Although these measures provide a powerful way of assessing the validity of conjoint studies, the results can be subject to a carry-over bias. In other words, once the respondents participate in a study, they tend to remember their answers and be consistent if they are required to participate in a similar study (Morwitz et al. 1993). This bias can be reduced by having a longer time period between the two studies. However, as the time gap gets larger, the conditions and individuals' preferences can change. Thus, we will not know whether the difference between the estimation and actual behavior is due to the method used or due to the changes in the conditions. Furthermore, these studies focused on predictive validity of the composite utilities, rather than on the measurement of preferences for each attribute

9.3   The Multitrait Multimethod (MTMM) Methodology

Because we are interested in comparing the validity of various conjoint method-ologies in measuring preferences for various attributes, we compared the methods within an MTMM framework. The MTMM analysis was first introduced by Campbell and Fiske (1959) for construct validation. A typical MTMM matrix includes correlations among multiple traits (concepts) measured by multiple methods and enables researchers to determine the extent of similarities of the methods (convergence) and the extent of uniqueness of the traits (discrimination).

Campbell and Fiske (1959) also suggested specific criteria for *convergent* and *discriminant* validity in analyzing an MTMM matrix. *Convergent validity* is achieved when the correlations between attempts to measure the same concept with different methods (i.e., monotrait-heteromethod correlations) are significantly different from zero and sufficiently large. On the other hand, *discriminant validity* is achieved when:

1. the correlations between attempts to measure the same concept with different methods (i.e., the monotrait-heteromethod correlations) are larger than the correlations between attempts to measure different concepts with different methods (i.e., the heterotrait-hetereomethod correlations);
2. the correlations between attempts to measure the same concept with different methods (i.e., the monotrait-heteromethod correlations) are larger than the correlations between different concepts measured by the same method (i.e., the heterotrait-monomethod correlations); and finally
3. the patterns of correlations between different concepts are consistent under the same or different methods (Bagozzi and Yi 1991).

Despite providing these criteria, Campbell and Fiske (1959) did not specify any objective mechanism to test them. The criteria are subjectively assessed by researchers, thus leading to ambiguous interpretations. Researchers later developed statistical procedure to analyze MTMM matrices, most notably Confirmatory Factor Analysis (CFA) and direct product decomposition. CFA decomposes the total variation into (1) the variation due to differences in individual trait scores, (2) the variation due to differences in systematic biases induced by methods used and (3) the variation due to random error (Bagozzi and Yi 1991). The CFA methodology assumes that the total variation is a linear combination (additive) of the variations due to traits, methods and error. Researchers have questioned the validity of this assumption by showing some level of interaction between traits and methods (Campbell and O'Connell 1967; Lastovicka et al. 1990; Kumar and Dillon 1992).

As an alternative, Browne (1984) proposed a methodology called Direct Product Model for analyzing MTMM matrices based on a multiplicative decomposition of the trait and method effects. Under this methodology, the observed covariance matrix is expressed as

(1) $\quad \Sigma = Z(P_M \otimes P_T + E^2) Z$

Where Σ is the population covariance matrix for the observed scores; P_M and P_T are nonnegative definite matrices of method and trait correlations, respectively; E^2 is a nonnegative definite diagonal matrix for the unique variances; Z is a nonnegative definite diagonal matrix of scale constant; and $\otimes$ represents a right direct (Kronecker) product. Note that the elements of P_M and P_T represent multiplicative components of common score correlations, that is correlations corrected for attenuation as opposed to observed score correlations. In addition, the identification of scale factor estimates requires one equality constraint per method. For instance, one may select a trait and set all its scale parameters (corresponding diagonal elements of Z) equal to unity (Wothke and Browne 1990).

An important aspect of the direct product model is that the P_M and P_T matrices can be directly used to test the convergent and discriminant validity of constructs as suggested by Campbell and Fiske (1959). More specifically, convergent validity is achieved when the correlations among methods in P_M are positive and large. On the other hand, discriminant validity is achieved when (1) the correlations among traits in P_T are low; (2) the method correlations in P_M are greater than the trait correlations in P_T; and (3) the direct product model fits the data (Bagozzi and Yi 1991).

Previous studies have compared the additive and multiplicative approaches to analyzing MTMM matrices (Lastovicka et al. 1990; Bagozzi and Yi 1991; Kumar and Dillon 1992). Despite the inconclusive results, the studies suggested that the use of a particular methodology should be based on theory. Furthermore, Kumar and Dillon (1992) argued that when the primary purpose is to assess the extent to which the MTMM data satisfy the Campbell and Fiske (1959) criteria, the direct product model should suffice. As we will discuss it further in the following section in more details, we compare the partworth estimates of various conjoint models for banking services. In addition, we also compare the partworth estimates with actual behavior. Because we are using actual behavior as one of the methods the partworth estimates interact with the traits. In other words, the partworth estimates of the conjoint models should be different than actual behavior. Furthermore, because our primary focus is to test the criteria set by Campbell and Fiske (1959) we use a direct product model to conduct the MTMM analysis.

The following section briefly explains the research methodology and the various conjoint models used in the MTMM analysis. After that, we present the results of the MTMM analysis.

9.4   Description of Data and Methods

Our Multitrait Multi-Method analysis will be based on a comparison of partworth estimates for multiple attributes obtained from four different estimation methods, with actual behavior, directly related to the attributes preferences measured in the conjoint task, observed from the same consumers. For this purpose, we use the same data utilized by Kamakura et al. (1994) to illustrate their latent-class conjoint segmentation model. This commercial study involved four attributes for checking accounts, each manipulated in three levels:

- *MINBAL*: minimum balance required to exempt the customer from a monthly service fee ($0, $500 or $1,000)
- *CHECK*: cost to the customer per checked issued (0c, 15c or 35c)
- *FEE*: monthly service fee ($0, $3 or $6)
- *ATM*: availability and cost of ATM (no access, free ATM, or paid ATM @ 75c per transaction)

Two distinct but equivalent sets of 9 hypothetical checking accounts were generated using a fractional factorial design. A random sample of 269 customers from the bank was asked to rank the nine accounts from the first set in order of preference. After a series of other questions related to the same commercial study, the respondents were asked to rank the second set of profiles. These two similar tasks provided us the opportunity of replicating the test-retest reliability comparisons that are commonly reported in the conjoint literature.

In addition to the two conjoint data sets, we also obtained the following information (in disguised and anonymous format) from the bank, regarding the participants' banking behavior in the 6 months immediately prior to the conjoint task:

- BALANCE: average balance kept in the account (earning 5% interest)
- NCHECK: number of checks issued per month
- SRVFEE: number of times the customer paid a monthly service fee
- NATM: number of ATM transactions per month

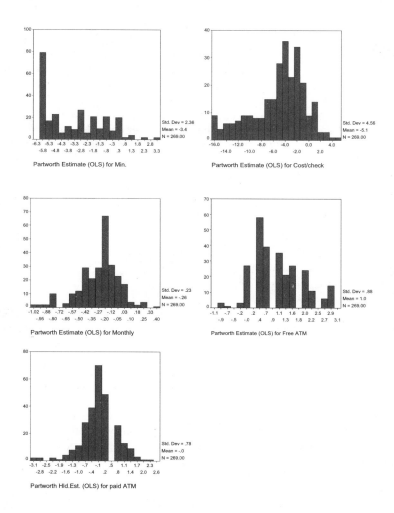

Figure 1:   Least squares regressions (OLS) to the data from each of the 269 subjects

This combination of conjoint and behavior data provides us with a rare opportunity of testing for the external validity of the preference measurements obtained from conjoint analysis using a variety of estimation methods. Preferences for the levels of the four attributes in the conjoint task can be viewed as multiple traits. On the other hand, measurements for each of these attributes obtained from different estimation methods, along with the actual banking behavior associated with these attributes represent multiple measurement methods, leading to the classic Multitrait Multi-methods approach for assessing the validity of measurement instruments. Given that we know the actual behavior of the respondents, we already have an idea of the inter-trait correlations. For instance, people who are sensitive to minimum balance should be more willing to pay a monthly fee whereas people who do not care about minimum balance (i.e., people who have money in their accounts) do not want to pay a monthly fee. In addition, given the inconclusive results of the previous comparative conjoint validation studies, we are more interested in the inter-method correlations. Moreover, one of our „methods" is the actual banking behavior observed immediately prior to the conjoint task, providing a benchmark for assessing predictive validity.

The following measurement methods are used in our MTMM analysis:

1. individual OLS estimates,
2. Kamakura's (1988) agglomerative hierarchical regression(KAM),
3. Hagerty's (1985) Q-factor methodology (HAG), and
4. Latent Class Rank Logit model (Kamakura et al. 1994).

   The first method (OLS) involves the estimation of a linear regression for each respondent across all nine profiles, using the (inverted) preference ranking as the dependent variable. The next two models (KAM and HAG) attempt to improve the predictive validity of the partworth estimates by estimating them within homogeneous groups of consumers (KAM), or by obtaining an optimal partitioning of the sample via Q-factor analysis. The emphasis in these two techniques is obtaining individual-level estimates that would maximize the ability to predict preferences. The main purpose of the latent-class rank logit model, on the other hand, is market segmentation, i.e., identify relatively groups of consumers who are relatively homogeneous in their preferences for the attributes.
   Application of least squares regressions (OLS) to the data from each of the 269 subjects leads to the partworth estimates displayed in Figure 1. The partworths for *MINBAL*, *CHECK* and *FEE* are the regression coefficients for the (mean-centered) attributes, while the partworths for ATM are the coefficients for the effects-coded dummies for *Free ATM* and *Paid ATM*.

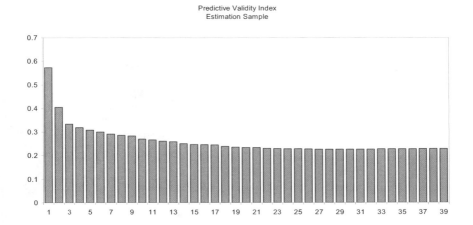

Figure 2:   Predictive validity indices

The hierarchical clusterwise regression approach (KAM) joins consumers into hierarchical segments to maximize a predictive validity index, which indicates the ability of predicting individual-level preferences using cluster-level estimates of partworths. Application of the model to our data led to the predictive validity indices displayed in Figure 2. Based on this figure, and on the purpose of maximizing predictive accuracy, we chose the 23-cluster solution, which is not appropriate for segmentation purposes, but produces the highest expected predictive accuracy. The distribution of partworth estimates across the 269 consumers are shown in Figure 3.

The method proposed by Hagerty (1985) (HAG) amounts to a Q-factor analysis of the between-subjects covariance matrix of preference ratings. The eigenvalues obtained from applying Hagerty's Q-factor analysis to our data are displayed in Figure 4. Based on these values, we decided for a 3-factor solution. The individual-level estimates of partworths are summarized in Figure 5.

Application of the latent-class rank logit model led to 4 latent classes, chosen on the basis of the ICOMP criterion (see Kamakura et al. 1994 for details on this analysis). The individual-level estimates, based on this 4-class solution are summarized in Figure 6. The reader should note that while the other approaches being compared specify a linear model relating the attributes to the observed preferences, the latent-class rank logit model is applied to preference rankings. Consequently, the relationship between the attributes and the observed preferences is non-linear, and the estimated partworths are not directly comparable to the ones obtained from the other approaches.

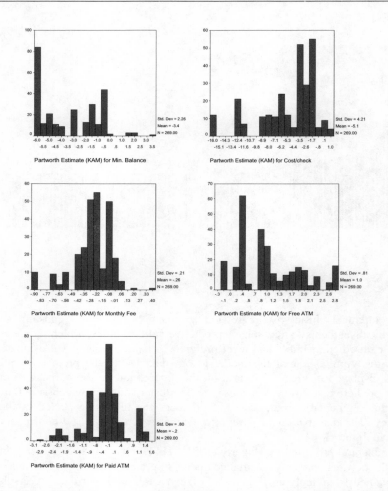

Figure 3: *Distribution of partworth estimates across the 269 consumers*

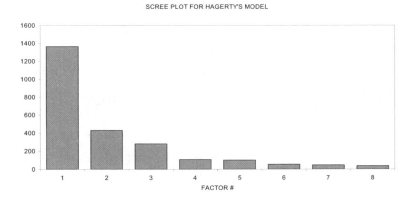

Figure 4: Eigenvalues obtained from applying Hagerty's Q-factor analysis

Aside from the estimates shown in Figures 1, 3, 5 and 6, we also obtained estimates for each of the models using the second set of conjoint profiles. The correlations between these two measurements for the same constructs and subjects using
the same method in two separate tasks provide us with the measures of test-retest
reliability for each construct (partworth) and method.

As mentioned earlier, we also had data on the actual banking behavior of each
of the 269 respondents on variables that are directly related to the estimated partworths. Consumers who are highly sensitive to minimum balance (extreme negative partworths for *MINBAL*) would be expected to have lower average balances
(BALANCE). Therefore, the partworths estimates for *MINBAL* obtained from any
method should be positively correlated to BALANCE.

Similarly, those who are highly sensitive to cost/check (extreme negative
partworths for *CHECK*) would be expected to issue more checks per month
(NCHECK). In order to maintain a positive correlation between partworth estimates and observed behavior, we invert the sign of the partworth estimates for
CHECK, which should then be positively correlated with NCHECK.

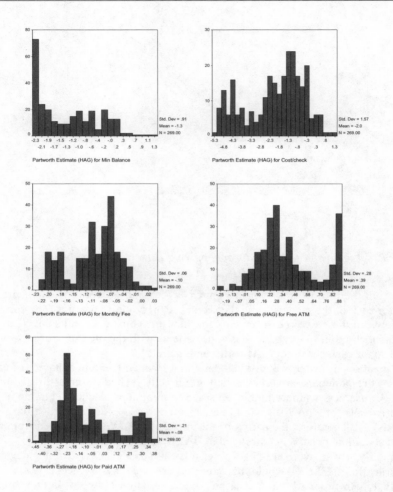

Figure 5:   The individual-level estimates of partworths

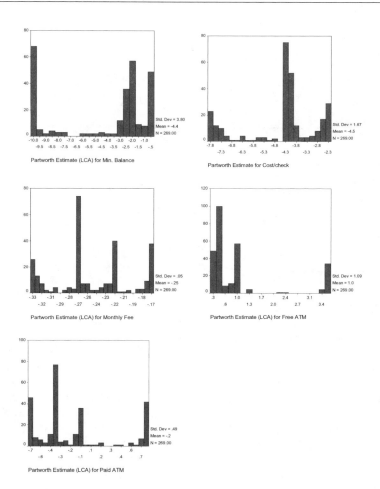

Figure 6:   The individual-level estimates based on this 4-class solution

Table 1:   *MTMM Matrix*

	MIN. BALANCE					COST/CHECK					MONTHLY FEE					ATM ACCESS				
	ACT	OLS	KAM	HAG	LCA	ACT	(OLS)	(KAM)	(HAG)	(LCA)	ACT	OLS	KAM	HAG	LCA	ACT	OLS	KAM	HAG	LCA
average balance in past year	100																			
OLS estimate for min. balance	39	87																		
KAM estimate for min. balance	39	94	76																	
HAG estimate for min. balance	39	99	93	86																
LCA estimate for min. balance	35	93	91	93	83															
checks issued per month	32	6	8	7	10	100														
(OLS estimate for cost/check)	33	51	47	55	58	17	68													
(KAM estimate for cost/check)	30	56	52	58	64	16	87	60												
(HAG estimate for cost/check)	38	64	60	65	69	13	89	86	73											
(LCA estimate for cost/check)	13	24	25	26	35	6	50	48	45	42										
number of times paid fee	-54	-38	-35	-39	-37	5	-35	-34	-42	-18	100									
OLS estimate for monthly fee	-16	-32	-31	-30	-37	7	-30	-41	-60	-23	26	56								
KAM estimate for monthly fee	-24	-38	-37	-37	-41	-3	-41	-50	-65	-22	25	81	37							
HAG estimate for monthly fee	-37	-59	-56	-60	-66	-15	-89	-85	-99	-45	40	61	66	70						
LCA estimate for monthly fee	-10	1	1	0	-13	-8	-45	-41	-43	-81	15	24	24	44	48					
number of ATM transactions	0	2	5	2	3	31	-15	-14	-16	-6	23	14	12	15	15	100				
OLS importance of ATM	10	26	28	19	14	10	-3	-1	9	-44	1	13	2	-7	39	13	39			
KAM importance of ATM	12	27	32	22	14	6	-4	-2	9	-43	-6	5	2	-7	39	10	83	24		
HAG importance of ATM	27	54	56	55	58	12	42	43	45	16	-21	-33	-32	-48	20	16	11	11	61	
LCA importance of ATM	-10	1	1	-1	-13	-8	-46	-41	-43	-82	16	24	23	44	100	15	39	39	19	15

Customers who already pay monthly service fees (SRVFEE) should show less resistance to monthly fees (*FEE*) than those who rarely pay monthly service fees. Therefore, the partworth estimates for *FEE* should be positively correlated with the observed behavior SRVFEE, irrespective of the estimation method.

One should also expect customers with a large number of ATM transactions (NATM) to value this service more than those who are light users or non-users of it. In order to measure respondents' perceived value for ATM's, we create a new measure (*ATMV*) by subtracting the partworth for *paid ATM* (75c) from the partworth for *free ATM*. This new measure of preference for ATM's (*ATMV*) should be positively correlated with the number of ATM transactions (NATM).

Because the relationships among the partworth estimates obtained from the various methods and the observed behaviors are not necessarily linear, we used Spearman rank correlations to obtain the Multitrait Multi-method matrix. The resulting MTMM matrix is shown in Table 1, organized by methods. We also include the test-retest reliability correlations in the diagonals. These test-retest correlations show that the OLS and HAG methods tend to produce more reliable measurement than the other two approaches.

9.5   MTMM Analysis

Once creating the MTMM matrix in Table 1, we conducted a conventional MTMM analysis as suggested by Campbell and Fiske (1959) and a direct product model. A visual inspection of the MTMM matrix indicates some evidence of convergent and discriminant validity among the estimation methods. Convergent validity among the four estimations is clearly evident for *MINBAL* and *CHECK*, for which the monotrait-heteromethod correlations are very strong. Convergent validity for *FEE* is not as strong, but still statistically significant at 0.01. Convergent validity for *ATMV* is only evident for OLS, KAM and LCA.

Discriminant validity is also generally established in Table 1 among the four estimation methods, for *MINBAL, CHECK* and *FEE*. Monotrait-heteromethod correlations are larger than the heterotrait-heteromethod and heterotrait-monomethods correlations. However, discriminant validity (especially for the third criterion discussed earlier in this chapter, regarding the patterns of heterotrait correlations) is more easily verified with the direct product model, as discussed below.

In order to establish a stronger comparison of the different conjoint models, we applied a direct product decomposition to the MTMM matrix. We used MUTMUM (Browne 1992) to test the convergent and discriminant validity of the MTMM matrix. Table 2 presents the matrices of correlations among methods, P_M, and traits, P_T. As can be seen from the P_M matrix, the correlations among the different conjoint methods are very large. More specifically, as can be seen from the matrix, the correlations are significantly different from zero and sufficiently large, indicating strong convergent validity among the estimation methods. However, when it comes to explaining actual behavior, the partworth estimates of the conjoint models have relatively low correlations with the actual banking behavior. This implies that even though the conjoint models are consistent in their predictions, they have a relatively lower explanatory power with respect to actual behavior. This can be due to many external factors affecting actual behavior that were not included in the conjoint models. Among the four methods, OLS and HAG produce slightly better correlations with actual behavior, while LCA produces the lowest correlation, which is understandable, because the latter method constrains the individual-level estimates to the convex hull of the latent-class estimates.

Table 2:   *PM and PT matrices*

a. P_M: Method Correlations

	ACT	OLS	KAM	HAG	LCA
ACT	1.000				
OLS	0.468	1.000			
KAM	0.441	1.000	1.000		
HAG	0.484	0.972	0.913	1.000	
LCA	0.371	0.875	0.843	0.858	1.000

ACT: Actual behavior,
OLS: OLS estimation,
KAM: Kamakura's methodology,
HAG: Hagerthy's methodology, and
LCA: Latent Class Analysis.

b. P_T: Trait Correlations

	MBAL	CHE	FEE	ATM
MBAL	1.000			
CHE	0.651	1.000		
FEE	-0.579	-0.912	1.000	
ATM	0.343	-0.111	0.168	1.000

MBAL: Minimum Balance,
CHE: Number of checks issued per month,
FEE: Number of times that the individuals paid a monthly fee, and
ATM: The number of ATM transactions.

On the other hand, a visual inspection of the P_T matrix indicates that the correlations among the different traits vary. For instance, consistent with our expectations, the amount of balance in the account is negatively correlated with the monthly fee paid (i.e., the less an individual has in his/her bank account, the more monthly fee he/she pays.) Similarly, the number of checks issued has a negative correlation with the number of monthly fee paid.

   One advantage of the direct product model is that we can directly test the convergent and discriminant validity criteria established by Campbell and Fiske (1959). Convergent validity is achieved when the correlations among the methods in the P_M matrix are positive and large. From the P_M matrix, it is evident that the correlations are positive and sufficiently large. Thus, the conjoint methods are in agreement with each other. Discriminant validity is achieved when (1) the correlations among traits in P_T are low; (2) the method correlations in P_M are greater than the trait correlations in P_T; and (3) the direct product model fits the data (Bagozzi and Yi 1991). As can be seen from the P_T matrix, the first two conditions for discriminant are only partially met. The trait correlation between *CHECK* (with inverted sign) and *FEE* is strong and negative, indicating that customers who are sensitive to charges per check are also sensitive to monthly fees. In order to assess the last condition for the discriminant validity, we looked at the fit indices for the direct product model. Based on the OLS estimation procedure of MUTMUM, the model's discrepancy function value was 6.438 with corresponding $\chi^2 = 1884.31$, d.f. = 159 and p = 0.00. In addition, the model's Root Mean Square Error of Approximation (RMSEA) was 0.201. All these indices suggest that the model does not fit the data. Overall, when we take into account all these three conditions we can conclude that the traits are not distinct. This is consistent with our initial expectations that the traits in this study should be correlated. Therefore, the lack of discriminant validity is a reflection of the traits being measured, rather than the measurement instruments.

   Although we have theoretical and empirical reasons for using the direct product model for conducting the MTMM analysis, we also wanted to use the CFA to see whether we could get similar results. Like the models of many other researchers (Kalleberg and Kluegel 1975; Lee 1980; Marsh and Hocevar 1983; and Lastovicka et al. 1990), our model, after more than a dozen attempts, also yielded uninterpretable results, such as correlations outside the -1 and $+1$ range, negative unique variances, and nonconverging solutions. As suggested by Bagozzi and Yi (1991), these types of solutions can also be considered as an indication of why an additive model (CFA) is not appropriate to analyze MTMM matrices such as ours.

9.6 Conclusions and Directions of Future Research

Conjoint analysis has been a popular methodology for both researchers and practitioners. One important aspect of conjoint analysis is the validity of the results. As we discussed earlier, previous studies provide quite a large number of ways of improving the validity of conjoint analysis. Previous literature also presents a number of comparative studies investigating the extent to which those methods improve the validity of conjoint analysis. The results of these comparative studies have been inconclusive. The inconclusive results might be due to various reasons. One of the important reasons is the validity measure used for comparison. Our literature review indicates that previous studies have primarily used holdout samples and simulations. Only a few rare studies validated conjoint analysis with actual behavior, observed after a certain time period such as three months.

We used actual banking behavior of individuals immediately prior to a conjoint experiment as a benchmark for comparison, eliminating the concerns about the validity measures. By using an MTMM framework, we compared the actual banking behavior on four dimensions with the part worth estimates generated by the OLS procedure, Kamakura's and Hagerthy's methodologies, and the latent class analysis. The results were consistent with the findings of Vriens et al. (1996), indicating that the methods had more or less similar predictive performance. However, one interesting result was that despite the strong consistency among the methods, the correlations between the estimates and the actual behavior were relatively low, which is understandable due to the multitude of factors affecting actual behavior, but are not considered in the conjoint design.

Another aspect of the partworth estimates rarely considered in conjoint validation studies is their logical consistency. For example, in our study one should expect customers to prefer to keep a lower minimum balance, pay less per check, pay lower monthly fees, and have free access to ATM's. Table 3 reports the percentage of the 269 respondents with logically consistent estimates for each of these attributes for the four methods we tested. One can see that all methods produced a high percentage of logically consistent estimates, but the segment-level models (KAM and LCA) performed slightly better.

Table 3:   *The percentage of the 269 respondents with logically consistent esti-*
              mates for each of these attributes for the four methods tested.

| | Proportion of cases with logically consistent estimates | | | |
	OLS	KAM	HAG	LCA
Minimum Balance	92.6%	96.7%	90.3%	100.0%
Cost/check	91.8%	95.2%	93.7%	100.0%
Monthly Fee	94.4%	97.4%	98.5%	100.0%
Free-Paid ATM	95.2%	92.9%	100.0%	100.0%
Overall	93.5%	95.5%	95.6%	100.0%

This is certainly just one attempt to cross-validate preference measurements obtained through various conjoint models. Replication of the Multitrait Multi-
method analysis for other applications of conjoint analysis, using real behavior as
a criterion for external validity, are needed before generalizable conclusions can
be drawn about the validity of preference measurements via conjoint analysis. In
addition, future research can extend this study by investigating other conjoint
models and other data collection modes.

9.7   References

Akaah, I. P. (1991), Predictive Performance of Self-Explicated, Traditional Conjoint and
    Hybrid Conjoint Models Under Alternative Data Collection Modes, *Journal of the
    Academy of Marketing Science*, 19, 309-314.

Bagozzi, R. P. and Yi, Y. (1991), Multitrait-Multimethod Matrices in Consumer Research,
    Journal of Consumer Research, 17, 426-439.

Browne, M. W. (1992), *MUTMUM User's Guide*, Version of April, 1992, The Ohio State
    University, Department of Psychology, Columbus, Ohio.

Browne, M. W. (1984), The Decomposition of Multitrait-Multimethod Matrices, *British
    Journal of Mathematical and Statistical Psychology*, 37, 1-21.

Campbell, D. T. and Fiske, D. F. (1959), Convergent and Discriminant Validation by the
    Multitrait-Multimethod Matrix, *Psychological Bulletin*, 56, 81-105.

Campbell, D. T. and O'Connell, E. J. (1967), Method Factors Multitrait-Multimethod
    Matrices: Multiplicative Rather than Additive?, *Multivariate Behavioral Research*, 2,
    409-426.

Darmon, R. Y. and Rouzies, D, (1991), Internal Validity Assessment of Conjoint Estimated
    Attribute Importance Weights, *Journal of the Academy of Marketing Science*, 19, 315-
    322.

Darmon, R. Y. and Rouzies, D. (1994), Reliability and Internal Validity of Conjoint Estimated Utility Functions Under Error-Free Versus Error-Full Conditions, *International Journal of Research in Marketing*, 11, 465-476.

DeSarbo, W. S., Wedel, M., Vriens, M. and Ramaswamy, V. (1992), Latent Class Metric Conjoint Analysis, *Marketing Letters*, 3, 273-289.

Green, P. E. and Helsen, K. (1989), Cross-Validation Assessment of Alternatives to Individual-Level Conjoint Analysis: A Case Study, *Journal of Marketing Research*, 26, 346-350.

Green, P. E., Krieger, A. M. and Agarwal, M. K. (1993), A Cross Test of Four Modelsfor Quantifying Multiattribute Preferences, *Marketing Letters*, 4, 369-380.

Green P. E., Krieger, A. and Schaffer, C. M. (1993), An Empirical Test of Optimal Respondent Weighting in Conjoint Analysis, *Journal of the Academy of Marketing Science*, 21, 345-351.

Hagerty, M. R. (1985), Improving the Predictive Power of Conjoint Analysis: The Use of Factor Analysis and Cluster Analysis, *Journal of Marketing Research*, 22, 168-184.

Hagerty, M. R. (1993), Can Segmentation Improve Predictive Accuracy in Conjoint Analysis? *Journal of the Academy of Marketing Science*, 21, 353-355.

Jain, A. K., Acito, F., Malhotra, N. K. and Mahajan, V. (1979), A Comparison of the Internal Validity of Alternative Parameter Estimation Methods in Decompositional Multiattribute Preference Models, *Journal of Marketing Research*, 16, 313-322.

Kalleberg, A. L. and Kluegel, J. R. (1975), Analysis of the Multitrait-Multimethod Matrix: Some Limitations and an Alternative, *Journal of Applied Psychology*, 60, 1-9.

Kamakura, W. A. (1988), A Least Squares Procedure for Benefit Segmentation with Conjoint Experiments, *Journal of Marketing Research*, 25, 157-167.

Kamakura, W. A., Wedel, M. and Agrawal, J. (1994), Concomitant Variable Latent Class Models for Conjoint Analysis, *International Journal of Research in Marketing*, 11, 451-464.

Krishnamurthi, L. (1989), Conjoint Models of Family Decision Making, *International Journal of Research in Marketing*, 5, 185-198.

Kumar, A. and Dillon, W. R. (1992), An Integrative Look at the use of Additive and Multiplicative Covariance Structure Models in the Analysis of MTMM Data, *Journal of Marketing Research*, 29, 51-64.

Lastovicka, J. L., Murry, J. P., and Joachimsthaler, E. A. (1990), Evaluating the Measurement Validity of Lifestyle Typologies with Qualitative Measures and Multiplicative Factoring, *Journal of Marketing Research*, 27, 11-23.

Lee, S. Y. (1980), Estimation of Covariance Structure Models with Parameters Subject to Functional Constrains, *Psychometrika*, 45, 309-324.

Leigh, T. W., MacKay, D. B. and Summers, J. O. (1984), Reliability and Validity of Conjoint Analysis and Self-Explicated Weights: A Comparison, *Journal of Marketing Research*, 21, 456-462.

Marsh, H. W. and Hocevar, D. (1983), Confirmatory Factor Analysis of Multimethod-Multitrait Matrices, *Journal of Educational Measurement*, 20, 231-248.

Morwitz, V. G., Johnson, E. and Schmittlein, D. (1993), Does Measuring Intend Change Behavior? *Journal of Consumer Behavior*, 20, 1-16.

Ogawa, K. (1987), An Approach to Simultaneous Estimation and Segmentation in Conjoint Analysis, *Marketing Science*, 6, 66-81.

Srinivasan, V. and Park, C. (1997), Surprising Robustness of the Self-Explicated Approach to Consumer Preference Structure Measurement, *Journal of Marketing Research*, 34, 286-291.

Wedel, M. and Steenkamp, J. B. (1989), Fuzzy Clusterwise Regression Approach to Benefit Segmentation, *International Journal of Research in Marketing*, 6, 241-258.

Vriens, M., Wedel, M. and Wilms, T. (1996), Metric Conjoint Segmentation Methods: A Monte Carlo Comparison, *Journal of Marketing Research*, 33, 73-85.

Wothke, W. and Browne, M. W. (1990), The Direct Product Model for the MTMM Matrix Parameterized as a Second Order Factor Analysis Model, *Psychometrika*, 55, 255-262.

10 Conjoint Preference Elicitation Methods in the Broader Context of Random Utility Theory Preference Elicitation Methods

Jordan Louviere, David Hensher and Joffre Swait

10.1 Introduction

The purpose of this chapter is to place conjoint analysis techniques within the broader framework of preference elicitation techniques that are consistent with the Random Utility Theory (RUT) paradigm. This allows us to accomplish the following objectives: explain how random utility theory provides a level playing field on which to compare preference elicitation methods, and why virtually all conjoint methods can be treated as a special case of a much broader theoretical framework. We achieve this by:

- discussing wider issues in modelling preferences in the RUT paradigm, the implications for understanding consumer decision processes and practical prediction, and how conjoint analysis methods fit into the bigger picture.
- discussing how a level playing field allows meaningful comparisons of a variety of preference elicitation methods and sources of preference data (conjoint methods are only one of many types), which in turn allows us to unify many disparate research streams;
- discussing how a level playing field allows sources of preference data from various elicitation methods to be combined, including the important case of relating sources of preference elicitation data to actual market behaviour;
- discussing the pros and cons of relaxing the simple error assumptions in basic choice models, and how these allow one to capture individual differences without needing individual-level effects;
- using three cases studies to illustrate the themes of the chapter.

Random Utility Theory is not new; Thurstone (1927) proposed it as a way to understand and model choices between pairs of stimuli. RUT languished until McFadden (1974) provided key theoretical and econometric insights necessary to extend the paradigm to the general case of multiple choices and comparisons (Rushton, 1969 independently developed a similar but less far-reaching approach to modelling revealed choices). Since then, RUT has been applied to a wide range of cases of human judgment, decision-making and choice behaviour, and now represents a general framework for understanding and modelling many types of human behaviour.

Thus, we adopt the view that almost all conjoint analysis techniques can be viewed as a special case of the more general RUT paradigm. Historically conjoint techniques have played an important role in understanding preference formation in marketing and other social sciences, so a contribution can be made by introducing and discussing a more general framework and the role of conjoint analysis methods within it. In fact, it could be argued that the term „conjoint analysis" has passed its „use-by" date, and should be replaced with more specific terms like „Random Utility Choice Modelling" to describe various ways to model preference and choices. This could help to counter the misconception that there is one unique

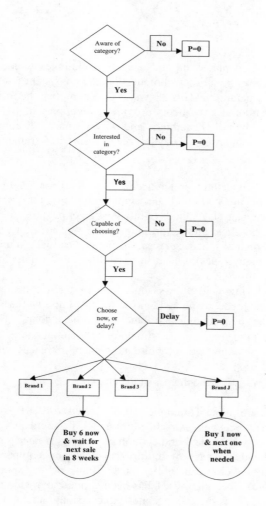

Figure 1:   A General Framework For Understanding Decision Sequences

technique called „conjoint," when, in fact, there are many forms and flavours of „conjoint analysis," each of which requires different assumptions and analytical techniques. For example, some conjoint theory and methods are consistent with economic theory but some are not, some methods permit one to combine experimental with actual marketplace choice data but many do not, etc.

Indeed, there are many ways to understand and model preferences and choices, some of which bear scant relation to one another and others that are incompatible, both theoretically and analytically. RUT offers a way to unify many seemingly disparate approaches to understand and model preference formation and choice. Figure 1 represents an overview of the general problems covered by RUT, which can assist our understanding of the role of conjoint analysis methods within RUT. Figure 1 should be regarded as a pedagogical vehicle to help explain why a more general view is required; it is not a theory per se.

Figure 1 suggests that many consumers make a series of sequential decisions en route to choosing products/services and brands. That is, a consumer first becomes aware that particular product or service categories are available and can satisfy needs/solve problems; if she is unaware of a category, the probability of purchasing brands in it is zero. Once aware, she evaluates benefits or problem solutions offered by category brands to determine her level of interest vis-à-vis purchase costs. If she is not interested in, does not value or cannot use the benefits (eg, she's allergic to certain ingredients) or perceives low value relative to cost, her category brand purchase probabilities will be zero. If she is interested in or perceives value, she then decides if she can purchase. For example, she may need a car, be interested in a luxury car but not be able to afford one or be put off by what her friends will say if she buys one. Thus, if not capable, her category choice probabilities may not be zero, but her brand choice probabilities in the luxury category will be zero. Finally, if aware, interested and capable, she must decide whether to buy now or wait. If she decides to wait, her current period brand purchase probabilities in the category will be zero. If she decides to buy now, she must decide which brand; and in many categories, she can buy more than one brand and more than one quantity of each brand. Thus, in general volume choices depend on brand choices, and inter-purchase times depend not only on brand and volume choices but also on a consumer's personal/household circumstances (eg, income, lifestyle, storage space, etc.).

Although simplistic, the framework allows some interesting and important insights into choice processes and the role of conjoint methods. In particular, many applications of traditional conjoint techniques deal with the evaluation of brands or „brand descriptions" (profiles), while others deal with generic category descriptions, or „concepts" (ie, benefits, problem solutions and costs that profile a category rather than a brand in that category). In the brand case, traditional conjoint methods model consumer evaluations of brand profiles near the end of the decision process sequence, which provides few insights about causally prior processes. Causally prior decision processes can play major roles in market choices, hence are of considerable strategic interest in their own right. In contrast, applications that involve category profile (concept) evaluations are causally prior to brand evaluations, so offer few insights into specific brand, volume or inter-purchase time choices. In general, therefore, they should have relatively low predictive accuracy forecasting trial and repeat choices, except possibly in quite mature categories.

To properly understand and characterise markets, one needs a comprehensive framework to explain and model the types of hierarchical (and temporal) sequences depicted by Figure 1. RUT is such a framework because it recognises that decisions at any stages in a sequence (or any other sequences, including simultaneous decisions not involving sequences) are random utility processes; hence decisions at advanced stages are conditional on decisions at prior stages. Figure 1 suggests why few researchers in marketing report significant individual differences associated with social, demographic, psychographic or similar factors, despite considerable evidence elsewhere that such differences often are significant, particularly in transport applications (Ben-Akiva and Lerman 1985; McFadden 1986; Ben-Akiva and Morikawa 1990). That is, individual differences, such as social and demographic factors, probably play key roles in early stages of decision-making, and explain fewer differences in choices in later stages.

For example, category and brand awareness may be influenced significantly by lifestyle, location of residence, media access and overall social and economic status (inter alia). As well, interest in and capability of purchasing in categories and decisions to delay purchases are likely also to be influenced by such factors. Failure to take such decision sequences and conditioning into account may lead to a wide variety of incorrect inferences and conclusions about decision and choice processes. For example, overall levels of price in categories may play causally prior roles in choices at earlier stages, such that those who choose brands are a „selected" sample of the market. Thus, it is unclear how to interpret price effects in many traditional conjoint or scanner data choice models because such effects are biased if one does not account for decisions not to purchase or delay purchase because of overall category price levels. Consumer income and other social and demographic factors may play roles in such causally prior processes, but are typically ignored, or at least under-represented, in many conjoint and choice modelling applications in marketing. Thus, it is hard to predict market behaviour and future outcomes well if one fails to take causally prior decisions into account when they matter. That is, RUT is not to blame for less than expected prediction accuracy; rather it is the application itself.

A more pragmatic assessment would suggest that decision processes in many markets are relatively stable because these markets are mature; hence, one can ignore prior processes if one's primary objective is short-run prediction. Although the latter observation often may be true, it begs the more general question, which is the object of this chapter: *How can we advance understanding of decision processes and develop better and more accurate approximations to them that will permit us to forecast market behaviour more accurately in both short and long terms?*

10.2   The Random Utility Theory Paradigm

The introduction provided insights into deficiencies in academic and applied research in decision and choice processes, including conjoint analysis methods. The purpose of this section is to introduce RUT and explain how it can enhance our understanding of decision processes, compare and contrast models from different sources of preference information, and relate models estimated from sources of stated preference data (eg, conjoint data) to market choices (revealed preferences). Preference, choice, or more generally, <u>dominance</u> data, come in many forms, such as:

- cross-sections of past, present or future preferences or choices (eg, consumer's last or next brand choices);
- preferences or choices expressed in controlled experiments that manipulate attribute levels and/or construct choice sets (eg, conjoint experiments);
- panels that supply temporal observations of preferences or choices (eg, scanner panels);
- cross-sectional or panel observations of consumer judgments (more generally, „evaluations") of products on latent dimensions like „attractiveness," „intent to purchase," etc. (eg, consumer brand evaluations on magnitude estimation or production scales, rating scales or rank orderings, or „forced" discrete choices involving selection of one or perhaps none of the products);
- direct observations of choices made by single persons or groups of people (eg, direct observation of purchases made from supermarket shelves);
- and many, many more.

This abbreviated list suggests that there are very many possible combinations of preference data types and decision contexts. To identify relationships among such preference data sources and test for regularity and order, one needs a unified way to compare as many types of preference „revelations" as possible on a level playing field. There has been little progress made in the comparison of such data sources, much less development of mechanisms that can explain differences in them. Indeed, there may be substantial regularities in preference and choice processes, but the lack of a unified framework with which to study and compare them has given rise to a veritable cottage industry of different techniques, measurement methods, experimental paradigms and „stories" used to study and explain decision processes (Louviere et al. 1999). As Louviere et al. (1999) explain, there has been limited substantive progress in understanding the processes themselves or regularities that may exist.

As in most scientific endeavours, little progress can be expected without fundamental theory, and empirical comparisons often are not meaningful without it. RUT provides a unified theoretical framework and a theoretically sound and relatively simple way to compare and contrast models estimated from many sources of preference data and develop models to account for real market choices (McFadden 1974; 1981;1986; Ben-Akiva and Lerman 1985; Louviere, Hensher and Swait

1999). In particular, RUT posits that the „*utility"* (or attractiveness) of product/service options can be decomposed into systematic (ie, observed) and random (ie, unobserved) components:

(1) $U_i = V_i + \varepsilon_i,$

where U_i is a latent measure of the attractiveness of option i, V_i is an observable, systematic or „explainable" component of the attractiveness of option i, and ε_i, is a random or „unexplainable" component of option i.

Randomness arises because researchers, scientists or analysts cannot „look" into consumers' heads and observe the true attractiveness of each alternative. Instead, they can indirectly observe indicators of the true attractiveness by designing elicitation procedures („preference elicitation procedures" or PEPs) to give insights into consumer preferences. Regardless of the time and effort one devotes to understanding preferences, some aspects of consumer preferences cannot be unexplained because all factors that drive preferences cannot be identified, unreliability is inherent in the measurement procedures one uses and preferences may vary at different times or situations for the same or different consumers.

Thus, viewed from the perspective of a scientist trying to explain consumers' decision-making processes and/or preferences, consumer preferences must be stochastic even if consumers themselves are perfectly deterministic. Consequently, we seek to model the probability that a randomly chosen consumer will do something like choose a brand, tick a box, report a choice frequency, etc. That is,

(2) $P(i|A) = P[\ (V_i + \varepsilon_i) > ... > (V_j + \varepsilon_j) > ... > (V_J + \varepsilon_J)],$ for all j in A,

where all terms are as previously defined, except for P(i|A), which is the probability that a consumer chooses action i from the set of all possible actions {A}, from which she might choose. RUT-based choice models are derived by making assumptions about distributions of the random component (ε_i) and deducing the consequences for equation 2. The effects of interest in the deduced model form are captured by specifying V_i to be a function of a set of observables. These observables can be attributes/levels systematically manipulated in conjoint or conjoint-like experiments and/or measures of quantities one hypothesises to explain or drive preferences in particular situations. Regardless of whether the effects are controlled, uncontrolled or some combination of both, V_i typically is expressed as a linear-in-the-parameters function of the observables:

(3) $V_i = \sum_k \beta_k X_{ki},$

where β is a K-element vector of parameters and X is an i by k vector (matrix) of observables that describe the actions that were available to be chosen and the consumers who make the choices (other relevant factors also can be included, like different situations, conditions, time periods, environments, cultures, etc.). RUT assumes that consumers try to choose those actions (options) that are the most attractive, subject to constraints like time, money, and peer pressure. We are unaware of other widely applied, scientifically accepted and empirically verified choice rules except the maximum utility rule, although others have been proposed from time-to-time (Simon 1983).

The foregoing discussion is well-known to many social scientists, and has been the basis for a vast amount of previous research in the RUT paradigm. However, what is less well-known and less-well appreciated is the fact that the random component itself plays a fundamental role in the behavioural outcomes in many sources of preference data. That is, random components play key roles in the statistical inferences made about model estimates (β's, or so-called „partworths") within data sources, as well as in comparisons of model estimates across data sources (Morikawa 1989; Swait and Louviere 1993; Louviere, Hensher and Swait 1998, 1999).

In particular, the random component (*specifically, the variability in the random component*) is inherently linked to estimates of the partworths, and cannot be separately identified in any one source of preference data (Ben-Akiva and Lerman 1985; Swait and Louviere 1993; Louviere, Hensher and Swait 1998, 1999). As explained by Ben-Akiva and Morikawa (1990) and Swait and Louviere (1993), the variance of the random component is inversely proportional to a constant that „scales" the β parameters in all RUT choice models. In fact, the systematic component is actually $\lambda\beta_k X_{ki}$, where λ is a multiplicative constant that is inversely proportional to the variability of the random component. A scalar λ is embedded in all choice models, regardless of the distributional assumption made about the ε's to derive any particular choice model specification. Thus, λ cannot be separately identified (estimated) in any one source of preference data. However, as explained by Ben-Akiva and Morikawa (1990) and Swait and Louviere (1993), ratios of λ's can be identified from two or more sources of preference data if one source of data is used as a constant reference. We note now, but leave for subsequent discussion, that identification of λ within a single data set is possible if exogenous information is introduced to allow for individual or alternative-specific differences or if variances can be freed up to identification limits (HEV models). We note that the present discussion assumes that the random components (ie, error terms) are independent and identically distributed.

These „variance-scale ratios" play crucial roles in comparing models estimated from different sources of preference data and testing hypotheses about how and why they might differ. That is, one must account for differences in random component variability to compare different sources of preference and choice data and rule out the possibility that data sources differ only in levels of error variability (ie, size of random components) before concluding that differences in model parameters are real. Swait and Louviere (1993) show how to test model and process hypotheses by controlling for and taking into account differences in random components.

The relevance of the preceding discussion to the objectives of this chapter is that RUT provides the basis for level playing field comparisons of many sources of preference and choice data. As Louviere (1994) noted, data from any conjoint experiment can be couched in a RUT framework, and modelled as a nested sub-model within the RUT family of choice models. This allows one to test if utility model parameters differ after accounting for differences in levels of error variability between tasks, task conditions, time periods, situations, etc., regardless of whether the observed data were generated from rating, ranking, binary, multiple choice or other types of judgment and choice tasks. The basis for this conclusion is the Luce and Suppes (1965) Ranking Theorem, which proves that any form of dominance data can be expressed as some type of weak or strong order, which are consistent with RUT and can be used to estimate RUT-based choice models. However, different sources of preference data generally will have different levels of random error variability, and hence different values of λ. As earlier noted, differences in λ must be taken into account to compare models estimated from different sources of preference data, and failure to do so can lead to misleading conclusions about differences in data sources, decision processes, etc.

The foregoing is now well-known in econometrics, transport and environmental and resource economics, but has been largely ignored in academic and applied marketing research. For example, Ben-Akiva, et al. (1994) discuss and Louviere, Fox and Moore (1993) show how to extend Louviere's (1994) argument to many forms of preference data, which in turn allows preference (utility) parameters to be compared and tested for different sources of preference data, types of decision tasks, task manipulations (eg, attribute or profile orderings), groups of people, time periods, etc. Louviere, et al. (1999) review a number of papers in this paradigm, such as Hensher and Bradley (1993); Swait and Louviere (1993); Swait, Louviere and Williams (1994); Adamowicz, et al. (1994, 1996); Swait, Adamowicz and Louviere (1998); Louviere, Hensher and Swait (1998) (to name only a few). As well, many of the basic issues are discussed in Carson, et al (1994); Keane (1997); and Louviere, Hensher and Swait (1998, 1999). Thus, the theory is well-established, there have been numerous empirical tests of the basic ideas discussed above and there is considerable empirical support for the general approach.

Moreover, comparisons of utility model parameters from different preference data sources have been the subject of considerable research attention for many years. A few examples include Meyer (1977), who examined profile order on attribute weights; Meyer and Eagle (1982), who studied the effect of attribute range on model parameters; Johnson (1989) who investigated attribute order effects; Olsen and Swait (1995) and Olsen, et al. (1995), who studied the effects on model parameters of differences in response mode, sequential vs simultaneous presentation, prior practice, etc; Oliphant, et al. (1992), who compared model parameter differences due to ratings and choices and profile or choice set order within tasks; Elrod, et al. (1993), who investigated the effects of Pareto Optimal sets on ratings and choices; Chrzan (1994), who studied order effects in choice tasks; and Ben-Akiva, et al. (1991) and Bradley and Daly (1994), who compared MNL model parameters estimated from different depths of preference ranking data (to name only a few papers). These references demonstrate that RUT now makes it possible to study these effects in a unified and systematic way.

Insights afforded by RUT as a unified framework for comparing sources of preference data extend to many other sources of preference data and types of research applications. For example, there have been a number of comparisons of models estimated from revealed (RP) and stated preference (SP) data sources, such as Ben-Akiva and Morikawa (1990) and Hensher and Bradley (1993), who compared RP and SP transport mode choice data; Louviere, Fox and Moore (1993) who compared several different RP and SP data sources for vacation trips; Swait, Louviere and Williams (1994), who compared RP and SP data sources for freight shipper choices in three cities; Adamowicz, et al. (1994, 1996), who compared RP and SP sources for water-based recreation and moose-hunting destination choices; and Louviere, Hensher and Swait (1998), who compared several RP and SP data sources (again, to name a few). The hypothesis of preference invariance across data sources generally was supported in these comparisons, although some minor discrepancies were found in some studies.

The preceding represent only a few of many new insights into consumer decision making and choice processes now possible from the RUT paradigm. Furthermore, our discussion suggests that many previously published results might bear re-examination. For example, Louviere, Hensher and Swait (1999, Chapter 13) reviewed a large number of published studies in marketing, transportation and environmental and resource economics that reported differences in model parameters or decision processes due to differences in product categories, context effects, latent segments, etc. They showed that in many cases the reported empirical differences most likely were due to differences in error variability (ie, sizes of random components), not real differences in model parameters or statistical effects. Hence, failure to recognise and understand the role of the random component may explain many published results. For example, Ainslie and Rossi (1998) recently reported a number of empirical regularities in choice model parameters estimated from different sources of scanner panel data for different product categories, but did not recognise that they were consistent with and could be explained by the error variability mechanism of RUT (they also did not reference the large literature on the role of the scale parameter).

10.3   A Theory of Preference Regularities/Invariance Based on RUT

The preceding discussion provides a conceptual basis to address the general problem of comparing and possibly combining sources of preference data, whether from conjoint analysis or other sources. That is, suppose a sample of consumers respond to a survey that (among other things) asks them to make choices from a designed set of paired-alternative scenarios that describe a product/service. We call this preference elicitation procedure one (PEP1), and it has an associated design matrix X_1. Suppose we also have data from a second sample of consumers for the same product/service consisting of self-reports about which product/service they last purchased (ie, PEP2). Associated with these self-reported choices is design matrix X_2 representing consumer's perceptions of attribute levels of each product/service. In general, X_1 and X_2 have some common attributes (say, X_{c1} and

X_{c2}), plus others that are data source-specific (eg, Z_1 and Z_2, respectively). Thus, $X_1=(X_{c1},Z_1)'$ and $X_2=(X_{c2},Z_2)'$.

We now specify the utility function for each data source in terms of common and data source-specific attributes. For pedagogical simplicity, let the utility expressions be strictly additive in all effects, let the common and data-source-specific attributes have separate error terms and let both data sources have different error components to account for typical statistical issues of measurement errors, omitted variables, wrong functional forms, etc. Denote these error components ζ_1, ζ_2, ζ_{c1}, ζ_{c2}, ε_1, and ε_2, respectively, so that we can write the utility expressions as follows:

$$(4) \qquad U_1=\theta_1+[V_{c1}(X_{c1},\beta_1)+\zeta_{c1}]+[W_1(Z_1,\gamma_1)+\zeta_1]+\varepsilon_1$$

$$(5) \qquad U_2=\theta_2+[V_{c2}(X_{c2},\beta_2)+\zeta_{c2}]+[W_2(Z_2,\gamma_2)+\zeta_2]+\varepsilon_2$$

where quantities V_{c1} and V_{c2} are the utility components of the common attributes with associated parameters (β_1, β_2); W_1 and W_2 are the utility components of the data source-specific attributes with associated parameters (γ_1 and γ_2); θ_1, θ_2 are intercepts that measure average preference levels in each data source; and the error components are as previously defined.
Rearranging we have:

$$(6) \qquad U_1=\theta_1+V_{c1}(X_{c1},\beta_1)+W_1(Z_1,\gamma_1)+(\zeta_{c1}+\zeta_1+\varepsilon_1)$$

$$(7) \qquad U_2=\theta_2+V_{c2}(X_{c2},\beta_2)+W_2(Z_2,\gamma_2)+(\zeta_{c2}+\zeta_2+\varepsilon_2)$$

The dimensionality of each data source is defined by its PEP. That is, U_1 has two rows per choice set because it is a paired choice task, but the number of rows of U_2 may vary from consumer-to-consumer because the number of brands that each reports were in their choice sets when they made their last purchase can vary between consumers.

A key issue suggested by the above discussion is whether responses obtained from different PEPs, contexts, etc., reflect the same underlying preference processes. That is, are the common utilities $V_{ck}(X_{ck},\beta_k)$ the same, despite being estimated from different PEPs, contexts, etc? In order to address this issue, a formal definition of preference regularity or invariance is needed. As discussed by Louviere, Hensher and Swait (1999), two or more PEPs exhibit preference regularity or invariance if the marginal common utilities for any (k,k') pair of data sources are proportional. That is, $\beta_k \propto \beta_{k'}$, and the constant of proportionality should be $\lambda_k/\lambda_{k'}$.

Strictly speaking, this definition holds only if the common attribute parameters are specified as linear-in-the-parameters. More generally, the marginal rates of substitution $(\partial V_{ck}(X_{ck},\beta_k)/\partial \ X_{ck})$ must be proportional. The linear-in-the-parameters case is more restrictive, but may be more applicable because most utility functions used in choice model applications are linear-in-the-parameters. A simple way to view preference regularity or invariance in RUT choice models is to graph one vector of estimated common utility parameters against a second. If invariance holds, the graphed points should lie on a straight line that intersects the origin. More generally, if there are two or more vectors of common model parameters, one must serve as a (reference) vector graphed on the X-Axis, with the other vectors on the Y-Axis. In this case, the vectors should plot as a fan of straight lines that intersect at the origin of the graph. The slope of each line is the constant of proportionality relative to the reference vector (ie, $\lambda_k/\lambda_{k'}$).

Put another way, if the parameter vectors plot as a fan of straight lines intersecting the origin (ie, preference invariance holds), they will be linear combinations of one another because they are proportional. Thus, a factor analysis of the vectors of model parameters (rows = parameters, columns = models) should yield a single factor (See Krijnen 1997 for a proof). Confirmatory factor analytic procedures could be used to test this hypothesis, but often there are few parameters and power is lost in aggregation (parameters are means).

Each common attribute utility parameter estimates $\partial V_{ck}(X_{ck},\beta_k)/\partial \ X_{ck}$; hence, graphs and factor analyses are not statistical tests, but instead are diagnostic aids. That is, one must take errors of sampling and estimation into account to properly test a preference invariance hypothesis that retains full statistical power. For example, one can generalise the test proposed by Swait and Louviere (1993) by treating parameter proportionality as a restriction tested by a Full Information Maximum Likelihood (FIML) procedure. In fact, model parameter proportionality is a very strong requirement, and its stringency increases with the number of attributes. For example, in the two data source case one first estimates separate models from each source, then pools both sources to estimate a single common vector of attribute parameters with the restriction that β's in data source 1 are proportional to β's in source 2. The pooled model will have K-1 fewer parameters if there are K total common β parameters. and twice the difference in the sum of the separate model likelihoods minus the pooled model likelihood is distributed as chi-square with K-1 degrees of freedom.

The null hypothesis in this test is that both β vectors are the same up to re-scaling by a constant of proportionality. This hypothesis should be rejected if there are differences in utility functions, choice sets (of alternatives) and/or decision (choice) rules used to select alternatives from choice sets, which might be due to differences in contexts, frames, orders, or any of a large number of other possibilities. Thus, it is both surprising and significant that there have been more than a dozen empirical tests of this hypothesis involving different sources of data collected under different conditions in different places at different times, etc., but few serious rejections. Thus, preference invariance or parameter proportionality (or its inverse, error variance proportionality) seems to account for a very wide range of differences in data sources. In fact, the success of this simple mechanism in explaining differences in empirical results in many published and unpublished cases now places the onus on consumer behaviour, judgment and decision making and behavioural decision theory researchers to demonstrate that *it cannot explain their findings*. Similarly, the onus is on conjoint analysis researchers and practitioners to demonstrate that *there is a compelling reason not to estimate and test RUT-based choice models* instead of traditional non-RUT flavours of conjoint given the consistent empirical success of the RUT paradigm.

It also is important to recognise that preference regularity or invariance does not require the alternative-specific constants (ASCs) of choice models from different PEPs to be comparable. That is, apart from the obvious fact that preference invariance is defined in terms of common attributes, ASCs are location parameters of the random utility component, hence not associated with attributes. ASCs capture average effects of omitted variables, which can vary between data sources. For example, in the case of the MNL choice model, including all ASCs in a model guarantees that aggregate predicted marginal choice distributions will exactly equal observed distributions (Ben-Akiva and Lerman 1985). Although other choice models may not have this property, ASCs still will be specific to data sources; hence should not be included in tests of preference regularity.

10.4   Generality of the Luce and Suppes Ranking Theorem

The preceding discussion provides a basis for understanding why and how many sources of preference data can be compared on a level playing field. Thus, we now briefly discuss how some common preference measures can be transformed to be consistent with RUT, such as the following:

1. *Discrete choices of one option from a set of options.* Discrete choices are observed in so-called „choice-based conjoint" experiments, more general choice experiments, self-reports of last brand purchased, self-reports of most preferred brand from a list of brands, and many other possibilities.
2. *„Pick-any" choices that indicate preference orderings*, such as „considered" or „liked" brands, and/or questions where more than one listed item can meet an implied threshold. These include responses to lists of brands or conjoint and/or tasks in which than one option meets some threshold preference value, etc.
3. *Complete or incomplete preference rankings* from ranking a list of brands in order of preference, ranking conjoint profiles, ranking options in choice experiments, etc. A ranking is „complete" if all options are ranked, and „incomplete" if only a subset are ranked (eg, „top four," „best and worst," „those that actually would be purchased," etc).
4. *Preferences expressed on (equal interval) category rating scales* or other scales assumed to yield cardinal measures (eg, magnitude estimation or ratio production scales). Examples include ubiquitous brand evaluations, responses to traditional conjoint analysis tasks and many more possibilities.

Each of the above PEPs provides data that can be transformed to be consistent with RUT. Comparisons of such data sources are important in their own right. That is, if a particular utility specification and/or choice process is hypothesised to underlie a particular response task, this hypothesis also must hold for any arbitrary monotone transformation of the response data into implied discrete choices, as we now explain. Suppose one posits that a utility function is additive and/or an attribute has a certain marginal rate of substitution (or other germane process hypotheses), and tests this by estimating a model from responses that are assumed to be ordinal or higher in measurement level (eg, interval or ratio measures). To generalise, the hypothesis also must hold for any arbitrary monotone transformation of the response data, and if not satisfied it cannot be generalised and results will be unique to certain measurement types and/or response modes.

For example, suppose one estimates a utility specification and associated marginal rates of substitution (MRS's) from a conjoint ratings task. If the ratings from that task are transformed to be consistent with discrete categorical, RUT-based choice models, one must obtain the same inferences about specification and MRS's from an analysis of the latter data for the former hypothesis to be generalised. If analytical results differ significantly, inferences from analyses requiring stronger metric assumptions (eg, ratings require equal interval, or at least ordinal, as opposed to categorical, discrete choice assumptions) would be rejected in favour of results based on weaker assumptions. We now demonstrate how to transform each data type previously discussed to be consistent with RUT (See Luce and Suppes 1965; Ben-Akiva and Lerman 1985):

1. Subjects in discrete choice tasks indicate one preferred or chosen option from a set of N total options. Choice sets are constructed such that chosen options are coded 1 and the N-1 unchosen options are coded 0. There may be only one choice set per subject (eg, consumers self-report their last purchased brand or most preferred brand in a list of N); or there may be several choice sets (eg, subjects in discrete choice experiments indicate one choice from N options in each of several choice sets).

2. Subjects in „pick-any" tasks indicate that 0, 1 or more of N total options meet a criterion. For example, „consideration" task subjects indicate all brands that they would „consider" from a list of N; or in choice experiments, indicate all options they would „consider" in each choice set of N options (ie, c options are „considered" and N-c are „not"). This implies that the c „considered" options are preferred to the remaining N-c options, which allows one to construct 0 (if c=0), 1 (if c=1), 2 (if c=2) or more (if c > 1) choice sets such that each of the c options is preferred to the remaining N-c options. In this way one can construct c total choice sets (if c=N no sets can be constructed).

3. Subjects in ranking tasks rank all or some subset, r, of N options. Here the first ranked option is preferred to the remaining N-1 options; the second ranked is preferred to the other N-2 options; and so forth (see also Chapman and Staelin 1982). This „rank-order explosion" procedure can be used to construct up to N-1 choice sets from a set of N rankings, or r-1 choice sets from a subset of r rankings of N options. Such data include lists of N brands ranked

in surveys, ranking of N conjoint-type profiles, ranking of N options in experimental choice sets, and many other possibilities.
4. The above procedure (3) can be used to construct choice sets from responses
    assumed to be cardinal measures, such as rating or magnitude estimation
    tasks, except that ties may arise if options receive equal numerical responses.
    If t items are tied, t choice sets should be constructed that include only one of
    the tied options per set.

In addition to the above transformation(s) of rating and ranking data, RUT
models can be derived from ratings or similar preference responses by treating
them as ordinal indicators of latent, underlying continua. That is, let the observed
response be Y_n (eg, a 1 to 7 category rating response), and let the latent scale be
U_{SP}.
Then we can write:

(8) $U_{SP}=\beta_{SP}X_{c,SP}+(\zeta_{c,SP}+\varepsilon_{SP})$,

with $v_{SP}=(\zeta_{c,SP}+\varepsilon_{SP})$ logistically distributed (location parameter 0 and standard
deviation σ_{SP}). The cumulative density function for U_{SP} is (Johnson, Kotz and
Balakrishnan, 1995)

(9) $G_{SP}(u)=\{1+\exp[\lambda_{SP}(\beta_{SP}X_{c,SP}-u)]\}^{-1}$, $-\infty<u<\infty$, and $\lambda_{SP}=\pi\sqrt{3}/\sigma_{SP}$.

We have to relate the latent scale to the observed responses (Y_n) to specify a
RUT model. This is achieved by noting that if U_{SP} is less than or equal to some
value τ_1, the subject answers $Y_n=1$, which event probability (Eqn. 9) =
$G_{SP}(\beta_{SP}X_{c,SP}+\tau_1)$. If U_{SP} lies between τ_1 and τ_2, the probability = $[G_{SP}(\beta_{SP}X_{c,SP}+\tau_2)$
- $G_{SP}(\beta_{SP}X_{c,SP}+\tau_1)]$, and the subject responds $Y_n=2$, and so forth. Thus, parameters
$\tau=(\tau_1, ..., \tau_6)'$ are cutpoints or response category boundaries, such that $\tau_1 \leq \tau_2 \leq ...$
$\leq\tau_6$. In this example, only five cutpoints can be identified, so one (eg, τ_1) must be
set to 0. Like all RUT models, the variance (or scale λ_{SP}) of the latent variable U_{SP}
cannot be identified and is confounded with parameter vectors β_{SP} and τ (equation
9). The same test procedures discussed above can be used to compare models
estimated from such responses with other preference data sources. Thus, conjoint
ratings data can be transformed to be consistent with RUT, models estimated from
each source of preference data can be compared and rigorous tests of preference
invariance or regularity can be performed.
For example, Morikawa (1994) combined and compared RP choice data with
preference ratings from a traditional conjoint task. RP data were choices between
rail and car for intercity travel in the Netherlands, and SP data were graded paired
comparisons for the same context. Morikawa tested parameter invariance between
data sources and found that the model parameters were proportional (95% confidence level). The estimated constant of proportionality (ie, $\lambda_{SP}/\lambda_{RP}$) was 0.27,
which implies an SP error variance approximately 4 times larger than the RP variance.

Now we use three case studies to illustrate the generality of RUT and how it can be applied to research problems involving conjoint and choice experiment data.

10.5   Case 1: Complex Models from Simple Conjoint Choice Experiments

This case study examines differences in marginal rates of substitution derived from simple and complex choice models, the results of which suggest caution in relying on simple choice models like MNL. Indeed, much progress has been made in relaxing the IID error assumptions that underlie simple models like MNL and Identity Probit, although some complex models are little more than mere statistical descriptions devoid of behavioural theory. Moreover, few complex models can forecast future behaviour because they include factors that cannot be forecast easily (if at all) and/or they are merely reduced form approximations of dynamic processes (Erdem and Keane 1996).

Worse yet, few advanced statistical choice specifications can be or have been used to model the full behavioural system of trial and repeat choices, volume decisions conditional on choice and/or inter-purchase time choices, etc. Thus, statistical and mathematical complexity is not a substitute for sound theory and rigorous thinking about process. Indeed, this case illustrates that a rush to complexity may be ill-conceived because recent Monte Carlo work by David Bunch (reported in Louviere et al. 1999) suggests that numbers of observations needed to satisfy asymptotic theory for complex models (eg, MNP) may be many times greater than simple models like MNL (eg, in some cases required sample sizes may exceed available human populations!).

The more complex the unobserved effects, such as variation and co-variation due to contemporaneous or temporal patterns between alternatives, the more likely it will be that one must simplify complex and often 'deep' parameters associated with covariance matrices to estimate models. Science seeks parsimonious and behaviourally meaningful models rather than complex statistical descriptions, which is why one must understand and appreciate model assumptions. For example, most discrete choice models estimated in conjoint analysis and other paradigms can be described by the following assumptions:

- A single cross-section (no lagged structure);
- Non-separation of attribute utilities from other component effects capturing the role of explanatory variables in utility expressions (due to confounds with scale);
- Constant scale parameters across alternatives (constant variance assumption);
- Random components that are not serially correlated (See Morikawa 1994)
- Fixed utility weights; and
- No unobserved heterogeneity.

A hierarchy of models has evolved that relax some of the above assumptions (Figure 2), and Case 1 focuses on refining the behavioural structure of choice models that treat variance-scale ratio parameters (ie, inverse of random component variances) as real behavioural processes. Specifically, we concentrate on three models: 1) random and fixed effects Heteroskedastic Extreme Value (HEV), 2) Random Parameter or Mixed Logit (RP/ML) and 3) Multi-Period Multinomial Probit (MPMNP).

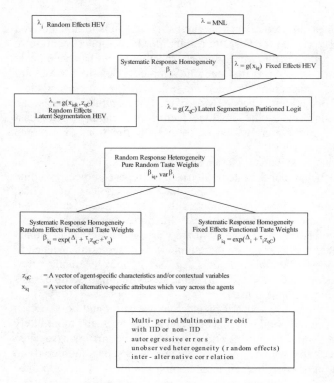

Figure 2:   Taxonomy of Behaviourally Progressive Models

10.5.1   Heteroskedastic Extreme Value (HEV) Models - Random Effects

If random component variances differ across alternatives, constant variance models will over- or under-estimate the indirect utility effects. HEV allows variance differences but retains zero inter-alternative correlations, hence variance scale ratios (hereafter λ's) can vary across alternatives (probit analogs involve normal distributions). HEV relaxes the IID property of MNL by allowing different variance scale-ratios (λ's) for alternatives, which in turn allows differential substitution among all pairs of alternatives. That is, changes in alternative l's utility affect utility differences in i and l, but the utility changes are affected by i's λ value. Specifically, the smaller i's λ value, the less effect utility difference changes have, and the smaller the effects on the probability of choosing i. Bhat (1995, 1997a), Allenby and Glinter (1995) and Hensher (1997, 1998a) discuss HEV.

10.5.2   Random Parameter Logit (RPL) or Mixed Logit models

Unlike MNL, RPL treats one or more utility parameters and/or alternative-specific constants as random parameters, the variance(s) and mean (s) of which are estimated. RPL will produce non-IID choice outcomes if random variation of individual parameters induces correlations among the utilities of alternatives (Bhat 1997, McFadden and Train 1996). RPL, or 'mixed logit,' is a mixture of a Gumbel distribution for the error component and a normal distribution for the utility parameters (Train, 1997) and can account for cross-correlation among alternatives. Revelt and Train (1996), Bhat (1996), McFadden and Train (1996) and Brownstone et al (1997) discuss RPL/Mixed logit models. More recently, Bhat (1997) extended RPL/Mixed Logit by including parameterised covariates (Z_{qk}) in the utility function.

10.5.3   Multi-Period Multinomial Probit

MultiPeriod-MultiNomial Probit (MPMNP) is the most general way to specify the variances and covariances of the random effects; hence HEV and RPL are special cases. MPMNP can relax most random component assumptions: eg, autoregressive structures, correlations of unobserved effects of alternatives and time periods, unobserved heterogeneity, variance differences in random components, etc. Parameter estimation is more complex for MNP models, and requires Simulated Maximum Likelihood (SML) methods that take pseudo-random draws from the underlying error process (Geweke et al 1994, McFadden and Ruud 1994; Boersch-Supan and Hajivassiliou 1990; Stern 1997) or some form of Bayesian estimation (eg, Wedel et al. 1999). The pros and cons of Bayesian estimation versus SML are not yet clear, but both have many similarities.

We now illustrate the behavioural implications of the three models by using them to analyse the results of a conjoint choice experiment used to forecast demand for a new high-speed rail system in Australia. The experiment was used to create high-speed rail profiles described by fare class (first, full economy, discount economy and off-peak), frequency of service (every 30, 60, 120 minutes) and parking cost ($2 - $20 per day). The choice task focused on each subject's most recent trip, offering a choice of four high-speed rail options or auto if that trip was made again. Subjects evaluated two or four profiles (355 evaluated two, and 81 other subjects did four scenarios). The number of scenarios is not germane to the case, hence is not discussed further.

Table 1:   Alternative error processes in models and values of travel time savings

Model	Error Processes	RAN	AR1	MNP	VTTS*	LogL
1	iid across periods, iid across alternatives	0	0	0	**4.63**	-1067.9
2	iid across periods, correlated across alternatives	0	0	1	**6.46**	-1050.71
3	random effects, iid across alternatives	1	0	0	**5.22**	-765.01
4	random effects, correlated across alternatives	1	0	1	**6.88**	759.57
5	AR1 errors, iid across alternatives	0	1	0	**4.98**	-811.46
6	AR1 errors, correlated across alternatives	0	1	1	**7.87**	770,38
7	random effects + AR1 errors, iid across alt's	1	1	0	**5.40**	-775.68
8	free variance, random effects, iid across alts	1	0	1	**8.37**	-759.71
9	free variance and iid across periods	0	0	1	**7.64**	-1040.25
10	free variance, iid across periods, correlated across alts	0	0	1	**8.06**	-1044.3
11	free variance, random effects, AR1 errors, correlated across alt's	1	1	1	**7.09**	-759.04

* Dollars per adult person hour, - = not able to identify an appropriate model

We estimated the mean values of non-business travel time savings (VTTS) from each model (Table 1). All models except Model 1 (MNL) were estimated using SML (100 replications). Table 1 reveals substantial and significant differences in VTTS, ranging from a low of \$4.63/adult person hours for MNL to \$8.37/adult person hour for a more complex model. Such large difference in VTTS can have major implications for go/no-go investment decisions in transport or marketing (which might estimate willingness-to-pay instead). Accounting for cross-alternative correlations and relaxing constant variance assumptions (Table 1) significantly reduce the evident downward bias in MNL mean VTTS estimates. In contrast, unobserved heterogeneity (random effects) and serial correlation have less effect on downward bias. This is consistent with McFadden's (1986) point that individual-level utility estimates rarely should be necessary to capture heterogeneity. As well, these results suggest that heterogeneity may result in less model bias than previously thought in conjoint and choice model applications in marketing.

10.6   Case 2: Extension to Multiple Conditional Choices and Combining Data Sources

Many behaviours of interest involve conditional decisions and/or what can be described as „coping strategies" to minimise hassles or losses. For example, commuters can cope with congestion by changing departure times and/or modes; travel mode choice models that ignore departure time choices will overestimate peak hour queuing and delays, increasing the implied value of new road investments. Billions of dollars are at stake in such investments; hence businesses and society have vested interests in development and application of accurate models of such choices. Similarly, investments in new products and services, product enhancements and extensions, etc, may risk many millions of dollars. Thus, firms also should seek more accurate models of choice processes, which often will in-volve more than the simple choice of a particular brand. Instead, they may involve conditional choices of brands, purchase quantities, inter-purchase timings and the like.

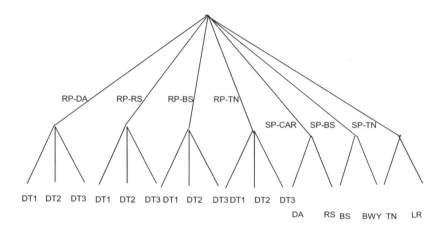

Figure 3:   The Nested Structure Used in Model Estimation

Case 2 illustrates the development and estimation of models of joint choice of departure time and travel mode. The case also illustrates how one can combine a choice (or stated preference, SP) experiment with real choice (or revealed prefer-ence, RP) data. The SP task has six travel options: Drive alone, Ride share, Bus, Busway, Train and Light rail (Figure 3). The Bus, Busway, Train and Light rail options are described by five attributes (total in vehicle time, service frequency, closest stop to home, closest stop to destination, and fare). Drive alone and Ride share options are described by five or six attributes (travel time, fuel cost, parking cost, travel time variability + departure time and toll charge for toll roads).

All attributes were assigned three levels, and a choice experiment was designed by treating all attributes as a collective factorial and selecting an orthogonal fraction from it (Louviere and Woodworth 1983). The selected fraction permits estimation of all main effects within alternatives, plus two-way bilinear interactions for both car options and generic two-way bilinear interactions for public transit options; and produces 81 choice sets, which were blocked into 27 versions of three choice sets due to task complexity. It is worth noting that the nature and number of attributes differ between options, posing design and implementation issues for traditional conjoint (Louviere 1988).

Nested Logit was used to model the departure time and mode choices to allow differential error variances and correlations between subsets of alternatives. RP options included Drive alone, Ride share, Train and Bus (toll and no toll options were combined); and SP options added two 'new' modes (buses on dedicated roads, or „busways", and light rail), and three departure times based on local data (before 7am, 7.01-8.30 am and after 8.30 am). The tree structure in Figure 3 was one of several investigated based on equivalent variances within partitions, which allows scale (variance) differences between partitions.

The model estimation results in Table 2 not only provide new insights into joint choices of departure time and mode, but also allow evaluation of a wide range of policy options to impact these choices. For example, Ride share and Bus unexplained utility components are significantly larger than the other modes that have about equal error variances. This suggests that variability in choice of Ride share and Bus is much greater than for other modes, or the model explains far less in choice. For example, preference heterogeneity is one source of the variability, and these results suggest that it is significantly larger for Ride share and Bus choices.

All attributes have the expected signs in both RP and SP data sources, and several individual difference effects also are significant (Table 1), which while common in transport applications of SP methods, is less so in marketing applications (but see Guadagni and Little 1983). The model in Table 3 is a very significant improvement over MNL, suggesting that accounting for variance and individual differences greatly improves MNL and offers other strategic insights. The parameter estimates associated with inclusive values are scale parameters for each partition of the tree. For example, scale parameters for RP-Ride share and RP-Bus (respectively, .278 and .256) imply less random component variance than RP-drive alone and RP-train (respectively, 1.075 and 1.00). We also note that in our experience scale parameters for subsets of RP and SP options often are more similar to one another than scale parameters within RP or SP choice sets.

STATISTICS:
- Groups (sets) = 4113
- Cases = 24678
- Free Parameters = 93
- Log LL(B) = -6961.90; Log LL(0) = -7369.51; -2[LL(0)-LL(B)] = 815.221
- Rho-Squared = 0.0553; AIC Rho-Squared = 0.0427

MNL models cannot account for these types of behavioural differences, suggesting many potential applications for models that can implement the framework in Figure 1: eg, joint brand and quantity choices, joint brand, quantity and inter-purchase time choices, brand and quantity choices conditional on category choice, etc. Thus, Case 2 may seem simple, but it serves to introduce and illustrate more complex tasks and model possibilities.

Table 2:   *Joint departure time and mode choice model for commuters*

Variable	Alts	Units	Estimated Parameter	t-value
Fuel cost (one-way trip)	All	$	.5745	-3.80
Door-to-door time (one-way trip)	rpda,rprs,spda,sprs	Mins	-.04224	-2.67
Parking cost	rpda,rprs,spda,sprs	$ per day	-.08978	-3.21
Car availability	rpda,spda		.3789	4.47
Personal income	rpda,spda	$'000	.00485	1.74
Drive alone constant	rpda		2.0433	1.84
Age <25 years	rprs dt3	years	.3234	1.64
Age 25-34 years	rprs, dt2	years	.1391	1.46
Age 35-54 years	rprs, dt2	years	.0734	1.53
Ride share constant	rprs		1.5412	0.79
Linehaul time	Rpbs,rptn,spbs,sptn, spbwy,splr	mins	-.05409	-5.92
Access and egress time	Rpbs,rptn,spbs,sptn, spbwy,splr	mins	-.03505	-3.47
Managers & Administrators	rpbs,dt1	1,0	8.743	1.83
Clerk	rpbs, dt2 & dt3	1,0	5.785	1.69
Full time employee	rpbs,dt3 & rptn	1,0	.5309	1.57
Age 35-54 years	rptn,dt1	years	-.02754	-1.94
Age 35-54 years	rptn,dt3	years	.01877	1.80
Professionals	rptn,dt2	1,0	-1.724	-3.25
Train specific constant	Rptn		3.088	3.57
Toll cost	spda,sprs	$	-.1466	-2.65
Travel time variability	spda,sprs	mins	-.1269	-2.89
Drive alone constant	Spda		.1289	.29
Ride share constant	Sprs		.1863	.41
Transit frequency	Spbs,sptn,spbwy,splr	mins	-.0267	-3.24
Train specific constant	Sptn		-.3777	-1.22
Light rail specific constant	Splr		-.2633	-.89
Busway specific constant	Spbwy		-.0722	-.67
DT1 specific constant	Rp all dt1's		-.1816	-1.01
DT3 specific constant	Rp all dt3's		.0958	.36
Inclusive Values:				
RP - Drive alone	Rpda		1.075	2.30
RP - Ride Share	Rprs		.278	2.00
RP - Bus	Rpbs		.256	2.01
RP - Train	Rptn		1.00	fixed
SP- Car (Drive alone & ride share)	Spda & Sprs		1.14	3.32
SP – Bus (Bus and Busway)	Spbs & Spbwy		1.07	3.85
SP – Train (Train and Light Rail)	Sptn & Splr		.925	3.91
Log-likelihood at convergence	-2500.82			
Pseudo-r^2	.659			
Sample	2688			

Note: rp=revealed preference, sp=stated preference, da=drive alone (for all departure times), rs=ride share (for all departure times), bs=bus (for all departure times), tn=train (for all departure times), bwy=busway, lr=light rail, dt1=departure time up to 7am, dt2=7.01-8.30am), dt3= after 8.30am. The sample was choice- based sample with RP choice set weights, respectively = .120, .064, .041, .023, .257, .181, .053, .060, .106, .047, .014, .034; all SP weights = 1.0. Estimation by the method of Simulated Maximum Likelihood.

Table 3: Baseline MNL model results for weekend recreation

	Parameter Estimate	Asymptotic t-Ratio		Parameter Estimate	Asymptotic t-Ratio
Campground	0	—	FishingC	0.0524	1.2
Rustic Cabin	-0.2142	-4.2	BoatingC	0.1723	3.8
Rustic Lodge	-0.6636	-10.7	HikingC	0.1825	4.0
Hotel/Motel	0.0665	1.5	PlayGrdC	0.252	5.5
SEMiss	0.0135	0.3	PicnicC	0.0717	1.6
SWMiss	0.185	3.7	TwoWeeksC	0.0886	2
SCMiss	-0.0145	-0.3	NumCabC	0.024	0.1
Vicinity	-0.0001	0.0	EntryFeeLC	0.0112	0.2
Rugged	-0.0289	-1	CampFeeLC	0.0229	0.5
Lake	0.1633	5.5	SEMissL	-0.2539	-5.5
RegXLake	-0.0354	-1.2	SWMissL	-0.1893	-2.0
VisSep	0.032	1.1	SCMissL	0.1765	2.0
Quiet	0.1564	5.2	VicinityL	0.1502	1.7
VisXQui	0.0377	1.3	RuggedL	0.0103	0.2
TownL	-0.0276	-2.1	LakeL	-0.0271	-0.5
TownQ	-0.041	-1.4	RegXLakeL	0.3169	5.9
Tents	-0.0844	-2.9	TownLL	-0.0053	-0.1
ShoNear	0.215	4.4	TownQL	-0.0201	-0.8
ShoCent	0.174	3.5	BBQL	-0.0925	-1.7
NoSho	-0.1637	-3.1	FishingL	-0.0129	-0.2
ElecHkUp	0.0695	2.3	BoatingL	0.2889	5.4
WaterHkUp	0.0245	0.8	HikingL	0.2352	4.4
BBQ	0.0622	2.1	PlayGrdL	0.2673	5.0
Fishing	0.2258	7.5	PicnicL	0.1005	1.9
Boating	0.1414	4.8	TwoWeeksL	0.0714	1.4
Hiking	0.0614	2.1	NumRoomL	0.0057	0.1
PlayGrd	0.0321	1.1	EntryFeeLL	-0.0272	-0.5
Picnic	0.0179	0.6	CampFeeLL	0.0596	1.1
Friday	-0.0034	-0.1	SEMissH	-0.371	-6.7
Anytime	-0.0839	-2.2	SWMissH	-0.0471	-0.7
TwoCG	0.0184	0.6	SCMissH	0.1713	2.5
Sites75	0.0021	0.1	VicinityH	0.0026	0.0
TwoX75	-0.02	-0.7	RuggedH	0.0716	1.7
NoFee	-0.0076	-0.4	LakeH	-0.0608	-1.5
EntryFeeL	-0.0547	-1.3	RegXLakeH	0.1481	3.6
EntryFeeQ	-0.0142	-0.6	FishingH	0.0158	0.4
CampFeeL	-0.0458	-3.5	BoatingH	0.0953	2.3
SEMissC	-0.0228	-0.8	HikingH	0.108	2.6
SWMissC	0.0417	0.5	PlayGrdH	0.0475	1.2
SCMissC	0.1021	1.4	TwoWeeksH	0.0383	0.9
VicinityC	0.0088	0.1	NumHotelH	-0.0151	-0.4
RuggedC	-0.0242	-0.5	CampFeeLH	-0.055	-1.3
LakeC	0.0514	1.1	CampxTowns	-0.093	-2.3
RegXLakeC	0.2105	4.7	CampxRustic	-0.1098	-3.5
TownLC	0.0781	1.7	CampxWith Roads	-0.015	-0.4
TownQC	-0.0553	-2.7	CampxNoRoads	0.5489	1.6
BBQC	-0.0439	-1.0	Campx Wildrness	0.6725	2.7

10.7   Case 3: Parameterising The Error Component In Choice Experiments

Case 3 illustrates the design and analysis of a fairly complex SP task. The research objective was to develop a model of weekend recreation accommodation choices in and near National Forests in two US states (Missouri and Arkansas) and estimate the likely effects of a wide range of policy changes on campgrounds managed by the US Forest Service. The study was funded by the USDA Forest Service (North Central Forest Experiment Station, Urban Forestry Project, Chicago), who wanted to consider policy changes not previously implemented or investigated systematically. A very large number of actual choice options and resource constraints precluded parallel RP data collection; hence, we discuss only the SP experiment and associated choice models.

Accommodation choices included four National/State Forest options (two campgrounds, rustic cabins and rustic lodges), hotels/motels in nearby towns/villages or staying home and/or doing something else. Each option was described by different attributes, with some attributes common to all options (attributes listed in model estimation results in Tables 3 and 4).

The SP task was designed by treating all attributes of all accommodation choice options (two campgrounds, rustic cabins, rustic lodges and hotel/motel/bed & breakfasts) as a common factorial $((2^{11} \times 4^8) \times (2^{11} \times 4^8) \times (2^{13} \times 4^3) \times (2^{13} \times 4^3) \times (2^9 \times 4) = 2^{57} \times 4^{23} \ (\times 8))$, from which we selected an orthogonal fraction to make 128 choice sets (Louviere and Woodworth, 1983; Louviere, Hensher and Swait, 1999). Choice sets were blocked into 16 versions of 8 choice sets using the additional 8-level factor. A university survey research center pre-recruited a random sample of Missouri residents by phone, and mailed the survey to those agreeing to participate (no incentive provided), randomly assigning each to one version of the experiment. This design approach was used to permit estimation and comparison of a variety of complex model forms (eg, Nested Logit, HEV, Mother Logit, MNP, etc.).

The survey contained questions additional to the choice experiment (eg, recent outdoor recreation behaviour, types of activities preferred, visits to National Forests and selected socio-demographics) not discussed for space reasons. The analysis and model comparison described below is based on approximately 520 subjects (some subjects omitted 1-2 choice sets; hence the approximation). Data were weighted to equalise sample sizes in the 16 versions (eg, let sample size average 32, with version 1 =20 and version 2 = 45 subjects; then versions 1 and 2 data are weighted by 1.6 and 0.71, respectively), which avoids over- or under-emphasis of design matrices associated with particular versions that can lead to biased parameters.

Table 4:   *HEV Model Results [Scale=f(Recreation Opportunity Scale)] for*
              weekend recreation

Attribute/Model Effect	Parameter Estimate	Asymptotic t-Ratio	Attribute/Model Effect	Parameter Estimate	Asymptotic t-Ratio
ASC-Campground	0.000	—	FishingC	0.025	1.1
ASC-Rustic Cabin	-0.277	-4.3	BoatingC	0.079	3.5
ASC-Rust. Lodge	-0.661	-4.8	HikingC	0.076	3.4
ASC-Hotel/Motel	-0.759	-14.7	Play GroundC	0.137	5.2
SE. Missouri	-0.002	-0.1	Picnic areasC	0.014	0.6
SW. Missouri	0.079	4.4	Reserve 2 WksC	0.037	1.7
SC. Missouri	-0.008	-0.5	No. CabinsC	-0.007	-0.3
NF in vicinity	-0.005	-0.5	Entry FeeLC	0.012	0.6
Rugged	-0.009	-0.9	Camping FeeLC	0.002	0.1
Lake	0.060	5.8	SE. MissouriL	-0.120	-4.8
Rugged x Lake	-0.013	-1.4	SW. MissouriL	-0.075	-1.3
Visually Separate	0.016	1.6	SC. MissouriL	0.053	1.0
Quiet	0.066	6.2	NF in vicinityL	0.095	1.8
VisSep x Quiet	0.016	1.7	RuggedL	0.032	1.0
Distance TownL	-0.006	-1.3	LakeL	-0.019	-0.6
Distance TownQ	-0.013	-1.3	Rugged x LakeL	0.164	4.4
Tents	-0.023	-2.3	Distance TownLL	0.006	0.2
Shower Near	0.092	5.1	Distance TownQL	-0.004	-0.3
Shower Cent	0.060	3.5	BBQsL	-0.057	-1.8
No Shower	-0.070	-3.8	FishingL	0.021	0.7
ElecHkUp	0.019	1.9	BoatingL	0.165	4.3
WaterHkUp	0.012	1.2	HikingL	0.126	3.7
BBQs	0.023	2.2	Play GroundL	0.138	3.9
Fishing	0.085	7.4	Picnic areasL	0.065	1.9
Boating	0.051	4.8	Reserve 2 WksL	0.050	1.6
Hiking	0.032	3.1	No. RoomsL	-0.010	-0.3
Play Ground	0.012	1.1	Entry FeeLL	-0.026	-0.8
Picnic Area	0.001	0.1	Camping FeeLL	0.010	0.3
Arrive Friday	-0.008	-0.5	SE. MissouriH	-0.214	-4.9
Arrive Anytime	0.006	0.5	SW. MissouriH	-0.007	-0.1
2 camp grounds	0.001	0.1	SC. MissouriH	0.099	1.6
75 Sites	-0.001	-0.1	In vicinityH	-0.018	-0.3
2 campg x 75 sites	-0.010	-1.0	RuggedH	0.041	1.1
No Fee	-0.004	-0.7	LakeH	-0.039	-1.0
Entry FeeL	-0.031	-2.2	Rugged x LakeH	0.110	2.9
Entry FeeQ	-0.003	-0.3	FishingH	-0.024	-0.6
Camping FeeL	-0.014	-3.3	BoatingH	0.079	2.1
SE. MissouriC	-0.008	-0.8	HikingH	0.077	2.0
SW. MissouriC	0.033	0.9	Play GroundH	0.052	1.4
SC. MissouriC	0.048	1.3	Reserve 2 WksH	0.027	0.7
NF in vicinityC	-0.017	-0.4	No. HotelsH	-0.042	-1.1
RuggedC	-0.007	-0.3	Camping FeeLH	-0.026	-0.7
LakeC	0.021	1.0	Camping x Towns	-0.095	-2.5
Rugged x LakeC	0.081	3.6	Camping x Rustic	-0.143	-4.2
Distance TownLC	0.035	1.6	Camping x Roads	0.198	5.8
Distance TownQC	-0.018	-1.8	Camp'g x 0Roads	0.091	2.8
BBQsC	-0.016	-0.7	Camp'g x Wilds	0.081	3.3

SCALE FUNCTION PARAMETERS

Main effects (variables) in error variance function	Parameter Estimate	Asymptotic t-Ratio
Campground	0.0607	3.4
Rustic Cabin	1.0997	18.1
Rustic Lodge	0.5296	6.0
Hotel/Motel	0.4168	3.7
Prefer Towns	0.0000	—
Prefer Rustic	-0.1062	-4.7
Prefer WithRoads	0.0834	3.8
Prefer NoRoads	-0.0042	-0.2
Prefer Wilderness	0.0640	2.6

Again, due to space, we discuss only a baseline MNL model and a parameterised HEV model that allows different random component variances for individuals and choice alternatives. Individual variance differences are a function of preferences for types of recreation environments (from primitive wilderness to developed, modern urban areas; an environment is coded 1 if subjects consider it and -1 otherwise). This variance component model is justified by the fact that many marketing activities and/or policies can impact not only mean utilities or preferences but also their variances (Swait and Louviere 1993; Louviere, Hensher and Swait 1999; Meyer, et al. 1999). Thus, the HEV model in Table 4 allows random component variance differences in both choice options and individuals.

STATISTICS:
- Groups (sets) = 4113
- Cases = 24678
- Free Parameters = 101
- Log LL(B) = -6748.85; Log LL(0) = -7369.51; -2[LL(0)-LL(B)] = 1241.32
- Rho-Squared = 0.0842; AIC Rho-Squared = 0.0705

The estimation results clearly favour the HEV model over MNL, even though MNL allowed individual differences in choices to be a function of recreation environment preferences (213 LL point difference for relatively few additional effects). Both models contain alternative-specific attribute effects: the first set of effects without capital letters behind them are generic effects for the two campgrounds, additional effects have capital letters („C" for cabins, „L" for lodges and „H" for hotels/motels/B&Bs). Recreation environments for which respondents expressed preferences are:

1. Developed urban and modern (cities and towns)
2. Rural, small towns, resorts, some development
3. Rustic, rural, limited development like cabins, lodges, farms, ranches
4. Natural, roads, trails, limited development like isolated cabins & homes

5. Natural, no roads, no established development & marked foot & horseback trails
6. Wilderness, undeveloped, foot and horseback access only, primitive trails

In the interests of brevity, we concentrate on the HEV scaling function results, and ignore most attribute results, except to note that each accommodation option has unique (ie, alternative-specific) attribute effects. For example, subjects who chose campgrounds preferred quiet SW Missouri locations on lakes with fishing and boating; but those who chose cabins, lodges and hotels/motels/B&Bs prefered rugged NW Arkansas locations on lakes with playgrounds, boating and hiking.

The scale (inversely proportional to variance) results reveal that rustic cabins have the least average error variance, „stay at home" and campground have the most average variance, and rustic lodges and hotels/motels/B&Bs have intermediate variances. Those preferring natural environments with roads (#4 above) or undeveloped wilderness (#6 above) exhibit more choice variability than those preferring rustic, rural areas with limited development (# 3 above), followed by those preferring developed modern areas (#1) or natural areas with no roads (#5). These results suggest that it will be harder for policies aimed at managing rustic cabins to produce consistent results for this sample, but campground management policies should yield more consistent results, particularly for those who prefer the rustic, rural environments that characterise Missouri National Forests. For example, those who chose campgrounds tended to prefer SW Missouri National Forest areas on lakes with visually separated and quiet camp sites, fishing, boating and hiking, RV sites, electrical hookups, conveniently located shower facilities and barbecues. They also seem fairly sensitive to both entry and camping fees, which suggests that the costs of providing such facilities should be considered carefully against likely revenues before deciding which strategy to pursue in each National Forest Division.

10.8   Conclusions

This chapter sought to expand the domain of conjoint analysis techniques by placing them within the more general framework of random utility theory (RUT) based stated preference methods. Thus, we explained that RUT provides a general theoretical framework to design and analyse simple and complex SP experiments to capture a wide array of interrelated behavioural phenomena of interest to marketers, transport planners, environmental economists and many other fields. Furthermore, we noted that RUT also provides a key theoretical link to real behaviour that allows one to pool SP and RP data sources, or more generally any data sources consistent with RUT. Furthermore, RUT provides a level playing field by which models and model results can be compared and rigorously tested.

We illustrated these ideas in three case studies that show that even simple RUT-based SP experiments can yield quite complex models; and complex SP experiments can provide new and different insights into the behaviour of the random component of utility. In fact, the latter case suggests that researchers should consider if the factors they vary in experiments and/or context or experimental differences impact only mean utilities (the traditional object of research interest), but instead also impact the variance in utilities and preferences, a heretofore neglected area of inquiry.

That is, individuals' mean preferences not only differ, but the variability with which they make choices or express preferences also can differ; and differences in variability can matter strategically and substantively (ie, empirically). For example, the more variable an organisation's implementation of a policy (eg, service variability), the more uncertainty individuals have about its true mean, and hence the more variable their response may be to the policy itself. Similarly, the harder for consumers to determine a policy outcome, the more uncertain they will be about what to expect; hence the more likely they will be to stay with what they know. Thus, new phone services, bank accounts, etc., that confuse consumers about fees are likely to struggle against competitors who make it easier for consumers to evaluate fees or established, „safe" competitors.

Likewise, some consumers are inherently (for reasons not yet understood) more variable in their choices and preferences than others. The more consistent a consumer's preferences, the more likely that a policy targeted at her will yield the effects suggested by research. Thus, opportunities exist to develop fundamental knowledge about variability in preferences and choices by developing theory and/or establishing empirical regularities that allow us to understand what drives differences in variability within and between choice options and individuals.

As McFadden (1986) noted, there are few instances in which one needs individual-level utility results to develop useful models of choice behaviour. More complex and behaviourally meaningful RUT-based choice models now provide powerful insights and ways to model and predict choice behaviour. RUT provides a rich and comprehensive theoretical framework with which to develop models, combine sources of preference and choice data, obtain behavioural insights and make more accurate forecasts. This chapter introduced these topics and used case examples to illustrate their potential to broadening our knowledge and ability to model and forecast complex behavioural systems.

10.9   References

Adamowicz, W.L., Louviere, J. and Williams, M. (1994), Combining Stated and Revealed Preference Methods for Valuing Environmental Amenities, *Journal of Environmental Economics and Management*, 26, 271-292.

Adamowicz, W. L., Swait, J., Boxall, P., Louviere, J. and Williams, M. (1996), Perceptions versus Objective Measures of Environmental Quality in Combined Revealed and Stated Preference Models of Environmental Valuation, *Journal of Environmental Economics and Management*, 32, 65-84.

Allenby, G. and Ginter, J. (1995), The effects of in-store Displays and feature Advertising on Consideration Sets, *International Journal of Research in Marketing*, 12, 67-80.

Ainslie, A. and Rossi, P.E. (1998), Similarities in Choice Behavior Across Product Categories, *Marketing Science*, 17, 91-106.

Ben-Akiva, M E and Lerman, S (1985), *Discrete Choice Analysis: Theory and Application to Travel Demand,* Cambridge.

Ben-Akiva, M. and Morikawa, T. (1990), Estimation of Switching Models From Revealed Preferences and Stated Intentions, *Transportation Research*, 24A, 485-495.

Ben-Akiva, M., Bradley, M., Morikawa, T., Benjamin, J., Novak, T., Oppewal, H. and Rao, V. (1994), Combining Revealed and Stated Preferences Data, *Marketing Letters: Special Issue on the Duke Invitational Conference on Consumer Decision-Making and Choice Behavior*, 5, 17-31.

Ben-Akiva, M., Morikawa, T. and Shiroishi, F. (1991), Analysis of the Reliability of Preference Ranking Data, *Journal of Business Research*, 23, 253-268.

Bhat, C. (1995), A heteroscedastic extreme value model of intercity travel mode choice, *Transportation Research*, 29, 471-483.

Bhat, C. (1996), Accommodating variations in responsiveness to level-of-service measures in travel mode choice modeling, *Transportation Research*.

Bhat, C. (1997a), Incorporating Observed and Unobserved Heterogeneity in Urban Mode Choice Models, *Transportation Science*, under review.

Bhat, C. (1997), Recent methodological advances relevant to activity and travel behavior analysis, Conference Pre-prints, IATBR'97, *The 8th Meeting of the International Association of Travel Behaviour Research*, Austin, Texas.

Boersch-Supan, A. and Hajvassiliou, V. (1990), Smooth unbiased multivariate probability simulators for maximum likelihood estimation of limited dependent variable models, *Journal of Econometrics*, 58, 347-368.

Bradley, M. and Daly, A. (1994), Use of the logit scaling approach to test rank-order and fatigue effects in stated preference data, *Transportation*, 21, 167-184.

Brownstone, D., Bunch, D. and Train, K. (1997), Joint mixed logit models of stated and revealed preferences for alternative-fuelled vehicles, Conference Pre-prints, IATBR'97, *The 8th Meeting of the International Association of Travel Behaviour Research*, Austin, Texas.

Carson, R. T., Louviere, J. J., Anderson, D. A., Arabie, P., Bunch, D. S., Hensher, D. A., Johnson, R. M., Kuhfeld, W. F., Steinberg, D., Swait, J. D., Timmermans, H. and Wiley, J. B. (1994), Experimental Analysis of Choice, *Marketing Letters: Special Issue on the Duke Invitational Conference on Consumer Decision-Making and Choice Behavior*, 5, 351-368.

Chapman, R. and Staelin, R. (1982), Exploiting Rank Ordered Choice Set Data Within the Stochastic Utility Model, *Journal of Marketing Research*, 19, 288-301.

Chrzan, K. (1994), Three Kinds of Order Effects in Choice-Based Conjoint Analysis, *Marketing Letters*, 5, 165-172

Elrod, T., Louviere, J. and Davey, K. (1993), A Comparison of Ratings-Based and Choice-Based Conjoint Models, *Journal of Marketing Research*, 24, 368-377.

Erdem T. and M.P. Keane (1996), Decision-making under Uncertainty: Capturing dynamic Brand Choice Processes in turbulent Consumer Goods Markets, *Marketing Science*, 15, 1-20.

Guadagni P. M. and J. D. Little (1983), A Logit Model of Brand Choice Calibrated on Scanner Data, *Marketing Science*, 2, 203-238.

Geweke, J., Keane, M. and Runkle, D. (1994), Alternative computational Approaches to inference in the multinomial Probit Model, *Review of Economics and Statistics*, 76, 609-632.

Hensher, D. and Bradley, M. (1993), Using Stated Response Choice Data to Enrich Revealed Preference Discrete Choice Models, *Marketing Letters*, 4, 139-151.

Hensher, D. A. (1997), A practical Approach to identifying the Market for high speed rail: a case study in the Sydney-Canberra corridor, *Transportation Research,* 31, 431-446.

Hensher, D. A. (1998a), Establishing a Fare Elasticity Regime for Urban Passenger Transport: Non-Concession Commuters, *Journal of Transport Economics and Policy,* 32, 221-246.

Hensher, D. A., Boersch-Supan, A. and Brewer, A. (1999*), Alternative behavioural perspectives on interactive Agency Choice,* Institute of Transport Studies University of Sydney and Department of Economics, Mannheim University, forthcoming.

Johnson, N., Kotz, S. and Balakrishnan, N. (1995), *Continuous Univariate Distribution*, New York.

Johnson, R. (1989), Making Decisions with Incomplete Information: The First Complete Test of the Inference Model, *Advances in Consumer Research*, 16, 522-528.

Keane, M.P. (1997), Current issues in discrete Choice Modelling, *Marketing Letters*, 8, 307-322.

Krijnen, W.P. (1997), Some Remarks To Using Single-Factor Analysis, As A Measurement Model, unpublished working paper, Department of Marketing, University of Groningen.

Louviere, J.J. (1988), *Analyzing Decision Making: Metric Conjoint Analysis*. Sage University Papers Series in Quintitative Applications in the Social Sciences, 67, Newbury Park.

Louviere, J. (1994), Conjoint Analysis, in: Bagozzi, R. ed., *Advances in Marketing Research*, London.

Louviere, J. and Woodworth, G. (1983), Design and Analysis of Simulated Consumer Choice or Allocation Experiments: An Approach Based on Aggregate Data, *Journal of Marketing Research*, 20, 350-367.

Louviere, J., Fox, M. and Moore, W. (1993), Cross-Task Validity Comparisons of Stated Preference Choice Models, *Marketing Letters*, 4, 205-213.

Louviere, J. J., Hensher, D.A. and Swait, J. (1998), Combining Sourcs of Preference Data, *Journal of Econometrics, Special Issue on Marketing and Econometrics,* forthcoming.

Louviere, J. J., Hensher, D. A. and Swait, J. (1999), *Stated Choice Methods: Analysis and Applications in Marketing, Transportation and Environmental Valuation*, New York.

Luce, R. D. and Suppes, P. (1965), Preference, utility and subjective probability, in: Luce R. D., Bush R. R., and Galanter E., eds., *Handbook of Mathematical Psychology*, New York.

McFadden, D. (1974), Conditional logit analysis of qualitative choice behaviour, in: Zarembka P., ed., *Frontiers in Econometrics*, New York, 105-142.

McFadden, D. (1986), The Choice Theory Approach to Marketing Research, *Marketing Science*, 5, 275-297.

McFadden, D. (1981), Econometric Models of probabilistic Choice, in: Manski, C.F. and McFadden, D., eds., *Structural Analysis of Discrete Data with Econometric Applications*, Cambridge, 198-272.

McFadden, D. and Ruud, P. A. (1994), Estimation by Simulation, *Review of Economics and Statistics*, 76, 591-608.

McFadden, D. and Train, K. (1996), Mixed MNL Models for discrete Response, Department of Economics, University of California at Berkeley.

Meyer, R. (1977), An Experimental Analysis of Student Apartment Selection Decisions Under Uncertainty, Special Issue on Human Judgment and Spatial Behavior, *Great Plains-Rocky Mountains Geographical Journal*, 6, 30-38.

Meyer, R. and Eagle, T. (1982), Context Induced Parameter Instability in a Disaggregate-Stochastic Model of Store Choice, *Journal of Marketing Research*, 19, 62-71.

Meyer, R., Louviere, J., Bunch, D., Carson, R., Delleart, B., Hanemann, M., Hensher, D. Irwin, J. (1999), Combining Sources of Preference Data, *Marketing Letters, Special Issue on the HEC Invitational Conference on Consumer Decision-Making and Choice Behaviour,* forthcoming.

Morikawa, T (1989), *Incorporating Stated Preference Data in Travel Demand Analysis*, PhD Dissertation, Department of Civil Engineering, M.I.T.

Morikawa, T. (1994), Correcting state dependence and serial correlation in the RP/SP combined estimation method, *Transportation*, 21, 153-166.

Oliphant, K., Eagle, T., Louviere, J. and Anderson, D. (1992), Crosspresented at the 1992 Advanced Research Techniques Forum of the American Marketing Association, Beaver Creek.

Olsen, G.D. and Swait, J. (1995), Nothing is Important, unpublished working paper, Faculty of Management, University of Calgary, Alberta.

Olsen, G.D., Swait, J., Johnson, R., Louviere, J. (1995), Response Mode Influences on Attribute Weight and Predictive Ability When Linear Models are Not Certain to be Robust, unpublished working paper, Faculty of Business, University of Calgary, Alberta.

Revelt, D. and Train, K. (1996), Incentives for Appliance Efficiency: random Parameters logit models for households' Choices, Department of Economics, University of California, Berkeley.

Rushton, G. (1969), Analysis of Spatial Behaviour by Revealed Space Preference, *Annals of the Association of American Geographers*, 59, 391-400.

Simon H.A. (1983), *Reason in Human Affairs,* Stanford.

Stern, S. (1997), Simulation-based Estimation, *Journal of Economic Literature*, 35, 2006-2039.

Swait, J. and Louviere, J. (1993), The Role of the Scale Parameter in The Estimation and Use of Multinomial Logit Models, *Journal of Marketing Research*, 30, 305-314.

Swait, J., Louviere, J. and Williams, M. (1994), A sequential Approach to exploiting the combined strengths of SP and RP data: Application to Freight Shipper Choice, *Transportation*, 21, 135-152.

Swait, J., Adamowicz, W. and Louviere, J. (1998), Attribute-based stated Choice Methods for resource Compensation: An Application to oil spill damage assessment, *Paper presented at the NOAA Workshop on Application of Stated Preference Methods to Resource Compensation*, Washington.

Thurstone, L. L. (1927), A Law of Comparative Judgment, *Psychological Review*, 34, 273-286.

Train, K. (1997), Mixed logit models for Recreation Demand, in: Kling, C. and Herriges, J., eds., *Valuing the Environment Using Recreation Demand Models*, New York.

Wedel, W., Kamakura, W., Arora, N., Bemmaor, A., Chiang, J., Elrod, T., Johnson, R., Lenk, P., Neslin, S., and Poulsen, C.S. (1999), Heterogeneity and Bayesian Methods in Choice Modeling, *Marketing Letters, Special Issue on the HEC Invitational Conference on Consumer Decision-Making and Choice Behaviour*, forthcoming.

11 Conjoint Choice Experiments: General Characteristics and Alternative Model Specifications

Rinus Haaijer and Michel Wedel

11.1 Introduction

Conjoint choice experimentation involves the design of product profiles on the basis of product attributes specified at certain levels, and requires respondents to repeatedly choose one alternative from different sets of profiles offered to them, instead of ranking or rating all profiles, as is usually done in various forms of classic metric conjoint studies. The Multinomial Logit (MNL) model has been the most frequently used model to analyze the 0/1 choice data arising from such conjoint choice experiments (e.g., Louviere and Woodworth 1983; Elrod, Louviere and Davey 1992). One of the first articles describing the potential advantages of a choice approach for conjoint analysis was by Madanski (1980). His conclusion was that conjoint analysts could adopt the random utility model approach to explain gross trends or predilections in decisions instead of each person's specific decision in each choice presented. The real breakthrough for conjoint choice came with the Louviere and Woodworth (1983) article in which they integrated the conjoint and discrete choice approaches.

The MNL model is the standard model for analyzing discrete choices, and can be derived from utility maximization (McFadden 1976). However, the MNL model does not accommodate heterogeneity of consumer choice behavior and potentially suffers from the Independence of Irrelevant Alternatives (IIA) property, which may be too restrictive in many practical situations. Latent class or mixture MNL models have been developed to accommodate heterogeneity (Kamakura, Wedel and Agrawal 1994). The Multinomial Probit (MNP) model does not suffer from IIA and deals with heterogeneity, but this model has some practical limitations related to identification, prediction and obtaining the choice probabilities. Haaijer et al. (1998) were the first to use a special specification of the MNP model for conjoint choice experiments.

In this chapter we review the alternative approaches to analyze conjoint choice experiments. But before doing that, we briefly describe in section 13.2 the general elements in conjoint analysis and the „classic" conjoint analysis approaches. Next, in section 13.3, the conjoint choice approach is discussed more extensively and an overview is given of recent conjoint choice applications in the marketing literature. Section 13.4 gives several approaches that can be used to estimate a conjoint choice experiment, including the MNL, the Latent Class MNL, and MNP models. These various models will be illustrated using an application to a conjoint choice experiment on coffee makers. Finally, section 13.5 compares the results of the various models and gives further discussion and conclusions.

11.2   General Concepts and Classic Conjoint Analysis

In marketing one wants to know which characteristics of products or services are important to consumers, for reasons of product optimization, new product design, price setting, market segmentation and competitive positioning amongst others. A technique, originally developed in the early 60's by Luce and Tukey (1964), that could eventually be applied to answer that question, is conjoint analysis. In conjoint analysis products or services are defined on a limited number of relevant attributes or characteristics each with a limited number of levels. These products, called profiles, have to be evaluated by respondents, who rank or rate them (as described in this section) or choose their most preferred ones from smaller choice sets (see section 13.3). As an introduction to conjoint choice experiments, in this section we describe briefly the general characteristics of conjoint analysis and the „classic" conjoint approaches, including ranking and rating conjoint. For a more extensive review see, e.g., Green and Srinivasan (1978, 1990), Louviere (1988) or Carroll and Green (1995).

The conjoint methodology is a decompositional approach to analyze consumer preferences. Product profiles are constructed from the product attributes, each defined at a certain number of levels, using factorial or fractional factorial designs (the latter to reduce the number of profiles and respondent burden in evaluating them). Respondents give an overall „score" to each product profile and the analyst has to find out what the preference contributions are for each separate attribute and level. Here it is commonly assumed that the overall utility of a profile is constructed by adding the preferences for the attribute-levels. This implies a compensatory preference model, in which a „low" score on a certain attribute can be compensated by a „high" score on another attribute. In conjoint experiments the contribution of an attribute (level) to the total utility is called a „*part-worth*", and the total utility of a profile in a compensatory, additive preference model is equal to the sum of the part-worths: $U = \sum_s X_s \beta_s$, where U is the utility of the profile, X_s the value of attribute-level s and β_s is the weight parameter of attribute-level s. The part-worths can be computed from $X_s \beta_s$. More complex constructions are possible, such as a multiplicative model for the overall utility or interaction effects in the utility function.

Based on the analysis of the observed data several marketing questions can be answered (e.g., Vriens 1994) such as: 1) What is the (relative) importance of attributes and levels?, 2) What is the overall utility of specific profiles?, and 3) Are their individual differences?. Cattin and Wittink (1982) identified five different purposes for conjoint analysis in commercial applications: new product or concept identification, pricing, market segmentation, advertising and distribution. Later, competitive analysis and repositioning were added to this list (Wittink and Cattin 1989). Because conjoint analysis can be used for so many purposes, it has become a very popular marketing technique, with many applications in (commercial) marketing research (Cattin and Wittink 1982; Wittink and Cattin 1989; Wittink, Vriens and Burhenne 1994).

In a conjoint study several steps have to be taken. First of all, the attributes and the levels for each attribute have to be selected. Based on these attributes and levels the set of possible profiles can be constructed. However, it is easy to see that the total number of possible profiles can be very large even for a relative small number of attributes and levels. When there are for instance 3 attributes with 4 levels and 2 with 3 levels 576 ($4^3 \cdot 3^2$) different profiles can be constructed, which is clearly a too large number for respondents to rank or rate. Therefore, fractional factorial designs can be used to limit the total number of profiles in the analysis, while the main effects and first order interaction effects can still be estimated independently in many of these designs. The design one uses, and therefore the total number of profiles in the analysis, depends on how many interaction terms one wants to be able to estimate. In principle all kind of attributes, including price and brand, can be used in a conjoint study. However, the inclusion of brand as an attribute may lead to complications since it may represent implicit attributes such as quality (e.g., Oliphant et al. 1992; Struhl 1994). Having price as a separate attribute, orthogonal to the other attributes, may lead to unrealistic profiles, and care must be taken that no unrealistic price-brand, or price-attribute, combinations appear in the design. The selection of the number of levels of the attributes may also have some important implications. When all attributes have the same number of levels, the (absolute) values of the estimated part-worths give an indication of the (relative) importance of the attributes. However, it is not always possible to have the same number of levels for all attributes, since some attributes may be binary (e.g., a Yes/No or Present/Absent attribute) while others may have (many) more levels (e.g., „Brand"). Furthermore, Wittink et al. (1991) showed that when an attribute has more levels it becomes more important. They called this the „Number of Levels Effect", an effect that has led to a substantial stream of research in its own.

Second, the evaluation task has to be selected. Above we mentioned ranking and rating tasks, but many more data collecting methods are available that all fall within the class of („classic") conjoint analysis (see, e.g., Vriens (1995) for a detailed description of these methods), such as the full profile method (Green and Rao 1971), the tradeoff matrix method (Johnson 1974), the paired comparison method, Adaptive Conjoint Analysis (ACA) (Johnson 1985), or Hybrid Conjoint (Green, Goldberg and Montemayor 1981; Green 1984). All of these approaches can be used to obtain individual (segment or aggregate) level part-worths. Individual-level results are obtained using the observed „scores" of a respondent on the profiles and the characteristics of these profiles, and are often derived with regression-type procedures applied to each subject's data. Subject characteristics or classification procedures may be used, however, for segmentation purposes, where respondents that perform similar on the conjoint task are put together in segments, which may be described using the subject characteristics.

Third, one has to choose the way the profiles are presented to the respondent and the way the data are collected (cf., e.g., Vriens 1995). The presentation of profiles can be done verbally, as a (printed) list of attributes and levels, with the use of pictorials, computer aided designs or actual products. Data collection can be done with a personal interview, a mailed questionnaire, over the telephone, or with a computer assisted procedure. Of course, some combinations of profile presentation and data collection are more suitable than others and some are not (always) possible. For instance, the construction of actual products is only possible for a very limited number of product categories because of the costs involved to actually produce all profiles in the experiment. See Vriens (1995) for a more extensive discussion on these issues.

Green and Srinivasan (1978) classified estimation methods for conjoint analysis in three categories. First, they described methods that assume that the dependent variable is, at most, ordinally scaled. In that case estimation methods like MONANOVA (Kruskal 1965), PREFMAP (Carroll 1972), or LINMAP (Srinivasan and Shocker 1973a/b; Pekelman and Sen 1974) can be used. Second, when it is assumed that the dependent variable is interval scaled, OLS regression techniques can be used. Third, for the paired comparison data in a choice context, the binary Logit or Probit model can be used. Tho se models arise as special cases of the models that we discuss more extensively later in this chapter.

In order to test the predictive ability of conjoint analysis, respondents most often have to evaluate a so-called holdout task after the main task. This task is usually similar to the main task, but the set of profiles differs. The responses on these holdout tasks are not used for estimation purposes but for prediction. The idea is of course that the estimated model should predict the holdout results as well as possible. Especially when no „real-life" data are available, the holdout task is simple way to test the predictive validity of a conjoint model. When no separate holdout task is obtained, predictive power can be tested by using the results of part of the respondents for estimation purposes to predict the results of the remaining respondents. However, this latter approach is only viable at the aggregate level.

The results of classic conjoint analyses are often used to predict choice or market share (Cattin and Wittink 1982). For instance, one may be interested to know what the predicted market shares of a specific product modification would be, or how the introduction of a new or modified product may affect the market shares of existing products in the market. To answer these kind of questions, market simulations have to be performed. In order to do this the individual level estimates have to be converted to choices to predict actual market behavior of the respondents. Many choice rules are possible, but one often-used method to achieve this employs the first-choice rule, where it is simply assumed that respondents choose the product with the highest utility. However, this approach may be inadequate because a deterministic rule is used to predict a probabilistic phenomenon (e.g., Louviere and Timmermans 1990). With the first-choice rule, the situation that an alternative has a probability of being selected over another alternative of 51% is treated the same as the situation that an alternative has a probability of 99% of being selected, which clearly present very different sets of preferences.

DeSarbo and Green (1984) listed five reasons why choice predictions constructed from the results of ranking or rating conjoint may not be accurate. They stated that (classic) conjoint studies are subject to incompleteness with respect to profiles, because the profile is never equal to the product, incompleteness with respect to model specification, because most often only main effects and some two-way interactions are estimated, and incompleteness with respect to situation, because conjoint assumes equal effects for marketing control variables across suppliers. Furthermore, they mentioned the artificiality of the conjoint analysis, caused by the fact that the amount of information in reality may be different from that in a conjoint experiment, and the instability of tastes and beliefs of consumers, because they may change over time. All of the above may be reasons that choice predictions are not accurate. However, DeSarbo and Green (1984) mention that aggregate market predictions from conjoint analysis can be quite good.

11.3 Conjoint Choice Experiments

11.3.1 Conceptual

Conjoint choice analysis has some advantages as compared to conventional conjoint analysis. There are no differences in response scales between individuals, choice tasks are more realistic than ranking or rating tasks, respondents can evaluate a larger number of profiles, choice probabilities can be directly estimated, and ad hoc and potentially incorrect assumptions to design choice simulators are avoided (Carroll and Green 1995). Several other authors point out similar (as well as some additional) advantages of the choice approach relative to the conventional approach (e.g., Louviere 1988; Elrod, Louviere and Davey 1992; Sawtooth Software Inc. 1995; DeSarbo, Ramaswamy and Cohen 1995; Cohen 1997; Vriens, Oppewal and Wedel 1998).

In the classic conjoint approaches described in the previous section, all profiles are presented to the respondent, while in the choice approach the total set of profiles is divided into several choice sets and respondents have to choose their most preferred alternative from each choice set. To set the scale of utilities between choice sets a base alternative often is added to each choice set. An advantage of the choice approach is that this base alternative not only can be one particular product profile, but it can also be a so-called „no-choice" option (see Haaijer, Kamakura and Wedel 2001 for a detailed discussion on the base alternative in conjoint choice experiments). In this case the choice probabilities can possibly be interpreted as market shares of the various profiles. The probability for the „no-choice" then might be interpreted as an indicator for the overall preference for the product category under research (e.g., Louviere and Woodworth 1983; Oppewal and Timmermans 1993). A disadvantage of including a no-choice alternative in the design is that respondents choosing that alternative provide no information on the alternatives and attributes and hence some information is lost (Elrod, Louviere and Davey 1992). Another potential problem with the no-choice option is the reason why respondents choose it. A reason could be that their preferred brand or price level is not in the choice set (or in general because of the presence -or absence- of a specific level of any attribute). Furthermore, a reason to choose the no-choice could be that respondents are not interested at all to do the task. Finally, they may find the choice too difficult and choose the no-choice if they decide not to spend more time on the choice task and avoid the difficult choice. In those cases one needs to be careful how to interpret the estimated no-choice probability. Johnson and Orme (1996) claim, after analyzing several conjoint choice experiments, that there is no evidence that the latter explanations may be true.

11.3.2 Design

The approach Louviere and Woodworth (1983) developed involved constructing conjoint choice experiments with the use of 2^J designs when there are J possible alternatives, obtained by generating all possible combinations of attribute levels. If there are, for instance, two attributes each with two levels, four alternatives can be constructed. The 2^J design used then contains all combinations of the four alternatives present or absent in the choice set. From the full 2^J design an orthogonal main effects experimental design is selected such that a relatively small number of choice sets remain for estimation purposes. A disadvantage of 2^J fractional factorial designs is that when there are many alternatives (J), this approach will result in large tasks for respondents where choice sets can contain (too) many alternatives. A more general version of the 2^J fractional factorial design can be used when each choice set contains a fixed number of alternatives (M) and each alternative has S attributes with each L levels. In that situation a $L^{M \cdot S}$ main effects, orthogonal, fractional factorial experimental design can be used to create joint combinations of attribute levels (e.g., Louviere and Woodworth 1983; Steenkamp 1985; Louviere and Timmermans 1990). In case the number of levels is not equal for all attributes a $L^{M \cdot S}$ design still can be used, where L now represents the maximum number of levels present in the study. Columns in the design representing attributes with fewer levels can be constructed by converting the columns with L levels to columns representing attributes with fewer levels.

The actual coding of levels in the choice designs can be done in several ways. For numerical attributes (e.g., price) actual values can be used in the design, which leads to so-called linear attributes. However, most of the time some dummy specification is used. This specification can involve „regular" dummy coding (e.g., „1" if a level is present and „0" if it is not present) or so-called effects-type coding. In the situation of 3 levels of an alternative, with effects-type coding, the first level is coded, e.g., as *[1 0]*, the second as *[0 1]* and the third as *[-1 -1]*. For attributes with 2 levels the codes are +1 and -1 respectively. This way of coding has as advantage, when all attributes are coded this way and each level appears with equal frequency in the design, that the sum of the part-worths for each level is equal to zero, so that the total model is centered around zero. Combinations of different ways of coding are possible.

A specific characteristic of conjoint choice experiments is that one needs two designs, instead of one design in the classic conjoint approach, to set up the experiment. One design is needed to construct the profiles, like in the classic conjoint approach, but an additional design is needed to put these profiles in various choice sets. It is beyond the scope of this chapter to discuss extensively how efficient designs for conjoint (choice) experiments should be constructed, but the key elements are described briefly. For much more detail the interested reader is referred to, e.g., Addelman (1962), Louviere and Woodworth (1983), Steenkamp (1985, in Dutch), Kuhfeld, Tobias and Garratt (1994) or Huber and Zwerina (1996). In principle one wants the main effects and interaction effects to be orthogonal in the design, however, Kuhfeld, Tobias and Garratt (1994) show that orthogonal designs are not always more efficient than non-orthogonal designs, hence a trade off has to be made between these two concepts. Furthermore, they show that the efficiency of a given design is affected by the coding of quantitative factors, even though the relative efficiency of competing designs is unaffected by coding (Kuhfeld, Tobias and Garratt 1994, p. 549).

The range of levels for quantitative factors should be as large as possible to maximize efficiency. However, the levels should of course not be implausible. Huber and Zwerina (1996) describe four properties that characterize efficient choice designs. They mention level balance, orthogonality, minimal overlap and utility balance. Level balance means that each level of an attribute appears with equal frequency. However, level balance and orthogonality are often conflicting. Choice sets should have minimal overlap since alternatives that have the same level of an alternative provide no information on the preference for that attribute. Hence, the probability that an attribute level repeats itself in each choice set should be as low as possible. Level balance, orthogonality and minimal overlap are used to construct optimal utility-neutral designs. The efficiency of such design can be improved by balancing the utilities of the alternatives in each choice set. This is important since choice sets that generate extreme probabilities are less effective at constraining the parameters of the choice model than are moderate ones (Huber and Zwerina 1996, p. 308), although they do have a big positive impact on the log-likelihood of a choice model. So, a high likelihood may go together with imprecise parameter estimates for choice sets with more extreme probabilities. One possible way to achieve more utility balanced designs is simply by re-labeling the levels of the attributes, which has as advantage that it does not affect orthogonality, in contrast to swapping techniques. One problem not solved yet is how efficient designs can be obtained when a base alternative (such as a nochoice) is present in the experiment (Huber and Zwerina 1996), another is that efficient designs for the MNP model have not been developed yet, although recently design procedures for the related mixed logit model have been proposed (Sándor and Wedel 1999).

Another issue that plays a role is the type of design to use in the analysis: a design with fixed, randomized or individualized choice sets. With a fixed choice set approach each respondent (or each group of respondents, in a slightly more general fixed approach) receives exactly the same choice sets at exactly the same stage of the choice task. In a randomized experiment each respondent (or group of respondents) also receives the same choice sets but in a different order to compensate for learning and fatigue effects that are expected to average out in this way. In an individualized experiment each respondent receives his own choice sets. An advantage of individualized choice sets is that it can be tested whether preferences, or attribute importance, change in later stages of the choice experiment (Johnson and Orme 1996), since for each choice set (i.e., the 1st, 2nd, ..., last for each respondent) estimates can be obtained in this situation. A study by Johnson and Orme (1996) showed, when comparing several conjoint choice experiments, that the importance of brand decreases throughout a conjoint choice experiment, while that of price increases. A disadvantage of using individualized choice sets is that no choice frequencies can be computed for alternatives in each choice set, since each set is only evaluated by one respondent. Another disadvantage of individualized choice sets is that comparison and clustering becomes more difficult (Oliphant et al. 1992), which would be possible when all (groups of) respondents receive the same choice sets. In that latter case, respondents that show similar choice patterns can be grouped together in segments. This problem is however alleviated by mixture model approaches to conjoint choice experiments, as detailed below. Depending on what type of analysis, the fixed, randomized or individualized approach can be the preferred choice.

11.3.3   Applications

In this section an overview is given of recent applications of conjoint choice experiments in the marketing literature. Some of the studies listed here have been already discussed briefly in the previous section. This overview is not intended to be complete, but the aim is to give an impression of possible applications of conjoint choice. In particular, we will show for each study several characteristics of the conjoint experiment. Table 1 lists the studies we present in this overview (it was not possible to retrieve all information for all studies) .

Table 1 shows that the range of products investigated in conjoint choice experiments is rather wide. The products range from fast-moving consumer goods, like toothpaste, to durable products, like houses and cars. The same holds for the number of choice sets presented to the respondents and the number of alternatives in the choice sets. In the various applications, respondents had to choose from 3 to 32 choice sets containing 2 to 8 alternatives. The profiles in these choice sets were defined on 2-12 attributes. In the Oppewal, Louviere and Timmermans (1994) study 33 attributes where used, but their aim was to reduce this number using Hierarchical Information Integration.

The number of respondents used in the various studies also shows a wide range from 64 up to almost 1000 respondents. There seems to be more agreement about the type of base alternatives to use in a conjoint choice study. Most of the studies listed in Table 1 used „none", „own" or „other" base alternatives and only a few used a fixed profile as base. Most of the studies that did use a fixed base alternative assume a specific situation (for instance like „given that you are going on a holiday, what would be your most preferred trip") and are less interested in obtaining market shares, which is the major advantage of including some sort of „no-choice" base alternative. This may be the main reason to include such a base alternative in the other applications. Note that for the studies with only two alternatives no base alternative was used. The number of levels of the attributes used in the studies also shows a rather consistent pattern. Most studies use attributes with 2-4 levels. In situations that more levels are used for an attribute, this most often is a brand-attribute.

Table 1: Conjoint Choice Applications

Authors	Product/ Product category	Attri- butes	Choice sets	Alter- natives[*]	Respon- dents	Base	Levels / Design
Elrod, Louviere and Davey (1992)	Rental apartments	4	27	3	115	Own	$2^4 \cdot 3^4$
Oliphant et al. (1992)	Insurance	9	20	5	149	None	$4^2 \cdot 2^8$
Oppewal and Timmermans (1992)	Shopping centers	4	8/16	3 /4	?	Other	4^4
Chrzan (1994)	Mail orders	5	8	3	605	None	2^5
	Fashion access.	?	16	6	300	Other	$8 \cdot 4^2 \cdot 3^4$
	Consumer fashion	10	16	3	876	Other	$4 \cdot 3 \cdot 2^8$
Oppewal, Louviere and Timmermans (1994)	Shopping centers	33	3	3 /4	396	None	$4^5 \cdot 2^3 + 4^8 \cdot 2^5$
Allenby, Arora and Ginter (1995)	Batteries	3	12/24	2	65	-	3^3
Allenby and Ginter (1995)	Credit cards	7	13-17	2	946	-	$4^2 \cdot 3^3 \cdot 2^2$
Dellaert, Borgers and Timmermans (1995)	Activity packages	4	5/6	3	221	Fixed	3^4
DeSarbo, Ramas- wamy and Cohen (1995)	Food	2	16	8	600	Fixed	?
Timmermans and Van Noortwijk (1995)	Houses	4	16	3	278	None	$4^4 \, (4^8)$
Dellaert, Borgers and Timmermans (1996)	Flower exhibits	3	?	3	64	Fixed	$3 \cdot 2^2$
Dellaert, Borgers and Timmermans (1997)	Tourist Portfolio	12	12	3	±660	Fixed	3^{12}
Moore, Gray-Lee and Louviere (1998)	Toothpaste	5	32	5	184	None	?
Vriens, Oppewal and Wedel (1998)	Coffee makers	5	4/8	5/3	185	Fixed	$3^3 \cdot 2^2$
Wedel et al. (1998)	Cars	6	9	4	200	None	$8 \cdot 3^3 \cdot 2^2$

*: Base included

The information in Table 1 shows that conjoint choice experiments can be and have been used for a wide range of possible applications. In almost any situation in which consumers have to choose between several options the conjoint approach can be used to determine which attributes of the product are important for the

respondent. In this case „product" can be some fast moving product like toothpaste, a durable like a car or a house, a service such as tourist attractions, and even
products that are not actually bought by respondents, like „shopping centers". In
most of the recent applications the number of attributes, levels and choice alternatives used in the design is rather low (attributes and alternatives around 4, levels
around 3), although there are some exceptions. The number of choice sets that can
be presented to respondents showed a wide range. A recent study by Sawtooth
Software (Johnson and Orme 1996) showed that given the rather short response
times in conjoint choice experiments, many choice sets can be offered to respondents even without reducing the quality of the choices. With modern computer
assisted data collecting methods for conjoint choice the response times can be
obtained very easily, and can actually be used to improve estimation of partworths, see Haaijer, Kamakura and Wedel (2000).

11.4   Conjoint Choice Models

11.4.1   Introduction

In this section we discuss several approaches to analyze conjoint choice experiments. First of all, the standard MNL approach is discussed in section 13.4.3.
Second, section 13.4.4 describes the Latent Class MNL model. Section 13.4.5
provides two MNP models, one in which choice sets are assumed independent,
and one where the choices from one individual are treated as correlated. But first
we specify the general structure of conjoint choice models in this section and
describe the data we will use as application in section 13.4.2.

In a conjoint choice model each respondent has to choose one alternative from
each of several choice sets. These choice sets are constructed by dividing the set
of profiles over K choice sets. In this chapter we assume that each choice set contains the same number of alternatives, without losing generality. In order to formulate models for conjoint choice experiments, we start from random utility maximization (McFadden 1976). The utility of alternative m in choice set k for individual
j is defined as:

(1) $U_{jkm} = X_{km}\beta + e_{jkm},$

where X_{km} is a (1xS) vector of variables representing characteristics of the mth
choice alternative in choice set k, β is a (Sx1) vector of unknown parameters, and
e_{jkm} is the error term. Note that we assume that the X-matrix in (1) does not depend on j, because in conjoint choice experiments no individual characteristics
appear in the analysis in general. Note, however, that when an individualized
design is used X does depend on j, but we omit this index here for convenience.

For each individual j, it is assumed that the alternative with the highest utility is chosen and a variable y_{jkm} is observed which is for each choice set k defined as:

$$(2) \qquad y_{jkm} = \begin{cases} 1 \ when \ U_{jkm} > U_{jkn} \ \forall \ n \neq m \\ 0 \ when \ \exists \ n \neq m : U_{jkn} > U_{jkm} \end{cases} , \ n = 1, .., M \ .$$

As mentioned in section 13.3.1, in conjoint choice experiments a base alternative is often used in each choice set k to scale the utility over choice sets. This base alternative cannot only be a regular profile, it also can be specified as a no-choice alternative („None of the above") or an „own-choice" alternative („I keep my own product"). This kind of base alternative, however, presents the problems of how to include it in the design of the choice experiment, and in what way to accommodate it in the choice model. Regular choice alternatives are most often coded in the design matrix with effect-type or dummy coding. Since the no-choice alternative does not possess any of the attributes in the design, it is often coded simply as a series of zero's, which makes the fixed part of its utility zero in each choice set. However, the utility level of the no-choice alternative still has to be specified when effect-type coding is used, since the zeros of the no-choice act as real levels in that case and this potentially leads to biased estimates. The no-choice alternative can be specified in two ways. The first specification is to include a no-choice constant in the design matrix X in (1). This introduces one additional parameter in the model to estimate. Note that when brand dummies (or other attribute specific dummies) are used for each level of the attribute, no additional parameter is needed since in that case the utility level of the no-choice is already set by those dummies. However, the total number of parameters to estimate is equal in both cases. The second specification is to formulate a nested MNL model, in which it is assumed that subjects first choose between the no-choice and the other choice alternatives in the choice set, and in a second stage make their choice among the alternatives when they decide to make a „real" choice. This also introduces one additional parameter in the model, the *dissimilarity coefficient* of the Nested MNL model. Which of these representations for the no-choice option is preferable is discussed in Haaijer, Kamakura and Wedel (2001).

11.4.2   The Data

The various models that will be introduced in the next sections to analyze the above conjoint choice structure will be illustrated with an application, which is a replication of part of an application reported by Haaijer et al. (1998), with coffee-makers as the product category. The five attributes, and their levels, for the coffee-makers are listed in Table 2. Using a factorial design, sixteen profiles were constructed. Data were collected from 185 respondents, divided into two groups that received different choice sets based on the same sixteen profiles. Respondents had to choose from eight sets of three alternatives. Each choice set included the same base alternative, which is a fixed regular alternative in this experiment. Furthermore, eight holdout profiles were constructed, which were divided into four holdout sets with three alternatives, where the same base alternative was used as in the estimation data. These holdout sets were offered to all respondents. The estimation and holdout designs were coded using effects-type coding.

For all models in subsequent sections we will obtain parameter estimates. Furthermore, to compare model performance, we report the log-likelihood value, AIC and BIC statistics, and Pseudo R^2 value (e.g., McFadden 1976) relative to a null-model in which the probabilities in a choice set are equal for all alternatives. The AIC criterium (Akaike 1973) is defined as: $AIC = -2 \ln L + 2n$ and the BIC criterium (Schwarz 1978) is defined as: $BIC = -2 \ln L + n \ln(O)$, where $\ln L$ is the log-likelihood in the optimum, n the total number of estimated parameters in the model, and O the number of independent observations in the experiment.

Table 2:   Attributes and Levels of Coffee-Makers

Attribute Level	Brand	Capacity	Price (Dfl)	Special Filter	Thermos-flask
1	Philips	6 cups	39,-	Yes	Yes
2	Braun	10 cups	69,-	No	No
3	Moulinex	15 cups	99,-		

11.4.3   Multinomial Logit

The most popular discrete choice model is the Multinomial Logit (MNL) model. It follows when the assumption is made that the error term in (1), e_{jkm}, is independently and identically distributed with a Weibull density function. A Weibull density function for a random variable Y is defined as (see, e.g., McFadden 1976):

(3) $P(Y \le y) = \exp^{-\exp^{-y}}$.

This distribution belongs to the class of double negative exponential distributions as are, e.g., the Type I extreme value distribution and the Gumbell distribution, which are sometimes also used to specify the MNL model. The MNL model treats observations coming from different choice sets for the same respondent as independent observations. Therefore, in estimating the MNL model, 100 respondents choosing from 10 choice sets yields the same computational burden as 1000 respondents choosing from 1 choice set. In the standard MNL model, with one choice observation for each individual, the choice probabilities have a simple closed form. The choice probabilities in the conjoint MNL approach can be obtained through a straightforward generalization of this standard model.

The probability p_{km} that alternative m is chosen from set k is in this case simply equal to (cf., e.g., Maddala 1983, p. 60-61; Ben-Akiva and Lerman 1985; Swait and Louviere 1993):

$$(4) \qquad p_{km} = \frac{\exp(X_{km}\beta)}{\sum\limits_{n=1}^{M} \exp(X_{kn}\beta)} .$$

The standard log-Likelihood for discrete choice models is in the conjoint context for the MNL model extended by adding a summation over choice sets:

$$(5) \qquad L_{MNL} = \sum\limits_{j=1}^{J} \sum\limits_{k=1}^{K} \sum\limits_{m=1}^{M} y_{jkm} \ln(p_{km}) .$$

The simple and easy to calculate form of the choice probabilities (4) in the MNL model has much contributed to its popularity in conjoint choice experiments. However, there is a serious limitation to the use of this model that is related to the *Independence of Irrelevant Alternatives* (IIA) property. This property arises from the assumption of independent random errors and equal variances for the choice alternatives, and implies that the odds of choosing one alternative over another alternative must be constant regardless of whatever other alternatives are present (e.g., Louviere and Woodworth 1983; Ben-Akiva and Lerman 1985), which may often be too restrictive in practical situations. If it is assumed that the IIA property holds and the MNL model is used, predicting the choice probabilities of new alternatives can simply be done by inserting the attribute values of these new alternatives in the closed form expressions for the choice probabilities (4). Green and Srinivasan (1978) stated that in consumer behavior contexts the IIA property might not be a realistic assumption, especially when some of the alternatives are close substitutes (cf. McFadden 1976). When covariances across alternatives are incorrectly assumed to be zero, the estimates for the effects of explanatory variables are inconsistent (Hausman and Wise 1978; Chintagunta 1992). When the IIA property does not hold, other models that avoid IIA, should be used instead of the standard MNL model, however, at the cost of computational complexity. One of the most general of these models is the Multinomial Probit (MNP) model, which is discussed in section 13.4.4.

When the IIA assumption is true, the parameters of the Logit model can be estimated when the sufficient condition is satisfied that the alternatives are independent across choice sets (Louviere and Woodworth 1983). So, choices between alternatives must be pairwise independent across choice sets. The alternatives in a conjoint choice experiment are obtained by using an orthogonal, fractional factorial main effects design (Louviere and Woodworth 1983; Louviere and Timmermans 1990). A constant base alternative is useful, because it preserves the design orthogonality of the attribute vectors of conjoint alternatives (Louviere 1988;

Elrod, Louviere and Davey 1992). However, in the case of the Logit model, design orthogonality does not imply information orthogonality, for which the parameters would be uncorrelated. When similarities across alternatives are incorrectly assumed to be zero, the estimates for the effects of marketing variables are incorrect (e.g., Chintagunta 1992).

The expression for the choice probabilities (4) may be expanded to accommodate ranking data, which is particularly useful in conjoint analysis (McFadden 1986; Kamakura, Wedel and Agrawal 1994). However, the assumptions needed to translate rankings into choices may not hold, especially when individuals use elimination and nesting strategies the IIA property does not hold (Louviere 1988). Also, the use of brand names in the conjoint design may result in correlations between the utilities of the alternatives, violating the IIA property. In order to be able to test for IIA, design plans that allow as many relevant two-way interactions as possible to be tested can be used (Louviere and Woodworth 1983).

Table 3:   MNL Estimation Results

Attribute (level)	Est.	S.e.
β_1 Brand (1)	0.040^*	.013
β_2 Brand (2)	-0.329^*	.013
β_3 Capacity (1)	-1.015^*	.014
β_4 Capacity (2)	0.494^*	.010
β_5 Price (1)	0.313^*	.018
β_6 Price (2)	0.372^*	.013
β_7 Filter (1)	0.340^*	.070
β_8 Thermos (1)	0.312^*	.010
Statistics		
Ln-likelihood	-1298.706	
AIC	2613.412	
BIC	2655.810	
Pseudo R^2	0.201	

*: $p < 0.05$.

The MNL specification was used to analyze the data set described in section 13.4.2. In Table 3 the parameter estimates and fit statistics are listed. With the effects-type coding used, the part-worth for the last level of each attribute can be constructed by taking the sum of the estimates of the other levels of that attribute and change the sign. The results show that respondents prefer a high capacity to a low capacity, a low price level over a high price level, and that they prefer the presence of a special filter and thermos flask to the absence of those attributes. Finally, the third brand is the most attractive brand and the second least. The pseudo R^2 has a value of 0.201, which for this kind of choice data is a reasonable value. The estimates in Table 3 were used to predict the holdout sets. This resulted in a predicted log-likelihood of -754.860 (Pseudo R^2 =0.072). This shows that the MNL model does not a very good job in predicting the holdout sets in this application, since the obtained Pseudo R^2 has a value much lower as those resulting from the estimation sample.

The standard MNL model described in this section assumes that all respondents act similar in their choice behavior. However, several groups of respondents may exist that show different choice behavior. The next section describes the Latent Class MNL model that can be used to obtain segments of respondents.

11.4.4   Latent Class MNL

Next to its disadvantages related to the IIA assumption, the MNL model also suffers from the problem that it treats all subjects in the sample as homogeneous, and does not deal with heterogeneity. The MNL model cannot be estimated at the individual level, and thus subject-specific part-worths cannot be obtained (e.g., Elrod, Louviere and Davey 1992). The issue of subject heterogeneity has received a lot of attention in the marketing literature and has become a topic of much research (cf. Wedel et al. 1999). Basically, there are two ways to accommodate heterogeneity. In this section we deal with one, where one specifies a discrete distribution of the response coefficients β_j across the population, that is, one postulates that groups of respondents exist with different part-worths. This leads to latent class or finite mixture discrete choice models, which have been applied to conjoint choice experiments by Kamakura, Wedel and Agrawal (1994), and De-Sarbo, Ramaswamy and Cohen (1995). In the subsequent sections we deal with Multinomial Probit models that specify a continuous distribution of heterogeneity. Finite mixture models connect very well to marketing theories of market segmentation (Wedel and Kamakura 1997) and have enjoyed considerable success. Managers seem comfortable with the idea of market segments, and the models appear to do a good job of identifying segments from conjoint choice data.

Kamakura, Wedel and Agrawal (1994) developed a unifying mixture regression model for segmentation of choice data. Their approach assumes that choices are based on random utility maximization. The observed choice variables y_{jkm}, are assumed to be independent multinomial, and to arise from a population that is a mixture of Q unobserved segments, in proportions $\pi_1, \ldots, \pi_Q$. We do not know in advance from which segment a particular subject arises. The probabilities π_q are subject to the following constraints.

$$(6) \qquad \sum_{q=1}^{Q} \pi_q = 1 \quad \pi_q \geq 0 \quad q = 1,\ldots,Q$$

Given segment q, the choice probability for profile m for choice set k is:

$$(7) \qquad P_{km|q} = Prob[U_{km|q} \geq U_{kn|q} \quad n = 1,\ldots,M, n \neq m],$$

where $U_{km|q}$ is the random utility derived from alternative m at k in segment s. Consumers are assumed to maximize their utility over the entire choice set, $U_{km|q} = \max\{ U_{kn|q}\ n = 1, \ldots M \}$. As before, the random utility for segment q is assumed to be a function of the attributes:

$$(8) \qquad U_{km|q} = X_{km}\ \beta_q + \varepsilon_{kmq} .$$

If the random components, ε_{kmq}, are assumed to be independent and identically Weibull distributed, the choice probabilities for segment q are:

$$(9) \qquad P_{km|q} = \frac{\exp[U_{km|q}]}{\sum\limits_{n=1}^{M}\exp[U_{kn|q}]}.$$

The idea behind the mixture model is that if the probability conditional upon knowing the segments have been formulated, the unconditional probability of observing the K choices is obtained as:

$$(10) \qquad P_j = \sum\limits_{q=1}^{Q}\pi_q \prod\limits_{k=1}^{K}\prod\limits_{m=1}^{M}P_{km|q}^{Y_{jkm}}.$$

As additional features of the model, the prior probabilities of segment membership can be reparameterized according to a concomitant variables model and the model can deal with rank-ordered data (Kamakura, Wedel and Agrawal 1994). Wedel et al. (1998) extended this mixture model for conjoint choice experiments by assuming that the brand can be decomposed into latent dimensions and segment-specific ideal points along those dimensions. The utility function further contains a linear combination of the attribute-level dummies. This model integrates conjoint analysis and multidimensional scaling, which makes it especially suited for product positioning.

The mixture regression model for conjoint choice experiments was applied to the coffee-maker data for $Q = 1$ up to 6 segments; the BIC statistic indicated $Q = 4$ segments as optimal. The four- segment solution was run ten times from different starts to overcome problems of local optima. Table 4 gives the estimated parameters for all 4 segments.

Table 4 shows that the four segments differ in their preferences for the attributes. The first segment (49,7% of the sample) wants a coffee-machine that contains as many features as possible, for a as low price as possible, but it does not matter what brand it is, since the brand parameters are not significant different from zero for this segment. So, this seems to be a price-sensitive segment. The second segment (17,4%) does not want a low capacity machine and prefers one with a thermos-flask, but this segment seems more quality seeking, since its partial utility for the lowest price level is negative, while that for the highest price level has the highest partial utility. This segment also has no preference for a particular brand. The third segment (13,5%) also likes only one feature (a special filter in this case), but does not want to pay a high price for it. This segment in addition has a preference for one of the brands (brand 2). Finally, the fourth segment (19,4%) finds the brand of the coffee-machine most important. It has a high preference for the first and third brand, and in addition for the presence of a special filter. So, this segment seems to be a real brand-seeking segment.

Table 4:   *LCMNL Estimation Results*

Attribute (level)	Segm. 1		Segm. 2		Segm. 3		Segm. 4	
	Est.	S.e.	Est.	S.e.	Est.	S.e.	Est.	S.e.
β_1 Brand (1)	0.005	.179	0.289	.188	-0.051	.316	0.920*	.202
β_2 Brand (2)	-0.224	.163	-0.321	.179	0.683*	.295	-1.673*	.346
β_3 Capacity (1)	-2.681*	.289	-0.956*	.247	-1.191*	.481	-0.001	.165
β_4 Capacity (2)	1.302*	.152	0.627*	.175	0.578*	.266	0.355	.203
β_5 Price (1)	1.263*	.284	-0.934*	.346	1.431*	.359	-0.322	.271
β_6 Price (2)	0.698*	.213	0.150	.193	0.605	.312	-0.064	.218
β_7 Filter (1)	0.630*	.132	0.134	.133	1.753*	.340	0.390*	.133
β_8 Thermos (1)	0.461*	.139	0.876*	.167	0.289	.159	-0.053	.167
Segment Size	0.497		0.174		0.135		0.194	
Statistics								
Ln-likelihood	-1040.271							
AIC	2115.542							
BIC	2336.058							
Pseudo R^2	0.360							

*: p < 0.05.

From the results of an Latent Class analysis different marketing strategies can be developed for the various segments, provided that these are big enough to make it profitable to develop a specific strategy. Table 4 shows that the smallest segment (segment 3) still contains 13.5% of the respondents, which may be big enough to target. The estimates in Table 4 were used to predict the likelihood of the holdout choice sets. This gives a predicted log-likelihood for the LCMNL model of -708.832 (Pseudo R^2 =0.128). Comparing this to the predictive fit of the MNL model (Pseudo R^2 =0.072) we see a substantial improvement. Thus the LCMNL model improves upon the MNL model by accommodating heterogeneity, by providing actionable information on market segments, and by providing better holdout predictive performance.

Although the LCMNL model accounts for consumer heterogeneity, it still treats choices made by the same respondent as independent. In the next section two versions of the MNP model will be developed. One in which it is still assumed that choice sets are independent, but choice alternatives within a choice set may be correlated, and one that in addition relaxes the independence of choice sets.

11.4.5 Multinomial Probit

Introduction

In the previous section we saw how latent class MNL model can be used to account for heterogeneity. The MNP model also presents a way to deal with continuous heterogeneity distributions of the part-worths across consumers. Specifically, the parameters are specified to follow a normal distribution, which by some has been argued to be a better representation of heterogeneity than a discrete mixing distribution (Allenby and Rossi 1999). The continuous heterogeneity distribution has several advantages: It has been argued to characterize the tails of heterogeneity distributions better and may predict individual choice behavior more accurately than finite mixture models, since the tails may have a substantial impact on the predictive performance of the models. It provides a parsimonious representation of heterogeneity and flexibility with regard to the appropriate choice of the distribution of heterogeneity (see, e.g., Arora, Allenby and Ginter 1998).

In the conjoint choice context, the Multinomial Probit model (MNP) offers the major advantage of allowing correlations among the repeated choices that consumers make from the multiple choice sets next to allowing correlation of random utilities of alternatives within choice sets. This follows since the MNP model relaxes the assumption of independence of the error terms in random utility models (e.g., Daganzo 1979; Kamakura 1989), and thereby alleviates IIA. Factors such as learning, boredom, or anchoring to earlier choice tasks may distort the measurement of preferences when these are assumed independent, like in the MNL model, and these effects should be tested and/or accounted for (McFadden 1986). Several studies showed that subjects' utilities for alternatives may indeed depend on the choice context (e.g., Huber, Payne and Puto 1992, Simonson and Tversky 1992; Nowlis and Simonson 1997), where „context" is defined as the particular set of alternatives evaluated. Since the design of conjoint choice analysis involves only a subset of all possible profiles (constructed by fractional factorial designs) and choice sets that vary in composition (constructed by blocking designs), context effects are likely to occur in those experiments. Simonson and Tversky (1992) distinguished *local contrast effects* and *background contrast effects*. Local contrast effects are caused by the alternatives in the offered set only, while background contrast effects are due to the influence of alternatives previously considered. In a conjoint choice experiment, local contrast effects may occur due to the composition of a particular choice set in terms of the attribute levels of the profiles, affecting attribute importance, inducing correlations among the utilities of profiles in the choice set and leading to a violation of IIA (Simonson and Tversky 1992). On the other hand, background contrast effects may occur in conjoint choice experiments if the attribute importance of profiles in a particular choice set are influenced by tradeoffs among profiles in previous choice sets. In this case covariance among the random utilities of alternatives in different choice sets may occur. This violates the assumption of independence of choices among alternatives in different sets, as assumed in the MNL model. For a more extensive discussion on context effects see, e.g., Tversky (1972), Huber, Payne and Puto (1982), Huber and Puto (1983), Simonson (1989), or Simonson and Tversky (1992).

Timmermans and Van Noortwijk (1995) explicitly modeled context effects in conjoint choice experiments by including cross effects in the design matrix such that the utility of an alternative depends on its own and other alternatives' attributes. However, they only model context effect within choice sets (i.e., the local context effects) and not between choice sets (i.e., the background context effects). Haaijer et al. (1998) applied the MNP model to conjoint choice experiments, accounting for both the local and the background context effects described above through a specific covariance structure. They showed that it is important to account for both types of context effects. Two sections below give a MNP model that deals with heterogeneity, IIA and local context effects, and a MNP model that in addition accounts for background context effects, respectively.

First we specify the MNP model in general, starting again from the utility function. Assume again that there are J respondents, each receiving the same H profiles which are divided into K smaller sets with M alternatives each. A base alternative that is common to all sets is added to the profiles and scales the utility levels between choice sets. This base alternative can be a no-choice alternative or a regular profile. The other profiles are unique to their particular choice set, so that $H = K(M1)+1$. The utilities of the alternatives for individual j are contained in the latent unobservable vector u_j, which satisfies:

(11) $u_j = X \beta_j + e_j$,

where X is a (HxS)-matrix containing the attributes of the alternatives, β_j is a (Sx1) vector of random weights, and e_j is the vector containing the random component of the utilities.

In the MNP model is it assumed that e_j is distributed as:

(12) $e_j \sim N_H (0, \Sigma_e)$,

independent between individuals; Σ_e is a (HxH) positive definite covariance matrix. In the MNP model not only the -parameters in (11) have to be estimated but also the parameters in the covariance matrix Σ_e.

A potential problem of the MNP model is that of identification. A model is identified when there is only one set of estimates that maximizes the likelihood. When different parameter estimates give the same results, interpretation of the estimates becomes difficult. Bunch and Kitamura (1989) demonstrated that nearly half of the published applications of MNP are based on non-identified models. It is easy to see that when the covariance matrix in (12) of the MNP model is multiplied with a factor β and all -estimates in (11) with a factor $\sqrt{\alpha}$, that this leads to the same results. So, at least one parameter in the MNP model must be fixed to scale the model and to identify the other parameters. Often, one of the variance parameters is used for this purpose, but this is not sufficient, however. In the standard MNP model with one choice set (K=1), only $M(M-1)/2-1$ of the $M(M+1)/2$ covariance parameters in Ω are identified (Dansie 1985; Bunch 1991; Keane 1992). So, $M+1$ restrictions must be imposed on the Ω-matrix in this situation.

Furthermore, in conjoint choice experiments, (holdout) predictions are often required. Another problem, besides identification, of the general MNP formulation is that these predictions for new profiles, not included in the conjoint design, cannot be made with the covariance matrix in (12) because in predicting choice probabilities for alternatives not included in the design of the experiment, estimates of the covariances of these new profiles are required and those are not available (cf., e.g., Pudney 1989 p.115; Elrod and Keane 1995; Haaijer et al. 1998).

In order to arrive at an MNP model for conjoint choice experiments that is both identified and that allows for predictions of new profiles, restrictions have to be imposed on the covariance matrix. We allow for heterogeneity in the attribute level coefficients by specifying β_j in equation (11) as (cf., e.g., Hausman and Wise 1978; Daganzo 1979; Ben-Akiva and Lerman 1985):

$$(13) \qquad \beta_j = \beta + \psi_j,$$

with $\psi_j \sim N_S\left(0, \Sigma_\psi\right)$, independent of e_j. Then

$$(14) \qquad u_j \sim N_H\left(X\beta, \Omega\right),$$

with:

$$(15) \qquad \Omega = \Sigma_e + X\,\Sigma_\psi\,X'.$$

The specification that enables the prediction of new alternatives that we use assumes $\Sigma_e = I_H$, and for reasons of parsimony and identification we parameterize Σ_ψ as a matrix of rank one: $\Sigma_\psi = \sigma\,\sigma'$, with an S-vector of parameters, where S is the number of columns in the X-matrix. The number of parameters in Ω now is equal to the number of β-parameters. Especially when the number of columns (S) in X or the number of profiles (H) is large, this specification for Ω is very parsimonious compared to a full random coefficients model or general Probit model. A more general specification for Ω results in an increase in the number of covariance parameters so that identification often becomes a problem. So, we now have:

$$(16) \qquad \Omega = I_H + X\,\sigma\,\sigma'\,X'.$$

This random coefficients model may account for heterogeneity, violations of IIA, and local and background context effects potentially caused by all attributes in the conjoint design. See Haaijer et al. (1998) and Haaijer (1999) for a more extensive discussion of this specification and its characteristics. Rossi, McCulloch and Allenby (1996) developed a related random coefficients Bayesian MNL model.

Like for the MNL and LCMNL model, estimates for the parameters are obtained for the MNP model by maximization of the likelihood (see below) over β and the parameters in the covariance matrix. However, when there are more than three alternatives in a choice set the choice probabilities cannot be evaluated numerically in the MNP model (cf., e.g., McFadden 1976; Maddala 1983; Kamakura 1989; Keane 1992). Simulation techniques have been developed that solve this problem of the MNP model. To obtain the estimates in the MNP models in the next two subsections, the Simulated Maximum Likelihood (SML) method is applied using the SRC simulator. A discussion of simulation techniques is beyond the scope of this chapter, for an extensive discussion see, e.g., Hajivassiliou (1993).

Multinomial Probit with independent choice sets

A straightforward way to apply the MNP model is to use it in the similar way as the MNL model. In this case we take an individual's utilities to be independent between the choice sets, and thus account for local, but not for background context effects. We then have JK independent observations, and the log-likelihood is again a straightforward generalization of the standard likelihood of choice models, where a summation over choice sets is introduced, similar as in the MNL model of section 13.4.3 Letting p_{km} denote the fraction of individuals choosing alternative m in set k, the log-likelihood is (in a slightly different notation as the log-likelihood (5) of the MNL model) equal to:

$$(17) \qquad L_{MNP_{csi}} = J \sum_{k=1}^{K} \sum_{m=1}^{M} p_{km} \ln \left(\pi_{km} \right),$$

where π_{km} is the probability that alternative m is chosen in set k. Note again that in conjoint choice models consumer characteristics or other individual specific variables are usually not included, hence π_{km} does not depend on j and each individual has the same probability of choosing any specific alternative, since we assumed that they all receive the same choice sets. This model is called the choice-set-independent MNP model (MNP$_{csi}$). For this MNP model, the assumption of utility maximization results in an expression for π_{km} that involves an $(M\text{-}1)$-dimensional integral:

$$(18) \quad \pi_{km} = P\left(u_{kn} - u_{km} \leq 0 \; \forall \; n \neq m \in \Delta_k \right) = P\left(\tilde{u}_{km} \leq 0 \right) = \int_{-\infty}^{0} d_{km}(t) \, dt$$

where Δ_k is the set of profiles in choice set k and $d_{km}(.)$ is the density of $\tilde{u}_{km}$. This specification accounts for local contrast effects only, since it allows utilities within choice sets to be correlated.

Table 5: MNP_{csi} Estimation Results

Attribute	β		σ	
(level)	Est.	S.e.	Est.	S.e.
1 Brand (1)	-0.106	.203	0.717	.386
2 Brand (2)	-0.179	.222	0.107	.665
3 Capacity (1)	-1.166*	.123	0.585*	.270
4 Capacity (2)	0.587*	.090	-0.001	.224
5 Price (1)	0.326	.497	-0.084	.599
6 Price (2)	0.378	.269	0.482	.473
7 Filter (1)	0.354*	.098	0.298	.372
8 Thermos (1)	0.269	.152	0.173	.259
Statistics				
Ln-likelihood	-1279.100			
AIC	2590.201			
BIC	2674.997			
Pseudo R^2	0.213			

*: $p < 0.05$.

In Table 5 the coffee-maker data results are listed for the structural parameters β and the covariance parameters σ, as well as the fit-statistics. It shows that the results of the MNP_{csi} model are a somewhat disappointing. Although it produces a better log-likelihood than the MNL model, due to the high standard errors only a few parameters are significantly different from zero with a p-value of 5%. The results indicate that the capacity and presence of a special filter are the only relevant attributes. Furthermore, the one significant covariance parameter (belonging to the first capacity level) is responsible for the increased fit of the MNP_{csi} model with respect to the MNL model, but no clear conclusions can be drawn from these results. In addition, the AIC and BIC statistics indicate that the LCMNL has better fit than the MNP_{csi} model. The estimates of Table 5 were use to predict the hold-out sets. The predicted log-likelihood is equal to -784.677 (Pseudo $R^2 = 0.035$), which is worse from the LCMNL model and even worse than those of the MNL model.

The results of the MNP_{csi} model indicate that allowing for heterogeneity and correlation of utilities within choice sets may help to improve model fit in terms of the log-likelihood value. However, this application also showed that the discrete (LCMNL) representation of heterogeneity seems to do better than the continuous (MNP) one. In the next subsection the MNP model that in addition allows for correlations between choice sets is developed.

Multinomial Probit with dependent choice sets

The MNP specification in the previous subsection only allowed for correlations within choice sets and not between. In this section we assume that utilities of the same individual are not independent over choice sets, but rather that utilities of alternatives in different choice sets are correlated. In this case a total probability has to be obtained for the complete choice observation of an individual. A simple example illustrates this. Assume we have two choice sets with each three alternatives (so, $H=5$). For each individual we observe two choices, one from each set. Consider an individual j choosing the second alternative from the first set and the base alternative from the second choice set. The resulting joint probability for this example is equal to (b represents the base alternative):

$$(19) \qquad \pi_{2b} = P \left(u_{j12} > u_{j11} , u_{j12} > u_{j1b} , u_{j2b} > u_{j21} , u_{j2b} > u_{j22} \right).$$

This probability can be expressed involving a four-dimensional integral. In the general case, a K-vector of choices is observed for each individual, and we have to consider M^K arrays containing the multiple choices from different choice sets. Each array corresponds to a joint probability, involving an $(H\text{-}1)$-dimensional integral that describes the probability of observing the array of choices from all choice sets (cf. Hausman and Wise 1978; Papatla 1996). In this case, the form of the probabilities for the MNP model becomes somewhat complicated, and we omit the formal presentation of these probabilities since the notation provides no additional insight.

The log-likelihood for this MNP approach is equal to:

$$(20) \qquad L_{MNP} = J \sum_{l=1}^{M^K} p_l \ln \left(\pi_l \right),$$

where l indexes the K-dimensional choice arrays, p_l denotes the observed fractions of the choice arrays, and π_l denotes the choice probabilities expressed as functions of the model parameters. This specification accounts for both the local and background contrast effect, because the choice probabilities, as in (19), depend on all profiles in the design or, alternatively, with heterogeneity of the parameters across choice sets. This is not the case with models that treat the choice sets as independent, such as the MNL model, LCMNL model and the MNP model of the previous subsection.

Table 6 lists the parameter estimates and fit statistics. After estimation, all eigenvalues of the final Hessian were positive, indicating that the model is identified (Bekker, Merckens and Wansbeek 1994).

Table 6 shows the same pattern of β-estimates as in the MNL model. However, the fit of the MNP model is much better than that of the MNL model. This is caused by the estimated covariance parameters. The log-likelihood of the MNP model is somewhat lower than that of the LCMNL model, and consequently also the Pseudo R^2 is lower. The AIC statistic would favor the LCMNL model over the

MNP model, but the BIC statistic, which penalties the likelihood more severely, indicates the MNP model as best. Table 6 shows that most attribute levels are potentially responsible for correlations between and within choice sets. Note, however, that because of the effects-type coding some effects may cancel out (see Haaijer (1999), chapter 5.2.4 for a discussion), so one has to investigate not only the estimated parameters but in addition the estimated covariance matrix (16).

Table 6:   *MNP Estimation Results*

Attribute (level)	β		σ	
	Est.	S.e.	Est.	S.e.
1 Brand (1)	-0.029	.101	0.417*	.096
2 Brand (2)	-0.240*	.078	-0.387*	.099
3 Capacity (1)	-1.075*	.092	0.850*	.094
4 Capacity (2)	0.565*	.060	-0.348*	.083
5 Price (1)	0.432*	.116	-0.562*	.139
6 Price (2)	0.244*	.082	-0.145	.100
7 Filter (1)	0.355*	.038	0.023	.058
8 Thermos (1)	0.393*	.054	-0.206*	.071
Statistics				
Ln-likelihood	-1086.622			
AIC	2205.245			
BIC	2256.770			
Pseudo R^2	0.332			

*: $p < 0.05$.

Interestingly, the covariance matrix of the MNP model reveals alternatives with near zero covariances with all other alternatives. This indicates that these are (almost) independent of the other alternatives. After constructing the Ω matrix the σ-estimates reveal what attribute (levels) are responsible for correlations within and between choice sets.

The estimates of the MNP model were again used to predict the holdout sets. For the MNP model the predicted log-likelihood is equal to -679.075 (Pseudo R^2 =0.165). This shows that it is very important to account for both kind of correlations, or context effects, which not only results in an improved model fit, with relatively few covariance parameters, but also in an improved holdout predictive fit, which is better than that of the MNL, MNP$_{csi}$, and LCMNL models.

11.5   Discussion and Conclusion

In the above sections we showed several models that can be used to analyze conjoint choice experiments. We discussed the standard MNL model, the Latent Class

MNL model and two versions of an MNP model with a specific covariance structure. The performance of the models was illustrated with an application. It is interesting to compare the results of the various models, although we realize that this comparison is based on only this one application, so some care must be taken with respect to drawing conclusions.

When we compare the estimated log-likelihood values, the LCMNL model gives the best result, followed by the MNP model. At some distance the MNP_{csi} model and MNL model follow. However, since the number of parameters in the LCMNL model is much larger than that in the MNP model (35 and 16 respectively), the BIC-statistic, that compensates for the number of parameters and observations in the model, ranks the MNP model as best. The AIC-statistic, that only puts a penalty on the number of parameters, still lists the LCMNL model as best. If we compare the predictive power of the models the MNP model comes out as best, followed by the LCMNL, MNL and MNP_{csi} models. Based on these results one could conclude that the using the MNL model for (conjoint) choice experiments may not be a good choice. It does not account for heterogeneity and correlated choice alternatives within and between choice sets. This results in an inferior model fit and predictive fit compared to models that do account for these elements. On the positive side, however, we saw that the estimates for the structural parameters do not differ much between the models. This is in line with findings by Börsch-Supan et al. (1990), who also found that differences in model fit, with respect to the log-likelihood value, is often caused by the error structure while the structural parameters are relatively left unaffected, although a misspecified covariance matrix not only affects the standard errors of the covariance parameters but also of the structural parameters. This is exactly what may have happened in the MNP_{csi} model. So, in terms of finding the „right" structural parameters the MNL model may do a reasonable job, but when these results are used to predict the performance of new alternatives, or holdout choice sets, the MNL model falls short to the LCMNL and MNP model. Of course, further research should be done to test the generalizability of these findings. Haaijer et al. (1998) tested three data sets, including the one in this chapter, and found in all three cases that the MNP model outperforms the Independent Probit model (which has similar characteristics as the MNL model) on estimation fit and holdout predictive power. Haaijer, Kamakura and Wedel (2000) support these findings for two other data sets.

Several authors have compared continuous and discrete specifications of heterogeneity (e.g., Lenk, DeSarbo, Green and Young 1996; Vriens, Wedel and Wilms 1996; Allenby, Arora and Ginter 1998; Allenby and Rossi 1999). These comparisons were made on scanner panel data rather than on conjoint choice data. Nevertheless, the conclusion from these studies is that for predictive purposes continuous (MNP) specifications may be preferable over discrete (LCMNL) specifications. From a substantive angle, the MNP-type of specification, particularly when applied in conjunction with the Gibbs sampler, that allows for individual level parameters to be estimated, seems preferable in direct marketing applications, where such individual level estimates are of great use in targeting individuals. However, advantages of the discrete model specification accrue in situations where managers are interested in targeting market segments (see Wedel and Ka-makura 1997 for an extensive discussion).

Several other issues need to be further investigated. The findings of this chapter that local and background context play a role in respondents' choices should be studied more closely. The importance of these effects in relation to the number of attributes, choice sets, levels of attributes and alternatives could be given additional attention. The attribute level effect found in the literature could be particularly related to context effects. Furthermore, the involvement of respondents and their knowledge on the product category, as well as the product category itself, could also influence the importance of these context effects. The influence of all these factors on the choice, and hence ultimately on the parameters of interest, should be minimized or at least be accounted for. Research should be done on the optimal design for conjoint choice experiments analyzed with Probit models, since optimal designs are not yet available. The results obtained from such an optimal conjoint experiments should lead to managerial more insightful and precise information on the product in question. In addition, one needs research on many product categories, designs, etcetera to investigate how generalizable findings are.

Furthermore, the performance of the Simulated Maximum Likelihood method explored in this chapter as optimization methods for the MNP models should be compared with Bayesian estimation using the Gibbs sampler. An interesting avenue for further research is in combining the Latent Class and MNP approaches, thus having the advantages of the predictive performance of the continuous and of the managerial appeal of segments of the discrete heterogeneity representation. It would be interesting to test the performance of such a Latent Class MNP model. In this chapter we already saw that the MNP model leads to better prediction results as compared to the LCMNL model. In addition accounting for different segments in an MNP context could further improve predictive performance and enhance managerial appeal, although the number of parameters to estimate may become a limiting factor, with respect to estimation time as well as their identification.

In any case, we may conclude that the MNL (or IP) model is no longer the preferred choice for analyzing conjoint choice experiments.

11.6   References

Addelman, S. (1962), Orthogonal Main-Effects Plans for Asymmetrical Factorial Experiments, *Technometrics*, 4, 21-46.

Akaike, H. (1973), Information Theory and an Extension of the Maximum Likelihood Principle, in: Petrov, B.N. and Csáki, F., eds., *2nd International Symposium on Information Theory*, Akadémiai Kiadó, Budapest, 267-281.

Allenby, G. M., Arora, N. and Ginter, J. L. (1995), Incorporating Prior Knowledge into the Analysis of Conjoint Studies, *Journal of Marketing Research*, 32, 152-162.

Allenby, G. M., Arora, N. and Ginter, J. L. (1998), On the Heterogeneity of Demand, *Journal of Marketing Research*, 35, 384-389.

Allenby, G. M. and Ginter, J. L. (1995), Using Extremes to Design Products and Segment Markets, *Journal of Marketing Research*, 32, 392-403.

Allenby, G. M. and Rossi, P. E. (1999), Marketing Models of Consumer Heterogeneity, *Journal of Econometrics*, 89, 57-78.

Arora, N., Allenby, G. M. and Ginter, J. L. (1998), A Hierarchical Bayes Model of Primary and Secondary Demand, *Marketing Science*, 17, 29-44.

Bekker, P. A., Merckens, A. and Wansbeek, T. J. (1994), *Identification, Equivalent Models, and Computer Algebra*, San Diego.

Ben-Akiva, M. and Lerman, S. R. (1985), *Discrete Choice Analysis: Theory and Application to Travel Demand*, Cambridge.

Börsch-Supan, A., Hajivassiliou, V. A., Kotlikoff, L. J. and Morris J. N. (1990), Health, Children, and Elderly Living Arrangements: A Multiperiod, Multinomial Probit Model with Unobserved Heterogeneity and Autocorrelated Errors, NBER working Paper 3343.

Bunch, D. S. (1991), Estimability in the Multinomial Probit Model, *Transportation Research B*, 25, 1-12.

Bunch, D. S. and Kitamura, R. (1989), Multinomial Probit Model Estimation Revisited: Testing Estimable Model Specifications, Maximum Likelihood Algorithms, and Probit Integral Approximations for Trinomial Models of Household Car Ownership, working paper, University of California at Davis.

Carroll, J. D. (1972), Individual Differences and Multidimensional Scaling, in: Shepard, R. N., Romney, A. K. and Nerlove, S. B., eds., *Multidimensional Scaling: Theory and Applications in the Behavioral Sciences*, New York.

Carroll, J. D. and Green, P. E. (1995), Psychometric Methods in Marketing Research: Part 1, Conjoint Analysis, *Journal of Marketing Research*, 32, 385-391.

Cattin, P. and Wittink, D. R. (1982), Commercial Use of Conjoint Analysis: A Survey, *Journal of Marketing*, 46, 44-53.

Chintagunta, P. K. (1992), Estimating A Multinomial Probit Model Of Brand Choice Using The Method Of Simulated Moments, *Marketing Science*, 11, 386-407.

Chrzan, K. (1994), Three Kinds of Order Effects in Choice-Based Conjoint Analysis, *Marketing Letters*, 5, 165-172.

Cohen, S. H. (1997), Perfect Union: CBCA Marries the Best of Conjoint and Discrete Choice Models, *Marketing Research*, 9, 12-17.

Daganzo, C. F. (1979), *Multinomial Probit, The Theory and Its Applications to Demand Forecasting*, New York.

Dansie, B. R. (1985), Parameter Estimability in the Multinomial Probit Model, *Transportation Research B*, 19, 526-528.

Dellaert, B. G. C., Borgers, A. W. J. and Timmermans, H. J. P. (1995), A Day in the City, Using Conjoint Choice Experiments to Model Tourists Choice of Activity Packages, *Tourism Management*, 16, 347-353.

Dellaert, B. G. C., Borgers, A. W. J. and Timmermans, H. J. P. (1996), Conjoint Choice Models of Joint Participation and Activity Choice, *International Journal of Research in Marketing*, 13, 251-264.

Dellaert, B. G. C., Borgers, A. W. J. and Timmermans, H. J. P. (1997), Conjoint Models of Tourist Portfolio Choice: Theory and Illustration, *Leisure Science*, 19, 31-58.

DeSarbo, W. S. and Green, P. E. (1984), Concepts, Theory, and Techniques, Choice-Constrained Conjoint Analysis, *Decision Science*, 15, 291-323.

DeSarbo, W. S., Ramaswamy, V. and Cohen, S. H. (1995), Market Segmentation with Choice-Based Conjoint Analysis, *Marketing Letters*, 6, 137-148.

Elrod, T. and Keane, M. P. (1995), A Factor-Analytic Probit Model for Representing the Market Structures in Panel Data, *Journal of Marketing Research*, 32, 1-16.

Elrod, T., Louviere, J. J. and Davey, K. S. (1992), An Empirical Comparison of Rating-Based and Choice-Based Conjoint Models, *Journal of Marketing Research*, 29, 368-377.

Green, P. E. (1984), Hybrid Models for Conjoint Analysis: An Expository Review, *Journal of Marketing Research*, 21, 155-169.

Green, P. E., Goldberg, S. M. and Montemayor, M. (1981), A Hybrid Utility Estimation Model for Conjoint Analysis, *Journal of Marketing*, 45, 33-41.

Green, P. E. and Rao, V. R. (1971), Conjoint Measurement for Quantifying Judgmental Data, *Journal of Marketing Research*, 8, 355-363.

Green, P. E. and Srinivasan, V. (1978), Conjoint Analysis in Consumer Research: Issues and Outlook, *Journal of Consumer Research*, 5, 103-123.

Green, P. E. and Srinivasan, V. (1990), Conjoint Analysis in Marketing: New Developments with Implications for Research and Practice, *Journal of Marketing*, 54, 3-19.

Haaijer, M. E. (1999), Modeling Conjoint Choice Experiments with the Probit Model, University of Groningen.

Haaijer, M. E., Kamakura, W. A. and Wedel, M. (2000), Response Latencies in the Analysis of conjoint Choice Experiments, Journal of Marketing Research, 37, 376-382.

Haaijer, M. E., Kamakura, W. A. and Wedel, M. (2001), The No-Choice Alternative in Conjoint Choice Experiments, International Journal of Market Research, 43, 93-106.

Haaijer, M. E., Wedel, M., Vriens, M. and Wansbeek, T. J. (1998), Utility Covariances and Context Effects in Conjoint MNP Models, *Marketing Science*, 17, 236-252.

Hajivassiliou, V. A. (1993), Simulation Estimation Methods for Limited Dependent Variable Models, in: Maddala, G. S., Rao, C. R. and Vinod, H.D., eds., *Handbook of Statistics*, 11, 519-543.

Hausman, J. A. and Wise, D. A. (1978), A Conditional Probit Model for Qualitative Choice: Discrete Decisions Recognizing Interdependence and Heterogeneous Preferences, *Econometrica*, 46, 403-426.

Huber, J., Payne, J. W. and Puto, C. (1982), Adding Asymmetrically Dominant Alternatives: Violations of Regularity and the Similarity Hypotheses, *Journal of Consumer Research*, 9, 90-98.

Huber, J. and Puto, C. (1983), Market Boundaries and Product Choice: Illustrating Attraction and Substitution Effects, *Journal of Consumer Research*, 10, 31-44.

Huber, J. and Zwerina, K. (1996), The Importance of Utility Balance in Efficient Choice Designs, *Journal of Marketing Research*, 33, 307-317.

Johnson, R. M. (1974), Trade-off Analysis of Consumer Values, *Journal of Marketing Research*, 11, 1221-1227.

Johnson R. M. (1985), Adaptive Conjoint Analysis, in: *Proceedings of the Sawtooth Software Conference on Perceptual Mapping, Conjoint Analysis and Computer Interviewing*, Ketchum, ID: Sawtooth Software, Inc., 253-265.

Johnson, R. M. and Orme, B. K. (1996), How Many Questions Should You Ask In Choice-Based Conjoint Studies?, Sawtooth Software Technical Paper.

Kamakura, W. A. (1989), The Estimation of Multinomial Probit Models: A New Calibration Algorithm, *Transportation Science*, 23, 253-265.

Kamakura, W. A., Wedel, M. and Agrawal, J. (1994), Concomitant Variable Latent Class Models for Conjoint Analysis, *International Journal of Research in Marketing*, 11, 451-464.

Keane, M. P. (1992), A Note on Identification in the Multinomial Probit Model, *Journal of Business & Economic Statistics*, 10, 193-200.

Kruskal, J. B. (1965), Analysis of Factorial Experiments by Estimating Monotone Transformations of the Data, *Journal of the Royal Statistical Society*, Series B, 251-263.

Kuhfeld, W. F., Tobias, R. D. and Garratt, M. (1994), Efficient Experimental Design with Marketing Research Applications, *Journal of Marketing Research*, 31, 545-557.

Lenk, P. J., DeSarbo, W. S., Green, P. E. and Young, M. R. (1996), Hierarchical Bayes Conjoint Analysis: Recovery of Partworth Heterogeneity from Reduced Experimental Designs, *Marketing Science*, 15, 173-191.

Louviere, J. J. (1988), Conjoint Analysis Modeling of Stated Preferences. A Review of Theory, Methods, Recent Developments and External Validity, *Journal of Transport Economics and Policy*, 10, 93-119.

Louviere, J. J. and Woodworth, G. (1983), Design and Analysis of Simulated Consumer Choice or Allocation Experiments: An Approach Based on Aggregate Data, *Journal of Marketing Research*, 20, 350-367.

Louviere, J. J. and Timmermans, H. J. P. (1990), A Review of Recent Advances in Decompositional Preference and Choice Models, *Tijdschrift voor Economische en Sociale Geografie*, 81, 214-225.

Luce, R. D. and Tukey, J. W. (1964), Simultaneous Conjoint Measurement: A New Type of Fundamental Measurement, *Journal of Mathematical Psychology*, 1, 1-27.

Madansky, A. (1980), On Conjoint Analysis and Quantal Choice Models, *Journal of Business*, 53, S37-S44.

Maddala, G. S. (1983), *Limited-Dependent and Qualitative Variables in Econometrics*, Cambridge University Press, Cambridge.

McFadden, D. (1976), Quantal Choice Analysis: A Survey, *Annals of Economic and Social Measurement*, 5, 363-390.

McFadden, D. (1986), The Choice Theory Approach to Market Research, *Marketing Science*, 5, 275-297.

Moore, W. L., Gray-Lee, J. and Louviere, J. J. (1998), A Cross-Validity Comparison of Conjoint Analysis and Choice Models at Different Levels of Aggregation, *Marketing Letters*, 9, 195-207.

Nowlis, S. M. and Simonson, I. (1997), Attribute-Task Compatibility as a Determinant of Consumer Preference Reversals, *Journal of Marketing Research*, 34, 205-218.

Oliphant, K., Eagle, T. C., Louviere, J. J. and Anderson, D. (1992), Cross-Task Comparison of Rating-Based and Choice-Based Conjoint, Proceedings of the Sawtooth Software Conference 1992.

Oppewal, H., Louviere, J. J. and Timmermans, H. J. P. (1994), Modeling Hierarchical Conjoint Processes with Integrated Choice Experiments, *Journal of Marketing Research*, 31, 92-105.

Oppewal, H. and Timmermans, H. J. P. (1993), Conjuncte Keuze-Experimenten: Achtergronden, Theorie, Toepassingen en Ontwikkelingen, *NVVM Jaarboek*, 33-58. (In Dutch).

Papatla, P. (1996), A Multiplicative Fixed-effects Model of Consumer Choice, *Marketing Science*, 15, 243-261.

Pekelman, D. and Sen, S. (1974), Mathematical Programming Models for the Determination of Attribute Weights, *Management Science*, 20, 1217-1229.

Pudney, S. (1989), *Modeling Individual Choice: The Econometrics of Corners, Kinks and Holes*, Basil Blackwell Inc., Oxford.

Rossi, P. E., McCulloch, R. E. and Allenby, G. M. (1996), The Value of Purchase History Data in Target Marketing, *Marketing Science*, 15, 321-340.

Sándor, Z. and Wedel, M. (1999), Robust Optimal Designs for Conjoint Choice Experiments, *SOM-Working Paper,* University of Groningen, Netherlands.

Sawtooth Software Inc. (1995), The CBC System for Choice-Based Conjoint Analysis, Sawtooth Software Technical Paper.

Schwarz, G. (1978), Estimating the Dimension of a Model, *Annals of Statistics*, 6, 461-464.

Simonson, I. (1989), Choice Based on Reasons: The Case of Attraction and Substitution Effects, *Journal of Consumer Research*, 16, 158-174.

Simonson, I. and Tversky, A. (1992), Choice in Context: Tradeoff Contrasts and Extremeness Aversion, *Journal of Marketing Research*, 29, 281-295.

Srinivasan, V. and Shocker, A. D. (1973a), Linear Programming Techniques for Multidimensional Analysis of Preferences, *Psychometrika*, 38, 337-369.

Srinivasan, V. and Shocker, A. D. (1973b), Estimating the Weights for Multiple Attributes in a Composite Criterion Using Pairwise Judgements, *Psychometrika*, 38, 473-493.

Steenkamp, J. E. B. M. (1985), De Constructie van Profielensets voor het Schatten van Hoofdeffecten en Interacties bij Conjunct Meten, *NVVM Jaarboek*, 125-155. (In Dutch).

Struhl, S. (1994), Discrete Choice Modelling: Understanding a Better Conjoint Than Conjoint, *Quirk's Marketing Research Review*, 36-39.

Swait, J. and Louviere, J. J. (1993), The Role of the Scale Parameter in the Estimation and Comparison of Multinomial Logit Models, *Journal of Marketing Research*, 30, 305-314.

Timmermans, H. J. P. and Van Noortwijk, L. (1995), Context Dependencies in Housing Choice Behavior, *Environment and Planning A*, 27, 181-192.

Tversky, A. (1972), Elimination by Aspects: A Theory of Choice, *Psychological Review*, 79, 281-299.

Vriens, M. (1994), Solving Marketing Problems With Conjoint Analysis, *Journal of Marketing Management*, 10, 37-55.

Vriens, M. (1995), *Conjoint Analysis in Marketing, Developments in Stimulus Representation and Segmentation Methods*, Thesis, University of Groningen.

Vriens, M., Oppewal, H. and Wedel, M. (1998), Ratings-Based versus Choice-Based Latent Class Conjoint Models - An Empirical Comparison, *Journal of the Market Research Society*, 40, 237-248.

Vriens, M., Wedel, M. and Wilms, T. (1996), Segmentation Methods for Metric Conjoint Analysis: A Monte Carlo Comparison, *Journal of Marketing Research*, 33, 73-85.

Wedel, M. and Kamakura, W.A. (1997), *Market Segmentation: Conceptual and Methodological Foundations*, Dordrecht, Kluwer.

Wedel, M., Kamakura, W., Arora, N., Bemmaor, A., Chiang, J., Elrod, T., Johnson, R., Lenk, P., Neslin, S. and Poulsen, C.S. (1999), Heterogeneity and Bayesian Methods in Choice Modeling, working paper, University of Groningen.

Wedel, M., Vriens, M., Bijmolt, T. H. A., Krijnen, W. and Leeflang, P. S. H. (1998), Assessing the Effects of Abstract Attributes and Brand Familiarity in Conjoint Choice Experiments, *International Journal of Research in Marketing*, 15, 71-78.

Wittink, D. R. and Cattin, P. (1989), Commercial Use of Conjoint Analysis: An Update, *Journal of Marketing*, 53, 91-96.

Wittink, D. R., Huber, J., Fiedler, J. A. and Miller, R. L. (1991), The Magnitude of and an Explanation/Solution for the Number of Levels Effect in Conjoint Analysis, working paper, Cornell University.

Wittink, D. R., Vriens, M. and Burhenne, W. (1994), Commercial Use of Conjoint Analysis in Europe: Results and Critical Reflections, *International Journal of Research in Marketing*, 11, 41-52.

12 Optimization-Based and Machine-Learning Methods for Conjoint Analysis: Estimation and Question Design

Olivier Toubia, Theodoros Evgeniou and John Hauser

12.1 Introduction to optimization and machine-learning conjoint analysis

Soon after the introduction of conjoint analysis into marketing by Green and Rao (1972), Srinivasan and Shocker (1973a, 1973b) introduced a conjoint analysis estimation method, Linmap, based on linear programming. Linmap has been applied successfully in many situations and has proven to be a viable alternative to statistical estimation (Jain, et. al. 1979, Wittink and Cattin 1981). Recent modification to deal with "strict pairs" has improved the estimation accuracy with the result that, on occasion, the modified Linmap predicts holdout data better than statistical estimation based on hierarchical Bayes methods (Srinivasan 1998, Hauser, et. al. 2006).

The last few years have seen a Renaissance of mathematical programming approaches to the design of questions for conjoint analysis and to the estimation of conjoint partworths. These methods have been made possible due to faster computers, web-based questionnaires, and new tools in both mathematical programming and machine learning. Empirical applications and Monte Carlo simulations with these methods show promise. While the development and philosophy of such approaches is nascent, the approaches show tremendous promise for predictive accuracy, efficient question design, and ease of computation.

This chapter provides a unified exposition for the reader interested in exploring these new methods. We focus on six papers: Toubia, Simester, Hauser and Dahan (TSHD), 2003; Toubia, Simester and Hauser (TSH), 2004; Evgeniou, Boussios and Zacharia (EBZ), 2005; Toubia, Hauser and Garcia (THG), 2006; Abernethy, Evgeniou, Toubia and Vert (AETV), 2006; Evgeniou, Pontil and Toubia (EPT), 2006. To avoid redundancy, we refer to each of the six reviewed papers by the initials of their authors after the first mention in each section.

We use a framework that clarifies the strengths and limitations of these methods as applied in today's online environment. Online conjoint analysis is often characterized by a lower number of observations per respondent, noisier data, and impatient respondents who have the power to terminate the questionnaire at any time. Such an environment favors methods that allow adaptive and interactive questionnaires, and that produce partworth estimates that are robust to response error even with few observations per respondent.

The framework is that of statistical machine learning (e.g., Vapnik 1998). Within this framework, we interpret recent attempts to improve robustness to response error and to decrease the number of observations required for estimation as an application of "complexity control." We complement this framework to review recent adaptive question design methods, by including experimental design principles which select questions to minimize the expected uncertainty in the estimates.

In the interest of brevity we focus on the conceptual aspects of the methods, and refer the reader to the published papers for implementation details.

12.1.1   Notation and Definitions

We assume I consumers indexed by i ($i=1,\ldots,I$) answering J_i conjoint questions each, indexed by j ($j=1,\ldots,J_i$). Let w_i denote a p-dimensional partworths vector for each consumer i. For ease of exposition, we assume binary features and a main effects specification. Neither of these assumptions are critical to the theory – the reviewed papers address multi-level features and interactions among features. Indeed, an important benefit of complexity control is that feature interactions of any degree may be estimated in an accurate and computationally efficient manner (EBZ; EPT).

The methods we review can be used for most conjoint data-collection formats. For simplicity we focus on the three most common: full-profile analysis, metric paired comparisons, and stated-choice questions.

For full profile rating conjoint data, we assume that the jth question to respondent i consists in rating a profile, x_{ij}. The respondent's answer by y_{ij}. The underlying model is $y_{ij} = x_{ij}.w_i + \varepsilon_{ij}$, where ε_{ij} is a response error term.

For metric paired-comparison conjoint data, we assume that the jth question asks respondent i to compare two profiles, x_{ij1} and x_{ij2}. We denote the respondent's answer by y_{ij}. The sign of y_{ij} determines which profile the respondent prefers; the magnitude of y_{ij} determines the strength of the preference. The underlying model is hence $y_{ij} = (x_{ij1} - x_{ij2}).w_i + \varepsilon_{ij}$ where ε_{ij} is a response error term.

For stated-preference (choice-based) conjoint data, each respondent is asked to choose among a set of profiles. For ease of exposition, we assume that the jth question asked the respondent to choose among two profiles, x_{ij1} and x_{ij2}. Without loss of generality, we code the data such that profile 1 is the chosen profile. (Binary choice simplifies exposition. Empirical applications and simulations use choices among more than two profiles.). The underlying model is that relative true utility, u_{ij}, is given by $u_{ij} = (x_{ij1} - x_{ij2}).w_i + \varepsilon_{ij}$ where ε_{ij} is a response error term. The respondent chooses profile 1 if $u_{ij} \geq 0$. The distribution of ε_{ij} implies alternative probabilistic models.

12.2   Using complexity control in conjoint analysis

In statistical estimation of partworths, researchers often worry about over-fitting the data. For example, if one were to use regression to estimate almost as many partworths as there are data points, then the conjoint model would fit the (calibration) data well, but we might expect that the partworths would be based, in part, on measurement error and would not be able to predict holdout data. Classical statistics address over-fitting by accounting for degrees of freedom and Bayesian statistics address over-fitting with hyper-parameters and the implied shrinkage toward the population mean. In statistical learning methods, over-fitting is addressed with the concept of complexity control. The conceptual idea is that if the model is too complex, it is too susceptible to over-fitting. To avoid this unwanted effect, we limit the complexity of the model by defining a measure of fit, a measure of complexity, and a method for determining the trade off between fit and complexity. Because the concept is important to understanding the philosophy of the new methods, we begin with a brief review of complexity control.

12.2.1   Ridge regression is an example of complexity control

There is a long history in models of consumer behavior that, in the presence of measurement error, unit partworths often predict well (e.g., Einhorn 1971, Dawes and Corrigan 1974.). One way to incorporate this concept in conjoint analysis is with ridge regression (e.g., Wahba 1990; Vapnik 1998; Hastie et al., 2003). Consider a simple ordinary least square regression resulting from a full-profile conjoint questionnaire. Such estimation involves minimizing the following loss function with respect to wi:

(1)
$$L(w_i) = \sum_{j=1}^{J} (y_{ij} - x_{ij}.w_i)^2$$

Minimizing loss function (1) results in the OLS estimate:

(2)
$$\hat{w}_i^{OLS} = (X_i^T.X_i)^{-1}.X_i^T Y_i$$

where X_i and Y_i are obtained by stacking all J observations for consumer i. If the number of profiles J is relatively small compared to the number of parameters to estimate p, this simple approach may suffer from over-fitting and the estimates may be very sensitive to small variations in the dependent variable. Mathematically, this instability comes from the poor conditioning of the matrix $(X_i^T X_i)$.

Ridge regression addresses instability and over-fitting by replacing $\hat{w}_i^{OLS}$ with:

(3) $\hat{w}_i^{Ridge} = (X_i^T.X_i + \gamma.I)^{-1}.X_i^T Y_i$

where I is the identity matrix and the parameter γ may be selected using various methods, such as cross-validation (which we will review later). Note that the matrix (XiT.Xi + γ.I) is better conditioned than (XiTXi): all its eigenvalues are greater than or equal to γ. It is easy to show that (3) is the solution to the following modification of the OLS problem (1), where the minimization is done over wi, given γ:

(4) $L(w_i \mid \gamma) = \frac{1}{\gamma} \sum_{j=1}^{J} (y_{ij} - x_{ij}.w_i)^2 + \| w_i \|^2$

where $\|w_i\|^2$ is the Euclidean norm of the vector w_i.

One interpretation of the term, $\|w_i\|^2$, is as a means to control the *complexity* of the estimate w_i. Complexity control may be viewed as an exogenous constraint imposed on w_i to effectively limit the set of possible estimates. The parameter y in (4) dictates the relative weight on complexity versus fit. As $y \rightarrow 0$, Equation 4 becomes equivalent to OLS regression; as $y \rightarrow +\infty$, Equation 4 simply minimizes complexity. If we had an additional constraint that the w_i's sum to a constant, the solution would be equal weights. Typically we observe a U-curve relationship between the parameter y and holdout accuracy (e.g., Evgeniou, Pontil, Toubia [EPT] 2006). Accuracy is poor when y is too small because of over-fitting. Similarly, accuracy is often poor when y is too large because the data are virtually ignored. Bootstrapping methods like cross-validation (reviewed in a later section), for example, offer a practical and effective way of searching for this optimal value of y, which is an issue extensively studied within statistical learning theory.

12.2.2   A Bayesian Interpretation of complexity control

We can use Bayes Theorem to provide another interpretation of complexity control. We augment the data likelihood with a Bayesian prior as follows:

(5)   Likelihood: $y_{ij} = x_{ij}.w_i + \varepsilon_{ij}$

                                        $\varepsilon_{ij} \sim N(0,\sigma^2)$

              Prior: $w_i \sim N(0, \beta.I)$

We compute the posterior distribution on wi conditioned on the data and a specific value of the parameters β and σ:

(6)

$$P(w_i \mid \{y_{ij}\}, \sigma, \beta) \propto P(\{y_{ij}\} \mid w_i, \sigma, \beta).P(w_i \mid \sigma, \beta)$$

$$\propto \exp\left(\sum_{j=1}^{J} -\frac{(y_{ij} - x_{ij}.w_i)^2}{2\sigma^2} \right).\exp\left(-\frac{\| w_i \|^2}{2.\beta^2} \right)$$

$$= \exp\left(-\frac{1}{2.\beta^2} \left[\frac{1}{\sigma^2/\beta^2} \sum_{j=1}^{J} (y_{ij} - x_{ij}.w_i)^2 + \| w_i \|^2 \right] \right)$$

The posterior likelihood in Equation 6 is now in the same form as the loss function in Equation 4 if $\gamma = \dfrac{\sigma^2}{\beta^2}$. Equation 6 provides a useful interpretation of the trade off parameter γ as the ratio of the uncertainty in the data (σ^2) relative to the uncertainty in the prior (β^2). We place more weight on the data when they are less noisy (small σ^2). We shrink our estimates more toward the prior when the data are noisy (large σ^2) or when we have a stronger belief in the prior (small β^2).

While there is a mathematical equivalence, the two approaches differ in philosophy and, in particular, in how γ is selected. In the Bayesian interpretation, γ is set by the prior beliefs – exogenously. In statistical machine learning γ is estimated endogenously from the calibration data. This also makes any interpretation of the methods as "maximum likelihood or a posteriori estimation" (i.e., estimation of the mode in Equation 6) not straight forward. This difference is a fundamental philosophical interpretation that leads to differences in estimation accuracy between statistical machine learning and Bayesian methods, as shown by EPT and discussed below.

12.2.3 General framework

Equations 4 and 6 are illustrative. The loss function in its general form, for a given γ, may be written as:

(7) $$L(w_i \mid \gamma) = \frac{1}{\gamma}.\sum_{j=1}^{J} V(w_i, data) + J(w_i)$$

The first term, $V(w_i, data)$, measures the fit between a candidate partworth estimate, w_i, and the observed data. The second term, $J(w_i)$, measures the complexity of w_i. The quadratic complexity function, $\|w_i\|^2$, is common, but any function may be used. In general the choice of $J(w_i)$ in Equation 7 may also depend on the data.

12.2.4   Minimization of the loss function

A potential (but not necessary) restriction is that both functions V and J in (7) should be convex. In that case, the large literature on convex optimization provides efficient methods to minimize the loss function given γ. Otherwise, non-convex (even combinatorial, for discrete decision variables) optimization methods can be used, leading to solutions that may be only locally optimal. Most of the reviewed papers use some variation of Newton's method and achieve convergence after few (e.g., 20) iterations. In some cases (Abernethy, Evgeniou, Toubia and Vert (AETV), 2006; EPT) the loss function is minimized using closed-form expressions. Computation time is rarely a limitation, and often an advantage compared to other methods such as hierarchical Bayes.

12.2.5   Trade of between fit and complexity

The tradeoff, γ, between maximizing fit and minimizing complexity can be set exogenously by the modeler or the Bayesian prior or endogenously, for example by means of cross-validation. For example, the polyhedral methods of Toubia, Simester, Hauser and Dahan (TSHD, 2003) and Toubia, Hauser and Simester (THS, 2004) implicitly assume an infinite weight on fit by maximizing fit first and then minimizing complexity among the set of estimates that maximize fit. The probabilistic polyhedral methods of Toubia, Hauser and Garcia (THG, 2006) use pretest information to select the tradeoff between fit and complexity, captured by a response error parameter α'. AETV set γ to the inverse of the number of questions, to ensure that the weight on fit increases as the amount of data increases (Vapnik 1998).

Of the conjoint analysis papers reviewed in this chapter, EBŻ and EPT select γ using cross-validation – a typical approach in statistical machine learning. (See for example Wahba 1990; Efron and Tibshirani 1993; Shao 1993; Vapnik 1998; Hastie et al., 2003, and references therein). It is important to stress that *cross-validation does not require any data beyond the calibration data.*

The parameter γ is set to the value that minimizes the cross-validation error, typically estimated as follows:

- Set Cross-Validation(γ)= 0.
- For $k = 1$ to J:
    - Consider the subset of the calibration data that consists of all questions except the kth one for each of the I respondents.[1]
    - Using only this subset of the calibration data, estimate the individual partworths $\{w_i^{-k}\}$ for the given γ.

---

[1] Variations exist. For example one can remove only one question in total from all I respondents and iterate $I \times J$ times instead of J times.

- Using the estimated partworths $\{w_i^{-k}\}$, predict the responses to the I questions (one per respondent) left out from the calibration data and let $CV(k)$ be the predictive performance achieved on these questions (e.g., root mean square error between observed and predicted responses for metric questions, logistic error for choice questions).
- Set Cross-Validation(γ) = Cross-Validation(γ) + $CV(k)$.

The parameter γ is set to the value that minimizes the cross-validation error, and is typically identified by using a line search. The cross-validation error is, effectively, a "simulation" of the out-of-sample error *without* using any out-of-sample data.

12.3   Recent optimization-based and machine-learning estimation methods

Five of the reviewed papers propose and test new estimation methods (Abernethy, Evgeniou, Toubia and Vert [AETV], 2006 is the only reviewed paper that focuses exclusively on questionnaire design and not on estimation). We examine these methods in light of the general framework outlined above. Each method may be viewed as a combination of a specific fit function, a specific complexity function, and a method for selecting the amount of trade off between fit and complexity.

12.3.1   Support vector machine estimation for choice-based conjoint analysis

Evgeniou, Boussios, and Zacharia (EBZ, 2005) focus on choice-based conjoint analysis and use a standard formulation known as the Support Vector Machine (SVM, Vapnik 1998). This has been arguably the most popular statistical machine learning method over the past 10 years, with numerous applications in various fields outside of marketing such as text mining, computational biology, speech recognition, or computer vision. An SVM uses the following loss function:

$$(8) \qquad L(w_i \mid \gamma) = \frac{1}{\gamma} \sum_{j=1}^{J} \theta\big(1 - (x_{ij1} - x_{ij2}).w_i\big)\big[1 - (x_{ij1} - x_{ij2}).w_i\big] + \| w_i \|^2$$

where the function θ is chosen such that $\theta(a) = 1$ if $a > 0$ and 0 otherwise. Equation 8 combines quadratic complexity control with a fit function that is slightly different from that normally used in conjoint analysis.

Recall that we assume, without loss of generality, that x_{ij1} is chosen over x_{ij2}. Hence a partworth vector w_i is consistent with choice j if $(x_{ij1} - x_{ij2}).w_i \geq 0$.

If $a = 1 - (x_{ij1} - x_{ij2}).w_i$, then $\theta(a) = 0$ if $(x_{ij1} - x_{ij2}).w_i \geq 1$, hence, the product $\theta(1 - (x_{ij1} - x_{ij2}).w_i)[1 - (x_{ij1} - x_{ij2}).w_i]$ equals   0   whenever $(x_{ij1} - x_{ij2}).w_i \geq 1$. This will happen whenever the observed choice j is predicted by wi with a margin of at least 1. If choice j is not predicted by a margin of at least 1, the loss function introduces a penalty equal to the distance between $(x_{ij1} - x_{ij2}).w_i$ and 1. Fit is measured by the sum of these penalties across choices. Setting the margin to 1 plays the role of scaling the magnitudes of the partworths; any other scaling number could be used. EBZ select the parameter γ using cross-validation.

This loss function may be related to the analytic center criterion reviewed below. In particular, if each choice is interpreted as a constraint $(x_{ij1} - x_{ij2}).w_i \geq 1$, then the set of points wi that satisfy all the constraints forms a polyhedron, and for each point wi in this polyhedron, the complexity term || wi||2 becomes the inverse of the radius of the largest sphere centered at wi inscribed in this polyhedron (Vapnik 1998). As a result, the value of wi that minimizes complexity is the center of the largest sphere inscribed in the polyhedron.

12.3.2   Analytic center estimation for metric paired-comparison conjoint analysis

Polyhedral methods introduced by Toubia, Dahan, Simester and Hauser (TDSH, 2003) and Toubia, Hauser and Simester (THS, 2004), and extended by Toubia, Hauser and Garcia (THG, 2006) were developed explicitly to improve adaptive question design. The primary application of these methods is to web-based conjoint analysis where respondents are free to leave the questionnaire at any time. Polyhedral methods provide means to gather the most efficient information from each question.

However, each of the three polyhedral methods provides an estimation method as a byproduct of question design. This estimation method is based on the analytic center of the set of feasible partworths – possibly probabilistic. We provide here an interpretation of analytic-center estimation within the framework of statistical machine learning.

We begin with TDSH, who assume a metric paired-comparison conjoint format. TDSH first consider the case in which there is no response error ($\varepsilon_{ij}=0$), and observe that the answer to each question may be interpreted as a constraint on w_i: $y_{ij} = (x_{ij1} - x_{ij2}).w_i$. The set of "feasible" estimates that satisfy all the constraints associated with all the questions is a *polyhedron*, defined as:

(9) $\Phi_{\{1,...J\}}=\{w_i, 0 \leq w_i \leq 100, (x_{ij1} - x_{ij2}).w_i = y_{ij}$ for $j=1,...J\}$

where the constraint, $0 \leq w_i \leq 100$, is chosen without loss of generality to establish the scale of the partworths. Out of all feasible estimates defined by this polyhedron, TDSH select the *analytic center* of the polyhedron as their working estimate, defined as:

(10)
$$\hat{w}_i^{AC} = \arg \max_{w_i} \sum_{k=1}^{p} \log(w_{ik}) + \log(100 - w_{ik})$$

subject to: $(x_{ij1} - x_{ij2}).w_i = y_{ij}$ for $j=1,\ldots J$

where w_{ik} is the kth element of w_i. The analytic center is the point that maximizes the geometric mean of the slack variables associated with the inequality constraints. The logarithmic function is called a "barrier function" in interior point programming. It prevents the expression inside the logarithm from being non-positive.

For small number of questions the feasible polyhedron will be non-empty, however, as the number of questions grows in the presence of response error, it will no longer be possible to find partworths that are consistent with all of the questions and the feasible polyhedron $\Phi_{\{1,\ldots,J\}}$ will become empty. Toubia et al. (2003) follow a two-step estimation procedure: (1) find the minimum amount of response error δ^* necessary for the polyhedron to become non-empty, (2) find the analytic center of the resulting polyhedron. In particular, they first find the minimum δ^* such that the polyhedron defined as:

$$\Phi_{\{1,\ldots,J\}} = \{w_i, 0 \leq w_i \leq 100, \ y_{ij} - \delta^* \leq (x_{ij1} - x_{ij2}).w_i \leq y_{ij} + \delta^* \ \text{for} \ j = 1,\ldots,J\}$$

is non empty, and then estimate the partworths using the analytic center of this new polyhedron:

(11)
$$\hat{w}_i^{AC} = \arg \max_{w_i} \sum_{k=1}^{p} \log(w_{ik}) + \log(100 - w_{ik}) +$$
$$\sum_{j=1}^{J} \log(y_{ij} + \delta^* - (x_{ij1} - x_{ij2}).w_i) + \log((x_{ij1} - x_{ij2}).w_i - y_{ij} + \delta^*)$$

We now reformulate Equation 7 within the general framework. We begin by rewriting the polyhedron $\Phi_{\{1,\ldots,J\}}$ in standard form:

$$\{\tilde{w}_i = (w_i, a_i, b_i, c_i); \tilde{w}_i \geq 0; w_i + a_i = 100; (x_{ij1} - x_{ij2}).w_i - b_{ij} = y_{ij} - \delta^*; (x_{ij1} - x_{ij2}).w_i + c_{ij} = y_{ij} + \delta^*\}$$

TDSH's fit measure becomes $V^{AC}(\widetilde{w}_i, data) = \delta *$ and their complexity control becomes:

$$(12) \qquad J^{AC}(\widetilde{w}_i) = \sum_{k=1}^{p} -\log(w_{ik}) - \log(a_{ik}) + \sum_{j=1}^{J} -\log(b_{ij}) - \log(c_{ij})$$

Their two-step procedure becomes the limiting case (when $\gamma \to 0$) of the following loss function:

$$(13) \qquad L(\widetilde{w}_i \mid \gamma) = \frac{1}{\gamma} V^{AC}(\widetilde{w}_i, data) + J^{AC}(\widetilde{w}_i)$$

If one wishes, one can generalize TDSH's analytic-center estimation by choosing a non-limiting parameter γ to balance fit and complexity.

12.3.3 Analytic center estimation for choice-based conjoint analysis

THS developed a choice-based polyhedral conjoint method. Each stated-choice question is interpreted as an *inequality* constraint of the form $(x_{ij1} - x_{ij2}).w_i \geq -\delta*$, where $\delta*$ is a non-negative parameter that captures response error. The polyhedron of feasible partworths becomes:

$$(14) \qquad \Phi_{\{1,\ldots J\}} = \{w_i, \ w_i \geq 0, \mathbf{1}.w_i = 100, (x_{ij1} - x_{ij2}).w_i \geq -\delta* \text{ for } j = 1,\ldots J\}$$

where $0 \leq w_i$ and $\mathbf{1}.w_i = 100$ are scaling constraints chosen without loss of generality. ($\mathbf{1}$ is a vector of one's, such that $\mathbf{1}.w_i$ is equal to the sum of the elements of w_i).

Like the metric version, the primary goal of polyhedral choice-based conjoint analysis is to select questions efficiently. Using the proposed method, THS select questions such that each choice by a respondent selects a subset of the feasible polyhedron of partworths. With this method, the feasible polyhedron never becomes empty. Ideally, with no measurement error the polyhedron will shrink toward the true value of a respondent's partworths. Intermediate estimates are the analytic center of the feasible polyhedron.

When choice-based polyhedral methods are not used to select questions, it is possible that the feasible polyhedron will become empty.

In this case, THS again follow a two-step estimation procedure: (1) find the minimum value of δ^* such that the polyhedron $\Phi_{\{1,...,J\}}$ is non-empty, (2) find the analytic center of the resulting polyhedron, defined as:

$$(15) \qquad \hat{w}_i^{AC} = \arg\max_{w_i} \sum_{k=1}^{p} \log(w_{ik}) + \sum_{j=1}^{J} \log((x_{ij1} - x_{ij2}).w_i + \delta^*)$$

subject to: $\mathbf{1}.w_i = 100$

The polyhedron may again be written in standard form as:

$$\Phi_{\{1,...,J\}} = \{\widetilde{w}_i = (w_i, a_i); \widetilde{w}_i \geq 0; \mathbf{1}.w_i = 100; (x_{ij1} - x_{ij2}).w_i - a_{ij} = -\delta^*\}.$$

The two-step estimation procedure becomes the limiting case ($\gamma \to 0$) of the following loss function:

$$(16) \qquad L(\widetilde{w}_i \mid \gamma) = \frac{1}{\gamma}.\delta^* + J^{AC}(\widetilde{w}_i)$$

subject to: $\mathbf{1}.w_i = 100$

where:

$$(17) \qquad J^{AC}(\widetilde{w}_i) = \sum_{k=1}^{p} -\log(w_{ik}) + \sum_{j=1}^{J} -\log(a_{ij})$$

12.3.4   Probabilistic analytic center estimation

THG offer a Bayesian interpretation of the method proposed by THS, which enables a richer treatment of response error and which allows capturing informative priors on the partworths. They consider prior distributions represented by mixtures of uniform distributions supported by polyhedra. (In one dimension, a uniform distribution supported by a polyhedron simply becomes a uniform distribution on an interval; in two dimensions, it is a uniform distribution on a rectangle, etc.) Mixtures of such distributions may be used to approximate any prior distribution. THG also provide a method by which prior beliefs are not directly captured by probability distributions, but rather by probabilistic constraints on some combinations of the parameters (e.g., the importance of feature A is greater than m with probability q). The general expression for this class of distributions is as follows:

$$P(w_i) = \sum_{m=1}^{M} \omega_m P_{\Psi_m}(w_i)$$

where M is any positive integer, $\{\omega_1,...,\omega_M\}$ is a set of positive weights such that $\sum_{m=1}^{M}\omega_m = 1$, $\{\Psi_1,...,\Psi_M\}$ is a set of polyhedra, and $P_{\Psi_m}(w_i)$ is the uniform probability distribution with support Ψ_m. The previous methods of TDSH and THS implicitly assume a uniform prior on the polyhedron defined by the scaling constraints.

THG combine this class of prior distributions with a conjugate class of likelihood function such that in each question, the profile with the highest deterministic utility is chosen with probability α', and the $(J\text{-}1)$ other profiles are chosen with probability $(1- \alpha')/(J\text{-}1)$ each. Such likelihood functions are step functions with two values, one taken by all points that are consistent with the choice, and the other taken by all points that are inconsistent with the choice. The specific values are driven by the parameter α'. This class of likelihood functions is attractive because the posterior distribution on the partworths is also equal to a mixture of uniform distributions supported by polyhedra. After J questions, the posterior distribution on w_i may be written as follows:

$$P(w_i) = \sum_{m=1}^{M} \sum_{s \in S_J} \omega_{ms} P_{\Phi_s \cap \Psi_m}(w_i),$$

where S_J is the set of all subsets of the questions $\{1, 2, ..., J\}$, and for a subset s of S_J, Φ_s is the polyhedron corresponding to the questions in s. The parameter ω_{ms} is the mixture weight on the polyhedron defined by the intersection between Φ_s and the prior polyhedron Ψ_m (see THG for a method to approximate these weights).

Although other techniques could be used as well, THG select the parameter α' from a pretest sample of respondents, following the tradition of aggregate customization (Arora and Huber 2001, Huber and Zwerina 1996).

Given the posterior distribution written as a mixture of uniform distributions supported by polyhedra, several methods could be used to produce point estimates of the partworths. For example, an algorithm could be developed that allows sampling from this posterior distribution and estimating the partworths as the mean of this distribution. For simplicity, THG estimate the partworths as the mixture of the analytic centers of the polyhedra involved in the mixture.

THG essentially shift the focus from the minimization of a loss function to the exploration of a posterior distribution. However their approach may be still be framed within statistical machine learning. In particular, complexity control is achieved by the prior distribution. The parameter α' effectively controls the trade off between fit and complexity. For example, $\alpha'=1$ implies no response error and the estimates fit the data perfectly; $\alpha'=1/J$ implies non-informative choices and all inference will be based only on the prior.

12.3.5   Using complexity control to model heterogeneity

Hierarchical Bayes has been one of the most successful developments in the estimation of conjoint-analysis partworths (Lenk et al., 1996; Allenby and Rossi
1999; Rossi and Allenby 2003; Rossi, Allenby and McCulloch., 2005).[2] Liu, Otter, and Allenby (2006) suggest that one reason for this accuracy is the likelihood
principle which states that the likelihood best summarizes the information in the
data. Another, less formal hypothesis is that Bayesian methods are accurate because they robustly shrink individual-level estimates toward the mean of the population. As motivated by the analogy of ridge regression and Bayesian priors, the
shrinkage in hierarchical Bayes can be seen as analogous to complexity control.

EPT explore this interpretation for both metric and choice data. In the metric
case, the loss function can be formulated as follows:

(18)

$$L(\{w_i\}, w_0, D \mid \gamma) = \frac{1}{\gamma} \sum_{i=1}^{I} \sum_{j=1}^{J} (y_{ij} - x_{ij}.w_i)^2 + \sum_{i=1}^{I} (w_i - w_0)^T D^{-1} (w_i - w_0)$$

subject to D being a positive semi-definite matrix scaled to have a trace of 1.

We note that this formulation is not identical to hierarchical Bayes methods. It
differs in both philosophy and computation. Nonetheless, it is an interesting
analogy.

There are a number of interesting characteristics associated with this loss
function: (1) estimates are obtained simultaneously for all respondents, (2)
estimates are shrunk toward a common partworth vector that may differ from the
unit vector, and (3) the parameter γ dictates the trade off between fit and
shrinkage.

Although the population vector w_0 is not defined to be the population means,
EPT show that the value of w_0 that minimizes the loss function must equal the
population mean. The matrix D is analogous to the covariance matrix of the
partworths; the shrinkage penalty is greater for partworths that are distant from the
mean w_0 along directions in which there is less variation across respondents. By
scaling D with its trace, the authors assure that the optimization problem is
convex. Although the actual minimization is beyond the scope of this chapter, we
note that, for a given γ, the optimal solution is in closed form and hence
computationally efficient (see paper for more details).

---

[2]   Technically, Bayesian methods sample from the posterior distribution of the parameters
rather than provide estimates in the classical sense. For simplicity, we refer to the mean
of the posterior distribution as the partworth estimates.

For choice data, EPT substitute the logit log-likelihood as the fit measure. The loss function becomes:

(19)

$$L(\{w_i\}, w_0, D \mid \gamma) = \frac{1}{\gamma}\sum_{i=1}^{I}\sum_{j=1}^{J}\left(-\log\frac{\exp(x_{ij1}.w_i)}{\exp(x_{ij1}.w_i) + \exp(x_{ij2}.w_i)}\right)$$

$$+ \sum_{i=1}^{I}(w_i - w_0)^T D^{-1}(w_i - w_0)$$

Because closed-form expressions are not available with this formulation, Newton's method is used (any other convex optimization method could be used) to minimize the loss function for a given γ.

To assess the impact of the differing philosophies, EPT compare their approach to hierarchical Bayes. In particular, they consider the following two HB models for metric and choice data respectively (in both cases a diffuse prior is assumed on w_0):

Metric data:

Likelihood: $y_{ij}=x_{ij}.w_i+\varepsilon_{ij}$, $\varepsilon_{ij}\sim N(0,\sigma^2)$
First-stage prior: $w_i\sim N(w_0,D)$
Second-stage priors: $\sigma^2\sim IG(r_0/2,s_0/2)$
$D^{-1}\sim W(\eta_0, \eta_0.\Delta_0)$

Choice data:

Likelihood: $\text{Prob}(x_{ij1}\text{ chosen})=\dfrac{\exp(x_{ij1}.w_i)}{\exp(x_{ij1}.w_i) + \exp(x_{ij2}.w_i)}$

First-stage prior: $w_i\sim N(w_0,D)$
Second-stage prior: $D^{-1}\sim W(\eta_0, \eta_0.\Delta_0)$,

where *IG* denotes the inverse gamma distribution and *W* the Wishart distribution.

Both the machine learning and hierarchical Bayes approaches shrink estimates toward the population mean. Moreover, in the case of metric data, EPT are able to show that the individual-level estimates *conditional* on D and w_0 are given by the exact same mathematical expressions.

However they identify two major and fundamental differences between their approach and HB. First, while the former involves the minimization of a loss function, the latter involves sampling from a posterior distribution. Hence in HB point estimates are only one of the many ways to summarize and describe the posterior distribution. Other important statistics include the standard deviation of this distribution. EPT illustrate that standard deviations and confidence intervals may also be obtained in their framework, using for example bootstrapping (Efron and Tibshirani, 1993).

Second, the two methods differ on how they select the amount of shrinkage. In HB the amount of shrinkage is selected, in part, by prior judgment embodied in the second-stage prior parameters (η_0, Δ_0, r_0, and s_0 in the metric case; η_0 and Δ_0 in the choice case); in machine-learning it is determined from the calibration data (γ). By selecting γ through cross-validation, it may not be surprising that the machine-learning approach can outperform HB unless, of course, the second-stage priors are chosen with prescience. See EPT for detailed results.

12.3.6 Summary of optimization and machine-learning estimation

Table 1 describes and contrasts the estimation methods reviewed in this section.

Table 1:   *Characteristics of the reviewed estimation methods*

Paper(s)	Fit measured by	Complexity measured by	Trade off fit / complexity
Evgeniou, Boussios, Zacharia (2005)	Support vector machine	Quadratic norm on the partworths	Determined by cross-validation
Toubia, Simester, Hauser, Dahan (2003)	Response error to obtain feasble polyhedron	Analytic center	Maximize fit first, then minimize complexity
Toubia, Simester, Hauser (2004)	Response error to obtain feasible polyhedron	Analytic center	Maximize fit first, then minimize complexity
Toubia, Hauser, Garcia (2006)	Polyhedral mixture	Informative prior	Based on pretest
Evgeniou, Pontil, Toubia (2006)	Sum of squared errors / logistic likelihood	Difference from population means	Determined by cross-validation

12.4 Recent optimization-based and machine-learning adaptive questionnaire design methods

One of the breakthroughs in the 1980s was the ability to adapt conjoint analysis questions to the observed responses of consumers. Algorithms developed by Johnson (1987, 1991) for Adaptive Conjoint Analysis (ACA) enabled researchers using computer-aided interviews to ask more efficient questions. For almost 20 years ACA was one of the most commonly applied methods, only recently surpassed by choice-based conjoint analysis. It is only in the past few years that we have seen a resurgence in adaptive questionnaire design. This resurgence has been made possible by the development of new efficient computational algorithms and the continued growth in computing power. It is now feasible to adapt questions in an on-line environment using sophisticated background computations that run in the time it takes to download the code for the next page display – the respondent notices little or no delay due to this computation. While the methods are still being perfected, the results to date suggest that in many applications these adaptive questioning methods enable researchers to design methods that ask fewer questions yet still provide estimates that are sufficiently accurate for important managerial decisions. The methods work for a variety of conjoint analysis formats, including both metric paired-comparison data and choice-based data.

In this chapter we review four newly proposed methods that enable researchers to adapt questions at the level of the individual respondent.

12.4.1   Experimental design principles

Non-adaptive questionnaire design builds primarily on the field of experimental design (Chaloner and Verdinelli 1995; Ford, Kitsos and Titterington 1989; Kuhfeld, Tobias and Garratt 1994; Pukelsheim 1993; Steinberg 1984). The approach can be summarized as minimizing a norm of the asymptotic covariance matrix of the parameter estimate $\hat{w}_i$. Under mild assumptions (Newey and McFadden 1994), it can be shown that the maximum likelihood estimate of w_i is asymptotically normal with covariance matrix equal to the inverse of the information matrix Ω, given by the Hessian (second-derivative matrix) of the loss function minimized in estimation.

Non-adaptive efficient designs maximize a norm of the information matrix Ω, the inverse of the covariance matrix. The most widely used norm is the determinant, giving rise to so-called D-efficient designs (Arora and Huber 2001; Huber and Zwerina 1996; Kuhfeld, Tobias and Garratt 1994; Kuhfeld 2005). D-efficiency minimizes the volume of the confidence ellipsoid around the maximum likelihood estimate $\hat{w}_i$, defined by $\{w : (w - \hat{w}_i)^T \Omega (w - \hat{w}_i) \leq 1\}$, and makes this ellipsoid as spherical as possible (Greene 2000). For example, the well-known orthogonal and balanced designs (Addelman 1962, Kuhfeld, Tobias and Garratt 1994), when they exist, maximize efficiency.

For stated-choice data, the information matrix depends on the true partworths w_i. In most cases, efficiency can be improved by attempting to achieve utility (or choice) balance such that the alternatives in each choice set are close in utility (close in probability of choice) where utility is often calculated based on prior beliefs about the partworths. There are many algorithms to increase efficiency: Arora and Huber (2001), Huber and Zwerina (1996), Kanninen (2002), Sandor and Wedel (2001), and Hauser and Toubia (2005). Abernethy, Evgeniou, Toubia and Vert (AETV, 2006) note that similar principles have been used in other fields such as active learning (Tong and Koller 2000).

The *adaptive* question design methods use similar fundamental principles. For example, Toubia, Dahan, Simester and Hauser (TDSH, 2004), Toubia, Hauser and

Garcia (THG, 2006), and AETV select the next questions to achieve utility balance based on estimates from the answers to previous questions. These methods attempt to minimize the amount of "uncertainty" around the estimate and to make uncertainty similar in all directions. Questions are chosen to reduce the uncertainty along the most uncertain dimension.

In polyhedral methods, uncertainty is characterized by the polyhedron of feasible estimates (which may conceptually be related to the confidence ellipsoid in maximum likelihood estimation), and questions are selected to maximally reduce the volume of this polyhedron and minimize the length of its longest axis (making it more spherical). In a similar vein, AETV characterize uncertainty by the inverse of the Hessian of the loss function (equal to the information matrix), and select questions to maximally increase the smallest positive eigenvalue of the Hessian. We now review these methods in greater detail.

12.4.2   Polyhedral question design

For ease of exposition, we describe the intuition for polyhedral methods when the feasible polyhedron is non-empty. The same intuition applies to the expanded polyhedron.

In polyhedral question design, the constraints imposed by the answers to previous questions form a polyhedron. All points in the polyhedron are consistent with prior answers. A smaller polyhedron implies a smaller set of feasible estimates and, hence, less uncertainty about the partworths. For example, the gray region in Figure 1 is the feasible polyhedron after a set of questions and all points (partworths) in that gray area are consistent with the answers to prior questions. Our goal is to select the next question such that when the question is answered, the resulting polyhedron is as small as possible.

Formally, let $\Phi\{1,...J\}$ denote the polyhedron defined by the answers to the first J questions asked of a given respondent. Let $\Phi\{1,...J+1\}$ denote the new polyhedron formed when the $J + 1$st answer constrains $\Phi\{1,...J\}$. Consider first metric paired-comparison questions. The new constraint will be of the form $(x_i(J+1)1-x_i(J+1)2).w_i = y_i(J+1)$. The set of points, w_i that satisfy this new constraint is a hyperplane perpendicular to the vector $(x_i(J+1)1-x_i(J+1)2)$. This is shown as the green surface in Figure 1. The new polyhedron, $\Phi\{1,...J+1\}$, is the intersection between the current polyhedron, $\Phi\{1,...J\}$, and this hyperplane.

We must now select a question that, when answered, minimizes the volume of the new polyhedron, $\Phi\{1,...J+1\}$. In addition we want to make it more spherical. Intuitively, we satisfy these criteria if we select the hyperplane to be orthogonal to the longest axis of the current polyhedron. Mathematically, this means that we select the two profiles in the next question such that the line, $(x_i(J+1)1-x_i(J+1)2)$, is as close as possible to the longest axis of the polyhedron. (At minimum, by intersecting the current polyhedron with a hyperplane perpendicular to the current longest axis will ensures that the longest axis of the next polyhedron will be strictly smaller than the longest axis of the current polyhedron.)

The mathematics are complex, but the basic idea is to find the analytic center of the polyhedron and choose the smallest ellipsoid such that the polyhedron is surrounded by the ellipsoid with its center at the polyhedron's analytical center. Then, by solving an eigenvalues problem, TDSH select the longest axis of the ellipsoid as representing the longest axis of the polyhedron.

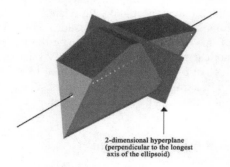

2-dimensional hyperplane
(perpendicular to the longest
axis of the ellipsoid)

Figure 1:   Cut perpendicular to the longest axis – metric data case
(From Toubia, Simester, Hauser, and Dahan 2003)

The methods and philosophy for choice-based data follow the same intuition, with a few modifications (THS, THG). For binary stated-choice data, new constraints are inequality constraints of the form $(x_i(J+1)1-x_i(J+1)2).w_i \geq 0$ (The method is extended easily to multiple alternatives in the choice set.). The set of points that satisfy the constraint implied by the J+1st answer is a half-space. If the boundary of his half-space intersects the feasible polyhedron, $\Phi\{1,...J\}$, it will divide the polyhedron into two sub-polyhedra. One sub-polyhedron corresponds to the choice of $x_i(J+1)1$ and the other to the choice of $x_i(J+1)2$. In other words, the respondent's choice in the J+1st question identifies one or the other sub-polyhedron. All points in the chosen sub-polyhedron are consistent with the answers to all J+1 questions.

THS again seek to choose questions such that the resulting sub-polyhedron will be as small and spherical as feasible. THS show that the expected volume of $\Phi\{1,...J+1\}$ is reduced efficiently if the separating hyperplane is chosen so that it goes through the center of the feasible polyhedron, such that each choice alternative is as equally likely as possible. Such choice balance assures that the resulting polyhedra are of approximately equal volume. This is illustrated in Figure 2a.

Of the many hyperplanes that split the feasible polyhedron, the hyperplane that will make the resulting sub-polyhedra as spherical as possible is the hyperplane that is perpendicular to the longest axis of the polyhedron. This is illustrated in Figure 2b.

The two points at which the longest axis intersects the boundary of the polyhedron provide two target partworth vectors. The final step is to construct one profile associated with each of them. Each profile is obtained by simply solving a budget constraint problem. That is, for each target partworth vector, THS construct a choice alternative that maximizes utility subject to a budget constraint.

A strength of adaptive polyhedral question design is that questions are chosen such that the resulting polyhedra are always feasible and non-empty. However, this strength is also a weakness. When there is response error, early errors propagate. A choice made in error forever assures that the true partworths are not in any subsequent polyhedra. As a result, early tests indicated that adaptive choice-based questions improved accuracy and efficiency when response error was small, but not when it was large.

THG address response error with a probabilistic generalization of polyhedral methods. They model potential response error by assuming that each constraint applies with probability α^3, where α is based on pretest data. They then show that polyhedral methods can be given a Bayesian interpretation such that the posterior distribution of the partworths is a mixture of polyhedra, each defined by a subset of the constraints imposed by the respondent's answers to the chosen questions (see details above). With this interpretation, it is simple conceptually to extend adaptive polyhedral choice-based question design. New questions are chosen based on the longest axis of the appropriate mixture of polyhedra.

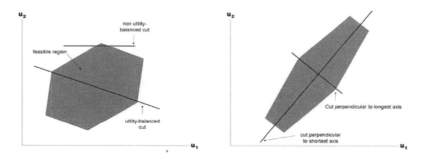

Figure 2:   Utility balance cuts and cuts perpendicular to the longest axis–
choice data case (from Toubia, Hauser, Simester 2004)

12.4.3 Hessian-based adaptive question design for choice-based conjoint analysis

Statistical learning methods also provide a means to adapt conjoint questions. AETV define loss functions that are convex and twice differentiable. For such loss functions, uncertainty with respect to the partworths is captured by the inverse of the Hessian of the loss function. Their goal is then to design a question by selecting a direction in parameter space that maximally decreases this matrix subject to enforcing utility balance.

In particular, AETV propose solving the following quadratic optimization problem in order to find a direction of maximal uncertainty:

(20)
$$\min_{z} z \nabla^2 L(\hat{w}_i \mid \gamma) z^T$$

subject to: $z.\hat{w}_i = 0, \quad z.z^T = 1$

where $\hat{w}_i$ is the value of the partworths that minimize the loss function, L, $\nabla^2 L(\hat{w}_i \mid \gamma)$ is the Hessian of the loss function at $\hat{w}_i$, and $z.z^T = 1$ is a scaling constraint. The optimal solution to Equation 20 is the eigenvector associated with the smallest positive eigenvalue of the matrix: $B_i = (I - \frac{\hat{w}_i.\hat{w}_i^T}{\hat{w}_i^T.\hat{w}_i}).\nabla^2 L(\hat{w}_i \mid \gamma)$ where I is the identity matrix.

The question-design algorithm is implemented as follows:

1. Find $\hat{w}_i$ such that $\hat{w}_i$ minimizes the loss function $L(w_i \mid \gamma)$. Because L is convex, there are many convex optimization methods that are efficient.
2. Find the (normalized) eigenvector z associated with the smallest positive eigenvalue of the matrix $B_i = (I - \frac{\hat{w}_i.\hat{w}_i^T}{\hat{w}_i^T.\hat{w}_i}).\nabla^2 L(\hat{w}_i \mid \gamma)$.
3. Find a pair of profiles such that $(x_{i(J+1)1} - x_{i(J+1)2})$ is as close as possible to being proportional to z and such that utility balance is preserved: $(x_{i(J+1)1} - x_{i(J+1)2}).\hat{w}_i \approx 0$.[3]

---

[3] AETV use the Knapsack approach of THS.

AETV illustrate the Hessian approach with a Ridge Regression loss function – similar to that used in support vector machines (where the constant, 1, scales the partworths):

(21)
$$L(w_i \mid \gamma) = \frac{1}{\gamma} \sum_{j=1}^{J} (1 - (x_{ij1} - x_{ij2}).w_i)^2 + \| w_i \|^2$$

With this loss function, the minimum $\hat{w}_i$ and the Hessian are given in closed form. To avoid the computational delays of cross-validation, γ is set equal to the inverse of the number of questions so that the data are weighed more heavily as more data become available. This specification is motivated by Vapnik (1998).

12.4.4   Summary of adaptive question design

Machine-learning and fast polyhedral algorithms have made it feasible to adapt both metric paired-comparison and choice-based conjoint questions to each respondent. Such questions promise to be more accurate and customized to focus precision where it is most needed. The basic concept is that each conjoint question constrains the set of feasible partworths. A researcher's goal is to find the questions that impose the most efficient constraints, where efficiency is defined as maximally decreasing the uncertainty in the estimated partworths.

To date, all question-design algorithms use information from a single respondent to select questions for that respondent. However, one of the lessons of both hierarchical Bayes and the machine learning approaches of EPT is that population-level information can improve accuracy at the individual level. We predict that such pooling methods will be feasible in the near future and make promising areas for research. For example one could adapt the Hessian method of AETV to a loss function like the ones in Equations 18 or 19 used by EPT.

12.5   Applications, simulations, and empirical tests

Conjoint analysis has a long history of validation and application. See, for example, Green (2004). Methods such as ACA, logit analysis of choice-based conjoint analysis, and hierarchical Bayes estimation have been improved through hundreds of applications. Such use and its related research have led to incremental improvement of these standard methods. By contrast, the methods reviewed in this paper are relatively new, each with only a few applications. On one hand, such tests usually involve only one or a few applications and, thus, must be considered experimental. On the other hand, we expect the performance on these tests to be lower bounds on eventual performance which is likely to improve with experience.

Despite the nascent nature of these methods, they have performed remarkably well in both Monte Carlo simulations and empirical applications. We review here applications, comparisons of estimation methods, and comparisons of question design methods.

12.5.1   Applications

Metric paired-comparison polyhedral methods. Toubia, Dahan, Simester and Hauser (TDSH, 2003) study preferences for the features of laptop computer bags. In their experiments, respondents were given the choice of real laptop bags worth approximately $100. Predictions were quite accurate. In addition, the models appear to have described market shares when the laptop bags were introduced to a real market.

Adaptive choice-based polyhedral conjoint methods. Toubia, Hauser, and Simester (THS, 2004) studied the preferences for the features of executive educational programs. The data were used to design MIT's 12-month executive program, which has since been implemented successfully. Toubia, Hauser and Garcia (THG, 2006) study the diffusion of non-traditional closures, "Stelvin" screw-tops, for premium wines by interviewing over 2,200 leading-edge wine consumers in the US, Australia and New-Zealand. They were able to identify the marketing actions that would be necessary to achieve market penetration in the US to match that in Australia and New Zealand.

Hessian-based adaptive choice-based conjoint analysis. Abernethy, Evgeniou, Toubia and Vert (AETV, 2006) study consumer preferences for digital cameras. They explore how respondents value different levels of price, resolution, battery life, optical zoom, and camera size.

Heterogeneous partworth estimation with complexity control. Evgeniou, Pontil and Toubia (EPT, 2006) test their method with a full-profile ratings study of personal computers collected by Lenk et al. (1996) and apply their method using data from a choice-based conjoint study of carbonated soft drinks collected by a professional market research company.

12.5.2   Comparisons of estimation methods

The basic results from the papers reviewed in this chapter are three-fold. (1) Individual-level optimization methods tend to outperform traditional individual-level methods that use neither complexity control nor shrinkage. (2) Individual-level methods often under-perform methods that use population-based shrinkage (either Bayesian or complexity-control shrinkage). (3) Complexity-control shrinkage often outperforms Bayesian shrinkage.

Metric paired-comparison analytic-center estimation. TDSH test metric analytic-center estimations with both Monte Carlo simulations and an empirical application. In the simulations they find that, for homogeneous populations, HB consistently performs better than analytic center estimation, likely because HB uses population-level data to moderate individual estimates. For heterogeneous populations, analytic-center estimation performs better, especially when paired with polyhedral question design. They also find that HB is relatively more accurate when response errors are high, but analytic center estimation is more accurate when response errors are low. For external validity tests, they found that HB outperforms analytic-center estimation for fixed, orthogonal questions, but that analytic-center estimation does better when matched with polyhedral questions.[4]

Adaptive choice-based analytic-center estimation. THS compare choice-based analytic-center estimation to HB on four metrics – root mean square error, hit rate, correlation among partworths, and the percent of respondents for whom a method predicts best. Analytic-center estimation performs well when matched with polyhedral question design in domains were there is high heterogeneity. Otherwise, HB does well in all domains. However, if one takes a convex combination of the population mean and the individual-level analytic center estimates, the resulting "shrinkage" estimates outperform HB.[5]

THG test the probabilistic interpretation of adaptive choice-based analytic-center estimation. Based on Evgeniou, Boussios and Zacharia (EBZ, 2005), their HB benchmark includes constraints that all partworths be positive. Such constraints improve predictive ability and are easily implemented with rejection sampling. To distinguish this method from standard HB, we label it HBP (P for positivity). THG find that taking response errors into account and using informative priors improve analytic-center estimation. At least one of the two improvements outperforms deterministic analytic-center estimation in all tests. Informative priors appear to provide the greater improvement. HBP is significantly better in most cases. We suspect that had HBP been applied in the earlier tests, it would have been best in most comparisons.

As a summary, analytic-center estimation is better than HB in some domains, but not as good as HBP. On the other hand, shrinkage-based analytic-center estimation shows considerable promise. We hypothesize that the dominant effect is the ability to use population-level information to improve individual-level estimates. If population-level information is used, analytic-center estimation may ultimately improve to be as accurate or more accurate than HBP.

Support vector machines. EBZ show that their method based on Support Vector Machines is more robust to response error compared to other individual-level methods. While their method does not perform as well as HBP in situations in which there is no interaction between attributes, it consistently outperforms HBP when interactions are present.

Heterogeneous partworth estimation with complexity control (HPECC). EPT show that their methods perform consistently better than HB (with relatively diffuse second-stage priors), both with choice and metric data, and both on

---

[4] We caution the reader that the HB method used as a benchmark in this paper was such that no external constraints were imposed. Subsequent research suggests that HB does much better if the partworths are constrained to be positive (Evgeniou, Boussios and Zacharia 2005). This caveat also applies to the simulation tests in THS.

5   THS do not estimate a γ through cross-validation but rather choose a γ based on out-of-sample performance. Their results are, thus, only suggestive.

simulated as well as field data.[6] In the case of metric data, they report simulations in which they vary heterogeneity, response error, and the number of questions per respondent. They find that their method significantly outperforms standard HB in 7 out of their 8 experimental conditions (2 levels per experimental factor). They further compare these two metric estimation methods using a metric-full-profile data set on the features of computers (from Lenk et al. 1996). Heterogeneous partworth estimation with complexity control (HPECC) significantly outperforms HB on holdout prediction, using both all 16 questions as well as a random subset of 8 questions per respondent (14 parameters are estimated per respondent). For choice data, they find that HPECC outperforms HB in 6 out of 8 experimental conditions. Empirically, HPECC outperforms HB with 16 questions per respondent for data on carbonated soft drinks, and does not perform significantly differently when 8 questions are used per respondent (17 parameters are estimated per respondent).

EPT's simulation and empirical validity tests reinforce the dominating effect of shrinkage/complexity-control. Population means clearly improve predictive performance by making the partworth estimates more robust. Their results also suggest that prediction is improved when γ is chosen endogenously rather than based on prior beliefs. Finally, EPT show that their approach allows modeling and estimating models with large numbers of attribute interactions. Estimates remain robust and significantly better than that of HB even if the total number of parameters becomes substantially larger than the number of observations per respondent. This result confirms earlier findings reported by EBZ for individual-level partworth estimation.

12.5.3   Comparisons of question design methods

The overall summary of the comparisons of adaptive question design methods is that adapting questionnaires at the individual level can improve performance.

Adaptive metric paired-comparison polyhedral question design. TDSH compare polyhedral question design to ACA as well as fixed designs and random designs. Monte Carlo simulations suggest that, when there are a small number of questions, polyhedral question design method outperforms the other three benchmarks. However, the performance may be due, in part, to endogeneity bias in ACA – prior, self-explicated questions are used in question design but standard HB estimation uses these only as constraints in estimation (Hauser and Toubia 2005; Liu, Otter, and Allenby 2006). When more questions are asked such that the questions cover the range of features more completely, fixed designs emerge as viable alternatives for some domains. In empirical tests, adaptive polyhedral questions outperform both fixed and ACA benchmarks.

---

[6] EPT do not consider positivity constraints on the partworths, neither for their methods nor for HB.

Adaptive choice-based polyhedral question design. THS simulations suggest that, when response error is low, choice-based polyhedral questions outperform random questions, fixed orthogonal questions, and questions chosen by aggregate customization (Arora and Huber 2001, Huber and Zwerina 1996). Furthermore, high heterogeneity tends to favor individual-level adaptation. When response error is high, the best method depends on the tradeoffs between response error and heterogeneity. THS apply their method empirically, but were not able to obtain validation data. However, they do show that the method achieves choice balance throughout the questioning sequence.

THG attempt to improve adaptive choice-based polyhedral methods so that they might handle high-response error domains. Their simulations suggest that taking response errors into account and using informative priors improve polyhedral question design. Compared to the THS's deterministic algorithm, random questions, fixed questions, and aggregate customization, at least one of the two probabilistic modifications is best or tied for best in all experimental cells. Their empirical tests (wine consumers) suggest that probabilistic polyhedral question design performs better than aggregate customization question design in three of the four panels and never significantly worse.

Hessian-based adaptive choice-based conjoint analysis. The Monte Carlo simulations and the field test reported by AETV confirm that individual-level adaptation outperforms random and non-adaptive benchmarks when response error is low and/or when respondent heterogeneity is high. Moreover, the use of complexity control in the loss function improves robustness to response error, hence largely overcoming possible endogeneity biases inherent to adaptive questionnaires (Hauser and Toubia 2005).

In summary, optimization-based adaptive question design for conjoint analysis shows considerable promise. In many cases, the tested methods outperform non-adaptive methods. Adaptation shows the most promise when response errors are low, when heterogeneity is high, and/or when relatively few questions are to be asked. However, the potential of individual-level adaptation is not limited to these domains. With application and incremental improvements we expect that the performance of these methods will improve further.

12.6   Conclusions and opportunities for future research

This chapter reviews some recent developments in the application of optimization methods and machine learning in conjoint estimation and question design. Although the many methods are disparate, they can be linked through a statistical learning framework and philosophy. This framework suggests that specific methods may be described by the choice of a measure of fit, a measure of complexity, and an approach for determining the trade off between fit and complexity. Adaptive questionnaire design is achieved by combining optimization and machine learning with principles of experimental design to select questions that minimize the uncertainty around the estimates.

We hope that this chapter will motivate future applications and research in this area. In particular, we hope that researchers will build upon the many successful methods in conjoint analysis that have been developed either to estimate partworths or to design questions. Complexity control, shrinkage, and adaptive optimization of questions all show considerable potential to improve extant methods and to develop new methods.

12.7 References

Abernethy, Jacob, Theodoros Evgeniou, Olivier Toubia, and Jean-Philippe Vert (AETV, 2006), "Eliciting Consumer Preferences using Robust Adaptive Choice Questionnaires," Working Paper, INSEAD, Fontainebleau, France.

Addelman, Sidney (1962), "Symmetrical and Asymmetrical Fractional Factorial Plans", *Technometrics*, 4 (February) 47-58.

Allenby, Greg M., Peter E. Rossi (1999), "Marketing Models of Consumer Heterogeneity," *Journal of Econometrics*, 89, March/April, p. 57 - 78.

Arora, Neeraj and Joel Huber (2001), "Improving Parameter Estimates and Model Prediction by Aggregate Customization in Choice Experiments," *Journal of Consumer Research*, 28, (September), 273-283.

Chaloner, Kathryn, and Isabella Verdinelli (1995), ``Bayesian Experimental Design: A Review", *Statistical Science*, 10(3), 273-304.

Dawes, R. M and B. Corrigan (1974), "Linear Models in Decision Making," *Psychological Bulletin*, 81, 95-106.

Efron, Bradley, and Robert Tibshirani (1993), *An Introduction to the Bootstrap*, (New York, NY: Chapman and Hall).

Einhorn, Hillel J. (1970), "The Use of Nonlinear, Noncompensatory Models in Decision Making," *Psychological Bulletin*, 73, 3, 221-230.

Evgeniou, Theodoros, Constantinos Boussios, and Giorgos Zacharia (EBZ, 2005), "Generalized Robust Conjoint Estimation," *Marketing Science*, 24(3), 415-429.

Evgeniou, Theodoros, Massimiliano Pontil, and Tomaso Poggio (2000), "Regularization Networks and Support Vector Machines," *Advances in Computational Mathematics*, 13, 1-50.

Evgeniou, Theodoros, Massimiliano Pontil, and Olivier Toubia (EPT, 2006), "A Convex Optimization Approach to Modeling Heterogeneity in Conjoint Estimation," Working Paper, INSEAD, Fontainebleau, France.

Ford, I., Kitsos, C.P. and Titterington, D.M. (1989) "Recent Advances in Nonlinear Experimental Designs," *Technometrics*, 31, 49-60.

Green, Paul E. (2004), "Thirty Years of Conjoint Analysis: Reflections and Prospects," *Conjoint Analysis, Related Modeling, and Applications: Market Research and Modeling: Progress and Prospects*, Jerry Wind and Paul Green, Eds., (Boston, MA: Kluwer Academic Publishers), 141-168.

Green, Paul E. and Vithala R. Rao (1971), "Conjoint Measurement for Quantifying Judgmental Data," *Journal of Marketing Research,* 8, (August), 355-63.

Greene, William (2003), *Econometric Analysis,* (Englewood Cliffs, NJ: Prentice Hall).

Hastie, Trevor, Robert Tibshirani, and Jerome H. Friedman (2003), *The Elements of Statistical Learning,* (New York, NY: Springer Series in Statistics).

Hauser, John R., Ely Dahan, Michael Yee, and James Orlin (2006), ""Must Have" Aspects vs. Tradeoff Aspects in Models of Customer Decisions," *Proceedings of the Sawtooth Software Conference in Del Ray Beach, FL,* March 29-31, 2006

Hauser, John R., and Olivier Toubia (2005), "The Impact of Endogeneity and Utility Balance in Conjoint Analysis," *Marketing Science,* Vol. 24, No. 3.

Huber, Joel and Klaus Zwerina (1996), "The Importance of Utility Balance in Efficient Choice Designs," *Journal of Marketing Research,* 33, (August), 307-317.

Jain, Arun K., Franklin Acito, Naresh K. Malhotra, and Vijay Mahajan (1979), "A Comparison of the Internal Validity of Alternative Parameter Estimation Methods in Decompositional Multiattribute Preference Models," *Journal of Marketing Research,* 16, (August), 313-322.

Johnson, Richard (1987), "Accuracy of Utility Estimation in ACA," Working Paper, Sawtooth Software, Sequim, WA, (April).

Johnson, Richard (1991), "Comment on `Adaptive Conjoint Analysis: Some Caveats and Suggestions," *Journal of Marketing Research,* 28, (May), 223-225.

Kanninen, Barbara (2002), "Optimal Design for Multinomial Choice Experiments," *Journal of Marketing Research,* 36 (May), 214-227.

Kuhfeld, Warren F. (2005), *Marketing Research Methods in SAS,* SAS Institute Inc., Cary, NC (USA). Available at http://support.sas.com/techsup/technote/ts722.pdf.

Kuhfeld, Warren F., Randall D. Tobias, and Mark Garratt (1994), "Efficient Experimental Design with Marketing Applications," *Journal of Marketing Research,* 31, 4(November), 545-557.

Lenk, Peter J., Wayne S. DeSarbo, Paul E. Green, Martin R. Young (1996), "Hierarchical Bayes Conjoint Analysis: Recovery of Partworth Heterogeneity from Reduced Experimental Designs," *Marketing Science,* 15(2), p. 173--91.

Liu, Qing, Thomas Otto, and Greg M. Allenby (2006), "Investigating Conjoint Analysis Bias in Conjoint Analysis," Working Paper, Ohio State University, Columbus, OH.

Newey, Whitney K., and Daniel McFadden (1994), "Large Sample Estimation and Hypothesis Testing," in *Handbook of Econometrics,* edited by R.F. Engle and D.L. McFadden, Elsevier Science.

Rossi, Peter E., Greg M. Allenby (2003), "Bayesian Statistics and Marketing," *Marketing Science,* 22(3), p. 304-328.

Rossi, Peter E., Greg M. Allenby, Robert McCulloch (2005), *Bayesian Statistics and Marketing.* (New York, NY: John Wiley and Sons).

Sandor, Zsolt, and Michel Wedel (2001), "Designing Conjoint Choice Experiments Using Managers' Prior Beliefs," *Journal of Marketing Research,* 38, 4, 430-444.

Shao, Jun (1993), "Linear model selection via cross-validation," *Journal of the American Statistical Association*, 88(422), p. 486--494.

Srinivasan, V., and Allan D. Shocker (1973a), "Linear Programming Techniques for Multidimensional Analysis of Preferences," *Psychometrika*, 38 (3), 337-369.

Srinivasan, V. and Allen D. Shocker (1973b), "Estimating the Weights for Multiple Attributes in a Composite Criterion Using Pairwise Judgments," *Psychometrika*, 38, 4, (December), 473-493.

Steinberg, D.M., and Hunter, W.G. (1984), "Experimental Design: Review and Comment," *Technometrics*, 26, 71-97.

Tikhonov, A., and V. Arsenin (1977), *Solutions of Ill-posed Problems*, W. H. Winston, Washington, D.C. (OLIVIER: add full first names)

Tong, S., and D. Koller (2000), "Support vector machine active learning with applications to text classification," *Proceedings of the Seventeenth International Conference on Machine Learning*, Stanford University, CA, USA.

Toubia, Olivier, John R. Hauser, and Rosanna Garcia (THG, 2006), "Probabilistic Polyhedral Methods for Adaptive Conjoint Analysis: Theory and Application," forthcoming, *Marketing Science*.

Toubia, Olivier, John R. Hauser, and Duncan I. Simester (THS, 2004), "Polyhedral Methods for Adaptive Choice-Based Conjoint Analysis," *Journal of Marketing Research*, 41, 116-131.

Toubia, Olivier, Duncan I. Simester, John R. Hauser, and Ely Dahan (TDSH, 2003), "Fast Polyhedral Adaptive Conjoint Estimation," *Marketing Science*, 22(3), 273-303.

Vapnik, Vladimir (1998), *Statistical Learning Theory*, (New York, NY: John Wiley and Sons).

Wahba, Grace (1990), "Splines Models for Observational Data," *Series in Applied Mathematics*, Vol. 59, SIAM, Philadelphia.

Wittink, Dick R. and Philippe Cattin (1981), "Alternative Estimation Methods for Conjoint Analysis: A Monte Carlo Study," *Journal of Marketing Research*, 18, (February), 101-106.

13 The Combinatorial Structure of Polyhedral Choice Based Conjoint Analysis

Joachim Giesen and Eva Schuberth

13.1 Introduction

In abstract terms conjoint analysis can be seen as fitting a model to preference information elicited from a group of respondents. That is, conjoint analysis comprises two tasks,

(1)   preference data elicitation, and

(2)   model fitting to the elicited data.

The model fitting phase is necessary since in general the elicited data tends to be very sparse and can be interpreted meaningfully only in the context of some model, which already encodes general assumptions on the structure of the preferences.

13.1.1 Conjoint structure and data elicitation

In conjoint analysis we are interested in preference information on a class of products that possesses a *conjoint structure*, i.e., that can be described in terms of attributes A_i and attribute levels $a_{ij} \in A_i$. That is, we consider sets of products whose profile is given as an element in a subset $P \subseteq A_1 \times \ldots \times A_n$, where the attribute set A_i has the levels $A_i = \{a_{i1}, \ldots, a_{im}\}$. A product profile $p \in P$ is just a vector $(a_{1j_1}, \ldots, a_{nj_n})$ of attribute levels $a_{ij_i} \in A_i$. Preference information can be elicited in many different ways. The most direct approach is to ask a respondent to state his valuation of a given product profile in terms of money. In choice based conjoint analysis we assume a more indirect elicitation procedure, namely, *discrete choice tasks*. A choice task consists of a small number of product profiles - typically between two and four - presented to a respondent, who has to state which one he is most likely to buy (often also a *none* choice option is included). Preference elicitation in the form of discrete choice tasks has two advantages, the cognitive burden on the respondent in each task is comparatively low, and choice tasks also simulate to a certain extent real buying situations. One drawback of preference elicitation with choice tasks is, that in order to be exhaustive, i.e., in order to derive a full product ranking from the choices of a respondent many choice tasks are necessary even if we assume that the respondent's choices are transitive, i.e., if he chooses p_1 over p_2 and p_2 over p_3, he should also choose

p_1 over p_3. *Adaptive* elicitation methods in conjoint analysis deal with this problem by trying to choose the next choice task dependent on the choices in previous tasks such that the information gained in the worst case outcome of the choice task is approximately maximized. Information gain maximization in the worst case means that the minimum of the information gain among all possible outcomes of the choice task is maximized. Polyhedral choice based conjoint analysis invented by Hauser, Toubia and Simester [1] is an intricate but elegant method to fit a linear model to discrete choice data elicited from one respondent, while at the same time providing information on a good next choice task, i.e., a choice task that provides a lot of information in the worst case.

13.1.2   Model and model fitting

In a linear model the preference information is encoded into a linear value function v, which assigns a value (partworth) λ_{ij} to every attribute level a_{ij}, i.e., for a given respondent his value for a product profile $p = (a_{1j_1}, \ldots, a_{nj_n})$ is given as

$$v(p) = \sum_{i=1}^{n} \lambda_{ij_i}.$$

The model fitting task now is to compute the partworths λ_{ij} from the choice data elicited from the respondent. Note that a linear model really makes an assumption on the structure of the respondent's preferences. In case that the attributes A_i are continuous sets, i.e., real intervals, this assumption can be made more explicit, namely, the linearity of a value function is equivalent to mutual preferentially independence of all attributes, see Keeney and Raiffa [2] for details.

13.1.3   Product sets without structure

As simple as it may seem a conjoint structure is quite intricate once one has a closer look. To make this more explicit we want to compare polyhedral choice based conjoint analysis with choice based preference analysis on product sets without any structure. In the latter case the product set P is just a finite set $\{p_1, \ldots, p_k\}$ of product (profiles) that does not possess any additional structure. A choice task in the structureless case is as in conjoint analysis a small subset of products that is presented to a respondent who has to indicate which of the products he is most likely to buy. Fitting a linear model to the elicited data now becomes assigning values μ_i to the products p_i.

13.2   Choice based polyhedral conjoint analysis

The insight that finally led to choice based polyhedral conjoint analysis is that the two tasks,

(1)   coming up with a next informative choice task, and

(2)   fitting the partworths in a linear model to the stated choices,

can be formulated as purely geometric problems. To this end one can assume (without loss of generality) that every partworth is a real number in the interval $[-1, 1]$. A valid fit of the partworths is a point in the cube $[-1, 1]^{nm}$, where n is the number of attributes and we assume (to keep the exposition simple) that every attribute has m levels. Of course a valid fit needs not to be a good fit. A good fit would allow to predict correctly the outcome of a choice task not encountered so far with high probability. If a respondent prefers product $p = (a_{1j_1}, \dots, a_{nj_n})$ over product $q = (a_{1l_1}, \dots, a_{nl_n})$ in a choice task, then the parameters of the linear model---the partworths---have to satisfy the following constraint

$$\sum_{i=1}^{n} \lambda_{ij_i} \geq \sum_{i=1}^{n} \lambda_{il_i} \Leftrightarrow \sum_{i=1}^{n} \lambda_{ij_i} - \sum_{i=1}^{n} \lambda_{il_i} \geq 0.$$

This constraint can be rewritten by using the inner product $\langle \cdot, \cdot \rangle$ on $\mathbb{R}^{nm}$ as

$$\langle h, \lambda \rangle \geq 0,$$

where λ is the partworth vector and h is a vector in $\{-1, 0, 1\}^{nm}$ whose entries are 1 at positions ij_i and -1 at positions il_i for all $i = 1, \dots, n$. All other entries in h are 0. This inequality defines a halfspace $H \subseteq \mathbb{R}^{nm}$,

$$H = \{\lambda \in \mathbb{R}^{nm} | \langle h, \lambda \rangle \geq 0\},$$

whose boundary, a hyperplane, contains the origin and has the inward pointing normal vector h. That is, all partworth vectors that are compliant with the comparison between p and q are contained in the intersection of $[-1, 1]^{nm}$ with the halfspace H. Every possible product comparison - there are only finitely many - leads to a hyperplane (bounding the corresponding halfspace). The arrangement of all these hyperplanes subdivides the cube $[-1, 1]^{nm}$ into polyhedral cells. All points in the same cell of the arrangement encode exactly the same ranking of all products with profile in $A_1 \times \dots \times A_n$, i.e., any such point is a perfect fit for the ranking. In other words using any point in such a cell as partworth vector gives the same ranking. Note however, that not all rankings of $A_1 \times \dots \times A_n$ can be expressed by a partworth vector, i.e. in the linear model. But once we assume that a respondent's preference structure can be faithfully represented by a partworth vector, the goal in choice based conjoint analysis becomes to set up the choice tasks such that one can identify a perfect (good) partworth vector from the respondent's choices in as few choice tasks as possible. The task to identify a perfect partworth vector from choice tasks is equivalent to identifying a cell in the hyperplane arrangement. Any vector in this cell can serve as a perfect fit for the linear model. The information provided in a sequence of choice tasks is in geometric terms a nested sequence of polyhedra: the first polyhedron is just the cube $[-1, 1]^{nm}$. Each choice task provides one or more halfspaces (a one out of k choice task provides $k - 1$ halfspaces). The common intersection of $[-1, 1]^{nm}$ with all the halfspaces provided up to a given choice task represents the information gathered up to that task. Two questions arise naturally:

1.   How can one find the the the cell that encodes the preference ranking efficiently, i.e., using as few choice tasks as possible.
2.   How to choose a 'good' representative point out of the unique cell once it has been identified.

In [1] the answers to these questions are intertwined: a deep point inside the cell, the so called analytic center of the polyhedral cell, is considered a good representative point and a comparison whose corresponding hyperplane is close to the analytic center and cuts the cell into two polyhedra of almost equal volume is considered to be a good next comparison.

13.3   The structureless case

We also have a purely geometric interpretation in the unstructured case. If we again assume the the values μ_i are contained in the interval $[-1, 1]$, then any point in the cube $[-1, 1]^k$ is a valid fit as long as we do not have any information about the ranking of the k different products. Information is gathered by product comparisons. A comparison of the i'th and the j'th product tells us which one of μ_i and μ_j is larger. In geometric terms this means, the comparison tells us on which side of the hyperplane passing through the origin and with normal $h \in \{-1, 0, 1\}^k$ the vector $\mu = (\mu_1, \dots, \mu_k)$ has to lie. The normal h has entry 1 at the i'th position, -1 at the j'th position and is 0 at all other positions. There are $\binom{k}{2}$ comparisons and thus $\binom{k}{2}$ hyperplanes. The arrangement of all these hyperplanes subdivides the cube $[-1, 1]^k$ into cells. Each cell of this arrangement corresponds to one of the $k!$ rankings of the μ_i. Hence determining the ranking of the k products from product comparisons is equivalent to determining a cell in the hyperplane arrangement. In Figure 1 we show two views on the subdivision of $[-1, 1]^3$ by the comparison hyperplanes for the case $k = 3$.

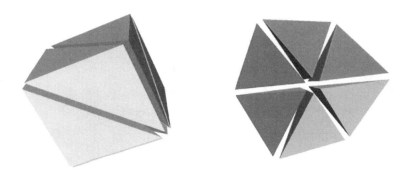

Figure 1:   *Subdivision of* $[-1, 1]^3$ *into the six cells that correspond to the six possible rankings of three products*

13.3.1   Information theoretic lower bound

We assume that we assess a respondent's preference ranking of n products from pairwise comparisons, i.e., from a sequence of choice tasks that each involves only two products. From the respondent's answers we compute values $\mu_1, \ldots, \mu_k$. These values are a perfect fit if they reproduce the respondent's preference ranking on the set of products. Therefore, if any query strategy to find the product ranking needs at least l comparisons, then also any strategy to find perfectly fitting values $\mu_1, \ldots, \mu_k$ needs at least l comparisons.

Information theory provides an answer to the question of how many product comparisons are needed in the worst case in order to infer a product ranking. In the information theoretic argument the notion of decision tree plays a central role. A decision tree for ranking k products represents a query strategy by describing all possible sequences of comparisons between products. In the end, each of these sequences leads to a different ranking of the products. Assume that we want to rank three products p_1, p_2, p_3 according to their values μ_1, μ_2, μ_3. In Figure 2 we show one possible decision tree, i.e., query strategy for that problem.

Every inner node - oval in Figure 2 - represents a product comparison. Depending on the outcome of the comparison the subsequent comparison is determined. After a sequence of comparisons one ends up in a leaf of the tree, rectangular node in Figure 2. This leaf corresponds to the product ranking compliant with the sequence of comparison outcomes. For a particular product ranking the number of inner nodes on the path from the root (i.e. the top most node) to the corresponding leaf is just the number of comparisons that is needed for that particular query strategy. The height of a tree is the maximum number of inner nodes that are visited when traversing the tree from the root to its leaves.

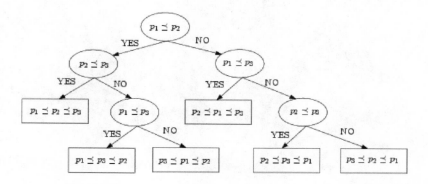

Figure 2:   A decision tree for ranking three products

In the example of Figure 2 the height is 3. It is obvious that the height of a decision tree is just the number of comparisons that the query strategy needs in the
worst case. We know that every decision tree for the sorting problem has $k!$ leaves
corresponding to the $k!$ possible rankings. The height of any binary tree on $k!$
leaves is at least $\log_2(k!)$ which can be lower bounded by $\frac{k}{2}\log_2(\frac{k}{2})$. Therefore
any query strategy for determining a ranking of k products needs at least $\frac{k}{2}\log_2(\frac{k}{2})$
comparisons. This is called the information theoretic lower bound in ranking. In
the following section we will show that the information theoretic lower bound can
be reached, i.e., there is a query strategy which can determine any ranking of k
products with no more than $ck\log_2(k)$ comparisons, where c is a constant independent of k. Later we will see that the same does not hold for the case that the
product profiles are described by a conjoint structure. In that case there is no algorithm that can reach the information theoretic lower bound.

13.3.2   Volume cuts

There are many query strategies known that reach the information theoretic lower
bound up to a constant, i.e., query strategies that always infer the ranking of k
products with at most $ck\log_2 k$ comparisons for some constant c. Here we describe such a strategy which is based on the geometric interpretation of the problem and the following two observations.

Observation 1 *Assume a respondent has performed already i comparisons.
Let P_i be the set of rankings of the products that are compatible with his answers.
Any query strategy that always reduces the set P_i for all i by at least a constant
fraction δ reaches the information theoretic lower bound. Ideally δ would be $1/2$,
but it can be shown that this is not always possible.*

Observation 2 *Every cell in the subdivision of* $[-1, 1]^k$ *by the hyperplanes corresponding to paired product comparisons is a simplex with volume* $2^n/n!$

In geometric terms a sequence of comparisons provides us with a nested sequence of polyhedra. The polyhedron at the beginning when no comparison was performed is just $[-1, 1]^k$. See Figure 3 for an example of such a nested sequence in the case $k = 3$.

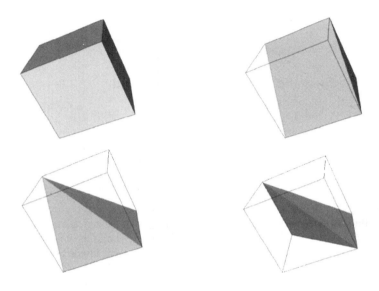

Figure 3:   Nested sequence of polyhedra compliant with a sequence of comparisons

The volume of each polyhedron multiplied with $n!/2^n$ gives us exactly the number of rankings that are compatible with the comparisons performed so far. More importantly, any comparison whose corresponding hyperplane in the worse of the two outcomes of the comparison cuts a δ-fraction of the volume of the polyhedron also cuts a δ-fraction of the rankings compatible with the comparisons so far. An application of the famous Brunn-Minkowski inequality shows that any comparison of two products whose average rank in the rankings compatible with the comparisons so far differs by only 1 cuts of at least a $1/2e \sim 0.184$ fraction of the volume (and thus also of the compatible rankings). Here the rank of a product in a ranking is the number of products that are ranked below the product plus 1. It can be shown that such a comparison always exists as long as there are at least two compatible rankings. Of course we are done once there is only one compatible ranking left. See Matousek [3] for details and a proof. At this moment we know that a good next comparison exists, but can we also find one efficiently? A heuristic to search for a good next comparison can be derived from the following observation: for any convex body in $\mathbb{R}^d$ any hyperplane that passes through the center of gravity cuts the body into two bodies whose volume is at least a $\left(\frac{d}{d+1}\right)^n$-fraction of the volume of the original body. Of course this leaves us with the problem to find the center of gravity of a polyhedron, which is not an easy task. The analytic center as used in [1] can be seen as an approximation to the center of gravity, but no guarantees are known for the latter.

13.4 The conjoint structure case

13.4.1 Information theoretic lower bound

According to the linear model each product p has a value $v(p) = \sum_{i=1}^{n} \lambda_{ij_i}$ where λ_{ij_i} is the respondent's partworth for the j_i-th level of attribute i. These values induce a ranking of the products in $A_1 \times \ldots \times A_n$. Like in the unstructured case we want to determine how many product comparisons are needed to infer this ranking. Fredman [4] has studied this question for the case when there are only two attributes. In the following we will generalize his results to the case with $n > 2$ attributes. But at first we want to determine the information theoretic lower bound. As in the unstructured case any query strategy can be represented by a decision tree. Every leaf of the tree corresponds to a ranking of the products in $A_1 \times \ldots \times A_n$. To determine the information theoretic lower bound one needs to determine the number of possible leaves of any decision tree, i.e., the number of possible product rankings. Let us call this number l. The height of a decision tree is lower bounded by $\log_2(l)$, which means that any query strategy to determine a ranking of $A_1 \times \ldots \times A_n$ needs at least $\log_2(l)$ product comparisons in the worst case. The total number of products in $A_1 \times \ldots \times A_n$ is m^n, but the number of possible rankings is substantially less than $m^n!$ -- as we would have in the unstructured case. To determine the number l of possible product rankings in the conjoint structure case we have a closer look at the hyperplane arrangement that corresponds to all comparisons of two products. This hyperplane arrangement gives us a subdivision of the cube $[-1, 1]^{nm}$ into cells and any cell corresponds to exactly one ranking of $A_1 \times \ldots \times A_n$. Hence, if we can count the number of cells we know the number of rankings and can therefore determine the information theoretic lower bound. Let us first count the number of hyperplanes: we have as many hyperplanes as we have possibilities to choose two products p and q. We can choose two products by choosing for every attribute A_i two levels a_{ij} and a_{ik}. There are $\binom{m}{2}$ possibilities to do so for one attribute and therefore $\binom{m}{2}^n$ possibilities to choose two products. It is known that h hyperplanes partition the d-dimensional space into at most $\binom{h}{d} + \binom{h}{d-1} + \ldots + \binom{h}{0}$ many regions and thus the number of cells in the hyperplane arrangement is at most $nm\binom{m^{2n}}{nm} \leq nm^{2n^2m+1}$.

Having found an upper bound for the number of cells we now can upper bound the information theoretic lower bound of the problem as the logarithm of this number. The information theoretic lower bound for ranking in the conjoint structure case is at most $(2n^2m + 1)\log_2(m) + \log_2(n)$. A query strategy that matches the information theoretic lower bound needs only polynomially many (in the problem parameters n and m) comparisons to find a ranking on $A_1 \times \ldots \times A_n$. In the unstructured case such a query strategy exists. Unfortunately, in the conjoint structure case such a query strategy does not exist as we will show in the next section.

13.4.2   Volume cuts

Here want to use a different technique than employed for information theoretic lower bounds to show a lower bound on the number of necessary comparisons that is dramatically larger than the latter bound, more precisely: any query strategy to determine a ranking obeying the linear model of the products in $A_1 \times \ldots \times A_n$ needs at least $(m - 1)^n$ comparisons in the worst case. Note, that this number grows exponentially in the number of attributes n. From a practical point of view it is infeasible to ask a respondent that many questions even for moderately large n and m. The exponential lower bound $(m - 1)^n$ was first shown by Fredman [4] for the case of two attributes. We are able to generalize his proof to $n > 2$ attributes, but since the generalization is very technical and hardly gives any new insights here we only restate Fredman's proof to give an impression of the type of argument.

Suppose we have the two attributes $A = \{a_1, a_2, \ldots, a_m\}$ and $B = \{b_1, b_2, \ldots, b_m\}$. We say that product $q \in A \times B$ is a successor of a product $p \in A \times B$ in the ranking if the rank of q is one higher than the rank of p. An outline of the lower bound construction is as follows: we start with a product ranking ω induced by carefully chosen partworths. For every product $(a_r, b_s) \in A \times B$ with $1 \leq r \leq m - 1$ and $2 \leq s \leq m$ we modify the partworths a little bit to get another ranking ω_{rs} which differs from ω only in the ranking of (a_r, b_s) and its successor in ω; in ω_{rs} the product (a_r, b_s) is preferred over this successor. This means that ω and ω_{rs} differ only in one transposition. To distinguish ω from ω_{rs} one definitely needs to compare (a_r, b_s) and its successor in ω. Since there are $(m - 1)^2$ possible rankings ω_{rs} that differ from ω by only one transposition one needs at least $(m - 1)^2$ comparisons to distinguish ω from them. So far we have not specified the ranking ω. Its defining property is that the product (a_{j_1}, b_{j_2}) is preferred over the product (a_{i_1}, b_{i_2}) if and only if $i_1 + i_2 < j_1 + j_2$ or $i_1 + i_2 = j_1 + j_2$ and $i_1 \leq j_1$. A ranking that satisfies the defining property can be derived from partworths if we choose for the a_i and b_i both the partworths to be i and break ties lexicographically (A before B) between products where the sum of partworths gives the same value. The lexicographic tie breaker can be encoded into the partworths as follows: choose ϵ such that

$0 < \epsilon < 1$ and modify the partworths of the a_i to be $i + i\epsilon$ and keep the part-worths of the b_i as i. The ranking induced from this partworth is ω. In Figure 4 we illustrate the ranking ω for the case that A and B have five levels each.

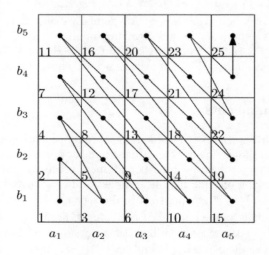

Figure 4: *Ranking ω*

In the figure every product is represented by a square in a rectangular diagram. Altogether there are $m^2 = 25$ products/squares. One can read off the levels that describe a particular product from the column and line labelling. The lower left square represents the product described by the levels a_1 and b_1. This product is the lowest ranking product. The products are connected in increasing order by an oriented path through the diagram that represents the ranking ω, i.e., (a_2, b_1) is the second least preferred product. One can easily verify that the illustrated ranking indeed satisfies the defining property.

Now let us describe how to derive the ranking ω_{rs} from the partworths that induce ω. For $1 \leq r \leq m - 1$ and $2 \leq s \leq m$ let the partworths of the a_i be

$$\begin{cases} i + i\epsilon & \text{if } 1 \leq i \leq r \\ i + i\epsilon - \frac{2}{3}\epsilon & \text{if } r + 1 \leq i \leq m \end{cases}$$

and the partworths of the b_i be

$$\begin{cases} i & \text{if } 1 \leq i \leq s - 1 \\ i + \frac{2}{3}\epsilon & \text{if } s \leq i \leq m \end{cases}$$

The ranking induced by these partworths is exactly ω_{rs}. In Figure 5 we illustrate the ranking ω_{rs} for $r = 2$ and $s = 3$. Observe that in ω_{rs} the product (a_2, b_3) is now preferred over (a_3, b_2).

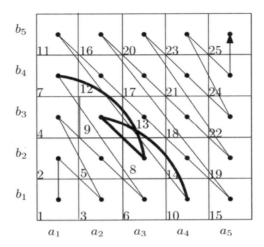

Figure 5:   Ranking ω_{rs}

The specification of partworths for ω and all possible ω_{rs} concludes the proof for the case of two attributes. That is, in the case of two attributes we now know that any query strategy to determine a ranking on $A \times B$ needs at least $(m - 1)^2$ comparisons in the worst case. The generalization of this result to the case of more than two attributes implies that any query strategy to determine a ranking on $A_1 \times A_2 \times \ldots \times A_n$ needs at least $(m - 1)^n$ comparisons in the worst case.

Finally, we want to discuss what the combinatorial insights mean for volume cut based query strategies like choice based polyhedral conjoint analysis. We have the following two observations. The first observation immediately follows from the exponential lower bound that we derived above.

Observation 3 *There does not exist a volume cut strategy that identifies a unique cell in the comparison hyperplane arrangement with only polynomially many (in n and m) comparisons in the worst case. Even stronger, in the worst case any volume cut query strategy needs at least $(m - 1)^n$ cuts (comparisons).*

The second observation is important if one wants to validate conjoint analysis methods on randomly generated partworth vectors. This observation has to be seen in contrast to Observation 2 for the structureless case.

Observation 4 *The cells in the subdivision of $[-1, 1]^{nm}$ by the hyperplanes corresponding to paired product comparisons have different combinatorial and thus also different geometric structures.*

An important consequence of this observation is that choosing partworth vectors uniformly at random from the cube $[-1, 1]^{nm}$ does not uniformly sample the space of rankings compliant with a linear structure. That is, a uniform geometric sampling strategy induces a combinatorial bias. Let us demonstrate the latter point by looking again at the case of two attributes A and B with m levels each. We consider the two purely lexicographic rankings on $A \times B$ and compare them to the ranking ω. The two lexicographic rankings are illustrated in Figure 6.

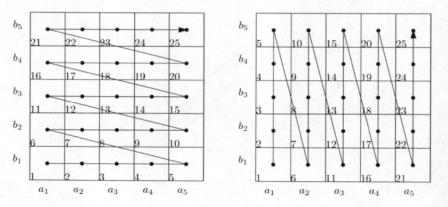

Figure 6:   *The two lexicographic rankings. In the left figure A is preferre-dover B and in the right figure B is preferred over A*

It is easy to see that both lexicographic rankings are linearly realizable. For example if A is preferred over B, then one can choose the partworths of the a_i to be im and the partworths of the b_i to be i. Observe that there are only $n - 1$ rankings that differ from the lexicographic rankings by one transposition - only the products at the turning points of the paths in Figure 6 can be exchanged to get another linearly representable ranking. Hence the cells in the subdivision of $[-1, 1]^{2m}$ by the comparison hyperplanes have only $n - 1$ facets, whereas the cell that corresponds to the ranking ω has $(m - 1)^2$ facets.

13.5   Conclusion

We shed some light on the geometric and combinatorial structure of polyhedral conjoint analysis. Our analysis shows that one has to be careful when transferring insights and ideas from the structureless case to the case with conjoint structure. In particular, we do not have a mathematical explanation of the impressive power of polyhedral conjoint analysis, whereas the structureless case is well understood by now. On the practical side we want to highlight that geometric random sampling strategies are probably not the best way to validate conjoint analysis methods.

13.6   References

[1] O. Toubia, J. R. Hauser, and D. I. Simester, Polyhedral Methods for Adaptive Choice-based Conjoint Analysis, *Journal of Marketing Research,* 41(1):116-131, 2004.

[2] R. L. Keeney and H. Raiffa. Decisions with Multiple Objectives: Preferences and Value Trade-Offs, *Cambridge University Press*, Cambridge, 1993.

[3] J. Matoušek. Lectures on *Discrete Geometry*, volume 212 of Graduate Texts in Mathematics, Springer Verlag, New York, 2002.

[4] M. L. Fredman. How Good is the Information Theory Bound in Sorting, *Theoretical Computer Science,* 1:355-361, 1976.

14 Using Conjoint Choice Experiments to Model Consumer Choices of Product Component Packages

Benedict G.C. Dellaert, Aloys W.J. Borgers,
Jordan J. Louviere and Harry J.P. Timmermans

14.1 Introduction

Recent advances in flexibility and automation allow a growing number of manufacturers and service providers to 'mass-customize' their products and offer modules from which consumers can create their own individualized products (e.g., Gilmore and Pine 1997). Traditional production processes limit consumer choices to fixed products defined by suppliers, but new mass-customization processes allow consumers to create their own optimal combination of product components. Although mass-customization offers consumers increased flexibility and consumption utility, little is known about how consumer choices to package or bundle separate components differ (if at all) from choices among traditional fixed product options, much less what the impact of packaging product components will be on the market shares of such products or a producer's overall share in the category.

The purpose of this paper is to resolve some of these issues by proposing a way to use conjoint choice experiments to model the impact of mass-customized product on consumer choices. Choice experiments have proved to be useful ways for researchers and managers to explore the potential impact of product modularization on consumer choice before implementation (e.g., see Louviere, Hensher and Swait 2000). We develop a formal way to model and predict how market shares are likely to shift when existing products are unbundled into different modules and/or new products are developed by adding new components.

To anticipate our approach, we hypothesize that module-level choices should result in smaller random component variances in choice models than choices of traditional products, and hat random component variances can differ for choices of different types of modules (c.f. Swait and Adamowicz 2001; Louviere et al. 2000, chapters 8 and 13). If this hypothesis is approximately true, it implies that impacts of changes in attribute levels will be greater for module-level choices than product-level choices and that impacts can differ among module types. We test this hypothesis empirically with consumer travel package choices. Our results show that consumer choices among modules exhibit less random component variation than choices among packages; however in our study the differences are significant only for one of two types of packages tested.

The rest of the paper is structured as follows: 1) we define terms and discuss the expected effects; 2) we propose and develop a model to capture fully and partly modularized choices; 3) we propose and develop a way to design choice experiments that allows us to test the proposed model; 4) we apply the approach to an empirical problem and present the results; 5) we use a series of simulations to illustrate the potential market share implications of our research for several marketing scenarios; 6) finally, we summarize our results, discuss the limitations of our empirical application and make some suggestions for potentially useful future research directions.

14.2   Conceptual framework

The following definitions and assumptions serve to formalize our analysis and the modeling of packaged product choices. First, let each *product g*, consist of *functions n_g* that the product provides to consumers. For each function, *modules j_{ng}* are available from which consumers can choose. We define *full modularization* to be the situation in which a consumer can choose from the complete range of possible modules or from the packages that can be obtained by combining all modules. Partial modularization also is possible, in which consumers can choose modules for some functions, but not all. Examples of partial modularization might include the following: automobiles for which only engine, heating system and display functions can be combined, clothing for which only design, fabric and fit functions can be combined, and travel packages for which only destination, transportation and tour functions can be combined. The number of functions typically will be smaller than the number of attributes because many functions are comprised of multiple attributes (e.g., price, color, and durability). Thus, modules differ from products and attributes because they are chosen independently (attributes are not) but not used independently (products may be).

Two aspects of modularized product choices differ from traditional 'fixed' product choices:

1. Consumers make separate module choices for each function (*'fully modularized choice'*), in which case we assume no restrictions with respect to the combinations that consumers can choose (i.e., the modules or packages they can organize and/or assemble).
2. Consumers choose separate modules for some but not all functions (*'partly modularized choice'*), in which case suppliers allow for some flexibility in product composition, but not for all functions.

We use random utility theory (RUT) to model consumer choice of modularized products. RUT-based choice models are based on the assumption that researchers cannot measure and model consumer preferences perfectly; hence, a random component must be included in consumer utility functions to capture unobserved effects. The latter effects include unobserved situational differences, omitted influences and consumer inability to express preferences perfectly and consistently (e.g., Ben-Akiva and Lerman 1985).

14.2.1 Hypotheses

Recently, Swait and Adamowicz (2001) showed that the complexity of choice sets measured by numbers of attributes that differ between options can affect the variance of the random component of consumer utility. Similarly, Dellaert et al. (1999) found that the absence or presence of price-level comparisons between products affected random component variance in consumer choices. Severin (2000) proposed that there was a tradeoff between experimental efficiency and respondent efficiency in choice experiments, and demonstrated that random component variability (or choice variability) increased with increasing numbers of attribute differences required to optimize efficiency in choice experiments (Street et al. 2000). Thus, it seems reasonable to hypothesize that module-level choices may be associated with less random component variance than traditional product-level choices. Furthermore, in the case of partly modularized choices, we expect that the number of modules present/absent in product comparisons should affect the size of the random component variance of consumer utility functions.

We also anticipate that differences in random component variances also may be associated with module choices for different functions. For example, options that involve more complex modules may represent more difficult choices than those with relatively simple modules and therefore may exhibit larger random component variances. We formalize these ideas below.

14.2.2 Model formulation

Fully modularized choices

We can specify a formal model as follows (omitting individual and product specific subscripts for notational simplicity): let U_{jn} be the utility of module j for function n, with $j_n \in \{1_n, ..., J_n\}$, the set of all modules that provide function n, and $n \in \{1, ..., N\}$, the set of all functions. Let V_{jn} be the structural component of utility U_{jn}, with $V_{jn} = \beta_n' x_{jn}$, where β_n and x_{jn} are function-specific vectors of utility parameters and product characteristics respectively.

First, we address the case of *full modularization* in which modules for all functions are sold separately. We make the following assumptions to develop the model:

1. Consumers select the module that constitutes their most preferred option for each function.
2. Random utility components of modules for each function are IID Gumbel (independently and identically distributed) and independent across functions.
3. Consumers choose no more than one module per function (e.g., they do not buy several types of heating systems for one car), but may not purchase any module for certain functions.

Based on these assumptions, consumer choices of packages of modularized functions can be expressed as a product of the choice probabilities P(jn) for each function n; hence the following utility and purchase probability functions apply for a module choice jn:

(1) $U_{jn} = \lambda_n \boldsymbol{\beta_n}' \mathbf{x_{jn}} + \varepsilon_{jn}$

(2) $P(j_n) = \dfrac{\exp(\lambda_n \boldsymbol{\beta_n}' \mathbf{x_{jn}})}{\displaystyle\sum_{j'=1}^{J} \exp(\lambda_n \boldsymbol{\beta_n}' \mathbf{x_{j'n}})}$

where, ε_{jn} is the error component in the utility of module j_n, λ_n is a function-specific scale parameter inversely related to the standard deviation of the Gumbel error distribution of the MNL model (Ben-Akiva and Lerman 1985, p.105). The choice probability function equals the product of the choice probabilities of each module contained in the product for products that consist of modules $\{j_1,...,j_N\}$:

(3) $P(\{j_1,...,j_N\}) = \displaystyle\prod_{n=1}^{N} P(j_n) = \prod_{n=1}^{N} \dfrac{\exp(\lambda_n \boldsymbol{\beta_n}' \mathbf{x_{jn}})}{\displaystyle\sum_{j'=1}^{J} \exp(\lambda_n \boldsymbol{\beta_n}' \mathbf{x_{j'n}})}$

where all components were previously defined.

Ben-Akiva and Lerman (1985, p.105) show that the formal relationship between λ and the variance of the Gumbel distribution is var$(\varepsilon) = \pi^2/6\lambda^2$. It is important to note that if the IID error assumption is satisfied in a given data set, the value of λ cannot be identified uniquely; only the combined effect of λ and β can be estimated (Swait and Louviere 1993), so λ typically is set (arbitrarily) to unity in empirical applications. However, random component variance may vary across functions; hence λ may differ between functions in at least some situations, which can be tested by allowing λ_n to be function specific.

Partly modularized choice
In order to test the expected effect on random component variance for the case of partly modularized choices, we need to allow the variance of the random component of utility for each product comparison to depend on the number and type of modules that differ between products. This is accomplished by making λ a function of the number and type of trade-offs that need to be made between products, which allows us to test whether the variance of the random component of utility is affected by the number of modules involved in comparing two products.

We formalize these ideas by using a variant of the heteroscedastic logit model (e.g., Allenby and Ginter 1995; Bhat 1995; Greene 1997; Louviere et al. 2000). Heteroscedastic logit (or HEV – heteroscedastic extreme value) relaxes the IID error assumption of the MNL model by allowing the random component variances of choice options to differ. In particular, HEV assumes that the random components of products are independently but not identically distributed. In the variant of the model that we propose, we specify λ to be a function of the number and type of modules that differ between pairs of products in choice sets. This approach is a restriction on HEV, such that the random component variances for particular product comparisons are a function of the number and type of modules that the products share (c.f. Dellaert et al. 1999).

We introduce one scale correction parameter for each module shared between products, and we assume IID holds for each binary comparison, while the variance of the random component can vary across comparisons between different products, depending on the number and functions of modules that differ between choice options. Our variant of HEV requires a total of N_g additional parameters (one for each function) compared to simple MNL. Our approach can be viewed as a way to estimate models jointly from different conditions (e.g., each product comparison is a condition), such that structural parameters are identical in each comparison but the variance of the random components of the conditions differ. Hensher and Bradley (1993) used a similar approach to combine revealed and stated preference data by including a random error scale correction between the two data conditions.

We need additional definitions to develop a model: let g be a product consisting of modules $\{j_{1g}, ...j_{Ng}\}$, with $g \in \{1, ...G\}$ the total set of products. Let $\mathbf{x_g}$ and ε_g, respectively, be a vector of characteristics of product g and associated random components; let $\lambda_{g,g'}$ be the scale of the comparison of products g and g', and γ_n be a scale function parameter to capture the effect of a difference in the nth function; let $\delta_n(p_g, p_{g'})$ be an indicator variable that takes equals zero if the module in function n differs between products g and g' and equals 1 if it does not differ; finally, let F be the standard cdf of the extreme value distribution and f the pdf.

Now, we can specify the following utility function, scale function λ and accompanying probability structure:

(4) $\qquad U g = \boldsymbol{\beta} \mathbf{x_g} + \varepsilon_g$

$\qquad P(g) = P(U g > U g'\cdot) \text{ for all } g' <> g$

(5)
$$P(g) = \int_{-\infty}^{\infty} F(\lambda_{1,g}(\boldsymbol{\beta}\mathbf{x_g} - \boldsymbol{\beta}\mathbf{x_1} + \varepsilon_g)) \times F(\lambda_{2,g}(\boldsymbol{\beta}\mathbf{x_g} - \boldsymbol{\beta}\mathbf{x_2} + \varepsilon_g))$$
$$\times ... \times F(\lambda_{G,g}(\boldsymbol{\beta}\mathbf{x_g} - \boldsymbol{\beta}\mathbf{x_G} + \varepsilon_g)) f(\varepsilon_g) d\varepsilon_g$$

(6) $\lambda_{g',g}$ = f(module difference between products)

$$= 1 + \sum_{n \in N} \gamma_n \delta_n (g', g)$$

The choice of these values of zero (for different modules) and 1 (for equal modules) for the indicator variable $\delta_n(g', g)$, fixes the scale equal to 1 for choices between products that differ on all modules (all indicator variables = 0). Scale should increase (i.e. random component variance should decrease) as the number of module differences becomes smaller; hence we can use the traditional choice condition as the control and estimate the effect of modularization on random component variance relative to it. Our model reduces to a joint MNL model with equal error variances if all parameters $\gamma_n = 0$. In the extreme, the model can also describe choices of single modules in which case the scaling in eq. 2 and eq. 5 is identical.

In some situations modularization is introduced only in part, such as when some functions can be purchased only separately (e.g., $\{j_{1g}, ..., j_{Mg}\}$), but other functions are packaged ($\{j_{Mg}, ..., j_{Ng}\}$). For example, this occurs when optional accessories are identical across brands but there are key differences between the main features of different brands. Choice probabilities for these situations are modeled as a combination of the choice rules in equations (2) and (5):

(7) $$P(g) = P(\{j_{1g}, ..., j_{Mg}, ..., j_{Ng}\}) = \prod_{n=1}^{M} P(j_{ng}) P(g_M)$$

where there are M functions ($M < N$) for which modules are sold separately. Module choices are modeled separately for each function, while the choice of functions $\{j_{Mg}, ..., j_{Ng}\}$ is modeled as a partly modularized product choice in which simultaneous trade offs are made between the packages of functions $\{j_{Mg}, ..., j_{Ng}\}$, summarized by (g_M).

The likelihood function of this model is:

(8) $$L = \prod_{c=1}^{C} \prod_{k=1}^{K_c} \prod_{g \in G_{kc}} P_{kc}(g)^{y_{gkc}}$$

where C is the total number of consumers, K_c is the total number of choice sets k_c faced by consumer c, and $g \in \{1, ..., G_{kc}\}$ the set of products in choice set k_c, and y_{gkc} is a dummy variable that equals 1 if product g_{kc} is chosen by consumer c in choice set k, and equals 0 otherwise.

14.3   Choice experiments for modularized choices

Choice experiments typically apply orthogonal, or nearly orthogonal, fractional factorial designs to create choice alternatives and choice sets simultaneously (e.g., Louviere and Woodworth 1983; Kuhfeld et al. 1994; Lazari and Anderson 1994;

Bunch et al. 1996; Huber and Zwierina 1996), which allow efficient estimation of effects of product variations on consumer choices. In this section we develop an experimental design heuristic to permit one to estimate and test the proposed HEV models of modularized and traditional consumer choices.

14.3.1   Proposed experimental design

The design strategy that we propose is simple, flexible and generally applicable but is not necessarily optimal for all design problems. We combine interrelated sub-designs for consumer choices in different random component variance conditions for modularized and traditional choices. That is, we construct sub-designs in such a way that the number of modules varying between products is fixed in any one sub-design but varies between sub-designs, which allows us to estimate differences in random component variances between sub-designs. For example, in the empirical application discussed later, respondents chose among modules and products separately, which allowed us to estimate differences in random component variances in these conditions. It is worth noting that this approach allows tests of random component variance differences as well as differences in structural preference parameters (response means) in modularized and traditional choices because the design allows one to estimate separate models for each condition as well as a combined model for all conditions.

We hypothesized that choices among products differing only in a single module should have lower levels of random component variance than complete products (i.e. products differing in all modules). Furthermore, choices of different functions should exhibit different levels of random component variance (e.g., variances for car heating system choices can differ from engine choices). The following design strategy is used to deal with these differences (Table 1):

1. Consumers first make choices in a 'control' sub-design describing choices among (traditional) products that differ on all modules. This design is similar to traditional choice designs, and can include relevant interactions between modules. It should be noted that comparisons should not include dominated options and/or options that share one or more modules. We expect choices in this sub-design to exhibit the highest levels of random component variance as all modules are present simultaneously. Random component variation in traditional product choice is expressed by the 'control' error term ε_{pg}, and set to an arbitrary fixed value to scale the model (e.g., 1.0).

2. Consumers then make choices in N additional sub-designs describing product options that differ only in one particular module. The objective of this stage is to estimate the effect of different levels of module variation on random component variance in consumer choices. The random component variance of each sub-design can vary depending on the functions that differentiate modules. In this way, if estimates differ for the 'traditional product' sub-design and each 'modularized' sub-design due to differences in levels of random component variance, one can estimate the variance contribution of

each module. Ways to estimate and test structural and random component variance differences in traditional and module-level product choices are described in section 4.

Table 1:   *Summary of experimental design strategy*

Strategy	Measurement objective	Number of subdesigns
Use one sub-design for traditional product choices that differ on all modules	Estimate structural parameters	1 (across all functions)
use N sub-designs to capture module choices between products that differ in only one function	Estimate error variance correction for module choices for each function	N (one for each function)

An attractive feature of the proposed design strategy is that each sub-design can be constructed using the same basic approach originally proposed by Louviere and Woodworth (1983) and subsequently extended by others (e.g., Bunch et al. 1996; Huber and Zwerina 1996). That is, each sub-design relies on traditional design theory because sub-designs are defined such that IID assumptions should be satisfied in each. This strategy allows one to test if choice set composition affects both random component variances and structural preferences of package choices, which may be important if structural preferences shift when alternatives are added to choice sets (e.g., Huber et al. 1982; Simonson and Tversky 1992). It is worth noting, however, that there is growing controversy as to whether the latter phenomenon can perhaps be explained by failure to take a variety of random component variance effects into account (see, e.g., Louviere et al. 1999; Louviere and Hensher 2001; Louviere 2001).

14.3.2   Model estimation

Separate module-level choice models (equation (2)) can be estimated using basic MNL estimation software. The traditional product choice HEV model (equation (6)) can be estimated with special purpose software or in the LIMDEP statistical package (Econometric Software 1998). Bhat (1995) discusses FIML estimation (full information maximum likelihood) of the HEV model by maximizing the log-likelihood of the model simultaneously with respect to the structural parameters β and the scale function λ. Allenby and Ginter (1995) develop and apply a Bayesian estimation procedure, while Swait and Louviere (1993) discuss a method that can be used if consumer choices are observed in each of the random error conditions that may occur. A detailed discussion of the HEV model and its estimation can be found in Louviere, et al (2000, pp.189-198).

In this paper we use the Swait and Louviere (1993) approach to estimate the model and make statistical comparisons. They note that if two data sources share common structural parameters, but different random component variances, the parameters will differ by a constant scale factor that is inversely proportional to the magnitude of the random component variance in each source. Hence, scale corrections (or more properly, variance-scale ratios) can be estimated for S-1 of S total conditions to capture differences in error variances between choice conditions.

One can estimate the ratios $r_{t,n}$ of the scales λ_t and λ_n of the parameter estimates for the control choice condition (i.e., traditional product choices t) relative to other choice conditions (i.e., module choices for function n). Scale ratios are expressed in terms of standard deviations of the random components of each choice condition; that is, if the scale of the random component in the control condition is set to one (i.e. λ_t=1, with all $\delta_n(p_{g'},p_g)$ taking on values of zero), the difference in scale between the control condition and the other conditions provides information about the random component variance for each module choice (λ_n). This measure is expressed as follows:

$$(9) \qquad r_{t,n} = \frac{\lambda_t}{\lambda_n} = \frac{\sigma_n}{\sigma_t}$$

Model estimates (β) are obtained from choice observations in all sub-designs, and γ_n is estimated from differences in scale between conditions (λ_n and λ_t).

The variance of the Gumbel distributed random components in the control condition equals $\pi^2/6$ if the scale λ_t is set to 1 (Ben-Akiva and Lerman, 1985); hence the variance in comparison n can be expressed as:

$$(10) \qquad \sigma_n^2 = \sigma_t^2 r_{t,n}^2 = \frac{\pi^2}{6} r_{t,n}^2$$

It should be noted that we adopt the so-called "average individual" approach and estimate models from the aggregated responses of all experimental subjects. Thus, error terms jointly capture unobserved differences in respondents and module-based random variations, and estimates of structural parameters represent average respondent utilities. This does not pose problems because respondents are randomly assigned to choice situations and presence/absence of different module options is balanced over subjects by design. Thus, if the model is correctly specified, unobserved heterogeneity represents only an efficiency issue, such that the structural estimates will be smaller than need be, but this effect applies systematically and equally to all conditions. That is, heterogeneity effects are orthogonal to estimates of module-based random component variance differences between conditions; hence they cannot affect tests of variance differences due to module-level differences (but they can affect inference quality due to less statistical efficiency). However, to the extent that unobserved heterogeneity is a problem, discrete or continuous preference parameter distribution methods can be used to capture these effects in conjunction with our proposed approach (e.g., Kamakura et al. 1996; Swait 1994; McFadden and Train 2000).

14.3.3   Hypothesis tests

The proposed HEV model can be tested by comparing the fit of a model that includes scale corrections to the fit of models with fewer or no scale corrections. The latter models are nested in the HEV model, which can be observed by setting relevant scale ratios to 1. If all scale ratios equal 1, our model reduces to simple MNL (cf. Ben-Akiva and Lerman 1985, p. 205). Therefore, we can use a likelihood ratio test to compare an HEV model with separate MNL models for each function (e.g., Theil 1971; Bhat 1995, uses this test in a similar context) by comparing the quantity $2*[L^*(model1) - L^*(model2)]$ which is asymptotically Chi-square distributed to the critical value of Chi-square for degrees of freedom equal to the difference in model parameters, where $L^*(model1)$ and $L^*(model2)$ are the adjusted log-likelihoods of models with and without variance corrections, respectively.

   Tests of structural parameter differences between conditions can be conducted in a similar way: if *model1* is the model with different structural parameters for each choice condition (i.e., parameters differ for traditional product choices and all N module choices), it can be tested against a model with identical structural preference parameters but unequal scale corrections (cf. Swait and Louviere 1993). For example, Ben-Akiva and Lerman (1985, p. 195) used this approach to test for structural parameter differences between market segments that could differ in terms of preferences.

14.4   Empirical application

We apply the proposed approach and test the hypothesized random component variance effects in a study of consumer choices of short-break city vacations consisting of transportation and destination modules.

14.4.1   Data

The study was conducted in a medium-sized European city. Surveys were administered door-to-door to 2040 randomly selected households and collected later in the same manner. The survey data were combined with data from a sample of 480 respondents contacted via travel organizations, who received the survey with their travel tickets. Respondent selection was based on making a short city break trip in the past three years. Response rates were 30.5% and 10.9%, respectively.

   Respondents were told to imagine that they were planning to take a short city break in the near future, and were asked to allocate one hundred points to three options in every choice set to indicate their preferences; the point allocations were rescaled later to the unit interval for estimation purposes. Each respondent received 12 choice sets from a larger experimental design based on a independent, uniform probability of equal expected assignment to each choice set, which produced an average of 27.9 observations per choice set (min. 16, max. 36). Responses were aggregated across respondents for purposes of analysis in this illustration.

The choice experiment was developed by identifying attributes that drive city break choices using consumer and expert interviews and previous research. Eight attributes described modules for the 'city destination' function (country, distance, restaurants and bars, shopping, special sights, hotel price, hotel quality and hotel location). Modules for 'transportation mode' functions were described by mode (bus, train) and two attributes (price and travel time). The respondent's own car was used as a base option for transportation choices in each choice set, and a relatively unattractive combination of attributes was used to define a base destination option. These considerations lead to the following experimental design:

1. One sub-design (*'Traditional package choice'*) was used to estimate model parameters for choices among different vacation packages. Each choice set in this sub-design represents a choice between a bus-destination package and a train-destination package and the base option. A 3^{10} fractional factorial design was used to generate 81 alternatives (or profiles) per transportation mode. Two of the 10 three-level attributes were transportation attributes and eight were destination attributes; all main effects were independent of interaction effects. Interactions between country and special sights as well as between distance and travel time were estimated but were not significant at the 95% confidence level. Options were randomly combined into choice sets.

2. A second sub-design (*'Transportation choice'*) described destination choices conditional on transportation mode, such that destinations were varied: a) within bus mode, and b) within train mode. This sub-design was treated as an $2*3^{10}$ fractional factorial design where the two level attribute defined transportation mode, two three-level attributes defined transportation price and travel times (specific for mode) and eight three-level attributes defined destination characteristics. 64 profiles were selected based on a 4^{12-9} orthogonal main effects design (one level of each three level attribute appeared twice as often as the other two). The profiles in this design described transportation-destination packages. Choice sets were developed by combining profiles from this design with those of an identical second design in such a way that transportation attributes did not vary within choice sets while destinations differed on all attributes.

3. A third sub-design (*'Destination choice'*) described transportation options conditional on destination; destinations were constant in each choice set and combined with one bus and one train alternative. The design problem was treated as a 3^{12} factorial design, and 64 profiles were selected based on a 4^{12-9} orthogonal main effects design (one level of each attribute appeared twice as

often as the other two). The eight destination attributes were varied systematically across choice sets, but were always present in the choice sets.

Thus, the total design comprised 209 (i.e., 81 + 2*32 + 64) paired option choice sets, to which a base option was added, which was not in the design. For the conditional choices in the design (second and third sub-design), destination and transportation attributes in the base option were changed to the same condition as the fixed component of the travel packages (e.g., if trips were conditional on a certain bus option, the base was changed to this option). Separate intercepts (alternative-specific constants, or ASC's) were estimated for each sub-design. Table 2 summarizes the design structure graphically.

Table 2: Summary of Experimental Design in Empirical Analysis[*]

Sub-design	Number of choice sets	First choice alternative		Second choice alternative		Base alternative	
1. Traditional package choice	81	D1	T2	D2	T2	D(base)	T(base)
2. Transportation choice	64	D(cond)	T1	D(cond)	T2	D(cond)	T(base)
3. Destination choice	64	D1	Tcond	D2	Tcond	D(base)	T(con)

14.4.2   Model estimation and testing

Model parameter estimation was conducted in two stages: a) separate MNL models were estimated from the choices in each experimental sub-design (3); b) the HEV model was estimated by pooling data across all three sub-designs, and

---

[*] D(cond) and T(cond) denote that destination and transportation modules respectively are conditional to the choice of the other function in each choice set while varying over choice sets. D(base) and T(base) are the base destination and transportation modules. D1, D2, T1 and T2 denote that destination and transportation modules vary within and between choice sets.

Table 3:   *Parameter estimates heteroscedastic logit model**

Attribute	Parameter estimate	t-value
Intercept traditional package choice	**0.78**	13.6
Intercept destination choice (train transportation)	**0.68**	7.7
Intercept destination choice (bus transportation)	**0.79**	8.9
Intercept transportation choice	**-0.27**	-15.9
Destination		
Country 1 (Holland vs. Belgium)	-0.01	- 0.2
Country 2 (Germany vs. Belgium)	-0.03	- 1.9
Distance (km)	-0.01	- 0.5
Restaurants and bars (few - very many)	**0.09**	3.3
Shopping facilities (few - very many)	**0.14**	5.3
Special sights (few - very many)	**0.25**	9.2
Hotel price per night (NLG 50 - 100)	**-0.10**	- 3.7
Hotel quality rating (2 star - 4 star)	**0.10**	3.5
Hotel location (city center - city border)	**-0.07**	-2.7
Transportation		
Difference between bus and train	-0.02	- 0.9
Price (bus) (NLG 30-60)	**-0.05**	- 2.1
Travel time (bus) (1.5-2.5 hrs)	-0.04	- 1.8
Price (train) (NLG 45-75)	-0.04	- 1.9
Travel time (train) (1.5-2.5 hrs)	-0.03	- 1.5
Random error difference		
γ_{des}	0.08	
(error variance destination choice = 1.39)		
γ_{trans}	0.43	
(error variance transportation choice = 0.53		

* **McFadden's RhoSq:** 0.400 γ parameters are estimated relative to a fixed scale of 1 for package choice (i.e., $\lambda_t = 1$ and error variance package choice = 1.64).

allowing for different random components in each. Because separate designs were used to create choice sets in each condition, differences in random components between the three conditions can be estimated independently.

14.4.3   Model results

Table 3 contains the HEV model parameter estimates and estimates of between-module random component variance differences. Only linear effects are reported because quadratic effects were not significant. The fit of the estimated model was satisfactory by traditional standards (McFadden's rho-squared = 0.40), and signs of all parameters were as expected.

We tested whether the random component variance corrections of the HEV model were needed by comparing HEV with simpler models with fewer variance corrections for the three conditions. These other models were: 1) an HEV model with a variance correction for transportation module choices only, 2) an HEV model with a variance correction for destination module choices only, and (iii) a joint MNL model with no variance corrections.

These results revealed that differences in model fits were fairly small, but differences in model structures were significant. Log-likelihood (LL) differences for each model are reported in Table 4. In particular, the LL for the HEV model was -757.28; LL's for simpler HEV forms were -759.29 (if only destination choices had a smaller random error) and -757.83 (if only transportation choices had a smaller random error). A Chi-square test (df = 1, for one omitted scale parameter) revealed a significant difference in random component variance between choice sets in which packages differed in both transportation and destination components ('traditional package choice') and choice sets in which packages differed only in transportation ('transportation choice'). This provides support for the hypothesis of differences in random error between traditional product choices and module-level choices. Random component variances did not differ significantly for choices that differed in both transportation and destination modules ('traditional package choice') and choices that differed only in destination modules ('destination choice'), but did differ for choices that differed only in transportation modules. The latter results provides partial support for the hypothesis that random component variance can differ between functions, and also suggests that destination module choice may be more important in travel package choices than transportation module choices. This result suggests that the appropriate model contain only a variance correction for transportation choices.

We next compared the cross-validity of the model with the variance correction for transportation module choices with a simpler MNL model without variance corrections using holdout choice set responses from a sample of 613 respondents. In this cross-validity exercise subjects were asked to choose between three options in which two options shared the same destination and a second two options shared the same transportation module. The results in Table 5 suggest that the HEV model with variance corrections only for transportation module choices outperforms an MNL model without variance corrections as well as models with variance corrections for both functions and for destination module choices only. A Chi-square test on the difference between observed and predicted choice frequencies was not significant for the HEV model with variance corrections for transportation module choices only; however, differences in observed and predicted frequencies were significant for all other models.

Table 4:   *Log-likelihood improvements for the various models*

	No of parameters	Model with transportation variance only	Model with destination variance only	Model without variance corrections
Model with variance correction for both functions	31	1.10	4.02 *	5.12 *
Model with variance correction only for transportation	30		2.92 *	4.02 *
Model with variance correction only for destination	30			1.10
Model without variance corrections	29			-

* significant at the 0.05 level

Table 5:   *Observed and predicted choices for hold out choice task*

	Observed	Model with variance correction for both functions*	Model with transportation variance correction only	Model with destination variance correction only*	Model without variance corrections*
alt D_1T_1	139	189	145	203	183
alt D_2T_2	333	323	318	231	242
alt D_1T_2	141	101	150	179	188
Total	613				

* Significantly different from observed shares in a Chi-square test at 95% confidence interval.

14.4.4   Using simulation to explore market share implications

The HEV model does not have a closed-form solution like MNL, hence, predictions have to be made using micro-simulation and the method of sample enumeration (Ben-Akiva and Lerman 1985). Thus, to illustrate how our results affect market share if modularization implemented, we ran several simulations to predict market shares in scenarios varying levels of modularization, function-specific random components and positions of competing brands. Each scenario described two brands (A, B) that offered one module for each of two functions ($A1$, $A2$ and $B1$, $B2$). Let the structural utility of a generic module or combination of modules 'x' be denoted as V_x. Then, the following variants summarize the structure of the simulations:

1. *Competitive position.* Two basic scenarios were constructed:
    a) A *'superior player'* scenario in which one brand provided a superior product for both functions ($V_{A1} > V_{B1}$ and $V_{A2} > V_{B2}$), and
    b) A *'specialists'* scenario in which each brand specializes in a different function, but with equal structural utilities ($V_{A1} > V_{B1}$, $V_{A2} < V_{B2}$, and $V_{A1A2} = V_{B1B2}$).
2. *Level of modularization* - Brands in each competitive scenario may wish to modularize different functions. The following options were explored:
    a) *Traditional product choice* – there is no modularization and product functions are sold only in fixed brand-specific combinations;
    b) *Fully modularized choice* - all functions can be purchased separately; and
    c) *Partly modularized choice* - a brand offers only one function as a separate module, so consumers can buy some, but not all, combinations of modules.
3. *Random error structure.* The empirical example reveals that random component differences can occur between functions and between module-level and product-level choices. The size of random component variances together with the specific utility structure of a brand may affect the success of a brand's modularization strategy. Hence, different random component structures were included in the simulations:
    a) Equal random components in all comparisons;
    b) Random component differences based only on one function (as observed in the empirical example); and
    c) Random component differences based on both functions (as hypothesized).

The simulation results are in Table 6, which reports market shares and the 'sales' percentage or the number of modules sold by brand A.

The simulated market shares were calculated as follows: shares for traditional and fully modularized choice scenarios were based on simple MNL models; results for partly modularized choice scenarios were based on 10,000 draws from Gumbel distributions with appropriate random component variance differences between products in each scenario. Specifically, model scales (λ) were varied for all combinations of 1 and 1.25 for choice sets in which these two scale differences were observed; a scale of 1 represents a traditional MNL model, while the value of 1.25 represents an intermediate value between the 1.08 and 1.43 observed in the module level choices.

Table 6:   *Simulations for modularization scenarios*

	Scenario	'superior player' $V_{A1}>V_{B1}$ and $V_{A2}>V_{B2}$	
	Brands A, B		
Module 1	V_{A1} V_{B1}	1.50	1.00
Module 2	V_{A2} V_{B2}	1.50	1.00

Traditional choice

Scale	var(error1-2)	P(A1A2)	P(B1B2)
1.00	1.64	0.73	0.27
1.25	1.05	0.78	0.22

Fully modularized choice

Scale1	Scale2	P(A1).P(A2)	P(B1).P(B2)	P(A1).P(B2)	P(B1).P(A2)	Sales(A)
1.00	1.00	0.38	0.14	0.24	0.24	62%
1.00	1.25	0.40	0.13	0.22	0.25	64%
1.25	1.00	0.40	0.13	0.25	0.22	64%
1.25	1.25	0.42	0.12	0.23	0.23	65%

Partly modularized choice

Scale1	Scale2	Scale all	P(A1A2)	P(B1B2)	P(A1B2)		Sales(A)
1.00	1.00	1.00	0.52	0.18	0.30	-	67%
1.00	1.25	1.00	0.57	0.15	0.28	-	71%
1.25	1.00	1.00	0.50	0.24	0.26	-	63%
1.25	1.25	1.00	0.58	0.21	0.21	-	69%

Partly modularized choice

Scale1	Scale2	Scale all	P(A1A2)	P(B1B2)		P(B1A2)	Sales(A)
1.00	1.00	1.00	0.52	0.18	-	0.30	67%
1.00	1.25	1.00	0.50	0.24	-	0.26	63%
1.25	1.00	1.00	0.57	0.15	-	0.28	71%
1.25	1.25	1.00	0.58	0.21	-	0.21	69%

'specialists'

$V_{A1}>V_{B1}$ and $V_{A2}<V_{B2}$

1.50	1.00
1.00	1.50

P(A1A2)	P(B1B2)
0.50	0.50
0.50	0.50

P(A1). P(A2)	P(B1). P(B2)	P(A1). P(B2)	P(B1). P(A2)	Sales(A)
0.24	0.24	0.38	0.14	50%
0.22	0.25	0.40	0.13	49%
0.25	0.22	0.40	0.13	51%
0.23	0.23	0.42	0.12	50%

P(A1A2)	P(B1B2)	P(A1B2)		Sales(A)
0.28	0.27	0.45	-	50%
0.33	0.23	0.44	-	55%
0.23	0.33	0.44	-	45%
0.30	0.30	0.40	-	50%

P(A1A2)	P(B1B2)		P(B1A2)	Sales(A)
0.39	0.39	-	0.22	50%
0.37	0.45	-	0.18	46%
0.44	0.37	-	0.19	54%
0.44	0.43	-	0.13	50%

The following conclusions can be drawn from the simulations:

1. Producers of products with higher structural utilities may lose market share in markets where modularization occurs (note differences between traditional choice scenarios and modularized and partly modularized choice scenarios for the 'superior player' scenarios).
2. Producers of products with higher structural utility who choose to modularize anyway are better off offering only one module as a separate option, and it should be the module that has the most random component variance. That is,

they should offer their 'weakest' module separately (see differences in market shares for cases in which scale differences exist for modules 1 or 2 only).
3. If there are no structural utility differences between products ('specialists' scenario), one should modularize only if one's strength is in a module with more random component variance.

14.5   Discussion and conclusions

We proposed and applied a way to study and model consumer choices of modularized products. Our approach offers ways to study consumer choices among products with several functions that may or may not require separate trade-offs. An empirical application in the area of consumer travel package choice supported the hypothesis that random component differences can exist between traditional and module-level product choices, such that module-level choices had smaller random component variances than traditional product choices. We also hypothesized that there should be random component variance differences between choices of modules for different functions, and obtained partial support for that hypothesis.

We used our empirical results to conduct a series of micro-simulation to illustrate the potential market share implications of non-constant random components. One interesting result of this simulation exercise was the finding that products that offer significant structural utility benefits can lose market share if they offer modularization; consequently, if they must adopt modularization, they should only offer their weakest modules as separate options.

The proposed approach can assist marketing researchers wanting to use designed choice experiments to study modularized choices by allowing them to investigate a wider and richer array of possible consumer choice processes using choice experiments. For marketing managers, our approach provides the opportunity to gain insights into complex consumer responses to marketing actions before implementing them. Experiments that support estimation of modularized choice models are especially relevant to address marketing management questions in areas such as branding, product innovation, bundling and packaging decisions and competitive analysis, because modularized choice structures are most likely to manifest themselves in areas characterized by comparisons of multiple functions between and/or within brands.

More generally, our analysis provides a modest step towards understanding and modeling the likely impacts of highly flexible and individualized marketing and production methods on consumer choices. Future research should investigate different degrees of modularization (e.g., the impact of limited availability of certain functions for certain brands or models), and conditions under which different degrees of modularization are most efficient from a social welfare point of view (i.e. the potential shifts in returns to producer and consumer due to modularization). Finally, choices of modularized products are one aspect of bundled choices, and we used a fairly restricted experiment in the sense that we deliberately limited the scope and combinations of products that we offered consumers. Future research could benefit from more work into higher dimensional choice options that would allow much larger bundles to be examined, and would provide greater scope for taking covariances among random components into account.

14.6   References

Allenby, G. M. and Ginter, J. L (1995), The effects of in-store displays and feature advertising on consideration sets, *International Journal of Research in Marketing,* 12, 67-80.

Ben-Akiva, M. and Lerman, S. R. (1985), *Discrete Choice Analysis: Theory and Application to Travel Demand,* Cambridge, Massachusetts.

Bhat, C. R. (1995), A Heteroscedastic Extreme Value Model of Intercity Mode Choice, *Transportation Research, B* 29, 471-483.

Bunch, D. S., Louviere, J. J. and Anderson, D. A. (1996), A Comparison of Experimental Design Strategies for Multinomial Logit Models: The Case of Generic Attributes, working paper University of California at Davis.

Chintagunta, P. K. and Honoré, B. E. (1996), Investigating the Effects of Marketing Variables and Unobserved Heterogeneity in a Multinomial Probit Model, *International Journal of Research in Marketing,* 13, 1-15.

Dellaert, B. G. C., Brazell, J. D. and Louviere, J. J. (1999), The Effect of Attribute Variation on Consumer Choice Consistency, *Marketing Letters,* 10, 139-147.

Econometric Software Inc. (1998), *LIMDEP version 7.0 users manual,* www.limdep.com, Econometric Software Inc.

Gilmore, J. H. and Pine II, B. J. (1997), The Four Faces of Mass Customization, *Harvard Business Review,* 75, 91-101.

Gönül, F. and Srinivasan, K. (1993), Modeling Multiple Sources of Heterogeneity in Multinomial Logit Models: Methodological and Managerial Issues, *Marketing Science,* 12, 213-227.

Greene, W. H. (1997), *Econometric Analysis* 3rd ed., Englewood Cliffs, NJ.

Hensher, D.A. and Bradley, M. (1993), Using Stated Response Choice Data to Enrich Revealed Preference Discrete Choice Data, *Marketing Letters,* 4, 139-151.

Huber, J., Payne, J. W. and Puto, C. (1982), Adding Assymetrically Dominated Alternatives: Violations of Regularity and the Similarity Hypothesis, *Journal of Consumer Research,* 9, 90-98.

Huber, J. and Zwerina, K. (1996), The Importance of Utility Balance in Efficient Choice Set Designs, *Journal of Marketing Research,* 33, 307-317.

Kamakura, W. A., Kim, B. D. and Lee, G. (1996), Modeling Preference and Structural Heterogeneity in Consumer Choice, *Marketing Science,* 15, 152-172.

Kuhfeld, W. F., Tobias, R. D. and Garrat, M. (1994), Efficient Experimental Design with Marketing Research Applications, *Journal of Marketing Research,* 31, 545-557.

Lazari, A. and Anderson, D. A. (1994), Designs of Discrete Choice Set Experiments for Estimating Both Attribute and Availability Cross Effects, *Journal of Marketing Research,* 31, 375-383.

Louviere, J. J. (2001), Response Variability as a Behavioral Phenomenon, *Journal of Consumer Research,* forthcoming.

Louviere, J. J. and Woodworth, G. (1983), Design and Analysis of Simulated Consumer Choice or Allocation Experiments: An Approach Based on Aggregate Data, *Journal of Marketing Research,* 20, 350-367.

Louviere, J. J. and Hensher, D. A. (2001) Combining Preference Data, in D.A. Hensher and J. King, eds., *The Leading Edge of Travel Behaviour Research,* Oxford, UK, *forthcoming.*

Louviere, J. J., Hensher, D. A and Swait, J. (1999) Conjoint Analysis Methods in the Broader Context of Preference Elicitation Methods, In A. Gustafsson, A. Herrmann and F. Huber, eds., *Conjoint Measurement: Methods and Applications,* Berlin, 279-318.

McFadden, D. and Train, K. (2000), Mixed Logit Models for Discrete Response, *Journal of Applied Econometrics,* forthcoming.

Severin, V. (2000), Comparing Statistical and Respondent Efficiency In Choice Experiments, Unpublished Ph.D. Dissertation, Department of Marketing, Faculty of Economics and Business, The University of Sydney.

Simonson, I. and Tversky, A. (1992), Choice in Context: Tradeoff Contrast and Extremeness Aversion, *Journal of Marketing Research,* 29, 281-295.

Street, D. J., Bunch, D. S. and Moore, B. (1999) Optimal Designs for 2^k Paired Comparison Experiments, Unpublished Working Paper, School of Mathematical Sciences, University of Technology, Sydney (Australia).

Swait, J. (1994), A Structural Equation Model of Latent Segmentation and Product Choice for Cross-Sectional Revealed Preference Choice Data, *Journal of Retailing and Consumer Services,* 1, 77-89.

Swait, J. and Louviere, J. J. (1993), The Role of the Scale Parameter in the Estimation and Use of Generalized Extreme Value Models, *Journal of Marketing Research,* 30, 305-314.

Swait, J. and Adamowicz, W. (2001), Choice Environment, Market Complexity and Consumer Behavior: A Theoretical and Empirical Approach for Incorporating Decision Complexity into Models of Consumer Choice, *Organizational Behavior and Human Decision Processes,* forthcoming.

Theil, H. (1971), *Principles of Econometrics,* New York.

15 Latent Class Models for Conjoint Analysis

Venkatram Ramaswamy and Steven H. Cohen

15.1 Introduction

Conjoint analysis was introduced to market researchers in the early 1970s as a means to understand the importance of product and service attributes and price as predictors of consumer preference (e.g., Green and Rao 1971; Green and Wind 1973). Since then it has received considerable attention in academic research (see Green and Srinivasan 1978, 1990 for exhaustive reviews; and Louviere 1994 for a review of the behavioral foundations of conjoint analysis). By systematically manipulating the product or service descriptions shown to a respondent with an experimental design, conjoint analysis allows decision-makers to understand consumer preferences in an enormous range of potential market situations (see Cattin and Wittink 1982; Wittink and Cattin 1989; and Wittink, Vriens, and Burhenne 1994 for surveys of industry usage of conjoint analysis).

15.2 Market Segmentation with Conjoint Analysis

As market segmentation is a cornerstone concept in strategic market planning, one of the major uses of conjoint analysis is for market segmentation (e.g., Green and Krieger 1991; Wedel and Kamakura 1997). The benefits that consumers derive from a product or service has been long recognized as one of the most powerful bases of market segmentation (Aaker 1998; Haley 1985; Wind 1978). It is not surprising then that with the growth in the use of conjoint analysis to understand consumer preferences, market researchers have employed it as a method to segment markets.

A more formal definition of the segmentation in conjoint analysis follows. Consider the following general formulation in metric conjoint analysis. Let:

i = 1, ... I consumers (respondents);
j = 1, ... J conjoint profiles;
m = 1, ... M conjoint design dummy variables;
s = 1, ... S segments;
Y_{ji} = the metric response rating to conjoint profile j elicited by consumer i;
Y = $((Y_{ji}))$, a (J x I) matrix containing the responses of the I consumers to the J profiles;
X_{jm} = the value of the m-th conjoint design variable in the j-th profile;

X = $((Y_{jm}))$, a $(J \times M)$ matrix containing the M conjoint design dummy vari-
       ables for the profiles;
B = a $(M \times I)$ matrix of regression coefficients
P = a $(I \times S)$ matrix representing a general segmentation scheme for assigning-
       consumers to segments;
E = a $(J \times I)$ matrix of random errors;

The general conjoint segmentation model is formulated as (Hagerty 1985;
Vriens, Wedel, and Wilms 1996):

(1) $$YP(P'P)^{-1}P' = XB + E$$

Note that if S=I, we obtain an individual-level model, and if S=1, we obtain an
aggregate-level model. The conjoint analysis literature has documented the potential instability of part-worth estimates derived at the individual level, especially in
highly fractionated designs (cf. Wedel and Kistemaker 1989). This has led to
segmentation procedures that weight „similar" consumers together (through **P**) to
reduce the variance of the estimates. However, to the extent that the within-
segment consumers are not identical in their true part-worths, bias is introduced
into the parameter estimates. Hence, there is a tradeoff between variance reduction
and increased bias in all conjoint segmentation methods.

Traditionally, segmentation in conjoint analysis has been accomplished in one
of two ways. In an *a priori* segmentation analysis, individual-level preference
judgments are combined at the segment level and the parameters are estimated.
However, problems typically arise in practice since demographic or psychographic
background information rarely adequately describe heterogeneous utility functions
(Moore 1980). In *post hoc* segmentation - sometimes called the *tandem approach*
(Green and Krieger 1991) - the analysis proceeds in two stages. In the first stage, a
conjoint model is estimated for each respondent and utilities for each level of each
feature are generated for each person. The individual-level utilities are then input
into a cluster analysis program to derive benefit segments. Thus, the estimation of
the conjoint analysis occurs first at the individual-level, and in the subsequent
step, the resulting individual-level part-worths are clustered to form market segments. The tandem approach, however, has problems: different clustering methods
will produce different results, and the initial utility estimation method (usually
regression) and the subsequent cluster analysis seek to optimize very different and
quite unrelated objective functions or aspects of the data (DeSarbo, Wedel, Vriens
and Ramaswamy 1992).

In response to the limitations of the tandem segmentation methods, several *integrated* conjoint segmentation methods have been proposed wherein the conjoint
estimation stage and the segmentation stage are simultaneously estimated, so that
a single criterion of interest is optimized under a set of restrictions (e.g., DeSarbo
et al. 1992; DeSarbo, Oliver and Rangaswamy 1989; Hagerty 1985; Kamakura
1988; Ogawa 1987; Wedel and Kistemaker 1989; Wedel and Steenkamp 1989). In
an excellent review and Monte Carlo comparison of traditional two-stage and

integrated metric conjoint segmentation methods, Vriens, Wedel and Wilms (1996) examine the relative performance of several such conjoint segmentation methods. These methods differ with respect to the segmentation scheme imposed, the algorithms and estimation procedures used to obtain **P** and **B**, and the criterion that is optimized. The authors conclude that most of the integrated segmentation methods outperform the tandem clustering procedures. Further, of the integrated segmentation methods, they found that *latent class metric conjoint analysis* (De-Sarbo et al. 1992) entailing a fuzzy segmentation scheme (**P**) and likelihood optimization using the EM algorithm (Dempster, Laird, and Rubin 1977) performed best, in terms of parameter recovery, segment membership recovery, and predictive accuracy.

15.3   Latent Segmentation Models

Latent class metric conjoint analysis is one of a broader class of models called latent segmentation models (see Cohen and Ramaswamy 1998, for illustrative applications). Strictly speaking, latent segmentation models (LSMs) are part of a more general class of statistical models called finite mixture models or unmixing models (e.g., Dillon and Kumar 1994; Wedel and DeSarbo 1994). These models assume that the observed data are really comprised of several homogeneous groups or segments which have been mixed together in unknown proportions. Because we don't know beforehand who belongs to which segment nor how many segments there really are - the segments are *latent* or unobserved, after all - we must *unmix* the data to discover their true number and definition. A brief comparison between LSMs and tandem approaches is given in Table 1.

LSMs have a great deal in common with traditional cluster analysis, namely the extraction of several relatively homogeneous groups of respondents from a heterogeneous set of data. What sets LSMs apart from cluster analysis is their ability to accommodate both categorical and continuous data, as well as descriptive or predictive models, all in a common framework. Unlike cluster analysis, which is relatively more data-driven, LSMs are model-based and true to the measurement level of the data. Perhaps the biggest difference between cluster analysis and LSMs is the types of problems they can be applied to. Cluster analysis is solely a descriptive methodology: there is no independent-dependent, or predictor-outcome relationship assumed in the analysis. While LSMs can also be used for descriptive segmentation, their big advantage over cluster analysis lies in *simultaneous segmentation and prediction*. An LSM prediction equation can be estimated - as in metric conjoint regression analysis - *at the same time* that the segments are uncovered. In the case of LSM regression, the segments consist of people whose regression coefficients or conjoint part-worths are relatively similar. So rather than having one aggregate regression equation describing the entire sample, a few equations capture several different predictor-outcome relationships - one equation for each latent segment.

Table 1:   *Comparison of Latent Segmentation Models with Traditional Tandem*
              Approaches

	Latent Segmentation Models (e.g., latent class metric conjoint analysis)	Tandem Approaches (e.g., metric conjoint – cluster analysis)
Creates segments	Yes	Yes
Statistical objectives	One: Fit model to original data using maximum likelihood	Two: Explain responses in original-data and then group entities in transformed space
Data used	Appropriate level of measure-ment based on original data	Proximity between entities defined in space other than original variables
Delineation of Segments	Penalty for overfitting tied to likelihood function; information heuristics guide number of segments to retain	Often ad hoc with no penalty for overfitting; goodness-of-fit typically assessed in transformed space, rather than based on original data

15.4   Latent Class Metric Conjoint Analysis

We now discuss the formulation of a LSM in the context of metric conjoint analysis. Returning to the model in (1), assume that the vector $\mathbf{Y}_i$ of dimension J has a probability density function that can be modeled as a finite mixture of the following conditional distributions (DeSarbo et al. 1992):

$$(2) \qquad f(Y_i; \alpha, X, \beta, \Sigma) = \sum_{s=1}^{S} \alpha_s g_{is}(Y_i | X, \beta_s, \Sigma_s),$$

where $\alpha = (\alpha_1, \alpha_2, ..., \alpha_{S-1})$ are S-1 independent mixing proportions of the finite mixture such that $0 \leq \alpha_s \leq 1$ with $\alpha_S = 1 - \sum_{s=1}^{S-1} \alpha_s$, β_s = the vector of conjoint part-worths for segment s, $\beta = ((\beta_{ms}))$, and $\Sigma = (\Sigma_1, \Sigma_2, ..., \Sigma_S)$ are the covariance matrices of the error terms estimated for each segment. Note that the specification of the error matrix E can accommodate correlations in errors across the J profiles.

Each of the conditional distributions, g_{is}, is specified as a conditional multi-variate normal distribution:

$$(3) \qquad g_{is}(Y_i | X, \beta_s, \Sigma_s) = (2\pi)^{-J/2} |\Sigma_s|^{-1/2} \exp[-1/2(Y_i - X\beta_s)\Sigma_s^{-1}(Y_i - X\beta_s)']$$

Given a sample of I independent consumers, the likelihood function can be expressed as:

(4)
$$L=\prod_{i=1}^{I}\left(\sum_{s=1}^{S}\alpha_s(2\pi)^{-J/2}|\Sigma_s|^{-1/2}\exp\{-1/2(Y_i-X_j\beta_s)\Sigma_s^{-1}(Y_i-X_j\beta_s)'\}\right)$$

or

(5)
$$\ln L = \sum_{i=1}^{I}\ln\left(\sum_{s=1}^{S}\alpha_s g_{is}(Y_i|X,\beta_s,\Sigma_s)\right)$$

Maximum likelihood estimation can be carried out via standard numerical optimization procedures or alternatively using the EM algorithm (Dempster, Laird, and Rubin 1977). EM is more popular because of its computational elegance, particularly for several finite mixture models (Titterington 1990). We outline the essential aspects of the EM algorithm below and refer the interested reader to Wedel and Kamakura (1997) who provide an excellent discussion of the applicability of the EM algorithm to a wide variety of mixture models.

15.4.1 Estimation of Latent Class Models

Put simply, the EM algorithm iteratively allocates respondents to segments and then estimates the segment-specific parameters of the model being estimated. Iterations continue so as to maximize the overall „fit" of both the segment sizes and the within-segment coefficients to the data at hand. The essential idea behind the EM algorithm in the context of latent class models is to augment the observed data (Y) with unobserved data (Z) representing the membership of consumers in the segments (equivalent to P in expression (1)), which simplifies the maximization of the log likelihood function in expression (5).

Let $Z = ((z_{is}))$ where $z_{is} = 1$ if consumer i belongs to latent segment s, and $z_{is} = 0$ otherwise. Assuming that z_{is} is independently multinomially distributed with probabilities α_s (s = 1, ..., S), the log likelihood function for the complete data Y and Z is given by:

(6)
$$\ln L_C(\theta) = \sum_{i=1}^{I}\sum_{s=1}^{S}\left[z_{is}\ln g_{is}(Y_i|X,\beta_s,\Sigma_s) + z_{is}\ln \alpha_s\right],$$

where θ denotes the parameter set (α_s, β_s, Σ_s). In the E-step, the expectation of ln $L_C(\theta)$ is computed with respect to the unobserved data Z, given the observed data and provisional estimates of θ. This expectation is obtained by replacing z_{is} by its current expected value $E(z_{is}|y, \theta)$ which is identical to the posterior probability P_{is}

that consumer i belongs to segment s as follows:

$$(7) \qquad P_{is} = \frac{\hat{\alpha}_s g_{is}(Y_i|X,\hat{\beta}_s,\hat{\Sigma}_s)}{\sum_{s=1}^{S} \hat{\alpha}_s g_{is}(Y_i|X,\hat{\beta}_s,\hat{\Sigma}_s)}.$$

In the M-step, the expectation of ln $L_C(\theta)$ is maximized with respect to the segment sizes α_s (under the constraints of these parameters), yielding:

$$(8) \qquad \hat{\alpha}_s = \sum_{i=1}^{I} \hat{P}_{is} / I.$$

Similarly, maximization of the expectation of ln $L_C(\theta)$ with respect to $\phi = (\beta_s, \Sigma_s)$ leads to independently solving each of the S expressions:

$$(9) \qquad \sum_{i=1}^{I} \hat{P}_{is} \frac{\partial \ln g_{is}(Y_i|X,\hat{\beta}_s,\hat{\Sigma}_s)}{\partial \phi_s} = 0.$$

In the case of the latent class metric conjoint model, the above equations have a closed form facilitating easy computation.

Once final estimates of $(\alpha_s, \beta_s, \Sigma_s)$ have been obtained, expression (7) is used to compute each consumer's posterior probability of consumer belonging to each of the S segments. Partitions may be formed by assigning each consumer to the market segment whose posterior probability P_{is} is largest. To examine centroid separation between the segments, one can compute the following entropy-based measure as suggested by Ramaswamy et al. (1993):

$$(10) \qquad E_S = 1 + \left(\sum_{i=1}^{I}\sum_{s=1}^{S} P_{is} \ln P_{is}\right) / I \ln S$$

E_S is a relative measure bounded between 0 and 1. A value close to 0 indicates that the centroids of these conditional parametric distributions are not sufficiently separated for the number of segments specified.

To determine the number of segments to retain, an information criterion, C, is utilized which imposes a penalty on the likelihood for estimating an increased number of parameters:

$$(11) \qquad C = -2\ln L + Qk,$$

where Q is the number of parameters estimated and k is a penalty constant. For instance the well known Akaike (1974) information criterion (AIC) arises when k=2, the modified AIC (MAIC) when k=3, the Bayesian information criterion (BIC) when k = ln I, and the consistent Akaike information criterion when k=ln(I+1). The larger the penalty, the fewer the number of segments that the criterion will recommend keeping. Wedel and Kamakura (1997) provide a discussion of these various criteria for determining the number of segments to retain in mixture models (see also Bockenholt et al. 1994). In practice, the final choice of the number of segments using these information criteria must be balanced against managerial interpretability and actionability of the results.

15.4.2   An Illustrative Application

A major automobile manufacturer was interested in investigating consumer preferences to determine which specific features to include in an automotive remote entry system (DeSarbo, Wedel, Vriens, and Ramaswamy 1992). A remote entry system allows the consumer to lock or unlock his vehicle remotely by activating a small transmitter, which is typically carried on a key chain. Based upon discussions with consumers, product engineers, and marketing managers, the following seven features were included in a metric conjoint study:

1. *Type of Transmitter*: This feature describes either a multi-button or single-button transmitter. The multi-button transmitter hangs from the key chain; each button activates a different feature of the system. The single-button is placed on the vehicle ignition key and can activate all the features of the system.
2. *Range of Operation*: The range of operation defines the maximum distance from the vehicle that the transmitter can be used to make the system active. The options tested are either 10 or 30 feet.
3. *Feedback*: A remote entry system may or may not provide feedback to the operator. A system with feedback sounds the horn every time a button on the transmitter is depressed.
4. *Panic Alarm*: A remote entry system may or may not include a panic alarm feature. When activated, this feature sounds the horn and flashes the lights to indicate danger.
5. *Keypad*: A remote entry system may or may not include a keypad on the vehicle below the door handle. This keypad offers an alternate means of locking or unlocking the vehicle by punching into the keypad a unique five-digit code.
6. *Memory*: A remote entry system may or may not include memory features that automatically set the driver's seat and the power mirrors when the doors are unlocked with the transmitter. Multiple transmitters for a given vehicle contain unique predefined settings for that driver.
7. *Trunk Release*: A remote entry system may or may not include a trunk release feature that unlocks the trunk .

Table 2 presents the levels of the seven attributes with their respective codings and the 2^7 fractional factorial design (Addelman 1962) used in the experiment for main effects estimation. During a pretest, conducted with 48 consumers, pictures were provided to describe each feature. In addition, to make the task more realistic, each feature level was assigned a price. Each full product profile shown to consumers displayed the total price that would be charged, so as to avoid the problem of the consumers uniformly preferring the profile containing the most features. These total prices and attribute level costs are also displayed in Table 2. Note that since the total price is a linear combination of each of the attributes, this variable was not explicitly included in the model estimation. The consumer was asked to rate each profile using a 10-point (metric) preference rating scale.

Table 3a presents the results from latent class metric conjoint analysis describing four segments with $\Sigma = ((\sigma_{js}^2))$ (log likelihood = -1586.7, AIC = 3371.32, E_S = 0.98), along with the aggregate conjoint results (S=1). The first latent class or segment representing 12% finds feedback, panic alarm, keypad, and memory all important, yet given that all these coefficients are negative, prefers a low price remote entry device with few features. This segment essentially prefers a basic, „no frills" product for $90. The second segment, consisting of 31% of the sample, values the memory and trunk release features as most important, and also prefers the „no memory" feature (perhaps due to its high price) and a trunk release option. The coefficients for feedback, panic alarm, and keypad are positive but not significant. The third segment, constituting 19% of the sample, shows a strong preference for the panic alarm, the keypad, and the trunk release options.

The fourth segment, representing a sizable 38% of the sample, finds the transmitter range, panic alarm, memory, and trunk release features most important, where higher utility is derived for the single button transmitter, 30 foot range, panic alarm, memory, and trunk release features at a relatively higher price of $230. This segment seemingly constitutes „feature creatures,." consumers who desire many features and also exhibit a willingness to pay for them. In summary, the latent class metric conjoint analysis results point to a market for three types of products: a low-end (no frills) product at $90, a mid-end product in the $120-$170 range (with the trunk release option included), and a high-end product for $230.

Contrast these findings with the aggregate results which suggest that the optimal design would include the multi-button transmitter, a 30-foot range, a panic alarm, no memory features, and a trunk release for $130. These results account for just 10% of the variance in the preference ratings. In contrast, the four group latent class metric conjoint model accounts for about 41% of the variance. Moreover, although not shown, the estimated variance matrix exhibits considerable heteroskedasticity in response, especially in segment 1 for profiles 5, 9, and 13, which offer a step up from the basic product of $90 to $110. The inequality in variance estimates both between and within latent classes attests to potential misspecification difficulties in applying other metric conjoint analysis techniques that assume homoskedasticity. Despite the differences in preferences, segment membership does not significantly relate to gender, previous ownership, and average yearly miles driven.

Table 2:   Remote Entry Design: Conjoint Attributes and Orthogonal Array

Attribute	Attribute levels
Transmitter	0 = Multi-Button ($90)
	1 = Single-Button ($90)
Range	0 = 10 Feet
	1 = 30 Feet (+$10)
Feedback	0 = No
	1 = Yes (+$10)
Panic Alarm	0 = No
	1 = Yes (+$20)
Keypad	0 = No
	1 = Yes (+$50)
Memory Features	0 = No
	1 = Yes (+$100)
Trunk Release	0 = No
	1 = Yes (+$10)

2^7 Orthogonal Array

	X-mit	Range	Feed-back	Panic	Key-pad	Mem-ory	Trunk	Price*
Card 1	0	0	0	0	0	0	0	90
Card 2	0	0	0	0	1	1	0	240
Card 3	0	0	0	1	0	1	1	220
Card 4	0	0	0	1	1	0	1	170
Card 5	0	1	1	0	0	0	0	110
Card 6	0	1	1	0	1	1	0	260
Card 7	0	1	1	1	0	1	1	240
Card 8	0	1	1	1	1	0	1	190
Card 9	1	0	1	0	0	0	1	110
Card10	1	0	1	0	1	1	1	260
Card11	1	0	1	1	0	1	0	220
Card12	1	0	1	1	1	0	0	170
Card13	1	1	0	0	0	0	1	110
Card14	1	1	0	0	1	1	1	260
Card15	1	1	0	1	0	1	0	220
Card16	1	1	0	1	1	0	0	170

* Total price was not included in the analyses; consumers only viewed total price and not individual, attribute level costs/prices (shown below).

Table 3b presents the within-cluster means from the four-group solution using a tandem approach,, in this case individual-level metric conjoint followed by cluster analysis of the individual-level coefficients using Ward's method (Punj and Stewart 1983). Table 3c crosstabulates the classifications from the cluster analysis with the latent class analysis after permuting label assignments to optimal congruence.

Only about 60% of consumers were assigned to the same group using both procedures. The coefficients from the cluster analysis indicate that Clusters 1 and 2 appear somewhat similar to latent segments 1 and 2 although their sizes are different. Clusters 3 and 4 do not exhibit much distinctiveness when compared to latent segments 3 and 4. When the means of the conjoint part-worths are substituted for β, the log likelihood was -2417.5 with α and P redefined accordingly, and assuming homoscedasticity in the error terms. This is much lower than the -1586.7 obtained from the latent class method (the variance accounted for was 33% which is also lower).

In addition to the results just described, DeSarbo et al. (1992) compared six other clustering methods to the latent class metric conjoint analysis. The clustering methods (and their associated congruence rates) were KMEANS (58.3%), Single Linkage (41.7%), Median Method (45.8%), Complete Linkage (54.2%), Centroid Method (43.8%), and Average Linkage (66.7%). In each case, the tandem approach performed less well than the latent class method, a finding later corroborated by Vriens, Wedel, and Wilms (1996) in their Monte Carlo study. These authors found that, for increasing numbers of parameters (e.g. regression coefficients and segment memberships), higher levels of error variance, and less well-separated segments, the overall performance of the tandem approach deteriorates much faster than does an integrated segmentation method like the latent class model.

Table 3a: Results of Latent Class Metric Conjoint Analysis

	Aggregate	Latent Class k=1	k=2	k=3	k=4
α	1.00	**0.12**	**0.31**	**0.19**	**0.38**
Transmitter	-0.51**	-0.22	0.35	-0.28	**-1.35****
Range	0.41*	-0.32	-0.08	0.58	**0.91****
Feedback	-0.10	**-1.54****	0.07	0.20	-0.04
Panic Alarm	0.62**	**-2.24****	0.14	**1.09****	**1.46****
Keypad	0.04	**-3.28****	0.33	**0.79****	0.38
Memory	-0.90**	**-2.99****	**-2.40****	**-1.24****	**1.00****
Trunk Release	1.04**	-0.04	**0.92****	**1.26****	**1.26****
Intercept	4.14	**9.28**	**5.73**	**1.76**	**2.83**

*p<0.05; ** p<0.01

Table 3b: Results of Tandem Method (Conjoint-Ward's Cluster Analysis)

	Aggregate	Cluster			
		k=1	k=2	k=3	k=4
α	1.00	0.25	0.19	0.33	0.23
Transmitter	-0.51**	-0.15	0.20	-0.22	-1.94
Range	0.41*	-0.63	0.45	0.66	1.03
Feedback	-0.10	-0.90	0.20	0.13	0.10
Panic Alarm	0.62**	-0.97	0.38	1.47	1.17
Keypad	0.04	-1.58	0.48	1.09	-0.28
Memory	-0.90**	-2.40	-2.80	0.22	0.72
Trunk Release	1.04**	0.00	1.28	1.75	0.78
Intercept	4.14	7.75	4.84	1.39	3.90

Table 3c: Cross Classification Frequencies: Latent Class (Rows) by Ward
(Columns)

	s=1	s=2	s=3	s=4	Total	
S=1	0	6	0	0	6	
S=2	0	6	2	7	15	*Congru-*
						encece:
S=3	1	0	6	2	9	*60.4%*
S=4	10	0	8	0	18	
Total	11	12	16	9	48	

In addition, unstable estimates at the individual-level compound misclassification during clustering (Kamakura 1988) and can negatively affect the goodness-of-fit and the power of significance tests. Fractionated designs, which are often used in individual-level conjoint models, generally leave few degrees of freedom for estimation of error at the individual-level (Cattin and Wittink 1982). Moreover, tandem methods are unable to estimate conjoint models that are overparameterized at the individual-level, and cannot deal with blocking designs. Fundamentally, even if there is enough data to obtain reliable individual-level estimates, the tandem approach uses two unrelated steps in which the procedures optimize different criteria. Thus, an emerging conclusion is that latent class metric conjoint analysis is superior to traditional tandem methods for market segmentation. Individual-level analysis may still be preferred if prediction is the primary purpose of the analysis (e.g., in market simulations with a first choice rule), since a limitation of latent class metric conjoint analysis is the assumption of homogeneous segments (with respect to the coefficients). In the concluding section of this chapter, we provide a brief discussion of a newer approach that delivers the benefits of latent class metric conjoint analysis while still retaining heterogeneity at the individual level.

15.5   Choice-based Conjoint Analysis

Choice-based conjoint analysis (CBCA) uses the basic ideas and designs of metric conjoint analysis, but instead asks the respondent to *choose one option* from several competing product or service alternatives (Cohen 1997). CBCA overcomes several issues encountered in traditional metric conjoint analysis. First, as researchers, we believe that research tasks which closely mimic what people do in the real world will produce more valid and reliable results than tasks which do not. So while metric conjoint analysis asks people to provide rankings or ratings, we know that people do something very different when selecting or purchasing products or services: they make *choices*.

Second, traditional metric conjoint analysis generates values for each product or service attribute which explain people's *preferences*. To obtain estimates of market share - which are just the sum of individual choices - the preference results from Conjoint Analysis must be used in a *share simulator*. Simulators are built on rules that translate the preference values into a predicted choice. Unfortunately there are many different share simulator rules and they do not yield the same answer. The analyst must select which set of rules he or she likes best for the situation at hand. Thus the traditional two-step traditional metric conjoint analysis procedure of predicting shares - which entails estimating preferences and then simulating shares - can yield different results, depending upon which simulator rule is used.

Third, performing the analysis for each individual assumes that we have measured the drivers of each consumer's preferences with certainty. Our earlier discussion of the potential instability of individual level models points out the dangers in this assumption. Fourth, interaction effects are typically ignored in most traditional metric conjoint analysis studies because including interactions will increase the number of profiles that each consumer must evaluate. Without interaction effects, we must make assumptions that may not make marketing sense. For example, without a term to estimate a brand-price interaction, consumers are assumed to be equally price-sensitive to every brand in the category.

Sixth, what if specific product features, or levels of specific product features, are unique to a brand or unique to products at a price point? For example, what if an 8X zoom lens can only appear on a camera which costs over $250, but you want consumers to evaluate cameras costing from $75 to $400? Traditional conjoint analysis cannot accommodate these restrictions without eliminating unacceptable profiles.

Finally, how does low purchase intent or a low ranking translate into non-purchase? Metric conjoint analysis simulations assume a share model where everyone will buy something. But what if some people do not wish to purchase, especially in those situations where the product is not fully featured or costs too much? Incorporating demand into a traditional metric conjoint model requires *ad hoc* assumptions about how a low purchase intent rating or ranking will translate into inaction (Bretton-Clark 1992; Oliphant et al. 1992).

Which Checking Account Would You Choose?

Services included with all four accounts	• ATM Card with free unlimited use of your bank's ATM machines • Unlimited free check writing with no per-check charges • Unlimited free access to automated account information over the telephone			
	ACCOUNT #1	**ACCOUNT #2**	**Account #3**	**ACCOUNT #4**
Monthly fee and minimum balance required	No minimum balance required Pay a monthly fee of $10 if your account balance drops below $0	Maintain a $500 minimum checking balance to avoid a $10 monthly fee	Maintain a $1,500 minimum checking balance to avoid a $10 monthly fee	Maintain a combined balance at least $15,000 in your checking and savings accounts to avoid a $25 monthly fee
Competitive interest paid on checking accounts	No	No	Yes	Yes
Use of other banks' ATM machines	$1.50 for each ATM visit	$1.00 for each ATM visit	$1.00 for each ATM visit	Free
Priority access telephone number	No	No	No	Yes
Choose the one account you prefer	9	9	9	9
	9 None of these			

Figure 1:   Simple Discrete Choice Task

Much of the credit for popularizing choice-based conjoint analysis must be given to Jordan Louviere and his colleagues (1983, 1988, 1994) who developed the idea of *choice experiments* by combining the seminal work on discrete choice models (e.g., logit and probit models) for behavioral data, originally developed in the econometric and transportation choice literature (Ben-Akiva and Lerman 1985; Ben-Akiva et al. 1997; McFadden 1986), with traditional conjoint analysis.

Figure 1 shows an example of a CBCA task that might be used to investigate the design of retail checking accounts. In this example, the consumer has five choices available. Account #1 on the far left is a no minimum, no fee account. Interest is not paid on the account and a fee is always charged for the use of another bank's automated teller machine (ATM). Account #4 on the far right is what bankers call a 'relationship' account. By keeping at least $15,000 in the account, interest is paid and the use of other banks' ATMs is free. A priority access telephone number is available to holders of this account.

In between these two are checking accounts that require intermediate amounts on deposit. Interest is included with one account and not with the other. The use of another bank's ATM machines is free for the first four transactions and is fee-based thereafter. No priority access number is available, however.

The fifth and final choice to the consumer illustrates a unique feature of CBCA: the consumer can choose „none of these," indicating that they would rather not have one of the described accounts. In a study using CBCA - just as in a traditional metric conjoint study - each respondent will perform several tasks. In this case, the consumer will evaluate several choice situations with the five alternatives, with the fees, account minimums and other benefits varying across them.

15.5.1   Advantages of Choice-based Conjoint Analysis

CBCA has several advantages over traditional conjoint models. First of all, in traditional conjoint analysis, each product or service profile is either rated one at a time, ranked in order of preference, or, at best, shown two at a time in a paired comparison. With CBCA, choice is made from a set of competing product or service alternatives. Second, a consumer performing a traditional conjoint analysis task will evaluate a few (12-16) product profiles. In a CBCA task, even though the consumer will make few (12-16) choices, since each choice situation contains several different alternatives, the total number of profiles seen is much greater. For example, if the consumer were to evaluate ten choice situations like the one shown in Figure 1, they would see and provide choices, or non-choices, for forty product descriptions, since each situation contains four different checking accounts.

Another limitation of traditional conjoint addressed by CBCA is that, in traditional conjoint analysis, every product or service being evaluated must share features and the levels of those features. By using CBCA, features can be unique to one alternative or the levels of a feature can be unique to each alternative.

A distinctive feature of CBCA is that the consumer can reject all alternatives and choose „none of the above" should none be appealing. In contrast, a traditional conjoint analysis requires that every product must be ranked or rated.

In traditional conjoint analysis, all features are assumed to have the same effect for each brand under study. With CBCA, price and feature sensitivity can be different for each alternative. In traditional conjoint analysis, only one product or service from each company is evaluated at a time. In CBCA, we can study how product features, prices, and availability affect the composition and market share of a vendor's entire product line in a single task.

Traditional conjoint analysis cannot explicitly test for different types of decision structures. Using CBCA, the nested logit model can be utilized to test for complex decisions. When traditional conjoint analysis is used to generate a utility equation for each person, characteristics of the individual are not typically used as predictors in the statistical model. Finally, only when traditional conjoint is estimated at an aggregate or segment level can individual characteristics be explicitly included in the analysis. With CBCA, we can explicitly test for differences in the impact of features or prices across a priori groups.

The major disadvantage of CBCA is that individual-level coefficients are rarely estimated (Elrod, Louviere, and Davey 1992; Struhl 1994). Since CBCA uses aggregate-level estimation, *post hoc* segmentation is impossible unless an LSM is applied to the data.

15.6 Latent Class CBCA

The absence of individual-level coefficients in CBCA of the type obtained from traditional individual-level conjoint analysis may actually be a blessing in disguise, considering the shortcomings of the tandem approach discussed above. While one can still perform a priori segmentation on choice data using ancillary variables such as demographics or based on the observed choice frequencies, there is no guarantee that the derived segments will exhibit different feature preferences or price sensitivity.

Recognizing the need to conduct post hoc market segmentation with CBCA, DeSarbo, Ramaswamy and Cohen (1995) combined LSMs with CBCA to introduce Latent Class CBCA, which permits the estimation of choice-based benefit segments with CBCA. A version of the CBCA approach has also been implemented in a commercial software package from Sawtooth Software (Johnson 1994).

Let:

i = 1, ... I consumers (respondents);

j = 1, ... J conjoint profiles of alternatives (e.g., brands);

m = 1, ... M conjoint attributes and dummy variables;

n = 1, ...N choice sets;

s = 1, ... S segments;

C_n = the specific brands in the n-th choice set;

X_{jm} = the value of the m-th conjoint design variable in the j-th profile;

Y_{ijn} = 1 if respondent i chooses brand j in the n-th choice set among C_n; 0 otherwise;

β_{ms} = the impact coefficient (or part-worth) for the m-th attribute for segments;

α_s = the size of segment s such that $0 \le \alpha_s \le 1$ with $\alpha_S = 1 - \sum_{s=1}^{S-1} \alpha_s$,

Louviere and Woodworth (1983) and Kuhfeld, Tobias, and Garratt (1994) discuss different approaches to the design and generation of the choice sets. Based on random utility theory (Ben-Akiva and Lerman 1985; McFadden 1986), a consumer's probability of choosing alternative j in the n-th choice set among Cn, conditional upon belonging to segment s, can be expressed as:

$$(12) \qquad P_s(j\varepsilon C_n) = \frac{\exp\left(\beta_{ojs} + \sum_{m=1}^{M} X_{jm}\beta_{ms}\right)}{\sum_{a\varepsilon C_n} \exp\left(\beta_{oas} + \sum_{m=1}^{M} X_{am}\beta_{ms}\right)}$$

where β_{ojs} is the intrinsic utility of alternative j to segment s. As in latent class metric conjoint analysis, segment composition is latent or unknown. The unconditional choice probability that a respondent chooses alternative j can be computed as:

$$(13) \qquad P(j\varepsilon C_n) = \sum_{s=1}^{S} \alpha_s P_s(j\varepsilon C_n)$$

where α_s, the size of segment s, may be construed as the initial probability of finding a respondent in segment s. The modeling framework thus entails a finite mixture of conditional logit models (Kamakura and Russell 1989; Ramaswamy and DeSarbo 1990) to estimate the latent segments with the observed choice data.

Given a sample of I independent consumers, the likelihood function can be expressed as:

$$(14) \qquad L = \prod_{i=1}^{I} \sum_{s=1}^{S} \alpha_s \prod_{n=1}^{N} \prod_{j\varepsilon C_n} \left(\frac{\exp\left(\beta_{ojs} + \sum_{m=1}^{M} X_{jm}\beta_{ms}\right)}{\sum_{a\varepsilon C_n} \exp\left(\beta_{oas} + \sum_{m=1}^{M} X_{am}\beta_{ms}\right)}\right)^{Y_{ijn}}$$

The goal of the estimation is to maximize the likelihood with respect to the segment-specific parameters, subject to the constraints on the segment sizes. As before, maximum likelihood estimation can be carried out using the EM algorithm, except that a numerical optimization routine is required for the M-step (see Wedel and Kamakura 1997 for a general discussion of estimation of logit mixture models).

Upon obtaining the parameter estimates, we can again compute the posterior probability of membership for each respondent i, $\hat{R}_{is}$:

(15)
$$\hat{R}_{is} = \frac{\hat{\alpha}_s \prod\limits_{n=1}^{N} \prod\limits_{j \varepsilon C_n} \left[\hat{P}_s(j)\right]^{Y_{ijn}}}{\sum\limits_{s=1}^{S} \hat{\alpha}_s \prod\limits_{n=1}^{N} \prod\limits_{j \varepsilon C_n} \left[\hat{P}_s(j)\right]^{Y_{ijn}}}.$$

Thus, the method described in DeSarbo, Ramaswamy and Cohen (1995) will simultaneously estimate the within-segment conjoint part-worths and the market segment sizes. As in latent class metric conjoint, consumers may be partitioned into discrete segments by assigning each respondent i to the group for which the value of $\hat{R}_{is}$ is largest. As always, information heuristics and managerial interpretation must guide the determination of the appropriate number of segments to retain.

15.6.1   An Illustrative Application

We briefly discuss a commercial application of a CBCA study conducted for a major packaged goods company as part of a new concept test (DeSarbo, Ramaswamy and Cohen 1995). This study concerned itself with the pricing of a new food product that was introduced into an existing market. We disguise the product category as diet and regular potato chips and assume that there are only three brands in the market: Wise, Lay's, and Ruffles.

Previous market research by the client had found that diet potato chips mostly appealed to the health conscious consumer and did not appeal to regular potato chip buyers because of its perceived poor taste. The study tested a new diet potato chip from Wise that promised „all the flavor of regular potato chips with one-quarter of the calories." This positioning was designed to attract both regular and diet chip buyers. 600 females who regularly purchased potato chips were interviewed in shopping malls around the country. Half the sample was recruited to reflect families with a concern about diet and health. All were presented with the new product concept and then asked various purchase intent and appeal questions.

Following this, each shopper engaged in a brand-and-price tradeoff exercise designed as a CBCA exercise. Everyone evaluated the same sixteen competitive buying situations, where the prices of the eight products were systematically rotated. While both linear and quadratic price effects were estimated, only the linear effects were statistically significant and retained in the final model.

As noted, CBCA typically uses a multinomial logit model, which is an „aggregate" data analysis technique. Estimating an individual-level multinomial logit model is not possible with as few as 16 profile, except in exceptional circumstances. Hence the traditional tandem approach of estimating individual conjoint utilities and then clustering them to form benefit segments *cannot* be done in practice with CBCA - or so it was until LSMs and Latent Class CBCA came along. Table 4 shows the aggregate CBCA results and those that describe four latent segments.

First examine the brand coefficients under the column marked Total Sample. Larger positive numbers indicate the brands, net of price, that are more appealing (the brand coefficient for the store-brand generic regular product is fixed at zero). The new product from Wise is the most appealing, followed by the existing Wise diet product and the Ruffles diet product. The overall price sensitivity is -1.32.

Using the sixteen choices from each respondent, four latent choice-based segments are uncovered. The first group exhibits high positive brand coefficients for all Wise products, either regular or diet. This group's price elasticity is the least steep of the four latent classes, giving further evidence of their high brand preference and loyalty. Members of the second segment are diet product buyers. The diet brand coefficients are more positive than the respective regular brand coefficients and their price sensitivity is near the aggregate average. The third segment consists of regular potato chip buyers. All the regular potato chip brand coefficients are more positive than the diet brand coefficients, with the exception of the new product. The new product's positioning statement seems to have had the desired effect of attracting regular chip buyers to a diet product. But the price elasticity for this group is much steeper than for either of the first two groups, indicative of the larger set of potential market choices available to regular chip buyers. The final segment contains those who prefer generic potato chips. The generic brand's coefficient is higher than the coefficient for any of the major brands, either diet or regular. Accompanying this preference for the generic brand is a very steep price sensitivity.

Additional data was collected in this study, including the respondents' evaluation of the new concept, past chip purchasing behavior, attitudes towards fitness and health, and demographics. Assigning respondents to the latent segment for which they had the highest probability of membership allowed detailed profiling. As might be expected, the Wise loyal and diet segments had higher top-box scores for purchase intent and uniqueness of the new concept. In contrast, members of the regular and generic segments were less favorable to the new product concept, with the generic segment having very low incidence of prior purchases of Wise products. Respondents belonging to the Wise and diet segments also appeared to have a strong orientation toward health and fitness and a basic commitment to watching their intake of calories and fat. This was in direct contrast to respondents in the regular and generic segments, who appeared to be less concerned about such issues.

However, there is weak differences between segments on demographics, which is not surprising given the nature of the product. The regular segment had relatively lower income and somewhat larger households, while the generic brand segment appeared to consist of „empty nesters" with higher-than-average incomes. In summary, the choice-based segments evaluate the new concept differently, hold different attitudes towards fitness and nutrition, and have different patterns of past category and brand purchase behavior. These results appear wholly consistent with the latent class CBCA results, thereby lending face validity to the choice-based segments.

Table 4:   *Latent Class Choice-based Conjoint Analysis Results*

	Brand	Type	Latent Purchasing Classes				
			Total Sample (600)	Wise Loyal (24%)	Diet Buyers (35%)	Regular Buyers (35%)	Generic Buyers (7%)
Brand Coefficients	Wise (New)	Diet	2.13*	**3.79**	**3.47**	**1.73**	-0.94
	Wise	Regular	0.43	**1.40**	-0.12	**1.42**	-3.62
	Wise	Diet	1.15	**3.03**	**2.26**	0.62	-2.94
	Lay's	Regular	0.48	-1.64	-1.09	**1.63**	-2.06
	Lay's	Diet	0.78	0.55	**2.58**	0.75	-2.20
	Ruffles	Regular	0.37	-1.45	-0.21	**1.53**	-2.15
	Ruffles	Diet	1.00	-0.19	**2.99**	0.79	-2.95
	Generic	Regular	0.00	0.00	0.00	0.00	**0.00**
Price sensitivity:			-1.32	-0.63	-1.33	-1.79	-2.83

*   Cell entries are multinomial logit coefficients.

15.7   Discussion and Future Directions

We have reviewed and presented applications of the basic framework of latent class conjoint analysis, for both metric conjoint and choice-based conjoint situations. As noted, these developments have enabled market researchers to conduct market segmentation using both traditional and newer conjoint analysis tools. Given the problems with the tandem approach to segmentation in traditional metric conjoint and the difficulty of obtaining individual-level coefficients in the choice-based conjoint context, LSMs have proved to be a boon to market researchers.

While we have focused on simultaneous segmentation and prediction, LSMs can also be used for descriptive segmentation (Cohen 1997; Dillon and Kumar 1994; Ramaswamy, Chatterjee and Cohen 1996). LSMs can easily and appropriately handle segmentation analyses with mixed levels of measurement. Instead of arbitrary rules of thumb about grouping algorithms, distances between respondents, or how many segments to retain, LSMs fit a statistical model based on a hypothesized number of segments. Tests of the goodness-of-fit of the model are generated.

Although LSMs used with metric conjoint or with CBCA offer substantial advantages, they are not without limitations. First, as an iterative procedure the estimation of large models can be very time-consuming, even on a fast computer. Rational starting values for the iterations are required to make sure a globally optimal solution is located. We have made good use of the traditional clustering procedures as a means to generate such rational starts. Second, while latent class metric conjoint or latent class CBCA provides guidance as to whether a particular solution fits the data better than one with more (or less) segments, selecting the best model still requires combining the statistical results with good judgement and category understanding. Third, as is true of any *post hoc* segmentation method, there is no guarantee that the derived segments will correlate with background descriptors or key behaviors of interest. Fourth, until very recently, widespread use of latent class metric conjoint and latent class CBCA by practicing researchers was hampered by the lack of readily available, easy-to-use software. This has been somewhat ameliorated, as witnessed by the excellent software review in Wedel and Kamakura (1997). Finally, some have criticized CBCA for not capturing heterogeneity adequately and for not delivering results at the individual level. Louviere, Hensher, and Swait (1999) discuss more complex model specifications which relax traditional logit assumptions and thereby provide a more comprehensive representation of consumer heterogeneity. While these model specifications move beyond simpler aggregate models, nothing less than individual-level results will suffice for some.

Two developments have attempted to address this last issue. Recently, Sawtooth Software has introduced a heuristic procedure called Individual Choice Estimation (ICE), which modifies the latent CBCA segmentation model described in equation (12) to deliver coefficients at the individual level (Johnson 1997). More experience with this procedure is needed before its usefulness is firmly established. The second development is the use of Bayesian methods to study consumer heterogeneity (see Allenby and Rossi 1999). In the context of choice-based conjoint analysis, these methods allow for the incorporation of prior knowledge (Allenby, Aurora, and Ginter 1995), estimation of the distribution of heterogeneity in part-worths, as well as the generation of individual-level estimates (Allenby and Ginter 1995).

Bayesian inference combines information contained in the data with prior knowledge to arrive at the posterior distribution of the model parameters. Typically, the posterior distributions of the parameters do not have a tractable closed form. Recent advances in Bayesian computation using Markov Chain Monte Carlo (MCMC) simulation (Gilks, Richardson and Spiegelhalter 1996) allow draws to be simulated from non-standard posterior distributions, given the knowledge of the full conditional distributions. In particular, implementation of the Gibbs sampler (e.g., Smith and Roberts 1993) requires knowledge of only the full conditionals, up to proportionality. Allenby, Aurora and Ginter (1998) discuss a mixture model specification that provides a flexible characterization of heterogeneity in part-worths, thereby simultaneously delivering market segment and individual-level information.

As progress in Bayesian methods enable increasingly flexible representations of heterogeneity in demand, there is considerable potential for marketers to not only obtain a detailed understanding of consumer diversity, but also to engage in more targeted marketing (e.g., Rossi, McCulloch and Allenby 1996). Advances in Bayesian estimation using more efficient computational methods such as the Slice sampler (Damien, Wakefield and Walker 1999; see Krishnan, Ramaswamy, Meyer, and Damien 1998 for an illustrative application), and reversible jump MCMC methods for finite mixture models (Damien, Dellaportas, and Ramaswamy 1998) hold much promise. More work is needed, we believe, to systematically compare the performance of Bayesian estimation methods with classic latent class models for conjoint analysis in terms of interpretability and managerial actionability. Work is also under way using Bayesian analysis (Liechty, Ramaswamy and Cohen 1999) to extend the capabilities of newer conjoint methods such as menu-based conjoint models (Ben-Akiva and Gershenfeld 1998).

We believe that the future holds much promise for using conjoint analysis for segmentation in marketing. Increased flexibility in experimental design, better representation of consumer heterogeneity, and more efficient statistical model estimation and computation will provide major benefits. In conjunction with rapid advances in information technology and the ability of marketers to engage in one-to-one marketing and mass customization, the new millenium will offer major opportunities for researchers and managers to segment markets in new ways, and thus to better understand and predict consumer behavior.

15.8   References

Aaker, D. (1998), *Strategic Marketing Management*, New York.

Addelman, S. (1962), Orthogonal Main-effect Plans for Asymmetrical Factorial Experiments, *Technometrics*, 4, 21-46.

Akaike, H. (1974), A New Look at Statistical Model Identification, *IEEE Transactions on Automatic Control*, 716-723.

Allenby, G. M., Aurora, N. and Ginter, J. L. (1995), Incorporating Prior Knowledge in Conjoint Analysis Studies, *Journal of Marketing Research*, 32, 152-162.

Allenby, G. M., Aurora, N. and Ginter, J. L. (1998), On the Heterogeneity of Demand, *Journal of Marketing Research*, 35, 384-389.

Allenby, G. M. and Ginter, J. L. (1995), Using Extremes to Design Products and Segment Markets, *Journal of Marketing Research*, 32, 392-403.

Allenby, G. M. and Rossi, P. E. (1999), Marketing Models of Consumer Heterogeneity, *Journal of Econometrics,* 89, 57-78.

Ben-Akiva, M., McFadden, D., Abe, M., Bockenholt, U., Bolduc, D., Gopinath, D., Mori-kawa, T., Ramaswamy, V., Rao, V., Revelt, D. and Steinberg, D. (1997), Modeling Methods for Discrete Choice Analysis, *Marketing Letters*, 8, 273-286.

Ben-Akiva, M. and Gershenfeld, S. (1998), Multi-featured Products and Services: Analyzing Pricing and Bundling Strategies, *Journal of Forecasting*, 17, 175-196.

Ben-Akiva, M. and Lerman, S. R. (1985), *Discrete Choice Analysis: Theory and Application to Travel Demand*, Cambridge.

Bockenholt, U., Bozdogan, H., DeSarbo, W. S., Dillon, W. R., Gupta, S., Kamakura, W., Kumar, A., Ramaswamy, V. and Zenor, M. (1994), Issues in the Specification and Application of Latent Structure Models of Choice, *Marketing Letters*, 5, 323-334.

Bretton-Clark (1992), *Conjoint Analyzer*, Morristown.

Cattin, P. and Wittink, D. (1982), Commercial Use of Conjoint Analysis: A Survey, *Journal of Marketing*, 46, 44-53.

Cohen, S. H. (1997), Perfect Union: CBCA Marries the Best of Conjoint and Discrete Choice Models, *Marketing Research Magazine*, 3, 12-17.

Cohen, S. H. and Ramaswamy, V. (1998), Latent Segmentation Models, *Marketing Research Magazine*, 10, 15-22.

Damien, P., Dellaportas, P. and Ramaswamy, V. (1998), How Many Segments?: A Full Bayesian Approach for Latent Segmentation Models, presentation made at the Advanced Research Techniques Forum, Beaver Creek.

Damien, P. S., Wakefield, J. and Walker, G. (1999), Gibbs Sampling for Bayesian Nonconjugate and Hierarchical Models Using Auxiliary Variables, *Journal of Royal Statistical Society*, 61, 331-344.

Dempster, A. P., Laird, N. M. and Rubin, D. B. (1977), Maximum Likelihood from Incomplete Data via the E.M. Algorithm, *Journal of the Royal Statistical Society*, 39, 1-38.

DeSarbo, W. S., Wedel, M., Vriens, M. and Ramaswamy, V. (1992), Latent Class Metric Conjoint Analysis, *Marketing Letters*, 3, 273-288.

DeSarbo, W. S., Oliver, R. L. and Rangaswamy, A. (1989), A Simulated Annealing Methodology for Clusterwise Linear Regression, *Psychometrika*, 54, 707-36.

DeSarbo, W. S., Ramaswamy, V. and Cohen, S. H. (1995), Market Segmentation with Choice-Based Conjoint Analysis, *Marketing Letters*, 6, 137-147.

Dillon, W. R. and Kumar, A. (1994), Latent Structure and Other Mixture Models in Marketing: An Integrative Survey and Overview, in: Bagozzi, R., ed., *Advanced Methods of Marketing Research*, Cambridge, 295-351.

Elrod, T., Louviere, J. J. and Davey, K. S. (1992), An Empirical Comparison of Ratings-based and Choice-based Conjoint Models, *Journal of Marketing Research*, 29, 368-377.

Gelfand, A. E., and Smith, A. F. M. (1990), Sampling-based Approaches to Calculating Marginal Densities, *Journal of the American Statistical Association*, 85, 398-409.

Gelman, A., Carlin, J. B., Stern, H. S. and Rubin, D. B. (1996), *Bayesian Data Analysis*, London.

Gilks, W. R., Richardson, S. and Spiegelhalter, D. (1996), *Markov Chain Monte Carlo in Practice*, London.

Green, P. E. and Krieger, A. M. (1991), Segmenting Markets with Conjoint Analysis, *Journal of Marketing*, 55, 20-31.

Green, P. E. and Rao, V. R. (1971), Conjoint Measurement for Quantifying Judgmental Data, *Journal of Marketing Research,* 8, 355-363.

Green, P. E. and Srinivasan, V. (1990), Conjoint Analysis in Marketing Research: New Developments and Directions, *Journal of Marketing* 54, 3-19.

Green, P. E. and Srinivasan, V. (1978), Conjoint Analysis in Consumer Research: Issues & Outlook, *Journal of Consumer Research*, 5, 103-123.

Green, P. E. and Wind, Y. (1973), *Multiattribute Decisions in Marketing: A Measurement Approach*, Hinsdale.

Hagerty, M. R. (1985), The Cost of Simplifying Preference Models, *Marketing Science*, 5, 298-319.

Haley, R. I. (1985), *Developing Effective Communications Strategy: A Benefit Segmentation Approach*, New York.

Johnson, R. M. (1994), *The CBC System for Choice-based Conjoint Analysis*, Sawtooth Software.

Johnson, R. M. (1997), *Individual Utilities from Choice Data: A New Method*, Washington.

Kamakura, W. A. and Russell, G. J. (1989), A Probabilistic Choice Model for Market Segmentation and Elasticity Structure, *Journal of Marketing Research*, 26, 379-390.

Kamakura, W. A. (1988), A Least Squares Procedure for Benefit Segmentation with Conjoint Experiments, *Journal of Marketing Research*, 25, 157-167.

Krishnan, M., Ramaswamy, V., Meyer, M. C. and Damien, P. (1998), Customer Satisfaction for Financial Services: The Role of Products, Services, and Technology, *Management Science*, forthcoming.

Kuhfeld, W. F., Tobias, R. D. and Garratt, M. (1994), Efficient Experimental Designs with Marketing Research Applications, *Journal of Marketing Research*, 31, 545-557.

Liechty, J., Ramaswamy, V., and Cohen, S. H. (1999), Menu-based Conjoint Analysis for Mass Customization: An Application to a Web-based Information Service, working paper, Ann Arbor.

Louviere, J. J. (1988), *Analyzing Individual Decision Making: Metric Conjoint Analysis*, Sage University Series on Quantitative Applications in the Social Sciences, Series #67, Newbury Park.

Louviere, J. J. (1994), Conjoint Analysis, in: Bagozzi, R., ed., *Advanced Methods of Marketing Research*, Cambridge, 223-259.

Louviere, J. J., Hensher, D. and Swait, J. (1999), Conjoint Preference Elicitation Methods in the Broader Context of Random Utility Theory Preference Elicitation Methods, Working paper, Sydney.

Louviere, J. J. and Woodworth, G. G. (1983), Design and Analysis of Simulated Consumer Choice or Allocation Experiments: An Approach Based on Aggregate Data, *Journal of Marketing Research*, 20, 350-367.

McFadden, D. (1986), The Choice Theory Approach to Marketing Research, *Marketing Science*, 5, 275-297.

Moore, W. L. (1980), Levels of Aggregation in Conjoint Analysis: An Empirical Comparison, *Journal of Marketing Research*, 17, 516-523.

Ogawa, K. (1987), An Approach to Simultaneous Estimation and Segmentation in Conjoint Analysis, *Marketing Science*, 6, 66-81.

Oliphant, K., Eagle, T. C., Louviere, J. J. and Anderson, D. (1992), Cross-task Comparison of Ratings-based and Choice-based Conjoint, Sun Valley, ID: *Sawtooth Software Conference Proceedings*, 383-394.

Punj, G. and Stewart, D. W. (1983), Cluster Analysis in Marketing Research: A Review and Suggestions for Applications, *Journal of Marketing Research*, 20, 134-148.

Ramaswamy, V. and DeSarbo, W. S. (1990), SCULPTRE: A New Methodology for Deriving and Analyzing Hierarchical Product-Market Structures from Panel Data, *Journal of Marketing Research*, 27, 418-427.

Ramaswamy, V., DeSarbo, W. S., Reibstein, D. J. and Robinson, W. T. (1993), An Empirical Pooling Approach for Estimating Marketing Mix Elasticities with PIMS Data, *Marketing Science*, 12, 103-124.

Ramaswamy, V., Chatterjee, R. and Cohen, S. H. (1996), Joint Segmentation on Distinct Interdependent Bases with Categorical Data, *Journal of Marketing Research*, 32, 337-350.

Rossi, P. E., McCulloch, R. E. and Allenby, G. M. (1996), The Value of Purchase History Data in Target Marketing, *Marketing Science*, 15, 321-340.

Smith, A. F. M., and Roberts, G. O. (1993), Bayesian Computations via the Gibbs Sampler and Related Markov Chain Monte Carlo Methods, *Journal of the Royal Statistical Society*, 55, 3-23.

Struhl, S. (1994), Discrete Choice Modeling: Understanding a 'Better Conjoint than Conjoint', *Quirk's Marketing Research Review*, 8, 6-12.

Titterington, D. M. (1990), Some Recent Research in the Analysis of Mixture Distributions, *Statistics*, 4, 619-641.

Vriens, M., Wedel, M. and Wilms, T. (1996), Metric Conjoint Segmentation Methods: A Monte Carlo Comparison, *Journal of Marketing Research*, 23, 73-85.

Wedel, M. and DeSarbo, W. S. (1994), A Review of Recent Developments in Latent Class Regression Models, in: Bagozzi, R. P., ed., *Advanced Methods of Marketing Research*, Cambridge, 352-388.

Wedel, M. and Kamakura, W. (1997), *Market Segmentation: Conceptual and Methodological Foundations,* Boston.

Wedel, M. and Kistemaker, C. (1989), Consumer Benefit Segmentation using Clusterwise Linear Regression, *International Journal of Research in Marketing*, 6, 45-59.

Wedel, M. and Steenkamp, J. B. (1989), A Clusterwise Regression Method for Simultaneous Fuzzy Market Structuring and Benefit Segmentation, *Journal of Marketing Research*, 28, 385-396.

Wind, Y. (1978), Issues and Advances in Segmentation Research, *Journal of Marketing Research*, 15, 317-337.

Wittink, D. R. and Cattin, P. (1989), Commercial Use of Conjoint Analysis: An Update, *Journal of Marketing*, 53, 91-96.

Wittink, D. R., Vriens, M. and Burhenne, W. (1994), Commercial Use of Conjoint Analysis in Europe: Results and Critical Reflections, *International Journal of Research in Marketing*, 15, 41-52.

16 A Generalized Normative Segmentation Methodology Employing Conjoint Analysis

Wayne S. DeSarbo and Christian F. DeSarbo

16.1 Introduction

Since the pioneering research of Wendell Smith (1956), the concept of market segmentation has been one of the most pervasive activities in both the marketing academic literature and practice. In addition to being one of the major ways of operationalizing the marketing concept, marketing segmentation provides guidelines for a firm's marketing strategy and resource allocation among markets and products. Facing heterogeneous markets, a firm employing a market segmentation strategy can typically increase expected profitability as suggested by the classic price discrimination model which provides the major theoretical rationale for market segmentation (cf. Frank, Massey and Wind 1972).

Market segmentation can be defined as the subdividing of a market into distinct, but possibly overlapping subsets, where any subset may be selected as a market target to be reached with a distinct marketing mix (Kotler 1995). It is one of the initial phases in marketing strategy for both consumer and industrial markets. However, prior to implementing such a strategy, the derived market segment scheme must satisfy a number of criteria (cf. DeSarbo and Grisaffee 1998; Wedel and Kamakura 2001):

1. **Differential Behavior** - the members of different market segments should behave differently either towards the brand or product class, or towards the marketing mix activity oriented towards them. For example, different segments typically purchase more or less of different brands/services;
2. **Membership Identification** - the marketer should be able to classify each customer in the market place into one or more segments on the basis of obtainable information;
3. **Reachability** - the marketer should be able to reach the members of target market segment(s) by a distinct marketing mix strategy (e.g., media vehicles, promotional strategy, advertising copy, etc.);
4. **Feasibility** - market segmentation should be a feasible endeavor. Feasibility here refers to the formation of market segments that obey or satisfy application-specific technological, environmental, and managerial constraints. For example, it may not be feasible to group customers in vastly different geographical locations in the same market segment due to the difficulty and costs of marketing to them.
5. **Profitability** - there are additional administrative and marketing costs associated with implementing market segmentation, as well as incremental

expected revenues. Profitability refers to the fact that the revenues must exceed the costs associated with the implementation of such a segmentation strategy.

6. **Substantiality** - the derived segments must be of different size and magnitude to be taken seriously from a marketing perspective. Segments with less than 5-10% of the population are typically artifacts of the particular methodology employed to derive segments.

7. **Responsiveness** - the derived market segments should respond uniquely to the marketing efforts targeted at them.

8. **Stability** - market segments should be stable over time at least during the period for identification of members and implementation of associated strategies.

9. **Actionability** - the formation of market segments should lead to the specification of associated marketing strategies towards segment targets.

10. **Projectability** - the results of a market segmentation study should be projectable to the entire marketplace at hand.

To date, few market segmentation studies or techniques are able to insure and verify these criteria in the actual operationalization of market segmentation. Frank, Massey, and Wind (1972) were among the first to acknowledge some of these criteria in what they called "normative segmentation", or the "development of normative models for the application of segmentation research findings to marketing decisions (p. 20)". These authors consider the basis, formation, and associated decision making concerning market segments all simultaneous as a conceptual entity. Mahajan and Jain (1978) and Winter (1979) later proposed conceptual and mathematical frameworks for operationalizing normative segmentation in terms of allowing for constraints, budgets, differential costs and revenues, etc. DeSarbo and Mahajan (1984) were the first to provide a constrained classification procedure, CONCLUS, to implement some of these aspects of normative market segmentation. More recently, DeSarbo and Grisaffee (1998) proposed a general, but flexible, methodological framework (NORMCLUS) for constrained market segmentation for either consumer or industrial markets. Given the nuances of each and every type of market segmentation application, NORMCLUS is completely flexible in terms of accommodating user-specified objective function(s) (including expected profit as in normative segmentation), single or multi-criterion objective functions, a variety of user-specified constraints, different forms or types of segments, multiple sets of data collected on the same consumers, and alternative models of market segmentation. This book chapter modifies the NORMCLUS approach by accommodating conjoint analysis in a market segmentation context.

The next section reviews the general NORMCLUS model, constraints, and optimization methodology employing various combinatorial optimization algorithms. Section III discusses the role of conjoint analysis in benefit segmentation schemes and describes many recent developments. Section IV presents an industrial marketing application including the specific concerns and needs of this manufacturing firm and how these were translated into an appropriate mathematical model (that was utilized for the specific application presented in this manuscript). Finally, the conclusion section lists several areas for future research.

16.2   Methodology

16.2.1   The NORMCLUS Framework

As mentioned in DeSarbo and Grisaffee (1998), NORMCLUS can accommodate any user specified objective function(s), including expected profit. In the more general case of multi-objective optimization, NORMCLUS can be formulated to utilize either utility function, global criterion methods, etc. to derive Pareto optimal solutions. Suppose there are m = 1, ..., M objective functions that are comparably scaled as to range and distribution, and that a particular segmentation problem implies their joint minimization (or maximization). In the utility function method, a utility function $U_m(f_m)$ is defined for each objective, f_m, depending on the importance of f_m compared to the other objective functions. Then, one can define a total utility function U as:

$$(1) \qquad U = \sum_{m=1}^{M} U_m(f_m)$$

A solution vector $\underline{\theta}^*$ is then found by optimizing U subject to user given constraints:

$$(2) \qquad h_j(\underline{\theta}) = 0 \quad j = 1, ..., J,$$

$$(3) \qquad g_s(\underline{\theta}) \leq 0 \quad s = 1, ..., S.$$

A specific form for (1) above can be given by:

$$(4) \qquad U = \sum_{m=1}^{M} U_m = \sum_{m=1}^{M} \alpha_m f_m(\underline{\theta}),$$

where α_m is a scalar weighting factor associated with the *m*-th objective function, $f_m(\underline{\theta})$, with $\sum_m \alpha_m = 1$, and $h_j(\underline{\theta})$ and $g_s(\underline{\theta})$ are linear or non-linear equality and inequality constraints respectively. Rao (1996) calls this the "weighting function method" for solving multi-criteria optimization problems which typically generate Pareto optimal solutions. Rao (1996) describes a number of alternative multi-criteria optimization frameworks such as the inverted utility method, the global criterion method, the bounded objective function method, lexicographic method, etc. which can all be accommodated in NORMCLUS.

16.2.2 Constraint Implementation

The parameter vector $\underline{\theta}$ can include segment membership information, as well as other parameters (e.g., segment level regression coefficients as in a cluster-wise regression framework). As mentioned, NORMCLUS can accommodate ordinary cluster analysis where, for example, $f_1(\underline{\theta})$ can be specified as a ratio of between to within cluster sum-of-squares to be maximized with respect to binary $\underline{\theta}$ indicating cluster membership. Alternatively, $\underline{\theta}$ can include both cluster membership and segment level regression parameters as in a cluster-wise regression market segmentation approach (cf. DeSarbo, Oliver and Rangaswamy 1989; DeSarbo and Grisaffee 1998), where $f_1(\underline{\theta})$ can be specified as a residual sum-of-squares to be minimized. Or, in normative segmentation applications where costs and revenues are readily available, $f_1(\underline{\theta})$ can be an expected profit function to be maximized. Again, a variety of optimization frameworks are accommodated in NORMCLUS depending upon the nature of the segmentation application at hand.

The remaining flexibility in NORMCLUS can be best illustrated in terms of the user-specified constraints that can be accommodated in (2) and (3) above. Let:

$i = 1,...,$ I consumers
$k = 1,...,$ K variables
$r = 1,...,$ R segments (R is user specified);
X_i = the value of the k-th variable or characteristic for consumer i;
m_{ir} = the degree of membership of consumer i in segment r ($0 \le m_{ir} \le 1$);
S_r = the set of consumers in segment r;
I_r = the number of consumers (cardinality) in segment r;
$\overline{X}_k^{(r)}$ = the mean of variable k in segment r.

Then, for several types of cluster analysis applications, the following section discusses several types of possible constraints representing prior information specified by the user or institutional constraints which can be addressed (cf. Mahajan and Jain 1978; DeSarbo and Mahajan 1984; DeSarbo and Grisaffee 1998).

Type of Segments

(5) a. mir (1 - mir) = 0 $\quad \forall$ i = 1...I, $\quad \forall$ r = 1...R

This set of constraints restricts m_{ir} to be either 0 or 1.

(6) b. $\sum_{r=1}^{R} m_{ir} = 1 \quad \forall i = 1.....I$

This set of constraints, together with (a) above, provides for a non-overlapping segmentation analysis where each consumer can belong to one and only one segment. Note, without this set of constraints (i.e., only with this (b) set), one can allow for overlapping segments-that is, allow for cases where consumers can belong to more than one cluster.

(7)   c. $0 \leq m_{ir} \leq 1 \quad \forall i = 1...I, \quad \forall r = 1...R$

This set of constraints, together with those in (b) above, allow for "fuzzy-set" segments, where objects can be fractional members of all segments.

(8)   d. $\sum_{r=1}^{R} m_{ir} \overset{\leq}{\underset{\geq}{=}} c_i$

This constraint, together with constraints in (a), restrict the number of segments (c_i) consumer i can belong to in an overlapping scheme.

Constraints Concerning Segment Membership

We assume that the constraints in equation (5) hold in the following discussion.

(9)   a. $m_{sr}* + m_{nr}* = 2$

Here, one wants consumer s and n to belong to the same segment r^*.

(10)   b. $\sum_{i \in T_{r*}} m_{ir*} = c_{r*}$

This is a generalization of constraint (a) above in that one wants the consumers in some set T_{r*}, whose cardinality is c_{r*}, in the same cluster r^*.

(11)   c. $m_{sr} + m_{nr} \leq 1 \quad \forall r = 1,..., R$

This constraint forbids consumers s and n to be in the same segment.

(12)   d. (1). $\sum_{i=1}^{I} m_{ir} \geq Min_r$ (2). $\sum_{i=1}^{I} m_{ir} \leq Max_r$

These constraints allow one to restrict the number of consumers that get allocated to cluster r. Constraint (d.1) states that the number of members in segment r is to be greater than or equal to some minimum number Min_r. Conversely, constraint (d.2) restricts membership to be equal or less than some maximum number Max_r. This constraint may be used to insure minimum profitability.

(13)   e. $\sum_{i=1}^{I} m_{ir'} = \sum_{i=1}^{I} m_{ir} \quad \forall r \neq r' = 1...R$

This set of constraints restricts the number of consumers in any segments r and
r′ to be equal (e.g., for sales territory/segment definition).

(14)   f. $\left| \sum_{i=1}^{I} m_{ir} - \sum_{i=1}^{I} m_{ir'} \right| \leq \varepsilon_1 \quad \forall \, r \neq r' = 1...R$

These constraints restrict the range or distribution of acceptable differences
(ε_1) in the number of consumers in segments r and r'. This set of constraints is
basically equivalent to specifying *both* sets of constraints in (d.1) and (d.2) above
where all the ceiling values (Max$_r$) and all floor values (Min$_r$) are identical for all
segments.

Characteristics of Segments

(15)   a. $X_{ik} m_{ir} \geq V_{kr}^{\min} \quad \forall \, i \in S_r$

These constraints guarantee that all members of segment r possess at least
$V_{kr}^{\min}$ of characteristic or variable k. Similarly, one could generalize constraint to:

(16) $\dfrac{\sum\limits_{i \in S_r}^{I_r} X_{ik} m_{ir}}{I_r} \geq V_{kr}^{\min}$,

where the average segment value on variable k must be greater than some minimum value. Similar constraints can be constructed to insure that each member or
segment average be less than some maximum value $V_{kr}^{\max}$ by substituting "≤" and
"$V_{kr}^{\max}$" for "≥" and "$V_{kr}^{\min}$" respectively above. These constraints can insure a
stable amount of homogeneity amongst the segments.

(17)   b. $\left| \sum_{i \in S_r}^{I_r} X_{ik} m_{ir} - \sum_{i \in S_{r'}}^{I_{r'}} X_{ij} m_{ir'} \right| \overset{\leq}{\underset{\geq}{=}} \varepsilon_2$

This constraint establishes a range or distribution of acceptable differences
(ε_2) of characteristic k in segments $r \neq r'$. Similarly, one can generalize this to:

$$(18) \qquad \left| \frac{\displaystyle\sum_{i \in S_r}^{I_r} X_{ik} m_{ir}}{I_r} - \frac{\displaystyle\sum_{i \in S_{r'}}^{I_{r'}} X_{ij} m_{ir'}}{I_{r'}} \right| \begin{matrix} \leq \\ = \varepsilon_2, \\ \geq \end{matrix}$$

where the range of differences in mean values of characteristic k in segments $r \neq r'$ is constrained. For example, this constraint can be gainfully utilized for insuring segments will differ as to price sensitivity.

$$(19) \qquad \text{c.} \quad \left| m_j r m_{ir} (X_{jk} - X_{ik}) \right| \leq t_{rk}^{max} \qquad \forall j, i \in S_r$$

This set of constraints restricts the maximum deviation allowed (t_{rk}^{max}) on characteristic k for any two members of the same segment r. Accordingly one could also constrain the maximum distance or dissimilarity allowed (D_r) between any two objects in segment r via:

$$(20) \qquad \left[\sum_{k=1}^{K} (m_{jr} m_{lr} (X_{jk} - X_{lk}))^2 \right]^{1/2} \leq D_r .$$

$$(21) \qquad \text{b.} \quad \left| m_{jr} (X_{jk} - \overline{X}_k^{(r)}) \right| \leq \gamma_{kr}^{max} \qquad \forall j \in S_r$$

This set of constraints restricts the maximum deviation (γ_{kr}^{max}) on characteristic k between any object in segment r and segment r's mean value on variable k. Similarly, one could generalize this to all variables via:

$$(22) \qquad \left[\sum_{k=1}^{K} (m_{jr} (X_{jk} - \overline{X}_k^{(r)}))^2 \right]^{1/2} \leq \Gamma, \qquad \forall j \in Sr,$$

where there is a restriction placed on the maximum distance or dissimilarity allowed between any consumer j in segment r and the centroid of segment r. The constraints in sets (a) through (d) impose restrictions that affect the "compactness" of a segment-or the within sum-of-squares of a segment.

Such constraints can be used in a geographical based segmentation scheme.

$$(23) \qquad \text{c.} \quad \left| \overline{X}_k^{(r)} - \overline{X}_k^{(r')} \right| \geq B_{rr'}^{min}$$

This constraint restricts the "separability" (affecting the between sum-of-squares) between the mean of variable k in segment r and r'. This can be generalized to the case involving all variables via:

$$(24) \qquad \sum_{k=1}^{K} (\overline{X}_k^{(r)} - \overline{X}_k^{(r')})^2 \geq C_{rr'}^{\min} ,$$

where restrictions are made on the between sums of squares between segments r and r'.

Application Specific Constraints

Additional constraints are indeed possible given the particular application in mind. For example, one may possess geographical distances, costs, or travel times (δ_{it}) between all prospective clients and a salesman's home. As such, the sales manager may wish to restrict the average travel time/distance/cost for salesman t to visit customers in segment r via:

$$(25) \qquad \frac{\sum_{i \in S_r}^{I_r} m_{ir} \delta_{it}}{I_r} \leq \delta_t^{\max} ,$$

where δ_t^{max} is an upper limit to the amount of time, fare, or miles for salesman t. Also, in a cluster-wise regression context, one often wishes to place constraints on the regression coefficients such as:

$$(26) \qquad \boldsymbol{b}_r \geq 0 \quad \forall \, r = 1,...R$$

or

$$(27) \qquad \boldsymbol{h}_r \, \boldsymbol{b}_r = 0 \quad \forall \, r = 1,...R,$$

where $\boldsymbol{h}_r$ is a linear contrast vector, given the specific context of the market segmentation framework (e.g., in a benefit segmentation framework, increasing performance on desired attributes/benefits should increase customer utility).

16.2.3   Estimation Algorithms

A variety of optimization procedures are available in NORMCLUS for parameter estimation including ordinary least-squares, constrained least-squares, and a host of combinatorial optimization procedures employing genetic algorithms (c.f. Rao 1996, for a survey), simulated annealing (c.f. DeSarbo, Oliver and Rangaswamy 1989), lambda-opt procedures (c.f. Lin and Kernighan 1973), as well as a variety of heuristics such as greedy algorithms and taboo search. The particular selection of which combinatorial optimization procedure to use depends very much on the structure of the segmentation problem at hand. We will illustrate the NORMCLUS procedure concerning an actual benefit market segmentation study in a business-to-business context shortly.

16.3 Conjoint Analysis and Benefit Market Segmentation

For the estimation of market segments, both the segmentation basis and method that are specified are quite important. According to Vriens, Wedel, and Wilms (1996), of all the segmentation bases, the benefits that consumers derive from the attributes of a product or service have proved to be the most powerful variables (Haley 1968; Wind 1978). Perhaps the most popular approaches for assessing these benefits is through the use of conjoint analysis (Green and Srinivasan 1978, 1990). It is therefore not surprising that market segmentation in commercial applications is one of the primary purposes for conducting conjoint analysis (Wittink and Cattin 1989; Wittink, Vriends and Burhenne 1994). In commercial and academic applications (cf. Green and Krieger 1991), the segmentation of markets with conjoint analysis traditionally involves a two-stage approach, in which the identification of segments and the estimation of conjoint models are performed separately.

Traditionally, this has been typically accomplished in one of two ways. In an a priori segmentation scheme (Green 1977) where segments are known or defined prior to the research, an aggregation of individual level preference judgments occurs (by segment) and subsequent estimation of the conjoint model is performed at the segment level (cf. Green and Srinivasan 1978, 1990). In post hoc segmentation schemes (Green 1977), estimation of the conjoint analysis occurs at the individual level, and subsequent level part-worths are then clustered to form market segments. Here, problems typically arise since traditional demographic or psychographic background information that typically characterizes market segments rarely adequately describes heterogeneous utility functions at the individual or market segment level (Moore 1980). In addition, the traditional two-stage methodology described will often influence the results obtained. In particular, the multiple regression and subsequent cluster analysis procedures typically optimize different and unrelated objective functions/aspects of the structure of the data. Another major problem well documented in the psychometric and classification literature (cf. Hartigan 1975; Punj and Stewart 1983) is that different clustering methods often produce different cluster (segment) results when applied to the same data. Finally, the marketing literature on conjoint analysis has documented the potential instability of part-worth estimates derived at the individual level, especially in highly fractioned designs (cf. Wedel and Kistemaker 1989).

A number of procedures for performing post hoc market segmentation with conjoint analysis have been proposed. Hagerty (1985) developed a Q-factor analytic procedure that maximizes the predictive power of the derived segment level utility functions. His procedure models each customer as, in part, belonging to every market segment and shows that the degree of membership of each consumer in each of the segments is determined by the first eigenvector of the correlation matrix calculated across the observed preference ratings among consumers. However, as noted by Kamakura (1988), such factor analytic procedures lead to overlapping clusters that are rarely identifiable. In addition, Stewart (1981) has noted that the number of factors obtained in such Q-factor analyses of individual characteristics (here, preferences) is not truly indicative of the true number of clusters. Kamakura (1988) stated that one may have more or less clusters than factors and the identification of the homogeneous clusters is subjective and complex, especially when there are more than two factors present. Finally, as mentioned in Vriens, Wedel, and Wilms (1996), such factor analytic solutions identify prototypes and the correlations of individuals with these prototypes. These loadings are not equivalent to segment/prototype membership or probabilities of membership as they do not necessarily satisfy the row sum (to unity) constraints.

Kamakura (1988) later developed a least-squares procedure for performing segmentation in conjoint analysis, which attempts to group customers into homogenous segments such that their stated preferences are explained maximally by their group level performance functions. He developed a two-step procedure, conceptually similar to that of Spath (1985), where given a fixed number of segments and a binary indicator matrix designating membership of each individual in each market segment, part-worths are estimated in a least-squares fashion for each segment. Further, given these segment level part-worths, Kamakura (1988) develops an agglomerative hierarchical clustering procedure, which attempts to optimize the same error sums-of-squares of objective function. As noted by Vriens, Wedel, and Wilms (1996), two problems can be identified with this innovative approach. One, as noted by Kamakura (1988) himself, combining two individuals or clusters to form a new cluster early in this agglomerative scheme forces them to be in the same cluster in the latter stages of his algorithm. Thus, any misclassification in the earlier stages of the algorithm will be carried on to higher aggregation levels. Two, the hierarchical procedure imposes rather severe constraints on the aggregations: a hierarchy and the inability to allow overlapping or fuzzy cluster memberships. It is indeed interesting to point out that Green and Helsen (1989) have shown that neither the Hagerty nor Kamakura approaches lead to higher predictive validity than are obtained by conventional conjoint analysis applied to individual response data.

There are also a number of related approaches are relevant to mention here. Ogawa (1987) has developed a stochastic, nonmetric approach for simultaneously estimating part-worths and aggregating individuals into segments. First, using a logit choice model framework, Ogawa (1987) developed a ridge-like procedure for estimating individual part-worths for *rank ordered* preferences. Then, an information-theoretic criterion or index is posited as a means to aggregate individuals. DeSarbo, Oliver, and Rangaswamy (1989) present a simulated appealing based methodology to perform clusterwise regression. As stated to earlier, these authors demonstrate the flexibility of their approach in accommodating multivariate measures, constraints on the resulting classification, etc. Wedel and Kistemaker (1989) and Wedel and Steenkmap (1989, 1991) provide alternative clusterwise regression formulations for benefit segmentation that could also be adapted to perform such simultaneous estimation and segmentation in conjoint analysis.

Finally, a number of latent structure or finite mixture regression models have been applied to both traditional and choice-based conjoint data. DeSarbo, Wedel, Ramaswamy, and Vriens (1992) developed a conjoint segmentation model for metric data. The preference values of a customer were assumed to follow a multivariate normal distribution, allowing for possible covariances among preference judgments for the profiles. The authors applied their model to a conjoint experiment on remote entry controls for cars, simultaneously identified segments, estimated the part-worths, and provided covariance structures within those segments. Similar applications of a mixture regression model to conjoint experiments are provided by Wedel and DeSarbo (1994,1995) who analyzed conjoint data on the measurement of service quality and on customer satisfaction. A multinomial mixture model for both conjoint choice and rank-order experiments was developed by Kamakura, Wedel and Agrawal (1994). As an additional feature, those authors provided a simultaneous profiling of the segments with consumer descriptor variables (using a concomitant mixture model). The model was applied to the analysis of a conjoint experiment on banking services. A finite mixture model for conjoint choice experiments was proposed by DeSoete and DeSarbo (1991) and DeSarbo, Ramaswamy, and Cohen (1995). DeSarbo, Ramaswamy and Chatterjee (1995) proposed a model for constant-sum data collected in conjoint analysis, where consumers are asked to allocate a fixed number of points across the alternative profiles. They used a mixture of Dirichlet distributions to describe the constant sum data. Their model, like the preceding ones, simultaneously estimates segments and identifies the part-worth of the conjoint attributes within the segments. It was applied to a conjoint study on industrial purchasing, where profiles were constructed on the basis of supplier selection criteria.

Note, none of the above listed techniques for simultaneous conjoint and market segmentation analysis can explicitly guarantee any of the ten criteria listed earlier for effective market segmentation. The primary objective of this book chapter is to explore how many of the criteria can be effectively dealt with through the formation of an appropriate objective function, as well as through the inclusion of appropriate variable batteries and classification constraints using a modified version of the NORMCLUS methodology first described in DeSarbo and Grisaffee (1998).

16.4   Application: Industrial Cleaners

16.4.1   Study Background

Hair, Anderson, Tatham and Black (1995) discuss a segmentation study performed for a hypothetical industrial supplier called HATCO. In developing a new industrial cleaner, HATCO conducted a conjoint study of some 100 business customers to aid in the understanding of the needs of its industrial customers. Previous marketing research and consultation with the product development group identified five factors as the key determinant attributes in the industrial cleaner market. Table 1 depicts these five attributes as well as the levels tested in the conjoint analysis. HATCO utilized a full profile method of collecting metric respondent evaluations. The conjoint task was administered during a personal interview. The respondents were handed a set of 18 cards, each containing one of the full-profile stimulus descriptions. They were also given a foldout response form that had seven response categories, ranging from "Not at All Likely to Buy" to "Certain to Buy". Respondents were instructed to place each card in the response category best describing their purchase intentions. After initially placing the cards, they were asked to review their elected purchase intentions and rearrange any cards if necessary. Finally, some six purchaser characteristics were measured as described in Table 1.

Table 1:   Attributes and Levels for the HATCO Conjoint Analysis Experiment

Attribute	Description	Level
MIXTURE	Form of the product	Premixed liquid
		Concentrated liquid
		Powder
NUMAPP	Number of applications per container	50
		100
		200
GERMFREE	Addition of disinfectant to cleaner	Yes
		No
BIOPROT	Price per typical application	No
		Yes
PRICE	Price per typical application	35 cents
		49 cents
		79 cents

Purchaser Characteristics

Z_1 Size of firm-size of the firm relative to others in this market. This variable has two categories: 1 = large, and 0 = small

Z_2 Usage level- how much of the firm's total product is purchased from HATCO, measured on a 100-point percentage scale, ranging from 0 to 100 percent

Z_3 Satisfaction level-how satisfied the purchaser is with past purchases from HATCO, measured on a graphic rating scale

Z_4 Structure of procurement-method of procuring/purchasing products within a particular company. This variable has two categories: 1 = centralized procurement, and 0 = decentralized procurement

Z_5 Type of industry-industry classification in which a product purchaser belongs. This variable has two categories: 1 = industry A classification, and 0 = other industries

Z_6 Type of buying situation-type of situation facing the purchaser. This variable has three categories: 1 = new task, 2 = modified rebuy, and 3 = straight rebuy converted to dummy variables in the analysis

16.4.2   Aggregate Conjoint Results

Table 2 presents the regression results for the entire sample of N = 100 respondents, while Figures 1 and 2 display the resulting part-worth utility charts and factor importances graphically.

Table 2:   The Aggregate Conjoint Solution

intercept	3.77**
powder	-0.05
premix	-0.52**
100 apps	0.44**
200 apps	0.81**
germfree	0.97**
biodegradable	0.15
49¢	-0.89**
79¢	-1.99**
S.E.	1.72
R^2	0.26
adj R^2	0.25
F	79.27

* $p \leq .05$
** $p \leq .01$

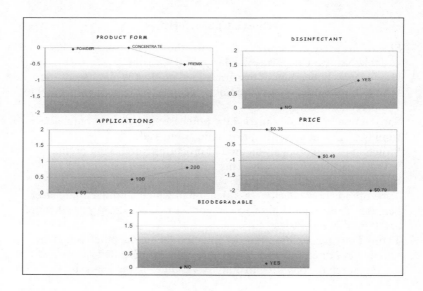

Figure 1:   Aggregate part-worth utility charts

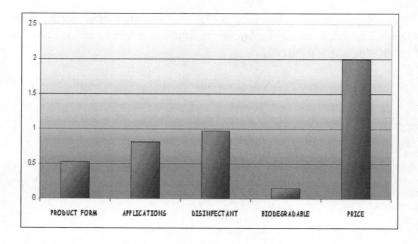

Figure 2:   Factor importance

As shown, price is the most important factor as is the case in most business-to-business studies. The disinfectant attribute appears next most important, followed by number of applications. While there is a notable aversion associated with a pre-mixed form of the product, the biodegradable feature effect is marginally significant.

16.4.3   Segment Level NORMCLUS Implementation

The primary objective for this illustrative market segmentation was to derive benefit market segments that satisfied many of the criteria discussed in Section I of this book chapter. More specifically, the client wants market segments whose benefit structures are different, whose purchase characteristics are different and identifiable, whose sizes are substantial (especially given the small sample size of 100 customers), and whose results can be easily projected to the entire customer base. Given these objectives, and the multidimensional nature of the problem, a multi-criteria objective function is defined as earlier described in the weighted utility function method. We use $\underline{X}$ to denote the design matrix converted to dummy variables, $\underline{Y}$ as the collected preference scores, and $\underline{Z}$ as the matrix of purchase characteristics. Here, we define two separate parts of the combined utility function that is to be maximized:

$$(28) \qquad f_1 = \sum_{r=1}^{R} w_r \overline{R}_r^2$$

and

$$(29) \qquad f_2 = \frac{|\mathbf{M}|}{|\mathbf{T}|} = 1 - \frac{\left|(\mathbf{Z} - \mathbf{E}\overline{\mathbf{Z}}_r)'(\mathbf{Z} - \mathbf{E}\overline{\mathbf{Z}}_r)\right|}{\left|(\mathbf{Z} - \overline{\mathbf{Z}})'(\mathbf{Z} - \overline{\mathbf{Z}})\right|}$$

where:

$$w_r = \frac{I_r}{I};$$

$\overline{R}_r^2$ = the adjusted R^2 for segment r;

M = the between segment sum-of-squares and cross-products for $\mathbf{Z}$;

T = the total sum-of-squares and cross-products for $\mathbf{Z}$.

   Thus, f_1 is the mean R-squares across each of the component segment level regressions, weighted by the fraction of the size of the sample in each segment. f_2 is an eta square measure which measures separation in the component segment purchaser characteristic variables. Note that Krieger and Green (1996) propose a bounded objective function approach to market segmentation using a K-means type of algorithm to maximize an R-square measure subject to a user specified maximum acceptable tolerance in eta square. While of interest, this EXCLU methodology cannot readily accommodate the previous constraints discussed, nor any other objective function (e.g., profit). Note that both f_1 and f_2 range between 0 and 1, and so does the combined function U in equation (1). Here, based on the available information about this manufacturing firm, we set $\alpha = .5$ to weigh each component of U equally given the nature of this specific application.

In addition, we imposed a number of other constraints on the final solutions. One, a mutually exclusive partitioning of the sample was desired into separate, non-overlapping segments. Two, no single segment should contain less than 10% of the sample in it due to financial considerations of administering to it. Finally, constraints on the segment level regression coefficients were forced in order to preserve the face validity of the study. The Appendix describes the modified lambda-opt constrained algorithm specially formulated for this particular application.

16.4.4   NORMCLUS Analysis

Table 3 depicts the combined goodness-of-fit statistic calculated for 1-4 segments. As shown, a dramatic increase occurs in moving from the aggregate (R=1) solution to two (R=2) segments. Very slight improvement is seen in moving from 3 to 4 segments. As such, we choose the R=3 segment solution to present.

Table 4 presents the regression coefficient for this three-segment solution, and Figures 3 and 4 display the contrasting part-worth utility charts and factor importances. Note the interesting pattern of part-worth heterogeneity that is captured by the methodology. The optimal product design is identical across all three segments. The regression coefficients in Table 4 look monotone increasing as one moves from segment one to two to three, with a few exceptions. All three segments find price as the most important attribute, although that importance increases near linearly across the three segments. Segment two finds the disinfectant attribute most highly relevant as compared across segments, while segment three appears to have the most sharpest preference structure of the three derived segments. This is especially pronounced with respect to price, which is over three times as important in that market segment.

Table 3:   Segment Level Goodness-of-Fit Statistics

R	Φ_R
1	0.13
2	0.63
3	0.68
4	0.70

Table 4:   The R=3 Conjoint Solution

	r = 1	r = 2	r = 3
intercept	3.85**	3.67**	3.76**
powder	-0.06	-0.11	0.04
premix	-0.40**	-0.51**	-0.78**
100 apps	0.21	0.56**	0.69**
200 apps	0.63**	0.91**	1.01**
germfree	0.95**	1.20**	0.68**
biodegradable	0.18	0.20	0.03
49¢	-0.43**	-0.72**	-2.01**
79¢	-1.28**	-2.06**	-3.22**
S.E.	1.56	1.76	1.46
R^2	0.20	0.28	0.50
adj R^2	0.19	0.28	0.50
F	23.37**	30.76**	53.55**
Size	43%	34%	23%

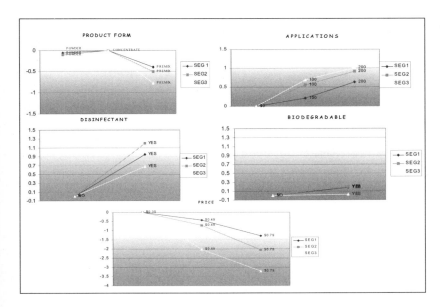

Figure 3:   Part-worth utility charts by segment

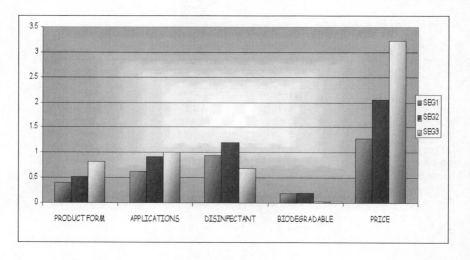

Figure 4:   Factor importance by segment

Table 5:   Segment Purchaser Characteristics

	r = 1	r = 2	r = 3
Large Size	0.26	0.71	0.22
Usage Level	51.44	36.91	49.70
Satisfaction	5.20	3.93	5.25
Centralized	0.40	0.77	0.30
Industry A	0.47	0.41	0.61
New Task	0.00	1.00	0.00
Straight Rebuy	0.56	0.00	0.44

Table 5 renders same insight as to whom these segments are (identifiability). Segment one contains smaller firms, with the largest percent usage of HATCO as a supplier, who find HATCO as a very satisfactory supplier, and are typically in a straight rebuy mode. Segment two members are the largest firms, who have the

lowest usage and satisfaction levels with HATCO, utilize very centralized purchase modes in a new task purchase scenario, and are least likely to belong to
Industry A. Finally, segment three members are your smallest firms with high
HATCO usage and satisfaction levels, utilizing non-centralized procurement, most
likely to be in Industry A, and never buy in a new task role.

16.4.5 Comparative Fits

We utilize KMEANS cluster analysis as a basis of comparison with the existing
methodology in three segments. The first analysis took the dependent variable
responses above and clustered those into three segments. The resulting goodness-
of-fit value was $\Phi = 0.129$. In the second cluster analysis, the background pur-
chaser characteristics alone were clustered into three segments producing $\Phi = 0.539$. Finally, both dependant variables and purchase characteristics were jointly
clustered into three segments producing $\Phi = 0.529$. In all cases, these naive ap-
proaches fail to out-perform the proposed combinational optimization approach on
objective mathematical criteria.

16.5 Conclusion

We have proposed a general approach to the segmentation of markets involving
conjoint analysis called NORMCLUS employing various methods in combinatorial optimization. The general approach accommodates multi-criterion objective
functions, alternative types of clustering respondents, model or profile based segmentation schemes, constraints on coefficients, constraints on segment memberships, etc. to adapt to the specific needs of the particular segmentation application
being dealt with. A variety of combinatorial algorithms are accommodated including genetic algorithms, simulated annealing, and various heuristics which are
selected according to their efficiency in dealing with the structure and goals of the
application at hand. We presented an industrial marketing application involving
benefit market segment and the development of a new industrial cleaner. A two
component utility function was formulated as a maximand and with equal weights
given the requirements in this application. In addition, a set of application specific
constraints was identified as important. The NORMCLUS three-segment solution
was presented and interpreted, with a favorable comparison made with another
traditional approach (KMEANS). We show that by trading off a small amount of
variance accounted for in the clusterwise regression portion of the multi-criterion
objective function, one can obtain describable, actionable segments that the client's management could verify/validate (based on their past experience) and gainfully utilize for marketing strategy.

Note that we have only provided one specialized application of NORMCLUS
to illustrate some of its features. In other contexts where costs and revenues are
known or reliably estimated, a more formal normative market segmentation
approach could be specified where expected profit would be a key objective to be

optimized. Future research involving such different market segmentation contexts is needed to examine NORMCLUS performance with comparisons to more traditional approaches.

16.6 Appendix

For the benefit market segmentation application discussed in Section IV, we attempt to estimate the segment membership indicators $\mathbf{M} = ((m_{ir}))$ and the cluster-wise regression coefficients $\mathbf{b}_r \geq 0$ in order to maximize:

(A-1) $\quad \Phi = \alpha_1 f_1 + \left(1 - \alpha_1\right) f_2,$

where f_1 and f_2 are defined in (28) and (29) respectively, $0<\alpha<1$ is user specified (as is R - the number of segments), and constraints (5), (6), and (12) are enforced. For this particular application, a modified lambda-opt combinatorial optimization procedure (cf. Lin and Kernighan, 1973) is devised, together with a constrained least-squares solver.
The general steps are as follows:

A Set J = 0; select n from (1,2,.....,I); Set the maximum number of iterations (MAXIT); generate random map of the sequence 1.....I, indicating the order in which customer segment memberships are altered. Evaluate Φ, and let $\Phi^*=\Phi$;

B For these n customers, change their segment memberships randomly (i.e., alter n row vectors in $\mathbf{M} = ((m_{ir}))$ and check for feasibility of all constraints. Iterate until feasibility is maintained;

C For these n customers, change their segment memberships randomly (i.e., alter n Estimate segment level regression coefficients (subject to positivity or monotonicity constraints if desired).

As an illustration, to enforce positivity constraints, a constrained optimizer must be utilized in each of the R least-squares problems implied by maximizing f_1 in (A-1), since $\mathbf{b}_r$ does not appear in (A-2). Here, we utilize a modification of the Lawson and Hansen (1972) procedure which follows directly from the Kuhn-Tucker conditions for constrained minimization. For a given r = 1,....., R, define:

(A-2) $\quad \mathbf{hr} = (hri) = M_{ir}^{1/2} \cdot y_i$

(A-3) $\quad \mathbf{Er} = \left(\left(E_{ik}^r\right)\right) = M_{ir}^{1/2} \cdot X_{ik},$

We can then reformulate this estimation problem in terms of r non-negative least-squares problems: Minimize $\|E_r b_r - h_r\|$ subject to $b_r \geq 0$, for $r = 1,\ldots,R$, (excluding such constraints on intercepts), which trivially can be shown to conditionally (holding M fixed) optimize (A-1). The algorithm, briefly outlined below follows directly from the Kuhn-Tucker conditions for constrained minimization. For a given r, we form the I x K matrix of "independent variables", E_r, and the I x 1 vector (acting as the dependent variable) h_r. In the description below, the K x 1 vectors w_r and z_r provide working spaces. Index sets P_r and Z_r will be defined and modified in the course of execution of the algorithm. Parameters indexed in the set Z_r will be held at the value zero. Parameters indexed in the set P_r will be free to take values greater than zero. If a parameter takes a non-positive value, the algorithm will either move the parameter to a positive value or else set the parameter to zero and move its index from set P_r to set Z_r. On termination, b_r will be the solution vector and w_r will be the dual vector.

1. Set $P_r := \text{Null}$, $Z_r := \{1,\ldots,K\}$, and $b_r := 0$.

2. Compute the vector $w_r := E_r'(h_r - E_r b_r)$

3. If the set Z_r is empty or if $w_{rj} \leq 0$ for all $k \in Z_r$, go to Step 12.

4. Find an index $a \in Z_r$ such that $w_{ra} = \max \{w_{rk} : k \in Z_r\}$.

5. Move the index a from set Z_r to set P_r

6. Let $E_P^{(r)} := $ denote the I x K matrix defined by

$$\text{Column k of } E_P^{(r)} := \begin{cases} \text{column k of } E_r \text{ if } k \in P_r \\ \\ 0 \text{ if } k \in Z_r \end{cases}$$

Compute the vector z_r as a solution of the least-squares problem $E_P^{(r)} z_r \cong h_r$. Note that only the components z_{rk}, $k \in P_r$, are determined by this problem. Define $z_{rk} = 0$ for $k \in Z_r$.

7. If $z_{rk} > 0$ for all $k \in P_r$, set $b_r := z_r$ and go to Step 2.

8. Find an index $v \in P_r$ such that $b_{rv}/(b_{rv} - z_{rv}) = \min \{b_{rk}/b_{rk} - z_{rk}) : z_{rk} \leq 0, k \in P_r\}$.

9. Set $Q_r := b_{rv}/(b_{rv} - z_{rv})$.

10. Set $b_r := b_r + Q_r(z_r - b_r)$.

11. Move from set P_r to set Z_r all indices $k \in P_r$ for which $\phi_{rk} = 0$. Go to Step 6.

12. Next r.

On termination, the solution vector $\mathbf{b}_r$ satisfies:

(A-4) $b_{rk} > 0, k \in P_r;$

and

(A-5) $b_{rk} = 0, k \in Z_r,$

and is a solution vector to the constrained least-squares problem:

(A-6) $\mathbf{E}_P^{(r)} \, \mathbf{br} \cong \mathbf{hr}$

The dual vector $\mathbf{w}_r$ satisfies:

(A-7) $w_{rk} = 0, k \in P_r;$

and

(A-8) $wrk \leq 0, k \in Zr,$

where:

(A-9) $\mathbf{wr} = \mathbf{E}_r \, (\mathbf{hr} - \mathbf{Erbr}).$

Equations (A-4), (A-5), (A-7), (A-8), and (A-9) constitute the Kuhn-Tucker conditions characterizing a solution vector $\mathbf{b}_r$ for this constrained least-squares problem. Equation (A-6) is a consequence of (A-5), (A-7), and (A-9). These twelve steps are then repeated for the next value of $r = 1, \ldots R$.

D   Set $J = J + 1$;

E   Evaluate Φ in trying to improve. If there is improvement, set $\Phi = \Phi^*$, store the
    M

F   and **B** that resulted in that solution, and go to step B. If no improvement, return
    to previous **M**, **B**, and Φ^* values and return to step B, unless $J > MAXIT$ in
    which case, output best solution.

16.7   References

DeSarbo, W. S. and Mahajan, V (1984), Constrained Classification: The Use of A Priori
    Information In Cluster Analysis, *Psychometrika*, 49,187-215.

DeSarbo, W. S. and Cron, W. (1988), A Conditional Mixture Maximum Likelihood Meth-
    odology for Clusterwise Linear Regression, *Journal of Classification*, 5, 249-289.

DeSarbo, W. S., Oliver, R. and Rangaswamy, A. (1989), A Simulated Annealing Methodology for Cluster-wise Linear Regression, *Psychometrika*, 54, 707-736.

DeSarbo, W. S., Wedel, M., Ramaswamy, V. and Vriens, M. (1992), Latent Class Metric Conjoint Analysis, *Marketing Letters*, 3, 273-288.

DeSarbo, W. S., Ramaswamy, V. and Cohen, S. H. (1995), Market Segmentation With Choice-Based Conjoint Analysis, *Marketing Letters*, 6, 137-47.

DeSarbo, W. S., Ramaswamy, V. and Chatterjee, R. (1995), Analyzing Constant Sum Multiple Criteria Data: A Segment Level Approach, *Journal of Marketing Research*, 32, 222-232.

DeSarbo, W. S. and Grisaffee, D. (1998), Combinatorial Optimization Approaches to Constrained Market Segmentation: An Application to Industrial Market Segmentation, *Marketing Letters*, 9, 115-134.

De Soete, G. and DeSarbo, W. S. (1991), A Latent Class Probit Model for Analyzing Pick Any/N Data, *Journal of Classification*, 8, 45-63.

Frank, R. E., Massy, W. F. and Wind, Y. (1972), *Market Segmentation*, Englewood Cliffs, NJ.

Green, P. E. (1977), A New Approach to Market Segmentation, *Business Horizons*, 20, 61-73.

Green, P. E. and Srinivasan, V. (1978), Conjoint Analysis in Consumer Research: Issues and Outlook, *Journal of Consumer Research*, 5, 103-23.

Green, P. E. and Helson, C. (1989), Cross-Validation Assessment of Alternatives to Individual Level Conjoint Analysis: A Case Study, *Journal of Marketing Research*, 26, 346-350.

Green, P. E. and Srinivasan, V. (1990), Conjoint Analysis in Marketing: New Developments with Implications for Research and Practice, *Journal of Marketing*, 54, 3-19.

Green, P. E. and Krieger, A. M. (1991), Segmenting Markets with Conjoint Analysis, *Journal of Marketing*, 55, 20-31.

Hagerty, M. R. (1985), Improving the Predictive Power of Conjoint Analysis: The Use of Factor Analysis and Cluster Analysis, *Journal of Marketing Research*, 22, 168-84.

Hair, J.F., Anderson, R.E., Tatham, R.L. and Black, W.C. (1995), *Multivariate Data Analysis*, Englewood Cliffs, N.J.

Haley, R. I. (1968), Benefit Segmentation: A Decision-Oriented Research Tool, *Journal of Marketing*, 32, 30-35.

Hartigan, J. (1975), *Clustering Algorithms*, New York.

Kamakura, W. (1988), A Least Squares Procedure for Benefit Segmentation with Conjoint Experiments, *Journal of Marketing Research*, 25, 157-67.

Kamakura, W., Wedel, M. and Agrawal, J. (1994), Concomitant Variable Latent Class Models for Conjoint Analysis, *International Journal of Research in Marketing*, 11, 451-64.

Kotler, P. (1995), *Marketing Management: Analysis, Planning, Implementation, and Control*, 9th Edition, Englewood Cliffs, NJ.

344 Wayne S. DeSarbo and Christian F. DeSarbo

Krieger, A. M. and Green, P.E. (1996), Modifying Cluster Based Segments to Enhance Agreement with an Exogenous Response Variable, *Journal of Marketing Research*, 33, 351-363.

Lawson, C. L. and Hanson, R. J. (1972), *Solving Least Squares Problems*, Englewood Cliffs, NJ.

Lin, S. and Kernighan, M. (1973), An Effective Heuristic Algorithm for the Traveling Salesman Problem, *Operations Research*, 21, 498-516.

Mahajan, V. and Jain, A. K. (1978), An Approach to Normative Segmentation, *Journal of Marketing Research*, 15, 338-345.

Moore, W. L. (1980), Levels of Aggregation in Conjoint Analysis: An Empirical Comparison, *Journal of Marketing Research*, 17, 516-523.

Ogawa, K. (1987), An Approach to Simultaneous Estimation and Segmentation in Conjoint Analysis, *Marketing Science*, 6, 66-81.

Punj, G. and Stewart, D. W. (1983), Cluster Analysis in Marketing Research: Review and Suggestions for Application, *Journal of Marketing Research*, 20, 134-48.

Rao, S. S. (1996), *Engineering Optimization, Theory and Practice*, 3rd Edition, New York, NY.

Smith, W. R. (1956), Product Differentiation and Market Segmentation as Alternative Marketing Strategies, *Journal of Marketing*, 21, 3-8.

Späth, H. (1985), *Cluster Dissection and Analysis*, New York.

Steenkamp, J.-B. and Wedel, M. (1992), Fuzzy Clusterwise Regression in Benefit Segmentation: Application and Investigation into its Validity, *Journal of Business Research*, 26, 237-49.

Stewart, D. (1981), The Application and Misapplication of Factor Analysis in Marketing Research, *Journal of Marketing Research*, 19, 51-62.

Vriens, M., Wedel, M. and Wilms, T. (1996), Metric Conjoint Segmentation Methods : A Monte Carlo Comparison, *Journal of Marketing Research*, 33, 73-85.

Wedel, M. and Kistemaker, C. (1989), Consumer Benefit Segmentation Using Clusterwise Linear Regression, *International Journal of Research in Marketing*, 6, 45-49.

Wedel, M. and Steenkamp, J.-B. (1989), Fuzzy Clusterwise Regression Approach to Benefit Segmentation, *International Journal of Research in Marketing*, 6, 241-58.

Wedel, M. and Steenkamp, J.-B. (1991), A Clusterwise Regression Method for Simultaneous Fuzzy Market Structuring and Benefit Segmentation, *Journal of Marketing Research*, 28, 385-96.

Wedel, M. and DeSarbo, W. S. (1994), A Review of Latent Class Regression Models and Their Applications, in *Advanced Methods for Marketing Research*, R. P. Bagozzi (ed.), London, 353-388.

Wedel, M. and DeSarbo, W. S. (1995), A Mixture Likelihood Approach for Generalized Linear Models, *Journal of Classification*, 12, 1-35.

Wedel, M. and Kamakura, W. (2001), *Market Segmentation: Conceptual and Methodological Foundations*, 2nd ed., Norwell, MA.

Wind, Y. (1978), Issues and Advances in Segmentation Research, *Journal of Marketing Research*, 15, 317-37.

Winter, F. W. (1979), A Cost-Benefit Approach To Market Segmentation, *Journal of Marketing*, 43, 103-111.

Wittink, D. R. and Cattin, P. (1981), Alternative Estimation Methods for Conjoint Analysis, A Monte Carlo Study, *Journal of Marketing Research*, 28, 101-06.

Wittink, D. R. and Cattin, P. (1989), Commercial Use of Conjoint Analysis: An Update, *Journal of Marketing*, 53, 91-96.

Wittink, D. R., Vriens, M. and Burhenne, W. (1994), Commercial Use of Conjoint Analysis in Europe, Results and Critical Reflections, *International Journal of Research in Marketing*, 11, 41-52.

17 Dealing with Product Similarity in Conjoint Simulations[1]

Joel Huber, Bryan Orme and Richard Miller

17.1 The Value of Choice Simulators

One of the reasons conjoint analysis has been so popular as a management decision tool has been the availability of a choice simulator. These simulators often arrive in the form of a software or spreadsheet program accompanying the output of a conjoint study. These simulators enable managers to perform 'what if' questions about their market - estimating market shares under various assumptions about competition and their own offerings. As examples, simulators can predict the market share of a new offering; they can estimate the direct and cross elasticity of price changes within a market, or they can form the logical guide to strategic simulations that anticipate short- and long-term competitive responses (Green and Krieger 1988).

Choice simulators have four stages. The first stage estimates a preference model for each individual or homogeneous segment in the survey. The second stage defines the characteristics of the competitors whose shares need to be estimated. The third stage applies the preference model to the competitive set to arrive at choice probabilities for each alternative and each segment or respondent. The final stage aggregates these probabilities across segments or individuals to predict choice shares for the market.

We pay the most attention to the third stage-estimating choice probabilities for each individual or segment. We explore the value of adjusting individual choice probabilities with two kinds of variability, each of which has a simple intuitive meaning. The first kind, product variability, occurs when a consumer simply chooses a different alternative on different choice occasions, typically through inconsistency in evaluating the alternatives. The second kind, attribute variability, occurs when a consumer is inconsistent in the relative weights or part worths applied to the attributes. As an example of this second kind of variability, consider a consumer who notices the nutrition label on breads in one shopping trip but is price sensitive in other trips. While most simulators do not distinguish between these two forms of variability, we will show that they differ strongly in their treatment of similarity. Attribute variability preserves appropriate similarity relationships among alternatives while product variability clouds them. However, attribute variability by itself allows for no residual error in choice once the part

---

[1] Originally presented at the Sawtooth Software Conference, February 2, 1999 and updated for this volume in 2006.

worth values have been simulated. Thus, to appropriately model individual choice it is necessary to include both sources of variability.

We present Randomized First Choice as a general way to „tune" conjoint simulators to market behavior. Conceptually, Randomized First Choice begins with the assumption of no variability - the highest utility alternative in the set is chosen all the time. Then it adds back levels of attribute and alternative variablity that best match choice shares in the environment. This process allows sufficient flexibility to approximate quite complex market behavior.

Mathematically, Randomized First Choice adds variation in the attribute values in addition to variation in the final product valuation. It begins with a random utility model with variability components on both the coefficients and the residual error:

(1) $U_i = X_i (\beta + E_A) + E_P$

where:

U_i = Utility of product i for an individual or homogeneous segment at a moment in time
X_i = Row vector of attribute scores for alternative i
β = Vector of part worths
E_A = Variability added to the part worths (same for all alternatives)
E_P = Variability added to product *i* (unique for each alternative)

In the simulator, the probability of choosing alternative *i* in choice set S is the probability that its randomized utility is the greatest in the set, or:

(2) $Pr(i|S) = Pr(U_i \geq U_j \text{ all } j \in S)$.

Equation 2 is estimated by using a simulator to draw U_i's from equation 1 and then simply enumerating the probabilities. To stabilize shares, group or individual choices are simulated numerous times.

Those familiar with logit will recognize that E_P is simply the error level in the logit model. The typical adjustment for scale in the logit model is mathematically equivalent to adjusting the variance of a Gumbel-distributed E_P in RFC simulations. The E_A term then reflects taste variation as has been found in models by Hausman and Wise (1978) and in work in mixed logit by Revelt and Train (1998).

The purpose of this paper is to provide an understanding of why including attribute variability is superior to just including product variability. The quick answer is that attribute variability is needed to account for expected similarity relationships whereas adding product variability clouds those relationships. The next section begins by detailing the desirable properties of any choice simulator. Then follows an experiment that demonstrates the effectiveness of adding attribute and product variability, particularly when applied to aggregate and latent class segments, but also for individual choice models generated by hierarchical Bayes and Sawtooth Software's ICE (Individual Choice Estimation).

17.2   Three Critical Properties of Market Simulators

Market simulators need three properties if they are to reflect the complexity of market behavior. First, the individual- or segment-level model must display differential impact - where the impact of a marketing action occurs as an alternative in a competitive set reaches the threshold for choice. Second, the model needs to exhibit differential substitution, a property where new alternatives take disproportionate share from similar competitors. Finally, the simulator must display differential enhancement, the idea that very similar pairs can produce disproportionately severe choice probabilities. Each of these is detailed below.

Differential Impact is a central requirement of an effective choice simulator. It reflects the property that the impact of a marketing action depends on the extent that the alternative is near the purchase threshold. This point of maximum sensitivity occurs when the value of an alternative is close to that of the most valued alternatives in the set - when the customer is on the cusp with respect to choosing the company's offering. At that time, an incremental feature or benefit is most likely to win the business.

The differential impact implicit in a threshold model can best be understood by examining three cases reflecting different kinds of thresholds. First we present the linear probability model which importantly defines the case of no threshold. Then we examine the other extreme, that of a first choice model, which has the most extreme step-like threshold. Finally we consider the standard choice models (logit, probit) whose threshold has been softened by the addition of variability.

If probability is a linear function of utility, then improving an attribute has the same effect on choice share regardless of how well it is liked. There are many problems with this linear probability model, the worst of which is a lack of differential impact. Under a linear probability model adding, say, an internal fax modem has the same share impact regardless of whether it is added to a high- or low-end computer. By contrast, a threshold choice model specifies that the benefit from adding the modem mainly affects those consumers who are likely to change their behavior. This makes good sense - adding the feature does not affect a person who would have bought the brand anyway, nor does it affect customers who would never consider it. Managerially, the differential impact brought about by a threshold model has the benefit of focusing managerial attention on the critical marginal customer, and thereby avoids expensive actions that are unlikely to alter market behavior.

The first-choice model offers an extreme contrast to the linear model. The first choice model is mathematically equivalent to Equation 1 with no variability ($\text{var}(E_P) = \text{var}(E_A) = 0$). In the first choice simulation, share of an alternative is zero until its value is greater than others in the set. Once its value exceeds that threshold, however, it receives 100%. The problem with the first choice model is that it is patently false. We know that people do not make choices without variability. In studies of experimental choices, given the same choice set (3-4 alternatives, 4-5 attributes) respondents choose a different alternative about 20% of the time. In our study, respondents chose a different alternative in the repeated task 19% of the time. One of the paradoxes we hope to resolve in this paper is why the first choice model operating on individual-level part worths works so well despite its counter-factual premise.

Standard logit and probit models reflect a compromise between the first-choice and linear model. Instead of the severe step function characteristic of the first choice model, the variablity implicit in these models moderates the step into a smooth s-shape or sigmoid function. As shown in Equations 1 and 2, these models are identical to first-choice models with variability added. For logit, E_P has a Gumbel, while for Probit, it has a Normal distribution. It is important to note, however, that these models are, to use a technical phrase, linear-in-the-parameters. Thus the *utility* of an item generally increases the same amount with a given improvement, however, the *probability of purchase* follows a threshold model.

A little-understood benefit of a threshold model is that it can reflect complex patterns of interactions between, say, a feature and a particular brand simply through the simulation process. An interaction term specifies that a particular feature has a differential impact on particular brands. While these interaction terms can be reflected in the utility function, we propose that many interactions can be better represented as arising from the aggregation of heterogeneous customers each following a threshold model. For example, consider a warranty x price interaction indicating that a warranty is more valuable for low- over high-priced appliances. The same effect could also emerge in a simulation of respondents under a threshold rule. Suppose there are two segments, one valuing low price and the other desiring high quality. Adding a warranty to the low-priced brand might not be sufficient to raise it past the purchase threshold of those desiring high quality. By contrast, the warranty pushes the alternative past the threshold of those desiring low prices. When these two segments are aggregated it appears that the warranty mainly helps the low priced brand and thus appears to justify an interaction term in the utility function. However, the same behavior can be reflected in a simulator with a threshold model. The heterogeneity account has the further advantage of being more managerial actionable than the curve-fitting exercise of the cross term.

The greatest difficulty with interaction terms is that their numbers can grow uncontrollably large. Above we illustrated an example of price tiers, but there can be many others. Consider combinations of brand tiers where customers are simply not interested in certain brands; size tiers where a large size never passes the threshold for certain segments, and feature tiers, where certain groups are only interested in certain features. Modeling these with interaction terms in the utility function is both complicated and can lead to problems with overfitting or misspecification. The beauty of a simulator operating on segmented or individual models is that it can approximate this behavior in the context of a simple main-effects additive model (e.g., see as Orme and Heft).

To summarize, differential impact is critical if we believe that impact on choice of, say, a new feature of a brand depends on values of the brands against which it competes. The threshold model within a random utility formulation focuses managerial attention on those alternatives that are on the cusp, and in that way places less emphasis on alternatives that are already chosen, or would never be. Further, applying the threshold model at the level of the individual or homogeneous segment confers the additional benefit of isolating the differential impact appropriately within each.

Differential Substitution is the second property critical to an effective choice simulator. Its intuition follows from the idea that a new offering takes share disproportionately from similar ones. Differential substitution is particularly important because the dominant choice model, aggregate logit displays *no* differential substitution. The logit assumption of proportionality implies that a new offering that gets, say, 20% of a market will take from each competitor in proportion to its initial share. Thus a brand with an initial 40% share loses 8 percentage points (40% x .2) and one with 10% share loses 2 percentage points (10% x .2). Proportionality provides a naive estimate of substitution effects and can result in managerially distorted projections where there are large differences in the degree of similarity among brands in the market. For example, a product line extension can be expected to take proportionately most share from its sibling brands. Managers recognize this problem. Successful companies manage their portfolios with new brands that are strategically designed to maximize share taken from competitors and minimize internal share losses. By contrast, proportionality glosses over such strategically important distinctions. Ignoring differential substitution could lead to the managerial nightmare of numerous line extensions whose cost to current brands is regularly underestimated.

An extreme, if instructive, example of differential substitution is the presence of a duplicate offering in the choice set. Economic theory often posits that a duplicate offering should take half the share of its twin, but none from its competitor. However, in practice this expectation is rarely met. If some consumers randomly pick a brand without deleting duplicates, then having a duplicate could increase total choice share. Indeed, the fight for shelf space is directed at capturing that random choice in the marketplace. To the extent that a duplicate brand increases the total share for that brand, we label the increase in total share from a duplicate *share inflation*. Clearly some share inflation is needed, but it is unclear how much. In the empirical test we measure the extent to which simulators reflect differential enhancement by how well they correctly predict the combined share of near substitutes in the holdout choice sets.

Differential enhancement is the third property needed by choice simulators. It specifies a second, but less commonly recognized way product similarity affects choices. Under differential enhancement, pairs of highly similar alternatives display more severe choice differences. Psychologically, this phenomenon derives from the idea that similar alternatives are often easier to compare than dissimilar ones. Consider the choice between French Roast coffee, Jamaican Blend coffee and English Breakfast tea. A change in the relative freshness of the coffees can be expected to enhance the relative share of the fresher coffee, while having relatively little impact on the proportion choosing tea.

In its extreme form, differential enhancement arises where one offering *dominates* another in the choice set. Rational economic theory typically posits that the dominated alternative receives no share, while the shares of the other brands are unaffected. Market behavior is rarely as neat. There are few purely dominated alternatives in the market. Even finding two otherwise identical cans of peas in the supermarket can lead to suspicion that the lower priced one is older. Determining dominance requires work that consumers may be unwilling or unable to perform. For that reason, manufacturers intentionally create differences between offerings (new line, different price, channel), so that dominance, or near dominance is less apparent. From a modeling perspective, the important point is that any choice simulator needs to allow both for dominance to produce cases of extreme probability differences and to allow consumers to be fallible in their ability to recognize that dominance.

The modeling implications of differential enhancement parallel those for differential substitution. The standard logit or probit models assume that the relative shares of any pair of alternatives only depend on their values, not on their relative similarity. Referring to a classic example, if trips to Paris and to London are equally valued, then a logit model predicts that adding a second trip to Paris with a one-dollar discount will result in one-third shares for the three alternatives. There are numerous ways researchers have attempted to solve this problem, from nested logit to correlated error terms within probit. Within the Sawtooth Software family Model 3 penalizes items that share attribute levels with other alternatives in the choice set. We will show that a simple first choice simulation with suitable variability added to both attributes and alternatives provides a robust way to mirror these complex market realities.

17.3   A Market Study to Validate Choice Simulators

As we approached the task of comparing the ability of different choice simulators to deal with varying degrees of alternative similarity, it became apparent that choice sets typically used for choice experiments would not work discriminate between models. For the sake of efficiency, most choice experiments feature alternatives where the numbers of levels differing among pairs of alternatives are relatively constant. For example, it would not typically make sense to include a near alternative twice since its inclusion adds so little additional information. In this study we deliberately add alternatives which are duplicates or near duplicates to be able to test the ability of various simulators to appropriately handle these difficult choices.

Three hundred ninety-eight respondents completed computerized surveys in a mall intercept conducted by Consumer Pulse, Inc. The survey involved preference for mid-sized televisions and was programmed using Sawtooth Software's Ci3 and CBC systems. Respondents over 18 who owned a television or were considering purchasing a mid-sized television set in the next 12 months qualified for the survey. The first part of the interview focused on attribute definitions (described in terms of benefits) for the six attributes included in the design. The main part of the survey involved 27 choices among televisions they might purchase. Each choice involved five televisions described with six attributes: brand name (3 levels), screen size (3 levels), picture-in-picture (available, not), channel blockout (available, not) and price (4 levels). Table 1 gives an example of a choice set that illustrates the levels. We gave respondents a $4.00 incentive to complete the survey, and urged them to respond carefully.

Table 1:   Example of a Holdout Choice Set

25" JVC, Stereo, Picture in Picture, No Blockout, $350	26" RCA, Surround Sound, Picture in Picture, Blockout, $400	25" JVC, Monaural, No Picture in Picture, No Blockout $300

27" Sony, Surround Sound, No Picture in Picture, No Blockout $450	25" JVC, Stereo, Picture in Picture, No Blockout, $350

Preliminary data from a small pre-test suggested that respondents were not giving sufficient effort to answer consistently. In an attempt to improve the quality of the data, we revised the survey. We told them that the computer would „learn" from their previous answers and know if they were answering carefully or not. The „computer" would reward them with an extra $1.00 at the end of the survey if they had „taken their time and done their task well." (We displayed a password for them to tell the attendant.) In terms of programming the survey logic, we rewarded them based on a combination of elapsed time for a particular section of the survey and test-retest reliability for a repeated holdout task. Though it is difficult to prove (given the small sample size of the pretest), we believe the revision resulted in cleaner data. Nearly two-thirds of the 398 respondents received the extra dollar. We discarded 46 respondents based on response times to choice tasks that were unusually low, leaving 352 for analysis.

The first 18 choice tasks were CBC randomized choice sets that did not include a „None" option. After completing the CBC tasks, respondents were shown an additional nine holdout choice tasks, again including five alternatives. The holdout tasks were different in two respects. First, to test the market share predictions of the different simulators, it was critical to have target sets for which market shares could be estimated. Respondents were randomly divided into four groups with approximately 90 in each group that would receive the same nine holdout choice tasks. Additionally, we designed the holdout choices to have some extremely similar alternatives. Four of the five alternatives in the holdout tasks were carefully designed to have approximate utility and level balance (Huber and Zwerina 1996). However, the fifth alternative duplicated another alternative in the set, or duplicated all attributes except the two judged least important in a pretest. To provide an estimate of test-retest reliability, each respondent evaluated two choice sets that were perfect replicates. Across respondents, the computer randomized both choice set and product concept order.

17.4   The Contenders

We analyzed the CBC data using four base methods for estimating respondent part worth utilities: Aggregate Logit, Latent Class, Sawtooth Software's ICE (Individual Choice Estimation) and Hierarchical Bayes (courtesy of Neeraj Arora, Virginia Tech). There is logic behind picking these four methods. Aggregate logit is important in that it reflects what happens when all respondents are pooled into one choice model. By contrast, latent class analysis seeks sets of latent segments (we used an eight-group solution) whose part worths best reflect the heterogeneity underlying the choices (Kamakura and Russell 1989; Chintagunta, Jain and Vilcassim 1991; DeSarbo, Ramaswamy and Cohen 1995). ICE then takes these segments and builds a logit model that predicts each individual's choices as a function of these segments (Johnson 1997). It thereby is able to estimate a utility function for each person. Hierarchical Bayes assumes respondents are random draws from a distribution of part worth utilities with a specific mean and variance. It produces a posterior estimate of each individual's part worths reflecting the heterogeneous prior conditioned by the particular choices each individual makes (Lenk, DeSarbo, Green and Young 1996; Arora, Allenby and Ginter 1998). Both ICE and hierarchical Bayes reflect current attempts to generate each individual's utility functions from choice data, while latent class and aggregate logit typify popular ways to deal with markets as groups.

For each of these base models we examine the impact of adding three levels of variability within the Randomized First Choice framework. The initial condition is the first choice rule that assumes respondents choose the highest valued alternative in a choice set with certainty. The second condition adds the level of product variability that best predicts holdout choice shares. This latter condition is identical to adjusting the scale under the logit rule to best predict these shares. The third condition tunes both product and attribute variability to best predict the holdout choice shares. The mechanism of the tuning process is simple but tedious: we use a grid search of different levels of each type of variability until we find those that minimize the mean absolute error in predicting holdout choice shares.

17.5   Results

We examine the ability of different simulators to handle product similarity from different perspectives. First, we measure deviations from predicted and actual share for the duplicates and near-duplicates that were included in the holdout choice sets. This focus enables us to uncover ways the various models appropriately account for differential substitution and differential enhancement. Then we broaden our perspective to consider the overall fit of the models - how well the models predict choice shares for all items in the choice set.

Differential substitution requires that similar items take disproportionate share from each other. Thus, our near and perfect substitutes should cannibalize share from each other. For example, if an alternative would receive 20% share individually, the joint share of the two alternatives should be only marginally more than 20%, since the new one takes most of its share from its twin. A first choice simulator, with its assumption of zero variability puts the joint share at exactly 20%, but in the marketplace this combined share is likely to be somewhat higher. Put differently, due to fundamental noise in the consumer choice processes we can expect some share inflation.

Table 2 gives predicted combined share of the near and perfect substitutes divided by the actual share. Thus, a value of 100% means that the degree of differential substitution reflected in the holdout choices was estimated perfectly. Notice that the first choice rule underestimates the joint share of the near substitutes by about 10%, indicating that the first choice rule of no variability is too severe. The next column shows the result of adding the level of product variability that best predicts the holdouts. In this case, adding that variability seriously overestimates the share inflation for the near substitutes, in effect, assuming too much variability. The third column then adjusts both product and attribute variability to optimally predict choice shares. By allowing some attribute variability to substitute for product variability, we are able to more closely track actual differential substitution in this data set for all models except ICE.

It is also instructive to compare the rows representing the four core models. The two aggregate models, logit and latent class, suffer most from overestimation of share inflation under product variability. However, when both forms of variability are combined, they do remarkably well. The two individual models appear both less sensitive to the addition of variation and less in need of it. We will discuss the implications of this phenomenon after the other results from the study are presented.

Differential enhancement occurs when a given quality difference results in a greater share difference between highly similar pairs. We examine the share difference between the alternative with higher expected share and its near duplicate. Table 3 gives the model's prediction of this difference as a percent of the actual difference. Once again a score of 100% indicates perfect level of differential enhancement relative to the actual choices.

The two aggregate models with product variability only are the least effective in representing the differential enhancement reflected in the holdout choices. In contrast, the first choice rule applied to the individual level models performs very well in this case. In all cases, adding the optimal level of product variability tends to understate desired levels of differential enhancement. Optimizing both kinds of variability has a small incremental benefit but results in predictions that still underestimate the appropriate level of differential enhancement.

Table 2:   *Differential Substitution: Predicted Combined Share of Near Substitutes As Percent of Actual Share*

	First Choice Rule	Product Variability	+Attribute Variability
Aggregate Logit	N/A	139%	108%
Latent Class	N/A	119%	105%
Hierarchical Bayes	91%	117%	104%
ICE	89%	101%	94%

Table 3:   *Differential Enhancement: Predicted Difference between Similar Alternatives As Percent of Actual Differences*

	First Choice Rule	Product Variability	+Attribute Variability
Aggregate Logit	N/A	63%	73%
Latent Class	N/A	71%	74%
Hierarchical Bayes	100%	73%	77%
ICE	90%	77%	79%

It needs to be emphasized that these measures of differential substitution and enhancement only relate to the shares of near substitutes. By contrast, the optimization to choice shares counts all five alternatives, not just the two most similar ones. The overestimation of differential substitution shown in the last column of Table 2 and the underestimation of differential enhancement in the last column of Table 3 could have been improved by decreasing the level of product variability, but overall fit would have suffered. An interesting implication of this result is that the actual variability around judgments relating to the share sums and share differences of these near substitutes may be smaller than for alternatives generally. An interesting path for future research involves allowing variability to change as a function of similarity of an alternative within each set.

Table 4:   Relative Error: Mean Absolute Error Predicting Market Share As Percent of Test-Retest

	First Choice Rule	Product Variability	+Attribute Variability
Aggregate Logit	N/A	151%	112%
Latent Class	N/A	117%	105%
Hierarchical Bayes	125%	110%	107%
ICE	112%	106%	106%

Relative error measures the degree that the different simulators predict the market shares across all alternatives in the holdout tasks for the study. Table 4 shows mean absolute error (MAE) predicting holdout stimuli as a percent of the test-retest MAE for repeated choice sets. For example, the 151% for aggregate logit indicates that adding product variability only results in an error that is about one and one-half times as great as for the choice replication. Adding attribute variability helps all models, but the greatest gains occur for the aggregate models.

The Table 4 offers several surprises. The first surprise is that Randomized First Choice applied to latent class does as well as any of the models. The positive impact of both kinds of variability on latent class makes sense because the original latent class model assumes that there is no heterogeneity within each latent class. By optimizing both product and attribute variability we are able to transform latent class from an elegant but counterfactual model into one that tracks choice shares remarkably well.

The second surprise is that the addition of attribute variability has very little impact on either of the individual level models. For both hierarchical Bayes and ICE the addition of product variability is the major benefit. We believe there is a simple reason for this result. The individual level models are not estimated with perfect accuracy, but have significant variation due to the noise in individual choices and the fact that many parameters are being estimated from relatively few observations. Thus, when estimates from these models are put in a simulator they act as if variability has already been added to the part worths. However, in this case instead of attribute variability coming from the RFC process, it comes from the inherent variability in the estimation model. This insight then leads to an important conclusion: where variability in the estimation technique is greater than in the market, then the optimal variability to add to the first choice model will be zero (see also Elrod and Kumar 1989).

The final surprise is that Randomized First Choice predictions are quite good regardless of the core estimation method used (except aggregate logit). That is, using RFC produces accuracy that is within 10% of what one would get asking the same question again. Clearly few techniques are going to do much better than that. There simply is not much room for further improvement.

Before concluding, it is important to briefly mention Sawtooth Software's Model 3, a long-available method that accounts for item similarity in a simulation. Model 3 operates by penalizing alternatives that have high numbers of levels in common with other attributes in a choice set. It does so in such a way that adding a perfect duplicate perfectly splits share with its twin when these duplicates share no levels in common with the other alternatives. Model 3 acts like the first choice model in assuming that there is zero share inflation from adding an identical alternative, thereby underestimating the joint share of the two identical alternatives for the holdout choices in our study. Further, Model 3 reflects a relatively simple (and inflexible) rule regarding differential substitution and does not address differential enhancement at all. Since Model 3 is not a theoretically complete model of similarity effects, it did not surprise us that for our study Model 3 was consistently outperformed by RFC. In our view, Sawtooth Software users should replace Model 3 with RFC.

17.6   Summary and Conclusions

The purpose of this paper has been to examine ways to build choice simulators that correctly reflect similarity effects. We began with the introduction of three principles needed for sound conjoint simulations, and in the light of those principles developed Randomized First Choice. RFC provides better choice share predictions by determining the optimal levels of attribute and product variability when generating simulated choices.

The first requirement of effective simulators is that they reflect differential impact. This property permits the simulator to focus managerial attention on those actions that are most likely to impact their customers. In addition, a little-known implication of the threshold model at the level of a segmented (e.g. latent class) or individual model is that it automatically allows for various kinds of price and offering tiers without the necessity of interaction terms. The cost of losing that benefit is best illustrated by the poor performance of the aggregate logit simulation, even with variability added. In simple, main-effects aggregate logit, there is no way the threshold effect can display the action of different segments. Either the homogeneous segments from latent class or individual models are necessary for that benefit.

Effective simulators also need to reflect differential substitution. Our analysis of the combined share of near and perfect substitutes indicates that the first choice model underestimates, while adding product variablity overestimates their combined share. The joint optimizations of both product and attribute variability then permit the estimates of combined share to closely approximate the actual choices. One can tune the appropriate balance of differential substitution/share inflation.

The third requirement of effective simulators is that they demonstrate differential enhancement. We illustrated this requirement by examining the share difference of nearly identical alternatives. The first choice rule overestimates differential enhancement in aggregate models by giving all share to the preferred alternative. By contrast, adding product variability underestimates the predicted share differences. Adjusting both kinds of variability improved this underestimation but did not solve it completely. Since differential enhancement comes in part from a psychological mechanism whereby decisions between similar alternatives are easier, a full solution to this problem may await models that adjust item variability to the difficulty in making the choice.

We demonstrated the benefits of RFC on a study in which the holdout choices included „difficult" alternatives that included near and true duplicates. However, a greater benefit for Sawtooth Software users may come in contexts where it is possible to project to actual market shares. Most markets will have far more complicated similarity structures than our simple problem, resulting from competition among family brands, different sizes, price tiers and subbrands. We believe that RFC with its two kinds of variability will be very useful in tuning the simulator to successfully account for market behavior in such cases.

17.7 References

Arora, N., Allenby, G. and Ginter, J. L. (1998), A Hierarchical Bayes Model of Primary and Secondary Demand, *Marketing Science,* 17, 29-44.

Chintagunta, P., Jain, D. C. and Vilcassim, N. J. (1991), Investigating Heterogeneity in Brand Preferences in Logit Models for Panel Data, *Journal of Marketing Research,* 28, 417-428.

DeSarbo, W. S., Ramaswamy, V. and Cohen, S. H. (1995), Market Segmentation with Choice-Based Conjoint Analysis, *Marketing Letters,* 6, 137-148.

Elrod, T. and Kumar, S. K. (1989), Bias in the First Choice Rule for Predicting Share, *Sawtooth Software Conference Proceedings.*

Green, P. E and Krieger, A. M. (1988), Choice Rules and Sensitivity Analysis in Conjoint Simulators, *Journal of the Academy of Marketing Science,* 16, 114-127.

Hausman, J. and Wise, G. (1978), A Conditional Probit Model for Quantitative Choice: Discrete Decisions Recognizing Interdependence and Heterogeneous Preferences, *Econometrica,* 43, 403-426.

Huber, J. and Zwerina, K. (1996), The Importance of Utility Balance in Efficient Choice Designs, *Journal of Marketing Research,* 23, 307-317.

Johnson, R. M. (1997), ICE: Individual Choice Estimation, *Sawtooth Software Technical Paper*.

Kamakura, W. A. and Russell, G. J. (1989), A Probabilistic Choice Model for Market Segmentation and Elasticity Structure, *Journal of Marketing Research*, 26, 339-390.

Lenk, P. J., DeSarbo, W. S., Green, P. E. and Young, M. R. (1996), Hierarchical Bayes Conjoint Analysis: Recovery of Partworth Heterogeneity from Reduced Experimental Designs *Marketing Science*, 15, 173-191.

Orme, B. K. and Heft, M. (1999), Predicting Actual Sales with CBC: How Capturing Heterogeneity Improves Results, *Sawtooth Software Conference Proceedings*.

Revelt, D. and Train, D. (1998), Mixed Logit with Repeated Choices: Household's Choices of Appliance Efficiency Level, *Review of Economics and Statistics*, forthcoming.

Rossi, P. and Allenby, G. (1993), A Bayesian Approach to Estimating Household Parameters, *Journal of Marketing Research*, 30, 171-182.

Addendum 2006

For this latest edition of *Conjoint Measurement*, the authors asked us to revisit this article and provide new insights and an update.

After publishing this article here and in the *1999 Sawtooth Software Proceedings* we later re-analyzed the data and published the results in *Marketing Research*, winter 2000. After writing the earlier articles, we had recognized that in tuning the two types of error in Randomized First Choice (RFC) to best predict holdouts, we were risking the possibility of overfitting and potentially overstating the benefit of RFC. We addressed this possibility in the 2000 *Marketing Research* article by splitting the sample into two matched replicates. We re-estimated the models within each of the replicates (this time using Sawtooth Software's commercial CBC/HB routine, which had not been available for the earlier work). We tuned the product and attribute errors for RFC on the first half of the sample and applied those error amounts to new respondents in the other half. Only the second group of respondents was used for predicting holdouts. The new overall error (relative to test-retest reliability) is given below, with the previous error rates as published in this article shown in parentheses:

	First Choice Rule	Product Variability	+Attribute Variability
Aggregate Logit	N/A	155% (151%)	121% (112%)
Latent Class	N/A	122% (117%)	113% (105%)
Hierarchical Bayes	116% (125%)	111% (110%)	107% (107%)

We were pleased to see that the essential findings held: RFC offered an improvement over tuning only for scale (product variability only). As before, the benefit was greatest for the aggregate models.

We have now had about eight years experience working with Randomized First Choice simulation models. Sawtooth Software added the capability to its commercial market simulator, even making it the default simulation method. In general, it has worked well. It should not surprise the reader that we have learned a few things: both how to improve RFC and also regarding weaknesses.

Eight years ago, the majority of Sawtooth Software customers were using aggregate models: logit or latent class. RFC clearly provided a benefit in these cases. Lately, the majority of Sawtooth Software customers are using part worths estimated under HB. For these customers, RFC provides modest improvements. Thus, the popularity and effectiveness of HB has in turn reduced the impact that RFC has in our industry.

Some HB users (especially academics) prefer to use the draws within choice simulators rather than the point estimates, as we applied in this research. It could be argued that HB provides more empirically correct draws of random error around point estimates (parameter-specific estimated variances) rather than RFC's simple assumption of uniform error variance across the parameters. In 2000, Orme and Baker compared the use of RFC to HB draws, again in terms of fitting holdout choices. They tuned both HB draws (product error only) and RFC operating on the HB point estimates (both product and attribute error) to best predict holdouts. The relative error rates were 107% and 109% for RFC and HB draws, respectively. The authors concluded that using the huge HB draws file was unnecessary, and RFC's simpler model performed equally well or better.

In the 2004 Sawtooth Software Conference, Allenby *et al.* pointed out that standard HB models can face what they termed "IIA Meltdown" when very many alternatives (such as 84 alternatives in a beverage category or even more alternatives in the automobile category) are in the choice design. Although they proposed a different model from RFC, their findings that the standard HB simulators face greater IIA troubles as the number of alternatives increased suggests that RFC may be even more useful in these cases.

We have also noted a weakness with RFC simulations. The simple RFC model assumes that all attributes involve a correction for product similarity. However, it is not clear that this should be the case. For instance, price represents an attribute for which it isn't clear that product similarity should apply. Some analysts like to derive demand curves via sensitivity analysis within choice simulators. Under RFC, if all products are first aligned on the average price (and the "test" product systematically varied across all price levels), an unwanted "kink" will occur in the demand curves around the point that was artificially chosen as the average price. When the test product is changed from the average to the next higher price point (and all others remain at the average price), it sometimes receives a boost in share due to its becoming less similar that nearly counteracts the penalty from becoming more expensive. One solution to this problem is to apply independent error to the price part worths for all alternatives in the simulation. This gives rise to a more sophisticated RFC simulator, where some attributes involve correlated error (when product alternatives share the same levels of these attributes) and other attributes involve uncorrelated errors (when product alternatives receive independent random error draws for these attributes, irrespective of shared levels).

There is another opportunity for analysts to improve RFC modeling. Some conjoint/choice designs involve many alternatives. Beverages and automobiles are good examples. Suppose we had conducted a choice study with 200 automobile makes, including trucks, minivans, sedans, and coupes. Further suppose that we had treated the makes (for part worth estimation) as independent levels of a 200-level attribute. However, we know that these 200 makes fall into four clear categories that should reflect increased competition within each category. One could assume a new attribute with four levels (truck, minivan, sedan, and coupe) for which we apply attribute-type error under RFC in choice simulations.

We should also note that as the number of alternatives in the simulated choice scenario increases, the number of draws used in RFC should also be increased. Otherwise, the random error involved with RFC may be uncomfortably large relative to the signal associated with some relatively tiny product shares.

Finally, given the strong performance of ICE (Individual Choice Estimation) for this data set, the reader might wonder why Sawtooth Software's ICE program is not used much any more and essentially has been abandoned by Sawtooth Software. Although it worked quite well for this dataset (and many others), it hasn't been as generally robust as HB. ICE can be problematic with sparse datasets (many parameters to estimate relative to the number of choice tasks at the individual level). HB has been widely embraced by the industry and is more theoretically appealing. Given the speed of computers today, it is also very manageable for most every practical data set, with run times seldom exceeding a few hours.

Additional References:

Allenby, Greg, Jeff Brazell, Tim Gilbride, and Thomas Otter (2004), Avoiding IIA Meltdown: Choice Modeling with Many Alternatives, *Sawtooth Software Conference Proceedings*.

Orme, Bryan and Gary Baker (2000), Comparing Hierarchical Bayes Draws and Randomized First Choice for Conjoint Simulations, *Sawtooth Software Conference Proceedings*.

Orme, Bryan and Joel Huber (2000), Improving the Value of Conjoint Simulations, *Marketing Research*, winter 2000.

18 Sales Forecasting with Conjoint Analysis by Addressing Its Key Assumptions with Sequential Game Theory and Macro-Flow Modeling

David B. Whitlark and Scott M. Smith

18.1   Introduction

Conjoint analysis is a research tool for assessing market potential, predicting market share and forecasting sales of new or improved products and services. In general, conjoint analysis follows a two-step process, i.e., (1) estimating utilities for varying levels of product features and (2) simulating marketplace preferences for established, improved, and/or new products. Conjoint analysis was introduced in the 1970s (Green and Rao 1971) and by 1980 had logged more than 1000 commercial applications (Cattin and Wittink 1982). During the 1980s usage increased tenfold (Wittink and Cattin 1989). Today it may be the most widely used quantitative product development tool in the U.S. and Europe (Wittink, Vriens, and Burhenne 1994).

Much of the research about conjoint analysis *as a method* has focused on different approaches for estimating utilities. The four most popular methods for collecting conjoint data and estimating utilities are the full-profile method (Green and Wind 1975), the self-explicated method (Srinivasan 1988; Srinivasan and Park 1997) the adaptive method (Johnson 1987) and the choice method (Louviere 1988). Each method has its strengths, weaknesses and optimal applications (Huber 1997).

Compared to the effort focused on utility estimation methods, over the past thirty years, preference simulation and its underlying dynamics such as competitive action-reaction sequences have been widely overlooked (Green, Krieger, and Wind 2001). Once moving past utility estimation, the conjoint analysis model actually has many key assumptions. In our experience, addressing these assumptions has a profound influence on estimates of market share and product sales.

Market share estimates and sales forecasts obtained from conjoint analysis simulations are often built upon broad, inaccurate assumptions, including; (1) no competitive reaction, (2) 100 percent product awareness, (3) 100 percent saturation of the distribution channels, i.e., 100 percent product availability, (4) uniform usage rates across all customers, and (5) 100 percent product repurchase rate To be accurate, sales forecasts based on conjoint data should take into account possible competitive reactions, changes in product awareness and availability,, and other marketplace realities such as varying usage rates and repurchase rates that unfold over time. The purpose of the article is to outline how sequential game theory and the macro-flow model can be applied to more accurately fit these assumptions when estimating market share and forecasting product sales.

18.2   The Impact of Competitive Reaction on Marketing Mix Decisions

Thinking one move ahead can make the difference between success and failure when managing the marketing mix. Business managers all have stories about how plans to gain competitive advantage have turned into a financial disaster because their "big marketing tactic" was matched by their competitors, or their marketing plan did not perform to plan.

A leading manufacturer of agricultural pesticides offers a sobering cautionary tale for managers that ignore competitive actions and reactions. To gain a marketing advantage, the pesticide manufacturer decided to add a performance assurance program to their marketing mix. The guarantee promised to re-spray agricultural crops for which their pesticide did not meet certain efficacy criteria. Managers felt confident the company would gain many new customers and retain old customers because of the assurance program. Unfortunately managers did not consider the potential impact of competitive reaction. Within a week of announcing their performance assurance program, the major competitors all announced similar assurance programs. The competitive advantage lasted less than a week. Incidentally, pesticide efficacy is heavily influenced by weather conditions. For the next two years unfavorable weather prevailed and pesticide manufacturers spent millions of dollars re-spraying crops. None of the manufacturers wanted to be the first to withdraw their guarantee. But in the end, the company that first offered the program became the first to end the program. The company lost profits, customers, and brand equity because they did not consider the potential impact of competitive reaction.

Conjoint analysis simulations do not automatically address the possibility of competitive reaction. Fortunately, once simulations are supplemented with sequential game theory and game trees, conjoint analysis can become a powerful tool for making managerial decisions in the context of competitive reaction.

18.3   Incorporating Competitive Reaction into Market Share Estimates

As a point for discussion of how to integrate competitive reaction into market share estimates, consider a leading packaged goods company, "Softy," that sells a premium line as well as a cost-conscious line of disposable diapers. The manufacturer believes their premium line of diapers is losing sales to competitors that have matched their premium features, but at a lower price point. The manufacturer does not want to reduce their own prices and risk losing sales on their cost-conscious line. Instead, they decide to re-engineer their premium diaper by adding new high-value features. Using conjoint analysis they identify two product alternatives, i.e., Diaper A and Diaper B. For each alternative, managers can anticipate a different market share, a different set of competitive reactions, and a different set of payoffs for the company and its main competitor. The situation fits the definition of a sequential game, that is, a situation for which opponents take turns, know what has happened in the past, and can look forward and then reason back (Osborne 2003). Sequential games are represented using a game tree and solved using backward induction. Predictions using sequential game theory are managerially conservative in that they normatively assume that competitors will respond with a solution that is best for them.

Figure 1:   Softy Diaper Game Tree

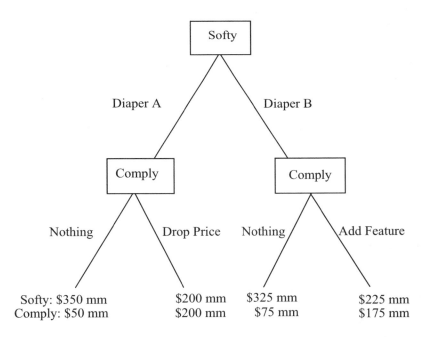

Figure 1 shows a game tree for the decisions facing the diaper manufacturer and their main competitor, "Comply". For each branch of the game tree, the conjoint analysis preference simulation generates a unique market share estimate for the diaper alternatives and, depending on the blend of price and features, it shows how the main competitor may respond and be affected by the product introduction.

Each diaper generates a different payoff for Softy and Comply. The payoffs can be calculated in terms of revenue or, better, in terms of contribution to profit over and above manufacturing costs. This is a simple example. More than one competitor can be included in a game tree as well as more than one action-reaction sequence.

We solve the game tree by working backwards from the payoffs. Again referring to the simple situation shown in Figure 1, if Softy introduces Diaper A, then Comply may do nothing resulting in a payoff of $50mm or could drop the price of their premium diaper resulting in a payoff of $200 mm. Based on "backwards induction," one can conclude that if Softy introduces Diaper A, then Comply will react with a price drop resulting in a $200 mm payoff for Softy. On the other hand, if Softy introduces Diaper B, then Comply may do nothing resulting in a payoff of $75 mm or could add a new feature to their premium diaper resulting in a payoff of $175mm. One can conclude that if Softy introduces Diaper B, then Comply will react by adding a new feature resulting in a $225 mm payoff for Softy. In this case, Softy should plan on introducing Diaper B. Diaper B is the optimal choice because the competitor's best reaction to Diaper B earns $225 mm for Softy which is $25 mm better than Softy could do from introducing Diaper A assuming the competitor acts in their own best interest.

18.4   Incorporating Time Dependent Market Changes

Game trees are a good place to start when anticipating competitive reaction. However, game trees are static. History shows the effectiveness of competitive reactions increase with time. When building sales forecasts we should try to account for the increasing effectiveness of competitive reactions.

Product awareness and availability, like competitive reactions, are also not static, they develop over time. It takes time for people to learn about a new product and for the product to appear in retail stores. The growth of awareness and availability of products is affected by the product category, marketing budget, media selection, advertising effectiveness, product uniqueness, product acceptance, promotional tactics, trade relationships, and choice of sales channels. Estimating how fast awareness and availability grows, like estimating competitive reaction, requires a mixture of practical experience and managerial judgment.

As an example, an advertising expenditure of approximately $50 million on a national media campaign for an environmental issue increased public awareness from 35 percent to 70 percent over a four year period. That this particular campaign won national awards for advertising efficiency, gives rise to expectations that different awareness growth rates may result depending on the efficiency and effectiveness of the campaign executions. Advertising agencies can help make these judgments. Account executives have access to historical records that relate growth in awareness to spending rates by product category. When combined with the company's own experience, advertising agency data can yield good estimates of awareness growth.

18.5   Incorporating Product Availability and Distribution Efficiency Effects

Product availability depends on the company's ability to manufacture inventory, their relationship with the trade, promotional budgets, choice of marketing channel and early sales results. Large, well-funded, and well-known companies such as Procter & Gamble, Kimberly-Clark, and Kraft Foods can expand product availability rapidly, particularly if initial product sales figures are favorable. Other companies with smaller budgets and limited market presence often expand availability very slowly. On the other hand, for the right type of products, e-tailing can quickly provide nearly universal availability to anyone with a credit card and access to the Internet. In any event, product availability will have a dramatic impact on sales and must be included along with estimates of customer preference when using conjoint analysis as a forecasting tool.

18.6   The Macro-Flow Model

The Macro-Flow model (Urban and Star 1991) is a simple sales forecasting approach that allows managers to incorporate market potential, customer preference, changes in awareness and availability, repurchase rates and usage rates into the same model. The macro-flow model has been used to forecast sales at companies such as General Motors and is more typically called the Funnel Model. As the name implies, it expresses product sales as an ever-narrowing funnel. At the top of the funnel is the total number of households, consumers or potential customers that could have any possible interest in buying the product, i.e., total potential buyers. When forecasting first-year sales, the number of potential buyers traveling down the funnel is reduced by (1) the percentage of people that become aware in the first year, (2) the percentage of people who have access to the product in the first year, and (3) the percentage of people that will choose to buy the product given the competitive situation modeled in the conjoint analysis simulation.

The number flowing out of the bottom of the funnel represents first-time buyers. If the product will be purchased several times during the year, we will multiply the number of first-time buyers by an estimate of the percentage of repeat buyers and the average number of product units we expect repeat buyers to purchase during the year based on usage tests and/or historical data. We add together the units sold to first-time buyers with the units sold to repeat buyers to estimate total units sold for the first year. The process can be repeated for several years to complete a sales forecast for whatever time horizon is necessary for business planning. For each additional year we update the number of potential buyers, awareness percentage, availability percentage, and choice probability. The choice probability, that is the market share estimate output derived from the conjoint analysis model, may change slowly or rapidly depending on how quickly we feel that competitors will react to our product introduction.

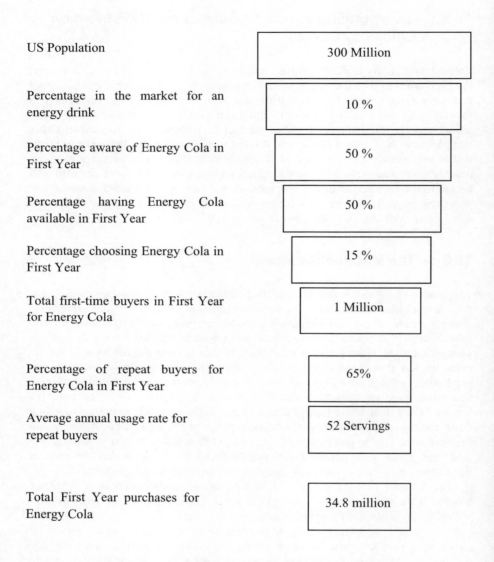

US Population — 300 Million

Percentage in the market for an energy drink — 10 %

Percentage aware of Energy Cola in First Year — 50 %

Percentage having Energy Cola available in First Year — 50 %

Percentage choosing Energy Cola in First Year — 15 %

Total first-time buyers in First Year for Energy Cola — 1 Million

Percentage of repeat buyers for Energy Cola in First Year — 65%

Average annual usage rate for repeat buyers — 52 Servings

Total First Year purchases for Energy Cola — 34.8 million

Figure 2:   Macro-Flow Sales Forecasting Model for Energy Cola

The macro-flow model allows managers to integrate choice probabilities estimated using conjoint analysis data with many other elements necessary for forecasting sales. It allows us to integrate the effects of competitive reaction, development of the marketing mix, and rates of repeat purchase. Such integration is necessary if the quality of market share estimates and sales forecasts are to continue to increase. Figure 2 illustrates the components of a macro-flow model for a fictitious energy drink we call Energy Cola.

The macro-flow model shown in Figure 2 estimates that 34.8 million servings of Energy Cola will be sold in its first year based on 15 percent "market share" derived from a conjoint analysis simulation. Because the current value of the energy drink market in the US exceeds $1.6 billion, managers ignoring or unaware of the underlying assumptions of conjoint analysis simulations may be tempted to estimate first year sales of Energy Cola at $240 million (15% of $1.6 billion) which translates to 240 million servings assuming the cost of an average serving is one dollar. That sales forecast would be off by a factor of almost seven, and disastrous for everyone involved. It would seem that such poor forecasts are never seen among sophisticated businesses. Yet it happens. First year sales for the Buick Reatta were forecast to be 20,000 cars. However, only about 20,000 total cars were sold over a four year period between 1988 and 1991 before production was halted.

18.7   Choice Probabilities Necessary but Not Sufficient

Conjoint analysis is a powerful tool for estimating utilities and choice probabilities, but choice probabilities are only one piece of the sales forecasting puzzle. These probabilities can change dramatically in the face of competitive reaction. Moreover, the speed and nature of competitive reaction can change based on the configuration of product we select. Different product configurations affect the sales of different competitors. Some competitors simply have more will and greater resources to react than others. Managers criticizing the accuracy of sales forecasts based on conjoint analysis data may want to consider incorporating competitive reaction into their models. Aside from competitive reaction, product awareness and availability also profoundly influence sales as will repurchase rates and usage rates. Accurate choice probabilities will not compensate for exaggerated levels of marketing support or misjudging growth in product awareness and access.

18.8   References

Cattin, Philippe and Dick R. Wittink (1982), "Commercial Use of Conjoint Analysis: A Survey," *Journal of Marketing*, 46 (Summer), 44-53.

Green, Paul E., Abba M. Krieger and Yoram Wind (2001), "Thirty years of conjoint analysis: Reflections and prospects," *Interfaces*, June, s56-s73.

Green, Paul E. and V. R. Rao (1971), "Conjoint Measurement for Quantifying Judgmental Data," *Journal of Marketing Research*, 8 (August), 355-363.

Green, Paul E. and V. Srinivasan (1978), "Conjoint Analysis in Consumer Research: issues and Outlook," *Journal of Consumer Research*, 5 (September), 103-123.

Green, Paul E. and Yoram Wind (1975), "New way to measure consumers' judgements," *Harvard Business Review*, Vol 53, 107-117.

Huber, Joel (1997), "What we have learned from 20 years of conjoint research: When to use self-explicated, graded pairs, full profiles or choice experiments," Sawtooth Software Research Paper Series

Johnson, Richard M. (1987), "Adaptive conjoint analysis," in *Sawtooth Software Conference on Perceptual Mapping, Conjoint Analysis, and Computer Interviewing.* Sawtooth Software, Ketchum, ID, 253-265.

Louviere, Jordan (1988), Analyzing Decision Making: Metric Conjoint Analysis, Newbery Park, CA: Sage Publications

Osborne, Milton J. (2003), An Introduction to Game Theory, Oxford University Press, 153-180.

Srinivasan, V. (1988), "A conjunctive-compensatory approach to the self-explication of multiattributed preferences," *Decision Sciences*, Vol 19, 295-305.

Srinivasan, V. and Chan Su Park (1997), "Surprising Robustness of the Self-Explicated Approach to Consumer Preference Structure Measurement," *Journal of Marketing Research*, 34 (May), 286-291.

Urban, Glen L. and Steven H. Star (1991), Advanced Marketing Strategy, Prentice Hall, Englewood Cliffs, New Jersey, 110-114, 385-386.

Wittink, Dick R. and Philippe Cattin (1989), "Commercial Use of Conjoint Analysis: An Update," *Journal of Marketing*, 53 (Summer), 91-96.

Wittink, Dick R., M. Vriens and W. Burhenne (1994), "Commercial Use of Conjoint Analysis in Europe: Results and Critical Reflections," *International Journal of Research in Marketing*, 11, 41-52.

Author Index

Baier, Daniel, Professor of Marketing and Innovation Management at the University of Cottbus, Germany.

Blomkvist, Ola, M. Sc., doctorial candidate at the Department of Quality Technology and Management at the Linköping University, Sweden, and ABB Switchgear, Ludvika, Sweden.

Borgers, Aloys W. J., Urban Planning Group at the Eindhoven University of Technology, Eindhoven, The Netherlands.

Chrzan, Keith, Manager at ZS Associates, Evanston, Illinois, USA.

Cohen, Steven H., President of Stratford Associates Marketing Research, Needham, USA.

Dellaert, Benedict G. C., Meteor Research Chair and Professor at the Department of Marketing and Marketing Research at the Maastricht University, The Netherlands.

DeSarbo, Christian F., Director of Marketing Research at Analytika Marketing Sciences, Inc. in Centre Hall, Pennsylvania, USA.

DeSarbo, Wayne S., Smeal Distinguished Research Professor of Marketing at the Smeal College of Business at the Pennsylvania State University in University Park, Pennsylvania, USA.

Ekdahl, Fredrik, Ph. D., ABB Corporate Research, Västerås, Sweden.

Elrod, Terry, Associate Professor of Marketing at the Faculty of Business at the University of Alberta, Edmonton, Canada.

Evgeniou, Theodoros, Assistant Professor of Technology Management and Decision Sciences at INSEAD, Fontainebleau Cedex, France.

Gaul, Wolfgang, Professor of Marketing at the Institute of Decision Theory and Management Science at the University of Karlsruhe, Germany.

Giesen, Joachim, Researcher at the Max Planck Insititute for Computer Sciences, Saarbrücken, Germany.

Gustafsson, Anders, Associate Professor of the Service Research Center at the Karlstad University and of the Department of Quality Technology and Management at the Linköping University, Sweden.

Haaijer, Rinus, doctorial candidate in Marketing Research, Faculty of Economics, Department of Marketing and Marketing Research at the University of Groningen, The Netherlands.

Hauser, John, Kirin Professor of Marketing and Head of the Marketing Group at M.I.T.'s Sloan School of Management, Cambridge, Massachusetts, USA.

Hensel-Börner, Susanne, doctorial candidate at the Unilever Chair of Marketing and Management Science at the University of Jena, Germany.

Hensher, David, Professor of Management and Director of the Institut of Transport Studies, Faculty of Economics at the University of Sydney, Australia.

Herrmann, Andreas, Professor of Business Metrics and Director of the Center of Business Metrics at the University of St. Gallen, Switzerland.

Huber, Frank, Professor of Marketing and Director of the Center of Market-Oriented Product and Production Management at the University of Mainz, Germany.

Huber, Joel, Professor of Marketing at The Fuqua School of Business, Duke University, Durham, North Carolina, USA.

Kamakura, Wagner, Wendel A. Smith Professor of Marketing at the University of Iowa, USA.

Louviere, Jordan J., Foundation Professor and Chair Department of Marketing at the Faculty of Economics at the University of Sydney, Australia.

Miller, Richard, Consumer Pulse, USA.

Orme, Bryan, Sawtooth Software, Inc., USA.

Ozer, Muammer, Assistant Professor of Marketing at the City University of Hong Kong, China.

Ramaswamy, Venkatram, Associate Professor of Marketing at the University of Michigan Business School, USA.

Rao, Vithala R., Deane W. Malott Professor of Management and Professor of Marketing and Quantitative Methods at the Johnson Graduate School of Management, Cornell University, USA.

Sattler, Henrik, Professor and Managing Director of the Institute of Marketing, Retailing and Management Science at the University of Hamburg, Germany.

Schuberth, Eva, doctorial candidate at the Institute of Theoretical Computer Science, Swiss Federal Institute of Technology, Zürich, Switzerland.

Shehu, Edlira, doctorial candidate at the Institute for Marketing and Media, University of Hamburg, Germany.

Smith, Scott M., James Passey Professor of Marketing and Director of the Institute of Marketing at the Marriott School of Management, Brigham Young University, Provo, Utah, USA.

Swait, Joffre, Partner of the Advanis Inc. and Associated Faculty Member at the College of Business at the University of Florida, USA.

Teichert, Thorsten, Professor of Marketing and Media, University of Hamburg, Germany.

Timmermans, Harry J. P., Urban Planning Group at the Eindhoven University of Technology, Eindhoven, The Netherlands.

Toubia, Oliver, Assistant Professor of Marketing at the Columbia University, New York, USA.

Wedel, Michel, Professor of Marketing Research at the Faculty of Economics, Department of Marketing and Marketing Research at the University of Groningen, The Netherlands.

Whitlark, David B., Professor of Business Management at the Marriott School of Management, Brigham Young University, Provo, Utah, USA.

Printing: Krips bv, Meppel
Binding: Stürtz, Würzburg